Weaving and Binding

Weaving and Binding

Immigrant Gods and Female Immortals
in Ancient Japan

Michael Como

UNIVERSITY OF HAWAI'I PRESS

HONOLULU

MICHAEL COMO is Tōshū Fukami Associate Professor of Shintō Studies at Columbia University. He is author of *Shōtoku: Ethnicity, Ritual and Violence in the Japanese Buddhist Tradition* (Oxford University Press, 2008) as well as numerous articles on the religions of ancient Japan.

© 2009 University of Hawai'i Press
All rights reserved
Printed in the United States of America

14 13 12 11 10 09   6 5 4 3 2 1

Library of Congress Cataloging-in-Publication Data
Como, Michael.
Weaving and binding : immigrant gods and female immortals in ancient Japan / Michael Como.
    p. cm.
Includes bibliographical references and index.
ISBN 978-0-8248-2957-5 (hard cover : alk. paper)
1. Japan—Religion. I. Title.
BL2202.3.C66 2010
299.5'6—dc22
                                        2009015371

University of Hawai'i Press books are printed on acid-free paper and meet the guidelines for permanence and durability of the Council on Library Resources.

Designed by University of Hawai'i Press production department
Printed by The Maple-Vail Book Manufacturing Group

For Hui-yu, Maggie, and Danny

Contents

Acknowledgments		ix
Introduction		xi
1	Immigrant Gods on the Road to Jindō	1
2	*Karakami* and Animal Sacrifice	25
3	Female Rulers and Female Immortals	55
4	The Queen Mother of the West and the Ghosts of the Buddhist Tradition	84
5	Shamanesses, Lavatories, and the Magic of Silk	109
6	Silkworms and Consorts	136
7	Silkworm Cults in the Heavenly Grotto: Amaterasu and the Children of Ama no Hoakari	155
Conclusion		193
Glossary of Names and Terms		197
Appendix: Notes on Sources		223
Notes and Abbreviations		237
Works Cited		279
Index		295

Acknowledgments

THROUGH EVERY STAGE of this project I have benefited enormously from the work of numerous friends and scholars whose generous assistance has made this a far better book than it otherwise would have been. During the formative stages of this project I was fortunate to receive the support and encouragement of such scholars as Jackie Stone of Princeton, Paul Groner of the University of Virginia, Terry Kleeman of the University of Colorado, and Hank Glassman of Haverford College. Without their assistance, it is doubtful that this project would ever have begun.

During the course of my research overseas I was also fortunate to meet with a number of scholars who unstintingly offered me their support and the fruits of their many academic labors. In all that I have done I have benefited enormously from the friendship and guidance of Professor Yoshikawa Shinji of Kyoto University, who both embodied the highest ideals of academic rigor and taught me how passion and curiosity should infuse all academic inquiry. I am also extremely grateful for the assistance of Professor Silvio Vita of the Italian School of Oriental Studies, who gave me an academic home in Kyoto, and Professor Wang Kuo-liang of the Academica Sinica, who provided me with a base of operations and introductions in Taipei.

Very special thanks must also go to Herman Ooms and Torquil Dulhe of UCLA, Tom Conlan of Bowdoin College, and Mark Teeuwen of the University of Oslo, each of whom spent countless hours and offered copious comments, criticisms, and corrections of various incarnations of the manuscript. Without the benefit of their assistance and insight, my own efforts would have been greatly impoverished.

Closer to home, those to whom I owe thanks at Barnard College and my own Columbia University are also legion. I will always be particularly grateful for the friendship and support of Wendi Adamek, Courtney Bender, Wiebke Denecke, Rachel McDermott, and Max Moerman. Very special thanks go to David Lurie, who as a friend, colleague, and critic, has done more for my work and my sanity than I shall ever be able to repay. I am also deeply indebted to Bob Hymes, Haruo Shirane, Chun-fang Yu, and Mark Taylor, upon each of whom I have relied for advice and encouragement for so very long. I would also like to express my deepest appreciation and gratitude for the aid, instruction, and encouragement given to me these many years by Bernard Faure, who as teacher, colleague, and friend has been all that anyone could hope for and more.

This project was also made possible by generous support by the U.S.-Japan Fulbright Commission, the Chiang Ching-kuo Foundation, and the Japanese Society for the Promotion of Science. To each of these institutions I offer my sincere thanks. I would also like to thank the editors of the journal *Asian Folklore Studies* for allowing me to include a revised version of an article that first appeared in the Fall 2005 edition of their journal as Chapter 6 of this work. I would also like to express my deepest thanks to Patricia Crosby and the staff of University of Hawai'i Press for their patience and assistance in the completion of this project.

Above all else, however, I would like to offer my deepest thanks to my wife Hui-yu and my children, Maggie and Danny. These past several years they have endured tribulations both large and small with extraordinary grace, patience, and love. To them I offer my most heartfelt thanks and the hope that someday, somehow, I may repay them for their many kindnesses.

Introduction

AMONG THE MOST exciting developments in the study of Japanese religion over the past two decades has been the discovery of tens of thousands of ritual vessels, implements, and scapegoat dolls (*hitogata*) from the Nara (710–784) and early Heian (794–1185) periods. Because inscriptions on many of these items are clearly derived from Chinese rites of spirit pacification, it is now evident that both the Japanese royal system and the Japanese Buddhist tradition developed against a background of continental rituals centered upon the manipulation of *yin* and *yang*, animal sacrifice, and spirit-quieting. Thus in spite of the longstanding tendency to approach Japanese religion according to a bivalent Buddhist/Shintō model, it is now clear that continental rites of purification and exorcism constituted a third major force in the development of the religious institutions of the Nara period.

The proliferation of these rites in the Japanese islands, in turn, was almost certainly related to the adoption of the Chinese festival calendar, a process that was apparently underway by the time of the court of Suiko (reigned 592–628), as envoys from the Chinese empire and the kingdoms of the Korean peninsula helped accelerate the diffusion of continental political, cultural, and religious norms.[1] As subsequent decades witnessed the accelerated transmission of Buddhism to the Japanese islands, they were also characterized by the rapid absorption of systems of knowledge based upon Chinese notions of medicine, astronomy, and ritual. This process was to influence virtually every aspect of court life for centuries to come.[2]

In light of the impressive number of continental-style effigies, ritual vessels, and clay figurines that have been unearthed, this book seeks to re-examine early Buddhist and "native" religious practice in the Japanese islands within the context of the rites, legends, and technologies associated with the Chinese festival calendar. Building upon recent archeological discoveries as well as textual sources, I chart the trajectory of this transformation in the religious culture through a study of the immigrant cults and deities that flourished during the Nara and early Heian periods.[3]

Throughout this work I argue that as the rites and legends of the Chinese festival calendar pervaded popular cultic practice across the Japanese islands, they also to a remarkable degree shaped the emerging Buddhist and royal traditions.[4] By highlighting the revolutionary effect of continental systems of technology, science, and material culture upon cultic development across the Japanese islands, I suggest new readings for a series of myths and legends related to the Sun Goddess Amaterasu, the formation of the royal line, and the foundational narrative of the Buddhist tradition in the Japanese islands. As a result, a new picture of cultic life in the period emerges that emphasizes the importance of animal sacrifice, weaving cults, and Chinese conceptions of medicine and immortality.

Inherent in this project are three overarching goals that have shaped both the structure and content of the work. At the most basic level, I wish to draw attention to the importance of continental technologies and the Chinese festival calendar for the development of purportedly native cultic practices and belief systems. Because continental technologies related to sericulture, medicine, and metalworking were firmly embedded in continental ritual and conceptual frameworks, their transmission necessitated the simultaneous transmission and adoption of a body of rites and legends that were part of the basic fabric of popular cultic practice in the Chinese empire(s) and in the Korean kingdoms. By focusing upon the primarily immigrant lineages most closely associated with this process, I hope both to explicate the primary mechanisms of this cultural transmission and to clarify the nature of the transformation that it engendered. Thus the diffusion of sericulture not only required adoption of new technologies and modes of social organization, but it also required the adoption of cults focused on silkworm goddesses and astral deities such as the Weaver Maiden and the Queen Mother of the West. Similarly, the practice of Chinese medicine required not only knowledge of human anatomy, but also an understanding of the relationship between body and spirit predicated upon Chinese conceptions of *yin* and *yang*. I argue that as a cluster of service groups and immigrant lineages incorporated continental tropes and cultic practices within their own ancestral cults and legends, the rites and legends of the Chinese festival calendar came to be embedded within the fabric of ritual practice across the Japanese islands. As immigrant ancestral deities became inscribed in local landscapes, continental conceptions of immortality, spirit pacification, and animal sacrifice became ubiquitous across the spectrum of cultic practice at court and in the countryside.

These considerations are closely related to a second, equally important goal, which is to highlight the role of gender issues in the formation of both economic and cultic systems during the period. Much of the narrative is devoted to the hitherto neglected consorts, shamanesses, goddesses, and female immortals who pervaded the cultic landscape of the Japanese islands.[5] The cultic identity of these figures, I argue, was closely related to the proliferation of weaving and sericulture, two heavily gendered activities that featured prominently in the rites of the Chinese festival calendar. As silks and fabrics became the commodity of choice for everything from taxes to offerings to deities, weaving maidens cum female deities, ancestors, and immortals played a major role in defining the nature of what would come to be known as "native" Japanese religion. I further argue that as these figures came to be intertwined with the newly emerging royal cult, the tropes and legends of the Chinese festival calendar came to play a major role in the construction of the lineal and cultic basis of the royal cult.

Finally, I relate these developments to the emergence of the Japanese Buddhist tradition, which took root during this period. Although obvious instances of cultic influences from the Chinese festival calendar have often been dismissed as preexisting accretions of popular cultic practices within the Chinese Buddhist tradition, I argue that continental rites and legends are best understood as integral elements of the technological and material transformation that was sweeping the Japanese islands during the period. Focusing on a series of legends drawn from popular tale collections as well as from court-sponsored accounts of the founding legend of Japanese Buddhism, I further argue that continental conceptions of medicine, spirit-quieting, and even animal sacrifice shaped a new religious ideal that involved the use of drugs and ascetic practices in pursuit of immortality and mastery of the superhuman world.

Iconoclasts and the Return of the Native

Exploring each of these issues in turn entails unraveling a series of methodological difficulties that may be traced to the continued influence of nationalist discourse from Japan's prewar period. One of the most important impediments has been an unspoken set of assumptions concerning a purportedly native Japanese identity that is closely associated either with the religious practices of the Japanese "folk" or with the Japanese royal house. In this view Buddhism was, by contrast, a "foreign" religion that was transformed as it gradually came to an accommodation with the "native" beliefs and practices associated with popular religious practice.

This paradigm is closely related to Meiji conceptions of the royal house as a central engine in the development of new cultic practices across the

Japanese islands. Because both the Nara and the prewar periods were typified by rhetoric heralding a dramatic centralization and then expansion of political power, Japanese rulers from the ancient period have almost invariably been presented as sponsors of technological and cultic changes/innovations to which local elites then responded. This has yielded a tendency to treat purportedly native practices as rooted in an essentialized Japanese identity, while the diffusion of "foreign" traditions has been seen as resulting from the activities of a small coterie of literate courtiers familiar with elite textual traditions from the continent.

These premises have greatly distorted our understanding of both Buddhist and popular cultic practices during the formative period of the Japanese Buddhist and royal traditions. A commitment to the category of "native" religious beliefs and practices has become increasingly difficult to sustain in recent years, however, in light of the large number of textual and archeological sources suggesting the clear influence of continental rites of spirit pacification and animal sacrifice in the cultic life of the period. In response to these developments, the traditional approach has in recent years been challenged from two directions. Scholars such as Fukunaga Mitsuji, Ueda Masaaki, Takigawa Masajirō, and Yoshino Hiroko have sparked heated debate within Japan by suggesting that numerous aspects of the royal cult and early "Shintō" were in fact Taoist in essence.[6] By emphasizing numerous instances in which cultic vocabulary found in Taoist sources was employed within court chronicles and court-sponsored rites, the work of these scholars represents an important breakthrough in the study of early Japanese religion. Criticisms by traditionalists angered at the thought of decoupling the royal cult from the Shintō tradition have often proven to be unconvincing.[7]

Unfortunately, the work of these scholars has proven to be vulnerable to methodological criticism on numerous other grounds. They have been distressingly vague if not silent on key questions concerning the actual mechanisms of transmission and on the lack of Taoist institutions during a period when Buddhist temples were being constructed with astonishing rapidity. Perhaps most problematic, proponents of the belief that the Taoist tradition flourished in the Japanese islands have also failed to provide a clear account of how practices that they have labeled "Taoist" differ from popular Chinese religious practices.[8] At times one suspects that virtually any aspect of Chinese popular religion related to conceptions of immortality and/or spirit-quieting could fall under the extremely broad and rather vague conception of Taoism proffered by Fukunaga.[9]

This approach stands in marked contrast to that of a long line of western scholars such as Anna Seidel, Rolf Stein, Michel Strickmann, Terry Kleeman, and Nathan Sivin. Each of these scholars has argued that the Taoist tradition, far from being a general Chinese religious orientation, was from at least the second century C.E. an elite, textually based religious movement that defined itself in terms of ritual lineages and that emerged at least in part in opposition to popular cultic practices.[10] I argue that such terminological issues are particularly important for understanding early Japanese religion; while it is highly doubtful, for instance, that Taoist liturgical institutions were transmitted to the Japanese islands, it appears highly likely that immigrant lineages from the Korean peninsula would have been familiar with popular continental cultic forms.

Adams and Horizons

More broadly speaking, the work of Fukunaga, Yoshino, and others is marred by a strong reliance upon what Wiebke Denecke has dubbed "Adamistic philology." This approach, Denecke argues, "traces every lexical unit to a point of origin, as if it had been 'quoted' directly from a Chinese source for the first time in the history of Japanese writing."[11] Rather than simply acknowledging a given text's or author's deep engagement with a canonical tradition that had continental roots, these scholars tend to reduce the meaning of any particular term to that which is found in the oldest Chinese source. In so doing, they tend to ignore the cultic horizon of reception in which such terms emerged and were then employed within the Japanese islands. Not surprisingly, this has had the additional effect of once again reinforcing the notion of the "foreignness" of such practices as opposed to the purportedly "native" practices that existed outside of the court.

This emphasis upon textual origins has thus served to reinforce the widely held belief that the appearance of cultic forms with continental roots was the work of intellectuals at court in the service of the royal house. This has in turn perpetuated the belief that continental influences must have come from the elite, textually based traditions of the continent. In this sense, at least, the fundamental premises of a pure, native folk religiosity, coupled with a dynamic royal house, could well be strengthened by the ostensibly iconoclastic approach of Fukunaga and Yoshino.

In contrast to Fukunaga and Yoshino, I take as a point of departure the premise that religious developments at the Yamato court are best understood against the horizon of reception that was constituted by lineages and cultic centers across the Japanese islands. In so doing I have benefited enormously from the work of a number of Japanese scholars, such as Murayama Shūichi, Shinkawa Tokio, and Wada Atsumu.[12] These scholars have been content for the most part to focus on the role of continental conceptions of *yin* and *yang* (*onmyōdō*) within the intellectual life of the period rather than seeking for their origins within the Taoist canon. I argue, however, that the prevalence of *onmyōdō* conceptions within court-sponsored literature represented not elite appropriations of continental knowledge, but the pervasive influence of commonly held cultic forms that had taken root throughout the Japanese islands. Once we abandon prewar paradigms that configured the royal cult as both the embodiment of native cultic identity and the chief producer of cultic innovation, it becomes possible to offer a new vision of the purportedly "native" popular cults of the Nara and Heian periods that formed within a variety of technological and social frameworks.[13]

Fabrics and Borders

In contrast to the works of the aforementioned authors, my principal concern here is not the meaning for the court of the images woven together within the (often divergent) court-sponsored texts that it sponsored, such as the *Kojiki, Nihon shoki,* and *Fudoki.* Although each of these texts can of course be read as representations of the royal or courtier imagination, I mainly focus on the degree to which all of them were permeated by elements associated with immigrant lineages and their assorted technological and cultic practices and interests. Without ignoring the content of the court-centered religious and ideological imaginaries that pervade the Nara and early Heian textual corpus, I am equally concerned with the fabric from which these imaginaries were fashioned. Bluntly put, I argue that to a very large degree immigrant and service lineages closely associated with continental technologies and cults shaped both the fabric and parameters, in terms of which courtiers and rulers conceived and expressed their visions of all under Heaven.

Inherent in this approach are several methodological premises, among the most prominent of which are the following. (1) Although the archeological record continues to improve yearly, we are fundamentally dependent upon textual sources that were products of courtiers and elite/literate elements of society. (2) Although we cannot assume that these texts speak with one voice or reflect a single, coherent ideological stance, reading them together can help elucidate points of commonality in terms of which divergent representations were conceived and expressed.[14] (3) Although it is not possible to "get outside" of these texts, it is possible (and essential) to recontextualize them. My readings are premised upon the belief that the court was not a discrete, unified identity, but rather a site of contestation among several lineages with discrete interests, cultic traditions, and ties to disparate regions, cultic centers, and deities. (4) Among the greatest factors giving impetus to textual production at court was an attempt to reconfigure both collective memories and cultic practices as they related to lineages and cultic centers across the Japanese islands. In describing this process, I therefore assume that the court was as much a consumer as a producer of new ideological and cultic forms. (5) To a large degree, the royal line and the figure of the *tennō* were constituted out of ideological and cultic materials at hand, not with imports from the continent or cultic practices that were created ex nihilo. Court-sponsored texts such as *Nihon shoki* and *Kojiki* were not merely imaginative constructions of a world that never was; they were also, and in large part, attempts to appropriate and transform preexisting narratives of ancestors, gods, and shrines that were drawn from written sources submitted by the most prominent lineages at court. (6) The ancestral cults of these lineages were, in turn, often deeply connected with legends of shrines, tombs, and deities inscribed in specific cultic landscapes. Prominent court lineages both maintained ancestral shrines in distant regions and participated in the process of assembling and editing materials for the court chronicles, and hence they were well positioned to mediate the process by which narratives from distant locales were transmuted into material for the royal imaginaries of Tenmu and his successors. (7) Because, prior to their appropriation, these narratives emerged within a wide variety of geographic and social contexts that were not controlled by the court, not only do we find important differences in orientation between texts such as the *Nihon shoki* and the *Kojiki*, but we also find multiple and often competing voices within each text as well. Seen from this perspective, it is therefore possible to view both the court and its ideological/textual production as themselves products of interactions with (and influences from) local concerns and elites.

In light of all this, I argue that the presence of continental literary and cultic tropes within court-sponsored rites and texts often reflects not direct literary quotations from continental texts, but rather the deployment of a cultic vocabulary that, while originally rooted in continental cultic discourses, was widely used at cultic centers across the Japanese islands. In Denecke's formulation, rather than searching for intertextual relationships between the Chinese classics and court-sponsored texts from Yamato, my concern is with the pervasive "intertopical" cultic relationships that can be shown to have existed between popular religious practices in China, the Korean peninsula, and the Japanese islands. Indeed, in some cases we shall see that cultic vocabulary associated with continental technologies and immortality cults constituted an essential element in the ancestral cults and local legends that appear throughout the earliest literature of the Japanese islands.

Put It Down to the Calendar

My focus, therefore, is not on rulers and their advisers per se, but on local cultic centers and lineages that appear to have been best placed to facilitate and mediate the diffusion of continental cultic traditions across the Japanese islands. I thus do not seek to trace the diffusion of continental technologies and cultic practices emanating out from the court towards the periphery. Rather, I focus on service groups and lineages that traced their descent to the Korean peninsula, were based in coastal regions, and were engaged in continental technological practices such as medicine, weaving, and sericulture. These groups, I argue, were best placed both to import cultic and technological practices from the continent and to transmit these practices at court and in the countryside. Once we examine the cultic geography of such groups and trace the movement of their ancestral legends and tutelary deities from coastal regions in Kyūshū, Tamba, Kii, and elsewhere towards the Yamato plain, it becomes possible to sketch, in at least very broad strokes, possible sources and routes of transmission for the continental cultic and technological forms that did so much to transform the political and religious culture of the Japanese islands.

Chapter 1 begins this process by tracing the role of the Hata, an immigrant kinship group from the Korean kingdom of Silla, in the complex interactions between rulers, *kami*, and buddhas during the Nara and early Heian periods. Because immigrant lineages such as the Hata played a major role both in the formative Buddhist tradition and in a series of local cults that were absorbed by the royal cult, their influence extended across the religious spectrum of the Nara period. As the court increasingly turned to lineages such as the Hata for Buddhist and non-Buddhist sources of protection from the hostile spirits that traveled the roadways of the land, members of the Hata came to pervade not only the upper echelons of the ecclesial hierarchy, but also some of the most powerful lineages at court. As a result, when Kammu *tennō* moved his court to the main Hata stronghold in Yamashiro province at the start of the Heian period, it was Hata monks and courtiers who propitiated the Hata shrines and deities that surrounded the court.

Because the ancestral deities of the Hata and other immigrant lineages were by definition "foreign" deities, or "*karakami*," Chapter 2 takes up the role of *karakami* and animal sacrifice in the construction of the "native" cultic paradigms and the formation of the Japanese Buddhist tradition. In contrast to the near-universal assertion that the "Shintō" and the Buddhist traditions of Japan abhor the shedding of blood, this chapter argues that animal sacrifice was a pervasive element in popular cultic practice in the Asuka and Nara periods. Beginning with a series of legends involving sacrifice and cowherd deities, the text explores the role of the cult of the Weaver Maiden and the Cowherd from the Chinese festival calendar in the diffusion of such legends. These cults, I argue, were directly related to rites of spirit pacification at roadsides and involved not only sacrifice but also the use of substitute bodies (*hitogata*) and ritual amulets. By focusing on legends involving meat offerings and the logic of substitution that pervaded even the Buddhist tale literature from the period, the chapter highlights the degree to which continental conceptions of spirit, sacrifice, and the logic of ritual substitution were important elements of continuity across the religious spectrum of the period.

Chapter 3 explores the influence of Chinese conceptions of medicine and immortality in the development of the ideal religious type, known as "*hijiri*." The chapter begins with a discussion of "medicine hunts" undertaken by the court in the Yoshino region of Yamato in accordance with the Chinese medical texts and the Chinese festival calendar. The chapter argues that a series of ancestral legends and cults from the region closely correlate with legends of female shamans from Chinese sources and that the topographical features of the Yoshino mountains were considered especially conducive to the pursuit of superhuman powers. Because female immortals frequently appear as ancestors of lineages closely associated with the transmission of continental medical technologies, the chapter argues that the development of both Buddhist and "native" cults in the region was in fact stimulated by the importation of continental conceptions of medicine and by the belief that a mix of drugs and ascetic practice could lead to the attainment of both immortality and control over the spirits of the dead.

In Chapter 4 I build upon this discussion by examining the role of continental conceptions of spirit pacification in shaping the founding legend of Japanese Buddhism. This chapter argues that because the establishment of the Buddhist tradition was deeply rooted in political violence and the subsequent need to propitiate hostile spirits, the tradition encountered a recurring "Atsumori effect," in which the gods of the vanquished claim the attention of the victors. Reading the founding legend of Japanese Buddhism in this light, the text examines the role of the vanquished Mononobe kinship group in the construction of the emerging Japanese Buddhist tradition. Focusing on the cultic practices of the Mononobe and their affiliated kinship groups, the chapter details a pervasive pattern of rites of spirit pacification based upon the Chinese cults of the Queen Mother of the West and the Weaver Maiden and the Cowherd.

Chapter 5 explores the role of sericulture cults from the Chinese festival calendar in the literary and cultic discourse of the period through an examination of a set of poems and legends that feature royal emissaries seeking to "call out" women with whom rulers have become enamored.[15] Because the motif of calling out appears to be related to rites of calling to the spirits of the recently deceased, these legends offer a small glimpse into the ways myths and legends associated with sericulture came to inform purportedly native funerary practices during the period. These legends, I argue, were directly rooted in Chinese rites of the fifteenth day of the first month, during which silkworm goddesses were called out using imagery based upon the silkworm's ability to "die" as it enters a cocoon only to re-emerge as a transformed being capable of flight.

In Chapter 6 I explore the role of these cults at a cluster of cultic centers at the heart of the royal cult of the Nara and Heian periods. As silks and woven items came to be used as a basic medium of exchange during the period, rites associated with sericulture and weaving assumed a major role in both the cultic and economic life across the Japanese islands. Because weaving and sericulture were heavily gendered activities across East Asia, the transmission of sericulture and weaving cults had a profound effect upon the construction of the cultic identity of female shamans and ancestors across the Japanese islands. Focusing on the sacerdotal lineages at such major cultic centers as the Kamo, Miwa, and Izushi shrines, I conclude with a discussion of the degree to which legends depicting "sacred marriages" between the female ancestors of these lineages and the deities and ancestors of the royal house helped the lineages shape the character and direction of court ritual for centuries to come.

Chapter 7 explores the role played by rites of sericulture and resurrection in the formation of the cult of Amaterasu no Ōmikami, the founding ancestor of the royal lineage. The chapter focuses on one version of the myth of the Heavenly Grotto, in which Amaterasu is called back from the land of the dead after she has impaled herself with a shuttle while weaving in a ritual chamber. Because this legend served as the mythic basis for the Rite of Spirit-quieting (Mitama Shizume Matsuri), one of the main pillars of court ritual, it was of enormous importance for the royal cult. The chapter reads the myth against a series of narratives from the third and fifth months of the Chinese festival calendar that call attention to a broader network of sericulture rites and legends centering upon the violent death of young maidens and the subsequent propitiation of their spirits. These legends, I suggest, so influenced the construction of Amaterasu as a royal ancestor that she is represented not only as a weaving maiden but also as a silkworm goddess spinning silk from cocoons in her mouth.

As these chapters trace the movements of *kami*, ancestors, immortals, and demons across the seas and highways of the Japanese islands, they often lead to obscure byways of Japanese religious history. By thus focusing on religious practices from the social and geographic margins as well as those of the courtly center, I have sought to present a fuller, more nuanced picture of the often violent ebb and flow that animated religious practice in this land of 80,000 deities. It is my hope that in charting the course of these developments I have done justice both to the tremendous social and religious ferment that characterized this period of Japanese history and to the profound, if often hidden, continuities that underlay the diverse responses of rulers, monks, courtiers, and provincials to the challenges engendered by the technological, cultural, and political upheavals of this pivotal epoch.

CHAPTER 1

Immigrant Gods on the Road to Jindō

ALTHOUGH FEW SCHOLARS of Japanese religion today would accept Meiji-period claims about the centrality of the royal cult for the spiritual life of the Japanese people, one of the most enduring legacies of prewar Japanese ideology has been the association of the Japanese royal house with Japanese nationalism. In this ideological configuration *tennō* and *kami* were represented as cornerstones of a purportedly continuous native Japanese cultural and religious identity with roots in pre-Buddhist antiquity. Perhaps because the Japanese university system and the academic study of religion began to take shape at just this time, to a large degree these ideological parameters have been absorbed into academic discourse and are found even within the self-representation of Japanese Buddhist institutions.

One of the most important presuppositions of this discourse has been the tacit assumption that while the relationship between the royal cult and the Buddhist tradition is a phenomenon that must be explained, the alliance between the *tennō* and the *kami* is something natural and in need of virtually no explanation. As a result, the bivalent Buddhist-Shintō framework for discussing Japanese religion still exerts a powerful influence in academic textbooks as well as in the broader academic discourse in Japan and the west. Central to this model are a series of historical claims rooted in a conception of Japanese Buddhism as an initially "foreign" tradition that was slowly absorbed by the Japanese as it reached an accommodation with the purportedly native *kami*. Because this model posits a horizon of reception for the Buddhist tradition that was dominated by native *kami*, it has also long been implicated in nativist discourses centering on the Nara (710–784) and early Heian (794–1185) periods, when many of the building blocks for the Japanese royal system were constructed.

Perhaps the greatest testament to the influence of prewar ideology can be seen in the emergence of two powerful countercurrents in the

1

scholarship of early Japanese religion that have more or less explicitly been presented in opposition to the bivalent model and its often distorting presuppositions. One of these movements, championed by such scholars as Fukunaga Mitsuji, Shinkawa Tokio, Herman Ooms, and David Bialock, has emphasized the prominence of continental cultic elements with little apparent connection to the Buddhist tradition in the ritual and cultural life of the early court. These scholars have tended to assert that much of what has long been labeled "Shintō" within the royal cult in fact represents early appropriations of rites and motifs found in Chinese Taoism.[1]

A second, equally powerful movement, led by scholars such as Kuroda Toshio and Mark Teeuwen, has directly challenged nativist understandings by arguing that Shintō is best understood as an important historical phenomenon with roots in mid-Heian period Buddhist discourses concerning the relationship between the buddhas and *kami* of the Japanese islands. Kuroda famously argued that the term "Shintō" itself was used only rarely in the ancient period and never in reference to a discreet religious system. Similarly, Teeuwen has argued that the term "Shintō," or *jindō*, as it would have been read at the time, was most likely taken from Chinese Buddhist discourses concerning deities in need of "taming" and Buddhist salvation. He notes that whereas court-sponsored rites at shrines were most commonly referred to by the term *"jingi,"* the term *jindō* appears almost exclusively in contexts related to such activities as the worship of *kami* at Buddhist temples or temple-shrine multiplexes (*jingūji*). Teeuwen therefore suggests that the origins of Shintō may lie not in court-sponsored *jingi* worship, but rather within *jindō*-style rites that were performed at temple-shrine multiplexes that had supplanted much of the *jingi* cult by the mid-Heian period.[2]

In this chapter I propose to build on the work of these and other scholars in order to delineate a few important turning points on the road that led from the establishment of the *tennō*-centered polity in the late seventh century towards the establishment of Jindō as an organizing principle of the royal cult in the mid-Heian period. This will require an examination of a complicated set of interactions between *tennō*, monk, and *kami* in which the often hostile relations between *tennō* and *kami* influenced the growth and direction of Buddhist movements on the one hand and the *tennō*'s still evolving political and cultic identity on the other.

Along the way we shall also repeatedly encounter—contrary to nativist assumptions regarding continuity in *kami* worship across the centuries— tremendous ferment in both the nature of the royal cult and in the cast of deities that formed its core. I shall argue that throughout the Nara and early Heian periods this ferment was both a product and cause of chronic conflict and antagonism between *tennō* and *kami*. As the court struggled to find the means to contain a number of volatile deities that threatened the well-being and even the lives of rulers and peasants alike, the consequences of this conflict proved to be both profound and long-lasting. Among the most notable can be seen in the development of court-sponsored Buddhist institutions, which took on the job of protecting the ruler and court at just this time.

Throughout this book I also argue that this religious ferment was inextricably linked to a dramatic transformation in the technological, material, and political cultures of the Japanese islands. We shall see that to a remarkable degree this transformation was closely related to the activities of the numerous immigrant lineages from the Korean peninsula, which served as principal conduits for the transmission and propagation of continental technologies related to weaving, sericulture, astrology, and writing. I therefore view these lineages as crucial for understanding the cultic ferment of the age. We shall also see that, even prior to the Nara period, both the royal cult and *kami* worship across the Japanese islands had been profoundly shaped by cults, deities, and legends from across the sea.[3]

In this chapter much of the discussion centers on the Hata, an immigrant kinship group from the Korean kingdom of Silla, which was prominent in both the political and cultic life of the period. Although significant work has been done on the role of the Hata and other immigrant kinship groups with regard to the introduction and formation of the Buddhist tradition in Japan, little effort has been expended to date to determine how the deities and cults associated with these kinship groups related to the royal cult and the development of Buddhism. If it is in fact the case that the same kinship groups that promoted the "foreign" Buddhist tradition also played a major role in the construction of the royal cult, then understanding the motivations and methods of these lineages promises to shed important light on the emergence of Jindō as a ritual and conceptual system from which *tennō*, *kami*, and monk could derive their various spheres of religious practice and cultic identity.

Towards this end I propose to investigate the role of the Hata in three pivotal moments in Japanese religious history: the construction of the provincial monastic network (*kokubunji*) during the Nara period, the Kusuko incident of 810, and the establishment of a court-sponsored network of temple-shrine multiplexes roughly one century later. Once we view the development of early Buddhist institutions in the context of immigrant *kami*, terrified rulers, and Hata priests and courtiers, it becomes possible to glimpse at least how and by whom the interlacing cultic networks of the *tennō*, monks, and *kami* were first constructed. Equally importantly, we shall also see that non-Buddhist cultic elements with roots in the Korean peninsula and the Chinese mainland may have played a major—at times perhaps even dominant—role in the development of the religious institutions of the Japanese islands.

Immigrants and *Kami* in the Kusuko Incident

One of the clearest illustrations of the importance of immigrant deities for the formation of Heian religious paradigms can be found in the so-called Kusuko incident of 810, in which the newly enthroned Saga *tennō* quelled an uprising led by his brother Heizei, who had just abdicated the throne. The source of the brothers' dispute was over the location of the court; Saga wished to remain in the recently completed Heian capital, while Heizei sought to return the capital to its former location on the Nara plain.[4]

In the midst of the uprising, Saga made a pilgrimage to the lower Kamo shrine, a large cultic center in the capital that was administered by the Hata and Kamo kinship groups. Because the Hata had helped construct the new capital in their home base in Yamashiro province, Saga, the Hata, and the shrine had a shared interest in keeping the capital in Heian. At the shrine Saga promised that if he were victorious, his descendants would thereafter send a princess, at the start of each reign, to serve as the shrine's chief priestess. He further promised to grant the shrine a rank equal to that of the royal house's ancestral shrine in Ise. Following Saga's victory, the Kamo shrine served for over 500 years as one of the main cultic centers for the royal house, responsible for the rites of blessing and spirit pacification that constituted a principal focus of the Heian royal cult.[5]

Although the story of Saga's establishment of the institution of the Kamo priestess is almost invariably discussed in terms of its importance for rulers and the court, for our purposes it is equally significant that at the time of the Kusuko incident the shrine and its deities were claimed as the domain of the Hata, an immigrant kinship group from the Korean kingdom of Silla. The degree to which the Kamo shrine was associated with the Hata can be seen in a remnant from the *Hatashi honkeichō*, a Hata document submitted to the court in 879. The text recounts the origins of the shrine as follows:

> In the beginning there was a Hata woman who came to the Kadono river to wash clothes. At that time an arrow came floating down from upstream. The girl took the arrow and returned home, where she stuck the arrow above the door [of her house]. At this the girl became

pregnant without any husband, and she subsequently gave birth to a boy. Her parents thought this strange, and asked her [how this could have happened]. The girl replied that she did not know. They asked her several times, but even after several months she still said she did not know. Her parents said "Even though she had no husband, a child could not have been born without a father. The father must be from among family and relatives or neighbors that frequent our house." They therefore prepared a feast and invited a great crowd of people. They then ordered the boy to take a cup and offer it to the man that he believed was his father.

At this the boy did not indicate anyone in the gathering, but instead he gazed over to the arrow above the door. He was then transformed into a thunder god and he burst through the roof of the building as he flew off into the sky. Therefore the [god of the] Upper Kamo Shrine is called Wake no Ikazuchi no Kami. The [god of the] Lower Kamo Shrine is called Mioya no Kami. The arrow above the door was the Matsuno'o Daimyōjin. Thus the Hata worship the gods in these three places.[6]

Although no one today would accept this account as historical reality, the text is remarkable for its bald assertion that all the deities of the Kamo shrines were Hata ancestors. Although the text does continue by noting that the Kamo frequently intermarried with the Hata and were therefore allowed to perform rites there, it is clear that during the period under discussion the Hata were asserting a claim of lineal privilege with regards to both the upper and lower Kamo shrines.[7] It also appears that the court, which replicated these claims in its own documents, accepted the Hata's account.

Encapsulated within the Kusuko incident and its aftermath are thus several clues concerning the role of immigrant lineages such as the Hata in the construction of the early royal cult. In the decades following the Kusuko incident the court moved to embrace a large network of Hata shrines and immigrant deities. Accompanying the rise of the Kamo shrines, for instance, was the similarly spectacular rise of the Matsuno'o shrine. Soon Hata deities at the Kamo, Matsuno'o, Hiyoshi, and Fushimi Inari shrines were among the highest ranking in all Japan.[8] As a result, the cultic practices of the Hata and their affiliated kinship groups were moved directly into the mainstream of royal cultic practice for centuries thereafter.

The Kusuko incident also illustrates the degree to which the *tennō*'s relationships with local *kami* could be characterized by dependence and/or antagonism. Although in this instance shared interests appear to have produced cooperation, for much of Japanese history local *kami* proved to be volatile, dangerous, and difficult for the royal house to control. As a result, the cultic agenda and identity of the royal house was to a surprisingly large degree shaped in response to local kinship groups and their gods. Because the Heian capital was constructed in the main Hata base in the Kadono district of Yamashiro province, Hata shrines and deities pervaded the cultic centers that surrounded rulers for the next thousand years.

These events were also essential background elements for a contemporaneous reformulation of relations between the court and Buddhist monastic institutions. Two central elements of this reformulation were the development of Kūkai's esoteric movement and the growth of Saichō's Tendai sect.[9] Saga's triumph was of crucial importance to the development of both movements if only because it averted a return to Nara and the rapprochement that existed before between the Japanese rulers and the Buddhist institutions of the Nara plain. Although distance did not necessarily indicate a rupture between the court and Nara Buddhist establishment, the new capital provided a new cultic as well as physical environment that directly influenced the development of fledgling Buddhist movements throughout the period. Henceforth *tennō* and monk alike would seek the protection of Hata deities as they took up residence in the new capital.

By ensuring the rapid rise of Hata cultic centers such as the Kamo and Matsuno'o shrines, Saga's triumph thus helped shape the cultic, political, and even physical terrain in which Heian Buddhist monasticism took shape. Brief glimpses of how this process unfolded can be seen in the development of Tōji and Enryakuji, two Buddhist institutions that adopted Buddhist cults and guardian deities that were closely associated with the Hata. As we shall see shortly, although there is no evidence that leaders at these institutions consciously sought the support of the Hata per se, there is ample reason to believe that immigrant lineages such as the Hata played a major role in constructing the horizons of reception of these movements. Thus although there is room for argument concerning the degree to which the Hata acted as the midwife of cultic change, there can be little doubt that they helped build its cradle.

Immigrants, Ancestors, and *Kami* in Heian Discourse

Perhaps the best place to begin approaching each of the above events is with the observation that each of them, in one way or another, was connected with a cluster of issues concerning the status of immigrant lineages and the ideology of the royal house. One manifestation of the importance of these issues for seventh- and eighth-century conceptions of kingship can be seen in the repeated references in the court chronicles to the arrival of immigrant "barbarians" from the Korean peninsula. As scholars such as Kōnoshi Takamitsu have pointed out, these passages were almost certainly motivated by Chinese conceptions of kingship in which tribute from distant lands was viewed as a confirmation of ruler's sage virtue and civilizing influence on all "under Heaven" (Ch. *t'ien hsia*, J. *tenka*).[10]

In spite of the persistence of such rhetoric, however, it is highly doubtful that this outlook ever accurately reflected the status of the immigrant lineages that controlled so many of the textual and technological resources from the continent that were most prized by the court. As these resources were utilized to fashion the narratives of kingship that permeated royal imaginaries for centuries, immigrant lineages came to play an extremely prominent role. This is vividly illustrated within the court chronicles in a series of legends that feature immigrant ancestors as sages and wise men with the unrivalled ability to discern and authenticate the sagely virtue of Yamato rulers.[11]

One indication of the depth and persistence of such tensions throughout the Nara and early Heian periods can be found in the *Shinsen shōjiroku*, a genealogical compendium from 814 that classifies some 1,182 lineages into the categories of "barbarian," "descendants of gods," and "members of the royal line." In the preface, which was composed less than four years after Saga *tennō* had made his pilgrimage to the Kamo shrines, the editors of the text made clear their desire to both standardize and clarify the boundaries that existed between the descendants of the gods of the Japanese islands and those whose lineages originated with figures from overseas:

> During the Shōhō era [749–757] there were from time to time edicts permitting the several immigrants to be granted [surnames] in accordance with their wishes. And so it came about that the characters for the older [Japanese] surnames and the newer surnames [granted to the immigrants] became thus alike; whether a family was immigrant or Japanese became doubtful; lowly families everywhere numbered themselves among the offshoots of the nobles; and foreign residents from Korea claimed descent from the gods of Japan.[12]

This text, insisting as it does that lineages that traced their roots to ancestors from across the sea were manipulating their genealogies, highlights several important aspects of the politics of immigration. By contrasting the category of "Japanese" with that of "immigrant," the authors of the *Shinsen shōjiroku* were seeking to set clear parameters for establishing native bona fides in both political and religious discourse. The concept of "immigrant" thus appears to have functioned at least in part as a repressed "other" that in later ages enabled the formulation of a nativist movement centered on the royal line.

This desire for clarity and standardization draws attention, however, to a central paradox of the politics of lineage; though lineal claims and ancestral cults were of tremendous significance in constructing social and political identities, they were also remarkably flexible. As the authors of the *Shinsen shōjiroku* realized to their apparent chagrin, it was all too easy to invent traditions that did not accurately represent the past, but rather met the needs of the present.

This paradox was, if anything, even more pronounced in the case of the *tennō*. One of the largest sources of authority for the *tennō* was the ability to bestow surnames and rank on individuals and lineages. Indeed, this power to bestow or withhold recognition of ancestors was in many ways integral to the definition of kingship during the period.[13] Equally important, however, the construction and manipulation of royal ancestral legends served as a vital political tool throughout the Nara and early Heian periods, as can be seen in the ongoing development throughout the period of the cult of Prince Shōtoku, a royal ancestor closely associated with the establishment of the Japanese Buddhist tradition.[14]

One final, though frequently overlooked corollary is the simple fact that immigrant kinship groups had ancestors just like everybody else, and several were *kami* at some of the largest shrines in Japan. As a result, many of the objects of veneration that Meiji ideologues assumed represented the core of a native Japanese spirit were often rooted in traditions and legends from across the sea. All of this suggests that the very same immigrant groups today credited with dissemination of the "foreign" Buddhist tradition almost certainly played a large role in the construction of major pillars of the purportedly native royal cult.[15]

The degree to which immigrant kinship groups such as the Hata were involved in construction of the royal cult was openly discussed in the *Kogoshūi*, a compendium of myth and legend that was completed in 810, at almost exactly the same time as the *Shinsen shōjiroku*. The author of this text, one Imbe no Hironari, laments:

> During the reign of the *tennō* at Toyoakira Palace in Karushima [Ōjin], the King of Paekche sent as tribute to the Imperial court a learned man named Wani, founder of the Fumi no Obito in Kawachi. The Hata no

Kimi ancestor Utsuki also immigrated to Japan along with a number of people under him who were living in his one hundred and twenty estates in Korea. . . . These immigrants who arrived from Ch'in, Aya and Paekche, became naturalized in this country. Each of these groups numbered in the tens of thousands. It is deeply regrettable that their services to Japan have, nevertheless, so far not been publicly recognized; and, still further, that the homage to the divine spirits of their respective ancestors is not yet paid with due religious ceremonies under the auspices of the Imperial Japanese Government.[16]

In light of the fact that Hironari bemoans the lack of recognition accorded to the Hata and others, it would appear that the desire to restrain the influence of immigrant kinship groups was not limited to the authors of the *Shinsen shōjiroku*. Hironari's protests indicate, however, that such views were not universally shared at court. Apparently by the advent of the Heian period conceptions of nativist culture were very much in flux.[17]

One possible reason for this may have been the increasing prominence of immigrant lineages at court. Of the 1,182 lineages listed in the *Shinsen shōjiroku*, roughly one-third are classified as immigrant. Even more to the point, members of immigrant kinship groups had begun breaking into the highest echelons of power during the final decades of the eighth century. This process was dramatically illustrated during the reign of Saga and Heizei's father, Kanmu, who had numerous consorts who claimed descent from the founding ancestors of the Korean kingdom of Paekche.[18]

Hironari's plea on behalf of lineages such as the Hata thus may have resulted not from a concern that such groups were weak, but rather from a calculation that they were powerful and potentially useful in promoting Hironari's agenda. This in turn suggests that the sense of urgency demonstrated by the *Shinsen shōjiroku* to delineate who was or was not descended from immigrant deities was itself spurred by the success and pervasiveness of lineages such as the Hata in cultural and political life.

Vengeful Gods and Buddhist Monasteries in Nara

Ironically, the influence of immigrant *kami* in the early Heian period in many ways shared common roots with those of the official monastic system established by Shōmu *tennō* in 741. Shōmu ordered the establishment of a network of provincial temples known as *kokubunji* across the Japanese islands for the purpose of safeguarding the *tennō* and the realm. The *kokubunji*, which were usually built in the immediate vicinity of provincial administrative centers, effectively dramatized the coextensive nature of the ruler's political and sacerdotal authority.

In so doing, the *kokubunji* helped define the cultic and political identities of Japanese rulers in several ways. As Piggott has noted, the Buddhist tradition offered rulers a new vocabulary with which to construct a cultic and political identity vis-à-vis their subjects. Thus the establishment of the *kokubunji* system and the construction of the Great Buddha at Tōdaiji created a ritual space in which Shōmu *tennō* could enact the role of leader of a Buddhist nation populated by devout—and loyal—believers. Piggott has also noted the role of Buddhist institutions in providing a suitable stage for a "theater of state," in which the performance of rituals elicited provincial participation in the political structures controlled by the court. Imposing monastic centers thus enhanced the prestige of the *tennō* even as they helped extend the court's control over the political and cultic resources offered by the Buddhist tradition.[19]

The political ramifications of the *kokubunji*, however, should not overshadow their stated purpose, which was to foster a community of monks charged with the task of producing karmic benefits and protection for the ruler and the realm. One example of the importance that the court placed on the ability of the Buddhist tradition to avert supernatural harm can be found in the 730s, not long before the court ordered the construction of the *kokubunji* network. At that time a plague originating in Chikuzen (northern Kyūshū) decimated both court and countryside. Among the plague's victims were the heads of all four sub-branches of the Fujiwara lineage. This event was interpreted as a spectacular illustration of the vulnerability of even the most powerful members of court to vengeful spirits.[20]

As might be expected, the plague had important ramifications for the cultic orientation of the Fujiwara. One of the most important consequences occurred when Shōmu's chief consort, Kōmyō, the de facto head of the Fujiwara, turned to the spirit of Prince Shōtoku, the hero of the battle for the establishment of Buddhism in Japan, for supernatural assistance. For our purposes, Kōmyō's appeal to the prince is of particular interest for two reasons. First, Kōmyō and the court were directly linking the Buddhist tradition with a royal ancestor in opposition to vengeful disease-bearing spirits. Second, the Shōtoku cult as it existed in Komyo's time would have been unimaginable without the efforts of immigrant lineages such as the Hata, who were among the cult's chief architects.[21]

One key figure in introducing Kōmyō to the Shōtoku cult was the monk Dōji, the leading intellectual of the day and one of the principal advocates of the *kokubunji* system. With Dōji's encouragement, Kōmyō in

733 began making repeated requests for Shōtoku's lineal temple Hōryūji to perform services for her own health and for the spirit of her mother. Several such rites were performed at Hōryūji by Dōji himself. These services did not go unrewarded. In 737, even as the heads of all four Fujiwara sublineages succumbed to the plague, work was begun on restoring several buildings at Hōryūji, which had burned to the ground some sixty years before. At the completion of the famed Yumedono, an octagonal structure that served as the prince's de facto mausoleum, Kōmyō, Shōmu, and the court sought the prince's protection from disasters. Shortly thereafter, Dōji successfully petitioned Kōmyō to establish yearly rites at his own temple, Daianji, which was at that time the administrative center for the ecclesial hierarchy and the *kokubunji* system. These rites were specifically designed to prevent disasters such as earthquakes, fires, and, of course, plagues.[22]

Chikuzen Deities and Terrified *Tennō*

Dōji's efforts to present Buddhist institutions as a means by which the court could find protection from vengeful spirits played upon longstanding fears on the part of *tennō* vis-à-vis hostile spirits from Chikuzen, the source of the plague that decimated the Fujiwara. One likely source of such fears lay in the fact that some seventy years earlier the ruler Saimei was thought to have been struck down in Chikuzen by hostile local deities. Saimei's death, as it is recorded in the *Nihon shoki*, a court chronicle completed in 720, is as follows:

> 5th month, 9th day. The *tennō* moved her residence to the Palace of Asakura no Tachibana no Hironiwa.
> At this time trees belonging to the Shrine of Asakura were cut down and cleared away in order to build this Palace. The god there was thus very angry and demolished the building. Within the Palace there were also mysterious fires. Because of this the Grand Treasurer and many of those in waiting took ill and died. . . .
> 6th Month. Prince Ise died.
> Autumn, 7th month, 24th day. The Empress died in the palace of Asakura. . . .
> 8th month, 1st day. The Crown Prince, waiting in attendance with the *tennō*'s remains, went back to the Palace of Iwase. That evening, on the top of Mount Asakura, there was a demon wearing a great hat who looked down on the funeral ceremonies. The people all uttered exclamations of astonishment.[23]

Saimei's death is not the only instance of a Japanese ruler believed to have been struck down by an angry deity. The *Nihon shoki*, for instance, states that the court attributed the death of Saimei's son Tenmu to the curse of the Kusanagi sword, which was the chief deity at the Atsuta shrine in Owari province.[24] Such events suggest that rulers during this period felt remarkably vulnerable to the wrath of deities ensconced in shrines located at some distance from the Yamato court; here we are told that in the space of less than thirty years, two sovereigns were believed to have been killed by such gods.

One by-product of the court's sense of vulnerability was that succeeding *tennō* turned to immigrant lineages such as the Hata for help in dealing with Chikuzen deities. This may have been due to the fact that the Hata, who had deep roots in Chikuzen, had already developed close relationships with several of the deities most likely to intimidate the court. Furthermore, the Hata's familiarity with continental culture meant that they were particularly well qualified to utilize cultic technologies developed in China and Korea for the pacification of spirits. Such rites, which were frequently rooted in continental *yin-yang* (*ommyōdō*) thought, offered Japanese rulers new and presumably more effective means of pacifying hostile deities and spirits.[25]

During the years that followed Tenmu's death, immigrant deities from Chikuzen and elsewhere entered the mainstream of the royal cult as legend cycles depicting royal ancestors propitiating Chikuzen deities proliferated rapidly. One of the best examples of this process can be seen in the role of the Sumiyoshi deities at the beginning of the Ōjin/Jingū legend cycle. Set in Chikuzen, the following *Kojiki* account details the terrible consequences that befell Jingū's husband Chūai when he refused to follow the instructions of Amaterasu and the Sumiyoshi gods:

> At this the Empress was possessed by gods who revealed to them the following command: "In the west there is a land of many rare and dazzling treasures beginning with gold and silver. I will now bestow it upon you." Then [Chūai] *tennō* replied, saying: "When I climb up to a high place and look westward, I see no land, but only the great sea." Then, saying, "They are lying deities," he pushed away his zither [*koto*], ceased playing it, and sat silently. At this the gods were very angry and said: "You should not rule this land! Go to the one road!" . . . Then [Chūai] slowly took back his zither and played on it listlessly. So almost immediately the sound of the zither became inaudible. When they then held up a light and looked, he was already dead.[26]

This legend, the third in the royal chronicles to record the death of a Japanese ruler at the hands of a vengeful god, does more than simply underscore the perceived need of Japanese rulers to reach an accommodation with vengeful spirits; here, in the starkest possible terms, we are told that propitiation of these deities brings glory, while failure to do so brings death.[27]

One important by-product of the court's policy of co-opting hostile deities from Chikuzen and elsewhere was the accelerated development of Hata cultic centers in Yamashiro province, where the Hata had their strongest base in the Kinki region. One example of this can be found in the *Nihon shoki*, which states that the ruler Kinmei ascended the throne in large part due to the efforts of a Hata ancestor and the deities of the Fushimi Inari shrine, yet another Hata cultic center in Yamashiro.[28]

The court's reliance on the Hata's sacerdotal abilities is also suggested in a remnant of the *Hatashi honkeichō*, which states that in 703 Monmu *tennō* ordered the Hata to bring Okitsushima Hime no Mikoto, one of the chief deities from the Munakata shrine in northern Kyūshū, to the Matsuno'o shrine in Yamashiro.[29] Although the text provides no background for this event, family registers from the Munakata district in Buzen province in northern Kyūshū suggest that the great majority of the area's population was Hata. Thus it would appear that the court turned to the Hata for assistance with the Munakata deities because of the Hata's own roots in Chikuzen.[30]

Further hints as to why the court would seek to bring the Munakata gods within the sphere of the royal cult can be found within the *Nihon shoki*, which portrays the Munakata deities as eminently capable of intimidating Japanese rulers when it suited them:

> 5th year, Spring, 3rd month, 1st day. The three deities who dwell in Tsukushi appeared within the palace and said, "Why were our people taken from us? We will now disgrace you." At this [Richū *tennō*] prayed, but his prayers were not answered....
>
> 19th day. There was a sound like a blast of wind calling out in the sky, saying "Oh! Prince the Sword!" ... Suddenly a minister came and said "The Imperial concubine is dead." The Emperor was greatly shocked, and immediately returned in his carriage....
>
> Winter, 10th month, 11th day. The Imperial concubine was buried. After this the *tennō*, regretting that he had not pacified the gods' wrath and had thus caused the death of the Imperial concubine, again sought after the offense [that caused the gods' anger].[31]

This legend, containing as it does the now-familiar pattern of deities from northern Kyūshū killing members of the court and intimidating a Japanese ruler, strongly suggests that less than twenty years before the formation of the *kokubunji* system the court was thoroughly cowed by a number of Chikuzen deities, many of which were closely associated with the Hata.

The capstone of this process came in 749, when the god Hachiman, yet another Chikuzen deity with close links to the Hata and other immigrant lineages, declared through an oracle that he wished to be brought to the capital to be the guardian deity of Tōdaiji, the ritual and administrative center of the *kokubunji* network. Shortly thereafter, the god was installed at the temple at the head of a procession of some 5,000 monks. By the early Heian period Hachiman and other Chikuzen deities permeated the royal cult to such a degree that the spirit of Jingū was worshipped in the Sumiyoshi shrine in Naniwa while the spirit of Ōjin was identified with Hachiman himself.[32]

All of this suggests two preliminary conclusions regarding the development of the royal cult. First, faced with seemingly implacable deities from northern Kyūshū, large portions of the cultic agenda of Japanese rulers were designed in response to powerful deities from the region. This led to some of the most dramatic cultic developments of the Nara period, as the court embraced a series of gods and kinship groups that traced their roots to the shores of the court's rivals across the sea. Second, and perhaps most important, Japanese rulers embraced these cults not from a position of strength but rather in fear and weakness.

Lineage and Buddhist Ancestors in Early Heian

In contrast to the dynamic of fear and propitiation that characterized relations between the *tennō* and the local cults and lineages at the core of the emerging royal cult, by the advent of the Heian period the legend cycle of the royal ancestor Shōtoku had become a cornerstone of the Japanese Buddhist tradition. New movements such as Saichō's Tendai sect were aggressively linking the figure of Shōtoku with their own sectarian agendas. A core element of Saichō's personal vocation, in fact, appears to have been his belief that he was a spiritual descendant of Shōtoku, whose teachings he held constituted the primary form of Japanese Buddhism. In 816, two years after the completion of the *Shinsen shōjiroku*, Saichō composed the following poem at Shitennōji, the first temple purportedly built by the prince:

> Seeking karmic strength and connection within the seas,
> I take refuge at the Palace of Shōtoku.

I now will spread the rare doctrine taught by the teacher and leave it
   neglected no longer . . .
I ask but to make [this] the teaching of the nation,
To protect it and help it flourish.³³

At the heart of Saichō's message was the belief that the prince had in fact been the incarnation of the Chinese monk Hui-ssu, the teacher of the famed T'ien-t'ai patriarch Chih-i. Apparently Saichō reasoned that importing T'ien-t'ai teachings from China to Japan constituted a recovery of the prince's Buddhist message, and thus the Tendai tradition was not a "foreign" tradition at all, but rather the product and teaching of a royal ancestor.³⁴

This claim to a special link with the prince was aggressively promoted even in China by Saichō's ecclesial descendants. On several occasions visiting Tendai monks gave their Chinese hosts copies of a commentary of the *Lotus Sutra* purportedly written by Shōtoku. Lest anyone fail to get the point, the inscription on the top of one said: "This is a work of Prince Kamitsumiya of Japan. It is not a foreign work."³⁵

All of this thus highlights one important means by which the politics of lineage and nativism influenced religious events of the period; here we find that even as the court was seeking to standardize the ancestral claims of lineages across the Japanese islands, a major concern of the fledgling Tendai movement was to establish and amplify a claim to direct spiritual descent from a royal prince. Other Buddhists made similar claims as they constructed a Buddhist lineage and cultic identity for Japanese rulers. Thus the *Nihon ryōiki*, a compilation of Buddhist legends that was completed sometime before 824, contains a statement that Saga himself was the reincarnation of Jakusen, a famed ascetic from Shikoku.³⁶ All of this suggests a triangular configuration of *tennō*, monk, and *kami* that contrasted sharply with the understanding of the period in the Meiji era, for here we see that at the start of the Heian period, the Japanese Buddhist tradition could claim that it was not in any sense foreign, but rather as native as the royal line itself.

Hata and Fujiwara in Nara Japan

Ironically, the heightened awareness of nativist issues at the start of the Heian was most likely directly related to the expanding influence of immigrant lineages and Chikuzen deities throughout the Nara period. Politically, the Nara era had been characterized by the adoption of continental conceptions of governance and sage kingship. Culturally, the era was characterized by the rapid diffusion of continental literary and architectural forms that were closely associated with the Buddhist tradition. Immigrant kinship groups such as the Hata were closely associated with each of these processes.

This political-religious context greatly served the interests of the Hata, who proved adept at transforming their facility with continental cultural forms into political influence. One of the best examples can be seen in the career of Benshō, a Hata monk who was sent to China as a student during the Taihō era (701–704). Benshō's career in China appears to have been remarkable; during his stay there he became a *go* companion of the future Chinese Emperor Hsüan-tsung. Although Benshō died in China, his son Hata no Asamoto returned, along with the monk Dōji, to Nara with great acclaim in 718.[37]

Asamoto transformed his cultural capital rather directly into political influence. He married two of his daughters to two sons of Fujiwara no Umakai, the head of the Shiki branch of the Fujiwara. In light of the fact that the Shiki Fujiwara constituted the main branch of the Fujiwara during the later Nara period, the importance of such an alliance can hardly be overstated.[38]

These alliances bore immediate fruit for the Hata. One of Asamoto's grandsons, Fujiwara no Tanetsugu, played a major role in engineering the rise of Kōnin *tennō* and a new branch of the royal line. Tanetsugu later served as a principal advisor for Kōnin's successor, Kanmu, and he is believed to have played a major role in the decision of the court to leave Nara for Yamashiro. Tanetsugu's line probably reached its apex of power under Heizei *tennō*, who took as his chief consort Tanetsugu's daughter Kusuko and whose chief advisor was Tanetsugu's son Nakanari. Thus at the start of the Heian period several of the most powerful courtiers at court called Hata women mother and grandmother.

The importation of continental cultic and governmental forms aided the rise of other Hata as well. As successive *tennō* constructed ever larger temples, roadways, canals, and even capitals, Hata wealth and engineering ability appear to have led to their direct involvement in a remarkable physical transformation of the topography of the Kinki region.[39] Perhaps the most spectacular example of this came in 740, when a revolt in Kyūshū led Shōmu *tennō* to seek to move his capital to the Kuni district of Yamashiro province. One figure charged with completing much of this project was Hata no Shimamaro. Within a year Shimamaro had completed his task, most likely through the expenditure of a substantial amount of Hata resources and labor and the conversion of Hata buildings into structures for use by the court. A similar process occurred some fifty years later, when Kanmu *tennō* moved his capital first to Nagaoka and then to the Kadono district in Yamashiro province.[40]

Although Shōmu soon abandoned the Kuni capital, Shimamaro had clearly made a large mark at court. In 742 the court rewarded Shimamaro by elevating him from eighth to fourth rank—a spectacular rise. Rank and wealth soon generated further alliances between the Hata and the Fujiwara. Shortly thereafter, Shimamaro married his daughter to Fujiwara no Oguromaro, the head of the northern branch of the Fujiwara until his death in 801. During Kanmu's lifetime Oguromaro may have been the single most influential Fujiwara at court. Although we can only speculate as to how Oguromaro viewed his alliance with the Hata, the fact that his eldest son Fujiwara no Kadono was named after the largest Hata base in Yamashiro suggests that the Hata played an active role in Kadono's upbringing. Kadono himself was prominent at court throughout his career, and he appears to have been directly involved in the planning of the Nagaoka and Heian capitals, both of which were in Yamashiro.[41]

This alliance would later prove to be of tremendous importance for Hata fortunes during the Heian period, as the northern branch of the Fujiwara replaced the Shiki branch in the aftermath of the Kusuko incident, for Hata influence proved broad and deep enough to survive even the fall of Kusuko and Nakanari. Although doubtless a severe blow, the fall of Heizei and Kusuko did not spell the end of Hata influence at court. Rather it meant that Hata influence was channeled through a different branch of the Fujiwara.

Several conclusions follow from all of this. First, by the time of the completion of the Great Buddha in 752, the Hata had succeeded in a type of marriage politics that is familiar to any student of the Heian period. Whereas, ironically, the Fujiwara are frequently noted for their ability to hold on to power by marrying Fujiwara women to rulers, we know that on at least three occasions Hata women were married to men at the highest echelons of the Fujiwara. These unions are notable not only for their quantity but for their quality—during the period the Hata were able to construct kinship relations with the courtiers at the very apex of the court hierarchy. Thus even as Fujiwara men learned to accumulate power by playing the role of the ruler's maternal grandfather, so too did the Hata accumulate influence through their prominence in the distaff lineages of powerful Fujiwara.

Second, such lineal affiliations had important consequences across several political and cultic registers. Figures such as Tanetsugu and Oguromaro are thought to have been key players in the elevation of Kanmu's father Kōnin to the throne. The Hata alliance with the Fujiwara was also undoubtedly a major—though by no means the only—factor in the decision to leave the Nara plain for Yamashiro.[42]

Third, these developments occurred during a period when the royal cult embraced a collection of cults and gods that included Hachiman, the Sumiyoshi and Munakata deities, as well as the deities of the Matsuno'o and Fushimi Inari shrines. Seen against this backdrop, Saga's decision during the Kusuko incident to incorporate the deities of the Kamo shrine within the heart of the royal cult suggests an intensification of a longstanding trend of royal dependence on Hata cults and deities.

Hata Monks, Kokūzō, and the Clerical Hierarchy

Hata involvement in the major shrine centers of the royal cult was mirrored by an equally large role in some of the most prominent Buddhist movements and lineages of the Nara and early Heian periods. Several clues concerning the extent of Hata influence can be found in the remains of Kokūzōji, a Hata temple in northern Kyūshū adjacent to the Usa Hachiman shrine. Archeological remains suggest that the temple was built at the end of the seventh century with the same architectural layout as that of Hōryūji, the kinship group temple of Prince Shōtoku.[43]

Kokūzōji is also of note because, as its name suggests, the Hata were from an early date involved in the cult of the bodhisattva Kokūzō (Skt. Akāśagarbha). Although we have no way of knowing when this temple first became involved with the Kokūzō cult, during the Nara and early Heian periods several prominent monks are known to have gone into the Yoshino mountains in order to perform a rite known as the Gumonjihō, an elaborate ritual of scriptural recitation performed before an image of Kokūzō. Further evidence suggesting Hata involvement in this practice—as well as for continuities in Hata Buddhist practice across large distances—can be found in the statuary of Kōryūji, the main Hata temple in Yamashiro, which housed a statue of Kokūzō from the early Heian period.[44]

For our purposes, the Kokūzō cult is of immediate interest for two reasons. First, Kūkai, easily the most successful monk of the early Heian period, traced the formation of his vocation to an experience he had while practicing the Gumonjihō.[45] Although, as Abe Ryūichi points out, there is no evidence that Kūkai regarded this moment as the starting point of his career in esoteric Buddhism per se, Kūkai's involvement with Kokūzō and the Gumonjihō persisted throughout his career.[46]

Second, the development of the Kokūzō cult is also revealing of the status of Hata monks and cults during the Nara and early Heian periods. In 859 the monk Dōsen, for instance, built a Kokūzō retreat center at Hōryūji, a center of the Shōtoku cult. Kukai's student Dōshō, similarly, was himself a Hata monk who eventually served as *shosōzu* (junior priest general) and confidant of Seiwa *tennō*. Dōshō's continuing affiliation with the Hata and Shōtoku was also reflected in his continuous service as chief administrator (*bettō*) of the Hata kinship group temple Kōryūji, where he installed the image of Kokūzō referred to above.[47]

Although Kūkai, Dōsen, and Dōshō are thought of today in conjunction with Japan's esoteric Buddhist tradition, several of the most prominent monks of the Nara and early Heian periods are known to have performed Gumonjihō rites. Sonoda traces one lineage of Gumonjihō practitioners beginning with Shin'ei, a monk from Gangōji who practiced at Hasedera in the Yoshino mountains. Although little is known about Shin'ei, he is said to have studied in the Korean kingdom of Silla prior to being named to the post of *risshi* (Vinaya master) in 717. Towards the end of his life Shin'ei, along with Dōji, was given a special stipend by the court in recognition of his knowledge of the Buddhist tradition.[48]

Sonoda also notes that after Shin'ei the careers of several Gangōji monks were characterized both by the study of Hossō doctrine and the practice of religious austerities in the Yoshino mountains. Noteworthy among these were Shōgo, who in 806 was named *daisōzu* (senior priest general), as well as Shōgo's disciple Gomyō. This lineage is particularly noteworthy in light of the fact that during the late Nara and early Heian periods, Gangōji Hossō came close to dominating the official clerical establishment. In this regard the figure of Gomyō is of immediate interest because he is known to have practiced Gumonjiō rites, he attained the top rank of the ecclesial hierarchy (*sōjō*, supreme priest), and because he was a member of the Hata.[49]

A second lineage of Gumonjihō practitioners can be traced to Daianji, the home of Dōji, whom, as we saw above, was a major advocate of both the Shōtoku cult and the *kokubunji* system.[50] Several Daianji monks are also known to have practiced in the Yoshino mountains, including the Chinese monk Dōsen, Dōji's disciple Zengi, and Zengi's disciple Gonsō. Gonsō is of special interest for us because, like Gomyō, he is known to have practiced the Gumonjihō, he also attained the rank of *sōjō*, and he was also a member of the Hata.

All of this suggests considerable Hata influence within the clerical hierarchy at the advent of the Heian period. Not only were several Hata monks at the cutting edge of the religious practices of the clerical elite, Hata monks were also near or at the pinnacle of several of the most prominent Buddhist lineages. Such influence was spectacularly illustrated in 827, when the Hata monk Gonsō was succeeded by his kinsmen Gomyō in the post of *sōjō*. Clearly Hata monks such as Gonsō and Gomyō played major roles in determining the court's response to the fledgling Buddhist movements of the period.[51]

The Hata and Immigrant Deities at Hiei and Tōji

The prominence of Hata-affiliated gods during the period also proved to be a key factor in the development of both Saichō's and Kūkai's movements. Tendai monks would later take advantage of the fact that the deity of the Hiyoshi shrine on the eastern base of Mount Hiei was Ōyamakui no kami, the Hata deity of the Matsuno'o shrine and the husband of Kamu Tamayori Hime, the goddess of the lower Kamo shrine. Tendai monks throughout the Heian period used their special relationship with Ōyamakui no kami as a point of entry into the Chikuzen/Hata network of gods embraced by Saga and his successors.[52] Sometime during the ninth century, for instance, a permanent shrine to Kamu Tamayori Hime was established on Mount Hiei's eastern slope.[53] Uwai notes that, according to the *Yōtenki*, by 965 such linkages had resulted in a series of rites that linked the gods of Mount Hiei with the Matsuno'o and Kamo shrines, for Ōyamakui no Kami was carried annually from Mount Hiei to the Matsuno'o shrine, where he was joined by his wife Kamu Tamayori Hime and their child, Wake no Ikazuchi no Kami.[54]

A similar process appears to have been at work at Tōji. Even as Hata monks such as Gonsō, Gomyō, and Dōshō received esoteric instruction from Kūkai, Kūkai's followers actively sought relationships with Chikuzen deities such as Hachiman, who was eventually enshrined as Tōji's guardian deity. Further linkages between shrine and monastery were created in 827, after a divination expert declared that Junna *tennō* had fallen ill as a result of court officials angering the Hata deity of the Fushimi Inari shrine. Shortly thereafter the Fushimi Inari deity appeared within the precincts of Tōji, where he was regularly propitiated. In the centuries that followed, the relationship between the Fushimi Inari deity and Tōji continued to strengthen as the Fushimi Inari deity became one of the most significant cultic figures for the burgeoning movement of mountain asceticism that would later be known as Shūgendō.[55] Thus even as the Tendai sect trumpeted its relationship with the Ōyamakui no Kami and the Matsuno'o shrine, so too did the Shingon movement come to embrace the Hata deity of the Fushimi Inari shrine.

The Hata and the Temple-Shrine Complexes of the Heian Period

If Saga's embrace of the Kamo shrine represented an emphatic affirmation of long-term cultic trends fueled by royal fear and Fujiwara/Hata cooperation, the early Heian period saw several further innovations in the royal cult that tended to solidify the position of Hata deities within the royal cult. One such innovation came a century later with a reorganization of the royal cult that centered on a network of officially sponsored temple-shrine complexes. These institutions served several important purposes. Theologically, they established a clear set of correspondences between several of the most prominent *kami* and buddhas of the realm. Institutionally, the system served to clarify the rank and services required of several of the most important shrines and temples in the land. But perhaps even more important, by binding prominent *kami* with monastic centers in the service of the *tennō*, this system helped domesticate several of the most volatile and dangerous deities in the Japanese islands. The degree to which Chikuzen/Hata deities were represented among these institutions can be seen in Table 1, which lists the twenty-two shrines that appeared in the three-tier system that was established by the court in 1039. With the exception of the Hirota shrine, however, all of the Chikuzen/Hata shrines were part of the network by 898. This group of shrines has been discussed by Alan Grapard, who is surely correct to point out the importance of Fujiwara institutions

Table 1 Twenty-two Shrines of the Heian Period

UPPER SEVEN	MIDDLE SEVEN	LOWER EIGHT
Ise	Ōharano (F)	**Hiyoshi**
Iwashimizu	Ōmiwa	Umenomiya
Kamo	Isonokami	Yoshida (F)
Matsuno'o	Yamato	**Hirota**
Hirano	Hirose	Gion
Inari	Tatsuta	Kitano
Kasuga (F)	**Sumiyoshi**	Nihunokawakami
		Kibune

Notes: Fujiwara shrines are indicated by (F). Shrines housing deities identified with Chikuzen or the Hata are in bold letters.
Source: Grapard, "Institution, Ritual and Ideology," 250.

on the list. As Grapard notes, one Fujiwara shrine is listed in each of the three tiers on the list, and the Fujiwara appear to have played a major role in constructing temples for several of the shrines. If we consider cases such as the Hiyoshi deity, which the Fujiwara worshipped from an early date, it is clear that Fujiwara influence was even greater.

Yet perhaps the most remarkable feature of the list is the large representation of deities that were closely identified with Chikuzen or the Hata. Shrines to such deities constitute the majority of the upper tier, with the Kamo, Matsuno'o, Inari, and Iwashimizu Hachiman shrines. In the second and third tiers we also find the Sumiyoshi shrine and the Hiyoshi shrines. In addition, the Hirota shrine, located near the port of Naniwa, was also closely associated with the Yamato ruler Jingū, with Hachiman, and with the Korean peninsula.[56]

Remarkably, when taken together, no less than five of the top seven shrines and ten of the total twenty-two shrines that the court chose for special attention were directly patronized by the Fujiwara or immigrant/Chikuzen lineages such as the Hata.[57] This suggests that the alliances between the Hata and Fujiwara that helped propel the court towards Yamashiro province at the end of the Nara period endured long enough to leave a definitive stamp on the deities to which the court turned for centuries to come. Although virtually no studies have been undertaken on the role of the Hata in mid- to late-Heian society, it is clear that whatever their subsequent fate, the Hata left a deep and enduring mark on the development of the royal cult and the dominant religio-political paradigms of the Heian period and beyond.

The picture that emerges is one of remarkable Hata influence across the religious and cultic spectrum during the very period when relations between *tennō*, monks, and *kami* were first being set. Hata monks such as Gonsō and Gomyō were chosen to head the monastic establishment, and several of the most powerful figures at court were children and grandchildren of Hata women. The court's embrace of the Hata shrine network and the Kamo Saiin similarly represented the culmination of a longstanding trend of royal dependence on immigrant shrines and *kami*.

In this context it is hardly surprising that as monks from Tōji or Mount Hiei competed for the court's support, they found it prudent to form alliances with cultic figures closely associated with the Hata. Simply put, the cultic horizon of reception during the period was dominated by Chikuzen and Hata gods to such a degree that the fledgling Buddhist movements could not ignore Hata deities, Hata cults, Hata monks, or Hata courtiers if they wished to survive and prosper. And because these institutions, in turn, later dominated the Buddhist world at court, they also helped set the trajectory of the Japanese Buddhist tradition for centuries to come.

Conclusion

The complex cultic interplay between *tennō*, monk, and *kami* that occurred during the Nara and early Heian periods was informed by notions of nativism that were in turn stimulated by the remarkable cultural and political success of immigrant lineages such as the Hata. One manifestation of the success of these groups was the central role played by a network of Hata cultic centers in the royal cult. The prominence of immigrant lineages and their deities within the royal cult had multiple roots, an important one being simple fear on the part of Japanese rulers that those volatile deities could and in fact had killed Japanese rulers and courtiers on multiple occasions.

These fears provided a powerful motivation for Japanese rulers to coopt the cults of the more powerful deities from Kyūshū, many of which were closely associated with the Hata or other immigrant kinship groups. As a result, throughout the Nara and early Heian periods shrines and deities with roots in Kyūshū and the Korean peninsula came to play an increasingly prominent role in the shrines patronized by the royal house and by prominent kinship groups such as the Fujiwara. They also helped accelerate a trend towards associating volatile immigrant *kami* with monastic institutions that offered protection for the person of the ruler and the court.

By the 730s these considerations, coupled with the Hata's command of cultural and technological traditions from the continent, helped spur the formation of the *kokubunji* monastic system and stimulated a pattern of intermarriage between the Fujiwara and Hata. By the latter half of the Nara period, leaders of the two most prominent sublineages of the Fujiwara counted members of the Hata among their closest distaff relatives. These figures were then instrumental in the elevation of the line of Kanmu *tennō*, who in turn made the decision to build the Heian capital in Yamashiro province, squarely in the middle of Hata territory.

In the years following the move to Heian, Hata deities and Hata monks played a pivotal role in shaping the still-developing royal cult, dominating both the court's cultic agenda as well as its hierarchy of shrines. Thus the flourishing shrines and temples of the Heian capital may have been the product not so much of a triumphalist court's self-confidence, but rather of the court's keenly felt fear and weakness in the face of gods and rivals from across the sea. The grand network of temple-shrine complexes of the

Heian period was both figuratively and literally rooted in ground prepared by the Hata.

Within this horizon of reception the fledgling Buddhist movements initiated by Kūkai and Saichō embraced Buddhist cultic forms closely associated with the Hata even as they established Hata *kami* as the guardian deities of their respective temples. Glimpses of Hata influence can also be seen in the long shadow cast by Hata monks such as Gonsō and Gomyō over the careers of both Kūkai and Saichō. Both of these younger monks, in turn, highlighted the role of figures such as Kokūzō and Shōtoku, respectively, in the formation of their religious vocations. As Hata deities were integrated into the ritual life of institutions such as Tōji and Enryakuji, immigrant gods then emerged at the heart of the nascent Jindō paradigm.

All of this suggests that a crucial thread of continuity across every leg of the Heian cultic triangle was the presence of immigrant lineages such as the Hata. Even as later generations sought to pluck apart the "foreign" Buddhist elements of this triangle, they did so only by embracing the very deities whose bullying had pushed a terrified court towards the protection of the Sangha a thousand years before.

CHAPTER 2

Karakami and Animal Sacrifice

> Up until now I have been enfeoffed as king and have received offerings of bloody victuals. It is through them that my might and blessings have been manifest. Now although my title of perfected lord is exalted, all sacrifice to me with vegetarian offerings. Deprived of the nourishment of bloody victuals, I consequently lack the numinous power of my awesome might and blessings.
> —Grumblings attributed to the god Li Er-lang after Taoists appropriated his cult and halted all meat offerings.[1]

BY THE EARLY Heian period several of the shrines and deities associated with the Hata and other immigrant kinship groups had already been adopted as primary figures of worship by the court—so many, in fact, that immigrant deities (*karakami*) constituted a major element within the court's cultic agenda. As a result, the cultic centers of immigrant lineages such as the Hata also came to play a major role in shaping the development of court ritual and what would later be thought of as the "Shintō" tradition.

The influence of immigrant lineages and deities, however, was not limited to the region of the capital. Because immigrant lineages were settled across the Japanese islands, their ancestral deities occupied an extremely wide geographic area. As a result, major local deities far from the court were also frequently *karakami*. Because the cultic practices and beliefs of the Yamato court were in constant interaction with cults and deities elsewhere, such distant *karakami* played a major role in shaping cultic life throughout the Japanese islands. One consequence was that long before the construction of the Heian capital, the Yamato court had already absorbed a host of immigrant deities and cultic practices from even the most distant regions of the realm. Local cults that were heavily influenced by immigrant lineages and their ancestral deities were thus an important driving force behind the proliferation of continental-style rites of spirit pacification and even animal sacrifice both within the royal cult and across the country.

In this chapter I propose to investigate two issues that were closely related to the prominence of immigrant lineages and deities within Japanese cultic life. The first concerns the degree to which cults of *karakami* and disease deities were embedded within the worldview of the Chinese festival calendar. My principal focus in this regard will be a cluster of ritual practices such as animal sacrifice, roadside rites of propitiation and pacification, and the cult of the Weaver Maiden and the Cowherd, two of the best-known astral deities in the Chinese pantheon. I will also examine a cluster of weaver and cowherd deities from locales across Japan that were adopted by the Yamato court prior to the Nara period.[2]

I will also suggest that because the Yamato court's adoption of the Buddhist tradition was closely linked to a broader appropriation of continental political and cultural forms, the early Buddhist tradition both helped promote and to a surprising degree was in turn shaped by continental ritual technologies for the propitiation of spirits. I focus particularly on a series of legends from the *Nihon ryōiki*, the oldest Buddhist tale collection in the Japanese islands. These legends suggest that the use of substitute bodies, the naming of spirits, and even meat offerings to spirits may have played an important role in the formation of popular Buddhist tales and beliefs.

Ritual Technologies and Popular Cultic Traditions

Although the worship of *karakami* and continental rites of spirit pacification are now widely recognized as important elements in the cultic life of the Nara period, for many years such cults were virtually ignored by scholars of early Japanese religion. This neglect is most likely attributable to two mutually reinforcing presuppositions from prewar Japanese imperial ideology. The first, and perhaps the most tenacious, was the simple notion that the religious practices of the Japanese "folk" and the royal cult lie at the core of Japanese identity. Since assigning an important role to *karakami* in the construction of such practices would be tantamount to admitting an important role for immigrant lineages in the construction of the royal cult, few scholars in prewar Japan dared venture near such controversial territory.

After the war a second, a more sophisticated approach was articulated in accordance with the need to put a more pacifist face on Japanese culture. In place of prewar declarations of the inherently martial spirit of Japanese religious life, postwar religious groups have frequently argued that a defining characteristic of both Shintō and Japanese Buddhism was an aversion to violence and bloodshed.[3] Others have focused on early conceptions of purity and pollution (*kegare*), which are often presented as distinctive if not defining elements of Japanese religious activity.[4] One consequence of this approach has been that cults and legends centering on blood sacrifice were long categorized as foreign influences beyond the range of native cultic practice. As a result, the performance of rites involving blood sacrifice, offerings of meat, and spirit pacification was for many years assumed to have been confined to immigrant cultic centers out of the mainstream of Nara and Heian religious life.

In support of this position, some scholars have frequently pointed to numerous edicts from the court that banned the practice of slaughtering animals. The first such recorded prohibition occurs in the *Nihon shoki* from 676, when Tenmu *tennō* ordered a comprehensive ban on the killing and consumption of all animals in the realm. The prohibition of the slaughter of cows and horses was subsequently codified within the Yōrō law codes, and edicts prohibiting the practice were also issued in Yōrō 6.7.7 (722), Tempyō 2.9 (730), Tempyō 4.7.5 (732), Tempyō 9.5.19 (737), and Tempyō 13.2.7 (741).[5] Similarly, within the Buddhist sphere throughout the Nara period and beyond, the court frequently ordered the performance of a rite known as a Hōjōe (Assembly of the Release of Sentient Beings) in response to droughts and other disasters. Edicts from Tempyō 9.8.2 (737) and Tempyō 13.3.24 (741) also forbade the killing of animals during the six Buddhist feast days.[6]

A closer examination of these injunctions, however, suggests that the court had a complicated approach to issues concerning the killing of animals, sacrifice, and ritual purity, one which was heavily influenced by continental rites and conceptions of spirit. As Ueda Masaaki and others have noted, the sheer number of prohibitions issued by the court itself strongly suggests that animal sacrifice was a common occurrence during the Nara period.[7] Further evidence suggesting that the practice was widespread can be seen in the following entry from the *Shoku Nihongi* from 792:

> Enryaku 10.19.6. The peasants [*hyakushō*] of Ise, Owari, Ōmi, Mino, Wakasa, Echizen, and Kii provinces are forbidden from sacrificing cattle for the use of worshipping *karakami*.[8]

This edict is noteworthy both for its statement that sacrifice was occurring within the Japanese islands and for its specific association with the worship of *karakami*. Perhaps even more important, however, given the number of provinces that are listed in the edict, it would appear that both the worship of *karakami* and the practice of animal sacrifice could be found across virtually the entire central Kinai region. It would also appear that whatever view the court may have held with respect to ritual impurity and the sanctity of life, throughout the Nara period animal sacrifice was a persistent and widespread element in cultic life.

Ueda has also argued that it is a mistake to assume that the court's injunctions against the killing of animals were simply motivated by concerns over ritual pollution; there is also good evidence suggesting that the court's motivations for prohibiting the killing of animals may have had a strong economic component. He notes, for instance, that several of the Tempyō and Enryaku bans were issued during periods when plagues were rampant among the populace.[9] Further support for this suggestion can be seen in an edict from Tempyō 13.2.7 (741), which condemns the practice on the grounds that it involves the destruction of valuable livestock:

> Horses and cattle do labor in the place of humans and nurture them. Because of this, We have previously made clear that the slaughter of animals is not permitted. Now, We hear that in some districts this prohibition has not been put into effect. Peasants are continuing to slaughter [animals]. Those who violate [this edict] shall, without regard to position or privilege, first be given 100 strokes, after which further punishments will be decided according to their guilt. We also hear that some district heads, without regard for public welfare, assemble people for the purpose of hunting. This hampers the industry of the populace and the damage is truly great. Henceforth this shall be banned. Those who violate this prohibition shall without fail be heavily punished.[10]

Here again although we find that the slaughter of animals has become sufficiently widespread as to cause the court concern, no mention is made of a need to avoid defilement from blood, nor is there any reference to Buddhist conceptions regarding killing. Rather, the edict explicitly states that the practice is to be stopped because of its deleterious economic consequences—in this case at least the court's concern is not the animals' spiritual well-being, but their labor. The edict also makes clear that over fifty years after Tenmu's injunction against the taking of life, and in spite of the fact that animal slaughter had been repeatedly banned during that same time period, the practice continued to flourish. Indeed, we are even told that local officials not only themselves engaged in the killing of game, but actually compelled others to aid them in the practice.

When read in conjunction with other edicts from this period, the timing of this edict also contains several important clues as to why the court so frequently banned a practice that persisted in spite of repeated injunctions. In an edict from Tempyō 13.3.24, for instance, the court announced that it was undertaking a major new ritual program involving the establishment of a network of provincial temples that would be charged with reciting Buddhist scriptures, thereby assuring the prosperity and well-being of the court and populace. In order to ensure the efficacy of the temples' efforts, the court also banned the killing of animals during any of the six Buddhist feast days that occurred each month. This edict is thus notable both for its direct linkage of the prohibition with the performance of Buddhist rites for the protection of the land and for what it indicates about the duration of the court's enforcement of its own edicts—this second ban on the killing of animals occurred less than two months after the court had threatened all who engaged in such practices with 100 blows and other, heavier punishments.

In light of all of this, Ueda convincingly argues that we cannot simply treat the court's repeated injunctions against the killing of animals as evidence of a continuous aversion to blood defilement and animal sacrifice. Rather, it would appear that animal sacrifice was a regular feature of the popular cultic life of the period. It would also appear that when the court banned such practices, it did so either to conserve resources during times of hardship or in the context of ritual responses to crises. Once the danger had passed, however, it appears that the killing of animals would continue apace until the next crisis.

In addition to all this, however, I would also suggest that the court's ambivalent approach to animal sacrifice was rooted in a belief that, while the act of banning animal slaughter was both meritorious and materially beneficial, the act of sponsoring meat offerings could also be ritually efficacious. Evidence for this can be seen in the Yōrō law codes, which mandated that the court itself regularly make meat offerings to spirits roaming the land. One such rite was the Michiae no Matsuri (Rite of Roadside Offerings), a rite for the propitiation of spirits on the highways of Yamato that was performed on the final days of the sixth and twelfth months of the year. According to the *Ryō no shūge*, a commentary on the Yōrō codes that is thought to have been composed sometime in the mid-ninth century, a central element of this rite consisted of offering the hides of cows and boar to potentially malevolent spirits on the roadsides in the four directions around the capital.[11] As we shall see shortly, there is also good reason to believe that the well-known Toshigoi Matsuri, which was performed at court-sponsored shrines throughout Japan at the advent of the New Year, also involved the sacrifice of animals and offerings of meat to roadside spirits.

It would thus appear that the court pursued multiple ritual strategies for dealing with crises and that, while some of these required the prohibition of killing, others required meat offerings. One of the clearest illustrations of the court's willingness to pursue multiple ritual strategies during a crisis can be found in the court's response to news that plague had broken out in Kyūshū in Tempyō 7.8.12 (735):

> In recent days, we have heard that there is currently a plague in Dazaifu and numerous people have died. We wish to eliminate this disease and save the lives of the people. In light of this, oblations shall be offered to the deities and prayers shall be offered for the populace. Further, the Great Temple at the headquarters and the many temples in the surrounding provinces shall read the *Kongō hannya kyō*. Envoys shall also be sent to aid the sick and provide medicines. Further, top officials and their assistants in provinces on this side of Nagato shall maintain ritual purity and perform the Michiae no Matsuri.[12]

This eclectic response is notable not only for the variety of measures that the court employed to stop the spread of the plague, but also for the court's willingness to pursue these measures in tandem. Buddhist rites such as the reading of the *Kongō hannya kyō* would normally entail a need for ritual purity, which includes, presumably, not shedding blood. And, indeed, such concerns are reflected in the instruction to local officials to abstain from all polluting activities. But because the court was also clearly worried that the plague would spread along the main highways leading from Kyūshū to the Yamato plain, it also ordered the performance of the Michiae no Matsuri in all provinces between the affected region and the court. Since this rite involved offerings of animal carcasses, it would appear that even as the court sought to eliminate the epidemic in Kyūshū by Buddhist means, it also believed that meat offerings to roadside spirits and deities were an effective means of preventing the spread of the disease from Kyūshū to the capital.

Let it Rain

Further clues suggesting the court's pragmatic embrace of multiple ritual systems may be found in the *Nihon shoki* in an account of a rainmaking competition between the Yamato ruler Kōgyoku and the leader of the powerful Soga kinship group. Although this text is of extremely dubious value as a historical account, it does illustrate the eclectic range of ritual practices that could be drawn upon in times of crisis:

> Kōgyoku 1.7.25. The Ministers discussed among themselves, saying "Following the teachings of the local shrine leaders [*hafuri*] in the villages, there have been some places where people have killed horses and cattle as a sacrifice to the gods of various shrines, and in other places there have been frequent relocations of the market places, while in others prayers have been offered to the River Earl. [Yet] none of these practices has had any effect." Then the Soga no Ōomi responded, saying, "The Mahayana sutras ought to be read in the temples and repentance rites should be performed in accordance with the Buddha's teachings. [We should then] reverently pray for rain."
>
> 27th day. In the southern courtyard of the Great Temple, images of buddhas, bodhisattvas, and the four Heavenly Kings were magnificently adorned. An assembly of priests was requested to read the *Great Cloud Sutra*. At this time the Soga no Ōomi himself took a censer in his hands, burnt incense in it, and petitioned [for rain].
>
> 28th day. A slight rain fell.
>
> 29th day. Because the prayers for rain had not succeeded, the reading of the sutras was discontinued.
>
> 8th month, 1st day. The *tennō* went to the source of the Minabuchi river and knelt down in worship towards the four quarters. Looking up to Heaven, she [then] prayed for rain. Thereupon there was thunder and a great rain which fell for five days, bestowing water across the land. *One writing says "For five days there was continuous rain, and the nine grains ripened."*
>
> At this the common people across the land cried out together, "Banzai!" and exclaimed, "An Emperor of supreme virtue!"[13]

Although this passage was once seen as asserting the superiority of native "Shintō" practices over the "foreign" Buddhist tradition, most scholars now believe that the final image of the populace hailing Kōgyoku as "a ruler of supreme virtue" suggests that the text was designed to contrast Kōgyoku's position as a rightful ruler with that of the Soga, who are presented in this chapter of the *Nihon shoki* as plotting to usurp royal prerogatives.

Read in this light, the text appears not as a triumphalist assertion of the superiority of native religious practice, but rather an affirmation of Chinese conceptions of Heaven and its responsiveness to the virtue of rulers.[14]

Indeed, both the content and the language of the text strongly suggest that such "foreign" notions were a basic part of the conceptual vocabulary of the court. The assertion that local shrine leaders wished to make offerings to the River Earl, the main water deity of the Chinese pantheon, for instance, can only be understood within the context of continental cultic traditions.[15] Similarly, the practice of changing the location of markets in order to produce rain makes sense only within the framework of Chinese concepts of *yin* and *yang*.[16] Although these and other such passages have for the most part been dismissed as embellishments by the editors of the text, there is no doubt that such practices did occur in such circumstances; one entry from the *Shoku nihongi*, for instance, shows that markets at the capital were moved in 705 in response to a drought.[17]

Perhaps most interesting of all, however, is the text's assertion that local shrine leaders, or *hafuri*, advocated the sacrifice of cows and horses in order to produce rain.[18] This passage is notable not only for the fact that the practice is not condemned, but also for what it reveals about how the court represented popular cultic practices of the time. Even if we dismiss the passage as nothing more than a literary invention, the fact that in 720 the editors of the *Nihon shoki* could plausibly assert that local religious leaders had recommended animal sacrifice in itself suggests that such practices enjoyed a substantial degree of popular currency within the Japanese islands at that time.[19] This is even more remarkable when we consider that every single ritual activity that the editors attributed to local religious leaders was clearly permeated by elements from continental cultic traditions.

Ritual Implements and Substitute Bodies

Several clues as to the nature of the continental ritual traditions that were most prevalent in the Japanese islands can be found in a wide variety of ritual implements and cultic technologies that have been found. Among the most prominent have been thousands of clay ritual vessels from the period. Because several of these vessels feature painted representations of disease-causing spirits or bear spells from Chinese texts that were designed to ward off the influences of the disease-bearing demons, there can be little doubt that continental elements played a central role in the rites. In several instances such vessels have also been found to contain the bones of sacrificed animals. Thousands of clay figurines of cows (*ushigata*), horses (*umagata*), and chickens (*torigata*) from the Nara period have also been found throughout Japan.[20] Such figurines, which are referred to in a number of textual sources from the period, were used for a variety of purposes including pacification of spirits and rainmaking.[21]

Ritual vessels and animal figurines were also often used in conjunction with human figurines (*hitogata*) that were used as substitute bodies.[22] Although still very poorly understood, thanks to the sheer volume of *hitogata*, *umagata*, and *ushigata* that have been unearthed to date, as well as the references to these objects in court liturgical sources such as the *Engishiki*, it is possible to speak in a general way about their use with a fair degree of confidence.

For our purposes three points are of particular interest. First, *hitogata* worked according to a logic of transference and substitution; in numerous court rituals of purification and healing, demons were offered a substitute human body, given food offerings, and admonished not to return. In others, *umagata* and *ushigata* were offered in lieu of actual livestock.[23] Second, a notable characteristic of many spells written on the *hitogata* was the name of the disease-bearing spirit. Within the Chinese ritual context, the identification of spirits by name appears to have been a central element in the ability to gain control over them. The proliferation of such rites in the Japanese islands appears to validate a veritable explosion in the number of superhuman figures that required the attention of ritual specialists.[24]

Finally, the discovery of large caches of *hitogata,* clay vessels, and other ritual implements at major crossroads (*chimata*) and riverbeds suggests that these ritual implements were also used in conjunction with roadside rites of purification. The close association between *chimata* and spirit pacification was almost certainly related to the belief that demons traveled along the roadways of the land.[25] Since, as we have already seen in the court's response to the plague that originated in Dazaifu in 735, epidemics did in fact spread quickly along major transportation arteries leading to the capital, it is not surprising that rites such as the Michiae no Matsuri came to occupy such an important position in the court's ritual arsenal.

Astrology and the Chinese Festival Calendar

One likely source for many of these practices can be found in Chinese astrological cults as well as in beliefs and practices related to the popular Chinese festival calendar. According to the *Nihon shoki*, Chinese astrological knowledge was transmitted to the Yamato court in the 10th year of the reign of Suiko (reigned 592–628), when a monk named Kwallŭk from the Korean kingdom of Paekche arrived at court and taught the arts of calendar-making, astronomy, and divination to members of the court.[26] The text further asserts that Kwallŭk was shortly thereafter named to the top post in a newly established bureaucracy charged with overseeing the development of Buddhist institutions in the Japanese islands.[27]

As the *Nihon shoki* account of Kwallŭk's arrival and reception suggests, the court's support of the Buddhist tradition was almost certainly closely related to a broader policy of accelerated importation of political and scientific technologies from China and the Korean peninsula. These in turn were ordered and given expression in the Chinese festival calendar, which organized everything from the motions of celestial bodies to political theatre to dicta concerning apparel into one comprehensive framework based upon the regular fluctuations of *yin* and *yang*. As a result, although the Suiko court is generally heralded as ushering in a new era dominated by Buddhist thought and institutions, in many ways the cults and legends of the Chinese festival calendar may have exerted an equal or greater impact upon the material and intellectual culture of the period. Because the rites of the Chinese festival calendar were predicated on a worldview in which the spirits of the dead were not only pervasive but also frequently hostile, rites of spirit pacification dominated much of the annual ritual cycle. By embracing the Chinese festival calendar, therefore, the court virtually guaranteed a sustained ritual focus at court on hostile spirits and the need for frequent rites to keep them at bay.

Chinese conceptions of astronomy and calendar-making, however, were deeply embedded within Chinese conceptions of politics and virtue, which were in turn understood in terms of concrete relationships between ruler and ruled on the one hand and between the ruler and Heaven on the other. In this worldview anomalous natural phenomena were seen as the means by which Heaven expressed, among other things, its pleasure or displeasure with the ruler. Judging by accounts from the *Nihon shoki*, the advent of divination texts triggered an explosion of discoveries of omens with political significance as various factions at court sought to demonstrate either Heaven's satisfaction with the ruler or its displeasure.[28] By the reign of Tenmu *tennō* the political ramifications of divination were considered so important that the court established an *onmyōdō* Divination Board with the exclusive right to perform divinations at the request of the court. Tenmu also ordered the construction of an astronomical observatory at virtually the same time.[29]

In addition to Tenmu's observatory, further archeological evidence for the diffusion of continental astrological knowledge can be found in the Takamatsuzuka and Kitora tombs in Yamato, which feature not only important astral configurations, but also representations of directional deities and figures from the Chinese zodiac.[30] Wooden tablets inscribed with spells and astral configurations that have been found in the short-lived Fujiwara capital also suggest that astrologically based rites were not simply limited to tomb worship.[31] Thus, although we have no way of ascertaining whether the *Nihon shoki* account of the transmission of astronomical and divinatory texts during the Suiko court actually corresponds with historical events, we can nonetheless state with a great degree of confidence that continental conceptions of astrology and divination had been transmitted to the Japanese islands by Tenmu's reign.

Sacrifice, Resonance, and the Calendar

The diffusion of the Chinese calendrical systems at court thus involved a dramatic shift in the ritual patterns by which power relations within the court and between the court and natural order were expressed and maintained. This involved far more than the tracking and observation of seasonal phenomena; it also, and perhaps primarily, involved the organization of a ritual regimen that incorporated rites of sacrifice and spirit pacification throughout the calendar year. While this emphasis upon spirit-quieting may at first glance appear surprising, it was in many ways consistent with fundamental Chinese conceptions of the relationship between the ruler, spirits, and the environment. Underlying the rites of the Chinese festival calendar was a sophisticated set of premises concerning the nature of spirits and their relationship to *yin* and *yang*. Two passages from the *Lun heng*, a rationalist treatise composed by Wang Ch'ung in the first century C.E., characterize early Chinese understandings of the formation and activities of *kuei* (demons) as follows:

> It is said that demons are a kind of visible *ch'i* that causes disease in humans. When *ch'i* is not in harmony, it harms people, and that which harms people [is called] demons. This *ch'i* appears in the form of humans. Thus people who are seriously ill have an abundance of [unbalanced] *ch'i*, and this *ch'i* arrives with a human appearance. When it [thus] arrives, the sick person will then see a demon.[32]
>
> . . . .
>
> When a person dies, his animate spirit ascends to Heaven, and his bones return to the earth. Therefore this [our human spirit] is called *kuei shen* 鬼神 ["demon and spirit"]. "*Kuei*" [demon] is [derived from] "*kuei*" [帰 return]. "Spirit" [*shen*] is that which is ineffable and without form. Some say that *kuei shen* is a different name for *yin* and *yang*. *Ch'i* that is *yin* hampers [life in] objects and returns [to the earth]. Thus it is called *kuei*. *Ch'i* that is *yang* leads objects to life, therefore it is called "spirit." "*Shen*" [spirit] means "*shen*" (申 extension).[33]

However idiosyncratic Wang Ch'ung's etymological derivations may seem, these accounts accurately reflect the fact that rites of spirit pacification (*chen kui*) in ancient China were ultimately premised on a desire to regulate the balance of *yin* and *yang* in order to prevent the proliferation of disease-causing spirits. Indeed, the Chinese festival calendar as a whole was in large part designed to recalibrate the balance of *yin* and *yang* in accordance with Chinese conceptions of numerology on the one hand and seasonal and agricultural cycles on the other.[34] Spirit pacification and the dispersal of excessive amounts of *yin* were thus even from pre-Confucian times basic responsibilities of government that went hand in hand with the creation of agricultural abundance and the prevention of disease.

Not surprisingly, these conceptions were strongly reflected within the Chinese festival calendar, in which rites of sacrifice were carefully timed to correspond with the waxing and waning of *yin* and *yang* elements in the seasonal/agricultural cycles. As we have just seen, because blood sacrifices were thought to directly affect the balance of *yin* and *yang* within a given environment, they were also considered important mechanisms for bringing about, or preventing, rainfall and a host of other natural phenomena.[35] Rites such as these formed an important part of the network of rites, rhythms, and legends associated with the Chinese festival calendar, which played a central role in shaping a remarkably wide range of religious phenomena.

From an early date the cultic activities in the Chinese festival calendar tended to cluster around five moments of transition within the regular cycle of alternating influence and decline between *yin* and *yang* elements throughout the course of each year. Known as the five nodes (Ch. *wu chieh*, J. *gosechi*), these dates represented important moments of flux within the forces of the cosmos and thus presented both dangers and opportunities for humans. From a very early point these moments were correlated with doubled odd-numbered days in the calendar. Thus roughly one month after the winter solstice, when *yin* reached its peak and then began a half-year period of decline, rites for the New Year began. New Year's rites, of course, focused on the first day of the first month, but they extended for a fifteen-day period, within which numerous rites were performed that attempted to influence the trajectory of the rest of the year. The third day of the third month and the fifth day of the fifth month were similarly related to major transitions in the balance of *yin* and *yang*, while the seventh day of the seventh month was closely correlated with the summer solstice and the subsequent ascendance of *yin* and the decline of *yang*. In this and other chapters we shall see repeatedly that across the Japanese islands these days served as major ritual foci for agriculture, industry, and, of course, the maintenance of proper relations with the superhuman world.[36]

From at least as far back as the reign of Chinese Emperor Han Wu-ti (140–87 B.C.E.), a core element of the Chinese court ritual programs was a regular series of rites of animal sacrifice that were designed to achieve a series of goals that, for heuristic purposes, can be divided into three types.[37] The first of these, aptly summed up in Confucius' memorable dictum that one should make offerings to one's ancestors "as if they were present," emphasized the transformative effect of the ritual process itself.[38] Seen in this light, sacrificial rites were a crucial mechanism for both the creation and expression of virtues such as filial piety, loyalty, and so forth. The virtue of the ruler, in this regard, was considered a matter of vital interest for the state if for no other reason than that virtuous performance of the rites was thought to resonate both within the human and superhuman worlds, thereby securing for the realm both harmonious human relations and the blessings of Heaven.

In spite of the enormous prestige that adhered to the Confucian tradition for much of the past two millennia, however, it is doubtful that this emphasis upon the performative dimension of sacrifice was ever the sole or even dominant paradigm for understanding sacrifice. Rites of sacrifice and meat offerings stood in sharp tension with contemporaneous Taoist practices that abhorred the impurities associated with the shedding of blood. Indeed, as the quote at the beginning of this chapter suggests, early Taoist liturgies appear to have developed at least in part as an effort to stamp out popular cultic practices involving the offerings of "bloody victuals."[39]

Both in China and Japan, however, bloody victuals constituted an important medium of exchange for the vast majority of the populace between the human and superhuman worlds; they could be used to propitiate ancestors and angry spirits alike. As Kleeman notes, such rites also constituted an important source of ritual empowerment for villages and individuals seeking the aid of the unquiet dead that wandered the roadways of the land:

> In spite of explicit regulations, few scholars think that the religious activity of the commoner at that time was in fact restricted to his ancestors. Rather, village and individual sacrifices were directed to the gods of the household, particularly the god of the hearth, nature spirits . . . and to the unquiet dead. It was this last category that posed the greatest perceived threat to the state.
>
> The unquiet dead were individuals who had died a violent death, who died away from home, whose bodies were not intact at death, or

who left behind no male descendants. Because these ghosts could not receive normal ancestral sacrifice, they wandered the world in search of food. Their liminal status, neither of the living nor among the safe, provided-for dead, gave them numinous power (*ling*). The absence of any effective ancestral sacrifice made them available to anyone, even nonrelations. Thus they were a reservoir of unclaimed spiritual power . . . more open to private, self-centered entreaties.[40]

Seen in this light, the apparently widespread use of roadside meat offerings and sacrifice in the Japanese islands constitutes an important piece of evidence concerning the roots and nature of continental practices that were appropriated by both the court and populace. Far from indicating the appropriation of Confucian or Taoist cosmologies, such rites strongly suggest the widespread adoption of popular continental practices and beliefs that both Confucian and Taoist elites within China actively sought to suppress.

The Weaver Maiden and the Cowherd

Perhaps the best-documented cult in Nara Japan with clear roots in the Chinese festival calendar was that of the Weaver Maiden and the Cowherd. Although from ancient times this cult was linked with an astral cult marking the annual meeting of the stars Vega and Altair, over time a legend cycle developed in which the Weaver Maiden, daughter of the Celestial Emperor, was said to have fallen in love with a cowherd and consequently neglected her weaving duties. As a result, the two lovers were condemned to spend the entire year on different sides of the Heavenly River (the Milky Way) until the seventh day of the seventh month, when the Cowherd was allowed to cross the Milky Way and be united with his lover for a single night.[41]

As set out in the *Ching ch'u sui shih chi*, the mythic basis for the cult of these literally star-crossed lovers was as follows:

> The Weaver Maiden is to the east of the Heavenly River. She is the daughter of the Celestial Emperor. Year after year she devoted herself to her weaving duties, weaving heavenly garments from fabrics made of clouds. The Celestial Emperor saw that his daughter was alone and felt sorry for her, so he married her to the Cowherd on the west of the Heavenly River. After becoming a bride, however, the Weaver Maiden completely stopped weaving. The Celestial Emperor was therefore angry and scolded her, forcing her to return to the east side of the Heavenly River. Each year she is allowed but one day to cross the Heavenly River and meet the Cowherd.[42]

Although both in China and in Japan this legend became a favorite subject of poets seeking to evoke images of tragic love, Kominami Ichirō, Nakamura Takashi, and others have argued that the meeting of the Weaver Maiden and Cowherd at a river suggests that the cult was most likely rooted not in romance, but in ancient Chinese rites of sacrifice and purification. Nakamura notes that in early Chinese sources the range of possible meanings for the term translated as "cowherd" includes not only officiants in charge of sacrificing cows, but also the sacrificial animals themselves.[43] He also points to a cluster of texts describing sacrificial offerings of young women as brides for the water deity known as the River Earl. He therefore concludes that the figures of the Weaver Maiden the Cowherd started not as exalted deities, but as sacrificial victims who were only later transformed into objects of worship. Kominami, in support of this view, points to later popular narratives in which the Cowherd is said to cross the river wearing the hide of his cow.[44]

Because the motif of the brief meeting of lovers followed by inevitable separation was popular with Japanese poets from the time of Tenmu's reign, Japanese scholars have long been interested in the literary significance of the "night of sevens" (*tanabata*) imagery within early Japanese literature.[45] Archeological discoveries suggesting that Chinese conceptions of astronomy were more pervasive in Japan than previously realized, however, have helped start a re-evaluation of the role of the *tanabata* cult in the mytho-religious life of the period. Hirabayashi, for instance, has emphasized the clear influence of this cult upon early representations of shamanesses (*miko*) in early Japanese mythology.[46]

Further hints as to the influence of the cult of the Weaver Maiden and Cowherd can also be seen in the prominent role that weaving implements played at cultic centers both at court and across the Japanese islands. Kaneko Hiroyuki notes that according to the *Engishiki*, four of the twenty-one sacred regalia of the Ise shrine are weaving elements and that a weaving implement was also one of the regalia of the upper Kamo shrine in modern Kyoto. Archeological evidence suggesting the widespread use of weaving implements as offerings has also been found at shrines at several sites near Ise in Mie prefecture as well as in Kagawa prefecture on the island of Shikoku. Probably the largest caches of weaving tools unearthed to date, however, have been at the Munakata shrine in Kyūshū and the Okinoshima shrine, an important island cultic center for the worship of the Munakata deities. This was an important stopover point for vessels traveling between Kyūshū and the Korean peninsula.[47] These discoveries are notable not only for the degree to which they bolster textual evidence for the use of weaving implements at shrines, but also for their geographic breadth, which includes not only central Japan, but also the island of Shikoku and several sites in Kyūshū at the southern end of the Japanese islands.

Further textual evidence concerning the ritual uses of these implements can be seen in the *Hizen fudoki*, an early eighth-century gazetteer from Hizen province in Kyūshū. There we find the following legend concerning propitiation of the vengeful Akaru Hime, a female deity whose cultic identity appears to have been closely related to weaving:

> Himegoso no sato. Of old, to the west of the river here there was a wild god that would kill travelers on the roadsides. Half [of those who passed by] would die, half would be allowed to escape. A divination was done to determine why the god was wreaking its vengeance [*tatari*] thus, and they were told "In the Munakata district of Chikuzen, have a man named Azeko build a shrine and worship me. If you do as I request, I will no longer have a violent heart." At this they found the man named Azeko. When they instructed him to build a shrine and worship the god, Azeko took a banner [*hata*] and raised it in his hands, praying "If my worship is truly needed, may this banner fly on the wind and fall at the place where the god who seeks me resides." At this the banner was suddenly taken up by the wind and flew away. It flew to the Mihara district and fell to the ground at the Himegoso shrine. It then once again flew up into the air and returned, falling to the earth in the fields near a small village by a small mountain river. Azeko thus knew where the wild deity resided, and at night he had a dream in which a loom [*kutsubiki*] and a shuttle [*tatari*] came dancing before Azeko, pushing him. At this he knew that the god was a female weaving deity and immediately built a shrine and worshipped her. After that travelers were no longer killed on the roadsides. For this reason, the shrine was called Himegoso (the princess's shrine) and today, the village takes its name from the shrine.[48]

This tale of divine wrath and propitiation speaks volumes about the role of weaving cults during the Nara period. Most noticeably, the text clearly illustrates how weaving implements could and were used for the pacification or propitiation of vengeful spirits. Not only does the liturgist Azeko locate the deity through the use of a flag, Akaru hime even represents herself to Azeko in the form of weaving implements. When taken together with textual and archeological evidence of similar activities at the Munakata, Okinoshima, Kamo, Ise, and other shrines, it would appear that weaving cults in Nara Japan were prominent even at the farthest reaches of the Japanese islands and that offerings of weaving implements were used to quiet the anger of female deities.[49]

Animal Sacrifice, Akaru Hime, and Mitoshi Kami

Although recent years have seen the accumulation of archeological evidence establishing the widespread use of both animal sacrifice and weaving implements in conjunction with rites of spirit pacification throughout Japan, there has to date been no convincing account of how, if at all, these phenomena might be linked. Fortunately, a small number of sources from the period suggests that female weaving deities who demanded offerings of weaving implements were also closely associated with cowherd deities who demanded animal sacrifice. I would therefore suggest that the worship of *karakami*, the use of continental spirit-pacification technologies, and the practice of animal sacrifice were all shaped by a common horizon of reception that was heavily influenced by the importation of continental technologies and the background beliefs and practices associated with the Chinese festival calendar.

Several clues as to the nature of this dynamic can be seen in the *Kogoshūi*, an early ninth-century text recounting the mythic and sacerdotal history of the Japanese islands. In the text we find the following legend recounting the origins of practices associated with the worship of Mitoshi no Kami during the Toshigoi Matsuri, a major rite performed at court-sponsored shrines throughout Japan at the start of each year:

> On one occasion in the Divine Age, when cultivating rice in the paddy field, Otokonushi no Kami served his men beef, while the son of the Rice God Mitoshi no Kami, when visiting that field, spat in disgust upon the dainty offered to him, and returning home, reported the matter to his father. Then Mitoshi no Kami in wrath sent a number of noxious insects, or locusts, to Otokonushi no Kami's paddy field to kill the young rice plants and in consequence the leafless rice-plants appeared like "*shino*" or short bamboo grass.
>
> When Otokonushi no Kami tried to ascertain the true cause of the incomprehensible disaster, he bade a "katakannai" or "hiji augur . . . " to ascertain the divine will. The augury ran thus: "Mitoshi no Kami has sent a curse, which makes the young rice plants die, so that you should not fail to appease the offended god with offerings of a white boar, two white horses and a pair of white domestic fowl." The conditions revealed in the divination being obeyed, the god was appeased.

> Mitoshi no Kami disclosed the secret in the following recipe: "It is I who brought the curse. Make a reel of hempen stalks, and therewith clear the rice plants, by expelling the locust with the hemp leaves . . . place some beef at the mouth of the ditch in the field together with a phallic symbol. . . .
> That autumn the people's hearts were gladdened by an abundant rice crop.
> The custom having been started, Mitoshi no Kami is still worshipped, in the present Shintō Bureau, with offerings of a white boar, a white horse, and a pair of white domestic fowls.[50]

Although this legend has attracted the attention of numerous Japanese scholars seeking to understand the role of animal sacrifice in Nara Japan, virtually all attempts to explain the text have foundered on the issue of why Mitoshi no Kami would in the first section be enraged at a meat offering, while at the end of the story his anger is appeased with the dedication of animals and offerings of meat. Yoshie Akiko has argued that the text in fact reflects two separate though common rites, the first being a New Year's agricultural rite involving the offering of a feast to laborers, the second being a rite for the propitiation of an angry deity.[51] Ueda Masaaki, on the other hand, has argued that the god is angry simply because the laborers should first have dedicated the animals to the deity before consuming the meat. Both scholars agree, however, that the legend most likely reflects contemporaneous practices concerning offerings of meat at roadsides to pacify angry deities.

A close examination of the text also suggests that this legend, the cult of Mitoshi no Kami and, by extension, popular religious practice, were also deeply colored by practices associated with immigrant kinship groups such as the Hata in regard to their *karakami* ancestral deities. Hints of this can be seen in Mitoshi no Kami's genealogy, which, as given in the *Kojiki*, includes half brothers named Kara no Kami (literally, "Korean deity") as well as Ōyamakui no Kami, the Hata deity that resided in the Matsuno'o and Hiyoshi shrines in Yamashiro province.[52] As we saw in Chapter 1, the Matsuno'o shrine also housed the spirit of Ōyamakui's wife, Okitsushima Hime no Mikoto, one of the chief deities of the Munakata shrine. Since there is good archeological evidence suggesting that the Munakata deity was regularly propitiated with weaving implements, it would appear that several deities with which the cult of Mitoshi no Kami was most closely associated were not only *karakami,* but also both cowherd and weaving deities.

Further evidence suggesting that rites of animal sacrifice and spirit pacification from China and the Korean peninsula had already entered the mainstream of popular Japanese religious activity is also apparent in the second half of the legend. The placement of meat offerings at roadsides, for instance, echoes not only continental ritual practices but also the practice of making offerings of animal hides during the Michiae no Matsuri, which also took place at the start of each year. The use of a ritual weaving implement (the reel) and hemp similarly mirrors the Mononobe liturgist Azeko's use of this same type of weaving implement as an offering to Akaru Hime. It would thus appear that such rites were not unique to the cult of Mitoshi no Kami in Yamato, but shared a number of important traits with other cults across the Japanese islands.

Other Cowherd Deities

Perhaps most important, however, the legend of Mitoshi no Kami is but one of a cluster from the period involving *karakami* that perform the function of cowherds. Another such figure was Ame no Hiboko, an immigrant deity from Silla who eventually became the object of one of the largest cults in Japan:

> In the land of Silla there was a pond called Agunuma. On the bank of the pond there was a poor young girl who was napping. As she was doing so the sun sparkled like a rainbow and penetrated her private parts. There was also a poor man there who thought this strange and so constantly observed her actions. Now from the time of her nap the girl became pregnant, and she gave birth to a red jewel. At this, the poor man who had been observing her begged her for the jewel, which he thereafter always kept tied around his waist.
>
> This man had a rice field in a valley. When he loaded food and drink for the field workers upon an ox and brought it into the valley, he met Ame no Hiboko, the son of the ruler of the country. [Ame no Hiboko] then asked the man "Why are you bringing this ox loaded with food and drink into the valley? You will surely kill the ox and eat it." He then seized the man and was going to put him in prison, when the man answered, saying "I wasn't going to kill the ox. I was just bringing food for the laborers in the field." However, [Ame no Hiboko] would still not release him. Therefore the man undid the jewel that was tied around his waist and offered it to the prince, who then released the man.
>
> [Ame no Hiboko] then took the jewel [home]. When he placed it beside his bed, it turned into a beautiful young woman. He immediately married her, and she became his chief wife. Now the

young woman would constantly make all sorts of delicacies that she would feed to her husband. When the prince therefore grew arrogant and scolded his wife, she said, "I am not a woman who should be wife to you. I will go to the land of my ancestors." She then secretly got into a small boat and fled [to the Japanese islands], where she stopped in Naniwa. *This is the deity called Akaru Hime, who resides in the Himegoso shrine in Naniwa.*[53]

Although the cult of Ame no Hiboko (Heavenly Sun Spear) has been characterized as a metalworking cult, as a sun cult and a sea cult, the legend is of direct interest to our discussion because of its close similarities with the legend of the Mitoshi no Kami. As with the *Kogoshūi* account discussed above, we have here the same fundamental structure of a god who is angered at the prospect of a landowner about to bring a cow to workers in the fields. Here, too, the deity is placated only after receiving an offering/bribe. Most important of all, however, the text concludes by stating that the deity who poses as the guardian of the cow then marries Akaru Hime, the very deity who, as we saw earlier, demanded offerings of weaving implements such as reels in Hizen province.

These same motifs also appear in the legend cycle of Tsunoga Arashito, yet another immigrant cowherd deity from the Korean peninsula. Indeed, accounts of this deity in the *Nihon shoki* and *Kojiki* bear such a striking resemblance to the legend of the immigrant deity Ame no Hiboko that there can be little doubt of extensive interaction between the two legend cycles; both gods are presented as nobles/cowherds who come to the Japanese islands from the Korean peninsula seeking an estranged bride, who in both cases is said to be the weaver maiden goddess Akaru Hime. Similarly, whereas Ame no Hiboko is said to have settled in Tajima province along the coast of the Japan/Eastern Sea, Tsunoga Arashito is said to have taken up residence in the port of Tsunoga, also along the coast of the Japan/Eastern Sea directly opposite from the Korean peninsula.[54] Perhaps most important of all, for our purposes, both Ame no Hiboko and Tsunoga Arashito appear to have been worshipped by the Hata and other immigrant lineages along the coast of the Japan/Eastern Sea.

The cults of these cowherding and weaving deities are thus of immediate note for a number of reasons. Most obviously, the location of these deities in Echizen, Tajima, Yamato, Yamashiro, and Hizen provinces once again suggests that cults of immigrant deities had diffused across an extremely large area of Japan even before the advent of the Nara period. It would also appear that each of these cults also served as a vehicle for the transmission of a wide range of continental beliefs and practices that closely integrated mythic and ritual patterns related to sacrifice, spirit pacification, weaving, and even astrology. In addition, I suggest that these cults may also have played a major role in the formation of the religious paradigms of the period; because the Hata and other immigrant lineages associated with these cults also played a major role in the transmission of Buddhism to the Japanese islands, it would appear that the earliest tropes and legends of the fledgling Japanese Buddhist tradition would have formed within a cultic context that was heavily influenced by such continental-style rites and legends.

Sacrifice and Spirit Propitiation in the *Nihon Ryōiki*

Probably the best place to begin approaching the question of how the adoption of the early Japanese Buddhist tradition related to continental technologies of spirit-quieting can be found in the *Nihon shoki* account of Kwallŭk's transmission of Chinese astrological and divinatory texts to the Suiko court. The fact that these texts are said to have been presented by a Buddhist monk very likely reflects the fact that continental conceptions of astronomy, divination, and spirit pacification permeated virtually every major strain of Buddhist thought in both China and the Korean peninsula at this time. The importance of Buddhist astral cults only increased over time, with such astral figures as the bodhisattva Myōken, Kichijō tenjo, and Jijōkō Buddha occupying the attention of the court and populace for centuries. Seen in this light, it appears that the early Japanese Buddhist tradition was a major engine for the transmission of continental astrological beliefs, even as it came to be shaped by them.[55]

In a similar vein the influence of Buddhist texts and rites on early conceptions of the nature of spirits is also readily apparent. Because Chinese conceptions of the nature of spirits and the means by which they might be pacified thoroughly pervaded the Buddhist traditions that entered the Japanese islands during the seventh and eighth centuries, Buddhist scriptures composed in China were a major source of spells and demon names in Nara Japan. Among the most important were scriptures of clearly Taoist provenance that had been adopted by Chinese Buddhists. One such recently discovered text, the *Scripture Spoken by the Buddha on the 7,000 Demon Amulets* (*Fo shuo ch'i ch'ien kuie fu ching*), contained, as its name suggests, literally thousands of spirit names that could be used to control the proliferating number of spirits believed to be roaming the land. It would thus appear that continental rites of spirit pacification and the diffusion of the Buddhist tradition at court were mutually reinforcing phenomena.[56]

The association of the Buddhist tradition with continental rites of spirit pacification and the Chinese festival calendar, however, was not a phenomenon limited to the court. One indication of the degree to which they populated popular Buddhist discourse can be seen in the following legend from the *Nihon ryōiki*, an early ninth-century Buddhist tale collection:

> Dōtō, a Buddhist scholar of Koryo, was a monk of Gangōji. He came from the Ema family in Yamashiro province. In the year of the horse, the second year of the Taika era, he built the Uji Bridge. Once, when he was passing through the valley in the Nara hills; he saw a skull that had been trampled by men and animals. In sorrow, he had his attendant Maro place it on a tree....
>
> On New Year's Eve of the same year, a man came to the temple gate, saying, "I would like to the see the venerable Dōtō's attendant Maro." When Maro came out to see him, he said, "Thanks to the mercy of your master, I have been happy and at peace. And I can repay your kindness only on this evening." Then he took Maro home with him. Through the closed gate they entered the back quarters of the house, where they found abundant food and drink already prepared. The man divided his fare with Maro, and they ate together. Shortly after midnight they heard a male voice, and the man said to Maro, "Go away quickly, for here comes my brother who killed me!" In wonder, Maro asked him about this, and he answered, "Once my brother and I were traveling on business, and I acquired about fifty pounds of silver in my trade. Out of envy and hate my brother killed me to take the silver...."
>
> It was at this point that the man's mother and elder brother entered the room to worship all spirits. Being surprised at the sight of Maro, they asked why he was there, and Maro told them what he had just heard. The mother thereupon accused her elder son, saying, "Ah! You killed my dear son. It was not a robber, but you!" Then she thanked Maro and gave him a feast. On his return, Maro reported this to his master.
>
> Even a spirit of the dead or a skeleton repays an act of kindness, how can a living man forget?[57]

Several elements of this legend illustrate the degree to which rites of spirit pacification from the Chinese festival calendar had come to pervade both Buddhist and non-Buddhist discourse by the early Heian period. We are told that the spirit returns to the human world on New Year's Eve, even as his brother appears to make offerings to "all spirits" on this same day.

The text makes it clear that the timing of these two elements is not simply coincidental; as the spirit of the skull tells Maro, "I can repay your kindness only on this evening." Such statements are all the more noteworthy in light of the fact that there is no suggestion in the text that this was a practice specifically identified with any Buddhist text or cultic tradition. Indeed, it appears far more likely that such offerings, much like court rituals such as the Michiae no Matsuri, were firmly rooted in the Chinese festival calendar. Perhaps even more significant, the practice of making offerings to spirits on the last evening of the year is treated simply as an accepted part of established ritual practice that needs no explanation or justification.

Although, again, it is impossible to know whether this legend accurately reflected popular religious beliefs from the period, there are several clues suggesting that the legend was indeed rooted in popular narratives from Yamashiro province. Among these is the assertion that the eminent monk Dōtō, who first takes pity on the skull, is from an immigrant kinship group from the Korean kingdom of Koguryō that had settled in the Uji district of Yamashiro during the mid-sixth century.[58] Because, as we shall see shortly, other legends from this area depict Buddhist practitioners engaging in rites of spirit pacification and animal sacrifice, I suggest that immigrant lineages such as the Ema, as well as monks such as Dōtō, represented important mechanisms for the absorption and transmission of such rites within the framework of Buddhist tale literature.

More broadly, the text's statement that Dōtō oversaw the construction of the Uji bridge, a major node of traffic across Yamashiro province also reflects an important element in the formation of the early Japanese Buddhist tradition. Regardless of the historical accuracy of this particular claim, there is little doubt that the propagation of the Buddhist tradition in Japan was vastly aided by the construction and expansion of road networks and bridges that had begun in earnest during the reign of Suiko.[59] Such construction projects greatly stimulated the expansion of centralized bureaucracy and central authority across the Yamato plain and beyond. One by-product of this process was the rapid diffusion of Buddhist rites and concepts.

An unexpected consequence of this dynamic, however, was the increased ease with which disease could travel large distances. Because, as the above legend makes clear, travelers were easy targets for robbers and prone to starvation, large numbers of corpses are believed to have littered the roads of early Japan. The obvious cultic concerns arising from so many corpses was almost certainly a powerful incentive for the court's frequent use of roadside rites of spirit propitiation. Yet as Buddhist monks traveled the highways of the Japanese islands, they as much as anyone needed protection from the vengeful spirits thought to be wandering the roadways. Seen in this light, this legend of a monk's encounter with a skull on a roadway would appear to reflect a strong awareness both at court and within the early Buddhist tradition of the need for cultic means to propitiate or pacify such spirits.[60] I suggest therefore that regardless of its historical accuracy, this legend most likely broadly reflects the material and ritual concerns of the age.

Weavers and Substitute Bodies

By the time of the composition of the *Nikon ryōiki*, the widespread use of *hitogata* and roadside rites of spirit pacification also appears to have been reflected in popular Buddhist discourse on demons and spirits of the dead. The following legend highlights the means by which the logic of substitution at the core of *hitogata* rites came to be represented in popular Buddhist conceptions of the afterlife:

> In Yamada district, Sanuki province, there lived a woman whose name was Nunoshiki no Omi Kinume. In the reign of Emperor Shōmu, she suddenly fell ill. Therefore, she laid all kinds of delicious offerings on both sides of her gate to give the deity of plagues a banquet as a bribe.
>
> There came a fiend, a messenger of King Yama, to seize her. Exhausted from searching for her, the fiend cast a covetous look at the offerings of delicacies and accepted them. Then he said to her, "As I have accepted your hospitality, I will repay your kindness. Do you know anyone with the same name as yours?" Kinume answered, "Yes, there is another Kinume in Utari district of the same province."
>
> Thereupon, he took her to the other Kinume's home in Utari district to see her, and, taking out a one-foot chisel from his red bag, drove it into the latter's forehead and arrested her. The former Kinume of Yamada district went home in secret.
>
> When King Yama, who had been waiting for them, examined her, he said, "This is not the Kinume I sent for. You have got the wrong person. Kinume, will you stay here for a while? Go and get the Kinume of the Yamada district."
>
> As he had failed in trying to conceal her, the fiend again went to Kinume of Yamada district to arrest her and came back with her. King Yama saw her and said, "This is the Kinume I sent for."
>
> Meanwhile, Kinume of Utari district went home only to find her corpse had been cremated during her three-day absence. She came

back and appealed to the king in grief, saying, "I have no body to enter into."

Then the king asked, "Is there the body of Kinume of Yamada district?"

There was, whereupon the king said, "Go and take her body as yours."

In this way Kinume of Utari district came back in the body of Kinume of Yamada district. She said, 'This is not my home. My home is in Utari district. . . . When she explained in detail what King Yama had told her, both sets of parents believed her and allowed her to inherit both fortunes. This is why the present Kinume had four parents and two inheritances.

There is sometimes merit in making offerings to a fiend as a bribe. If you have anything, you should offer it. This is another of the miraculous events.[61]

As with the legend of Dōtō and the skull, this narrative suggests that it was driven in large part by continental conceptions of spirit pacification. Most obviously, the susceptibility of demons to bribery, the efficacy of food offerings, and the ritual focus on names all suggest that continental motifs and ritual practices helped form the core of the legend. If, given the setting, we assume that the legend originated in Iyo province, then it would also appear that such rites were undertaken not only by the court but also by individuals even in comparatively remote regions of Japan. Perhaps most remarkable of all, Kyōkai, the Buddhist monk who compiled the *Nihon ryōiki*, actually advises laypeople to make such offerings to spirits.[62]

One further indication of the degree to which the conceptual apparatus underlying such rites had been appropriated by the Japanese Buddhist tradition can be seen in the names of the two heroines. The surname Nunoshiki, which literally means "spread cloth," was an appellation adopted by a weaving service group that traced its origins back to the Korean peninsula. Even more to the point, the given name, Kinume, is literally rendered as "Silk Maiden." Once we render the structure of the legend using the term "Silk Maiden," the legend's affinities with continental rites become obvious. In essence, this is a legend in which Emma, King of disease demons, sends for a Silk Maiden, who attempts to evade him by making roadside offerings to demons and finding a substitute body with the same name. Thus from start to finish the narrative is driven by the logic of substitution at the core of *hitogata* rites of spirit pacification.[63]

Just as the court frequently banned the slaughter of animals even as it regularly made offerings of animal hides on the roadsides, Kyōkai's attitude toward the practice of sacrifice appears to have been extremely complex. Although he concludes the above legend with a defense of making food offerings to spirits, elsewhere in the text he is harshly critical of the practice of sacrifice:

> In the village of Nadekubo, Higashinari district, Settsu province, there was a wealthy householder whose name is unknown. In the reign of ex-Emperor Shōmu, the householder, fearful of the evil influence of a Chinese deity, held services for seven years, sacrificing an ox each year until he had killed seven. At the end of seven years he contracted a serious disease, and, during the following seven years, neither doctor nor medicine could cure him. He called diviners to purify and pray for him, but his disease must have been caused by his past deeds of killing.[64]

For our purposes this legend is perhaps most significant not for Kyōkai's condemnation of the practice of animal sacrifice, but rather for his assumption that meat sacrifices were a common practice among the populace. Indeed, given the general tendency of this text to seek to illustrate the miraculous within the ordinary, it would appear that Kyōkai's main concern was not to condemn an aberrant practice, but rather to show that Buddhist methods of spirit-quieting were more effective than those of specialists from other traditions. Seen in this light, the text's casual reference to the use of non-Buddhist divination experts by members of the populace would thus also suggest that by the time of the completion of the *Nihon ryōiki*, such figures were also providing their services to people outside of the capital.

Although we have no way of knowing to what degree Kyōkai's text reflected actual Buddhist legends in circulation during his lifetime, the setting of the legend in the Nadekubo district suggests that there is a high probability the legend reflected located cultic realities. Nadekubo, located in Settsu province on the Inland Sea, appears to have been home to a number of immigrant lineages from the Korean peninsula. Although the text does not mention the name of the *karakami* to which the householder made his sacrifices, we do know that by far the largest cultic center in the Nadebuko district was none other than the Himegoso shrine wherein resided Akaru Hime, the vengeful weaving goddess and wife of the immigrant cowherd deity Tsunoga Arashito. It is therefore likely that here, as is often the case in the literature of the period, the very same immigrant lineages that are featured as protagonists in Buddhist morality tales are also actively engaged in continental-style rites of spirit-quieting and the worship of *karakami*. This, together with the discovery of archeological remains that show that animal sacrifices did indeed occur in this very area, strongly suggests that Kyōkai's concerns about the popularity of sacrifice and non-Buddhist practices of spirit pacification in the region may have been well founded.[65] It would thus appear that the legend provides further confirmation of the degree to which the early Japanese Buddhist tradition developed within a ritual context pervaded by *karakami* and continental-style rites of sacrifice and spirit propitiation.

This process of cultic interaction and transformation appears to have been repeated at numerous immigrant centers across Japan. Just as Akaru Hime was worshipped at an immigrant center in Settsu province, so was her spouse Tsunoga Arashito worshipped at the port of Tsunoga, a major point of entry for immigrant lineages from the Korean kingdoms of Koguryō and Silla. Because Tsunoga was connected by waterway directly to Yamashiro, it also appears to have served as an important conduit for immigrant lineages and their ancestral deities seeking to enter the Kinai region of central Japan. One such lineage was the Ema, which produced, as we saw above, not only artisans and shrine leaders, but also Buddhist monks such as Dōtō. Another such lineage was the Nara Osa, whom the *Shinsen shōjiroku* states were a sub-branch of the Hata that first arrived in the Japanese islands from Koguryō during the mid-fifth century.[66] The Nara Osa, in turn, are of note for, among other things, building the oldest known temple-shrine complex in the Japanese islands.[67]

The activities of the Nara Osa are particularly revealing about the process by which cults involving sacrifice to cowherds/*karakami* were able to penetrate even popular Buddhist discourse. One of the best examples of this can be seen in the following legend from the *Nihon ryōiki*, which, as in the case of the legend of the monk Dōtō's encounter with a skull, takes place at the Uji bridge in Yamashiro:

> Nara no Iwashima, lived at the Fifth Avenue, the Sixth Street, East Side of Nara, that is, in the village west of Daianji. In the reign of Emperor Shōmu he got a loan of thirty *kan* from the Sutra fund of Daianji, went to the port of Tsuruga in Echizen on business, and loaded the goods he had purchased on a boat to bring them home. On the way home he suddenly fell ill and got off the boat. Thinking he would go on alone, he hired a horse and set out.

When he reached Shiga no karasaki, Takashima district, Ōmi province, he looked around and saw three men half a furlong away running after him. At the Uji Bridge of Yamashiro, they caught up and went along with him. Iwashima asked them: "Where are you going?" They replied, "We are messengers from the office of King Yama sent for Nara no Iwashima." Then Iwashima said, "I am the very one you are sent for. But why do you want me?" The fiend messengers answered, "When we looked for you at your home, we were told, 'He has gone on a business tour.' Therefore, we went to the port so that we might meet and catch you there, but a messenger from the Four Divine Guardians implored us, saying, 'You should excuse him, since he is engaged in business with a loan from the temple.' So we let you go free for a while. We have spent so many days trying to catch you that we feel hungry and exhausted. . . ."

Eventually Iwashima took them home and gave them a feast. The fiends said to him: "We like the flavor of beef very much. Will you serve us beef? We are the fiends who steal cows." So he told them, "I have two brindled cows. Will you let me go free if I offer them to you?" They said . . . "Well, we have eaten much of your food. . . . Do you by chance know anyone of the same age?" "No, I don't," he answered. Then one of the three fiends, after thinking for a while said . . . "I heard that there is a diviner who was born in the same year at the shrine of Isakawa. He can be your substitute. We will take him instead. I urge you, however, to recite the *Kongō hannya haramitsu kyō* one hundred times, invoking our names. . . .

After three days the fiend messengers came to Iwashima, saying, "Owing to the power of the Mahayana scripture we escaped one hundred whipping strokes; besides, we were given half a bushel more rice than the usual ration. How happy and grateful we are! Please be virtuous and hold services for our sake hereafter on every holy day."[68]

One of the most remarkable aspects of this highly unusual legend is the degree to which it brings together the geographic and thematic elements from the legends of *karakami* and sacrifice discussed above. Most obviously, as in the case of Nunoshiki no Kinume, the text emphasizes the importance of determining the names of the living and the dead. Here again in a Buddhist apologetical text we find the logic of substitution that underlay the use of *hitogata* at the core of the narrative. Thus after an offering of animal flesh, demons are persuaded to take to the land of the dead a substitute figure known by the same name as their original target. By fusing the logic of sacrifice and meat offerings with the logic of substitution that underlay the use of scapegoat dolls, the text once again suggests that, to a surprising degree, continental ritual patterns had come to influence the Buddhist narratives of the period.

In addition, this text also illustrates the degree to which such ritual patterns served to provide continuity across the spectrum of ritual practice in the Japanese islands. At the level of immigrant cultic practice, here we find a member of a sublineage of the Hata making roadside offerings to spirits in order to fend off disease and death. The importance of such lineal orientations is reflected in the geographic construction of the legend, in which the protagonist travels from Tsunoga, home of the cowherd deity Tsunoga Arashito, to the Uji bridge, the very bridge that the *Nihon ryōiki* asserts was built by the monk Dōtō. More broadly, the text's casual reference to a *yin yang* diviner in residence at a nearby local shrine further highlights the degree to which immigrant deities and practices from the Chinese festival calendar had penetrated the cultic life of this area.[69] Most notably, however, the text also highlights the degree to which court ritual practices reflected popular cultic practice. Iwashima's ritual strategy is in its fundamentals no different from that employed by the court in the face of the plague of 735, for once again we see roadside meat offerings to disease spirits combined with the chanting of the *Kongō hannya haramitsu kyō*.

Conclusion

The evidence above suggests that immigrant kinship groups such as the Nara Osa, Hata, and Ema were responsible not only for the introduction of many of the earliest forms of Buddhism, but also for rites of animal sacrifice and spirit pacification associated with such *karakami* as Ame no Hiboko, Tsunoga Arashito, and Akaru Hime. Equally important, it would appear that these lineages were also closely associated with the transmission to Japan of continental technologies such as weaving, painting, and engineering. As these and other ancestors helped shape the cultic terrain in which local shrine rites and Buddhist hagiography took shape, the basic patterns, practices, and conceptual framework of the Chinese festival calendar came to be central elements in the ritual vocabulary of Japanese courtiers, shrine leaders, and even Buddhist monks.

In spite of the widespread presumption that "native" Japanese culture abhorred bloodshed, widespread archeological and textual evidence has established that animal sacrifice was frequently practiced during the Nara and Heian periods. By the Nara period such rites were practiced not only by immigrant kinship groups, but also by the population at large. By the advent of the Heian period, cults of *karakami* such as Tsunoga no Arashito, Ame no Hiboko, Akaru Hime, and others could be found both at court and across the countryside.

The cults of these and other immigrant deities were in turn closely associated with the rites of the Chinese festival calendar. Among the core practices of the Chinese calendar were rites of animal sacrifice designed to feed, and therefore propitiate, potentially hostile spirits. They also served to maintain the delicate equilibrium between *yin* and *yang* necessary for the proper functioning of the agricultural cycle. In addition, during the Nara period Chinese conceptions of demons as well as ritual practices involving the use of *hitogata*, or scapegoat dolls, proliferated rapidly across the Japanese islands. These rites were built upon a logic of substitution that involved the transference of disease-bearing spirits into substitute bodies.

All of this suggests that immigrant lineages associated with weaving and sericulture propagated a variety of continental cults and concepts centering not only on buddhas and scriptures, but also cults of cowherds and weaving maidens. Over time, these cultic practices appear to have played an increasingly large role across the spectrum of religious activity in the Japanese islands. As a result, by the advent of the Heian period even Buddhist apologetic texts such as the *Nihon ryōiki* endorsed at least in part practices involving meat offerings to spirits at roadsides and the logic of substitution. It would thus appear that by the time Kanmu moved the capital to the Hata base in Yamashiro province, "native" religious practices across the Japanese islands had been constructed to a surprising degree in terms of the patterns and practices of the Chinese festival calendar.

As weaving maidens and cowherds came to populate court and local mythologies, they also reflected broader material transformations engendered by the transmission of sericulture and weaving technologies. Yet sacrifice and sericulture were by no means the only cultic concerns addressed by the Chinese festival calendar. Of equal importance was the transmission of Chinese medical knowledge and the subsequent formation in the Japanese islands of a religious ideal based upon the attainment of immortality and control over the processes of life and death. Not surprisingly, many of the same lineages and social forces propelling the use of *hitogata* and other rites from the Chinese festival calendar also helped propel this development. In Chapter 3 we will take up the issue of how these conceptions took root in the seventh century in the red clay of the Yoshino region of Yamato as a series of political upheavals gave rise to the first self-proclaimed Heavenly Sovereigns of the realm.

CHAPTER 3

Female Rulers and Female Immortals

> Thus in ancient times, among those who practiced the way there were none who neglected the medical arts.
> —*Pao p'u tzu*[1]

BY THE START of the Nara period continental-style rites and deities were an established part of the cultic life of the Japanese islands. One by-product of the establishment of the *tennō*-centered polity that emerged following Tenmu's victory in the Jinshin war of 672 was substantial ferment in the worship of *kami*. As cults and deities from as far as distant Kyūshū entered the Yamato plain, *karakami* and ritual practices with roots in continental understandings of spirits and *yin* and *yang* proliferated both at court and across the countryside.

The diffusion of continental conceptions of spirit was not limited to the sphere of temples and shrines. Indeed, one of the most salient characteristics of popular cultic life both in China and in the Japanese islands was its high degree of integration with the most basic activities of daily life. In China, conceptions of *ch'i*, the five elements, and *yin* and *yang* underlay not only the worship of spirits and ancestors, but also an extremely wide range of activities involving the care of the human body, the production and consumption of food, and virtually all other essential activities of daily life. I therefore suggest that the appearance of rites of sacrifice, spirit pacification, and even the pursuit of immortality in the Japanese islands was most likely related to the spread of continental technologies related to sericulture, weaving, medicine, engineering, and the like. Crucially, for our purposes, each of these activities was in one way or another related to the Chinese festival calendar. All were also practiced to varying degrees by local lineages as well as by service groups of the court.

It is thus hardly surprising that in the court chronicles and across multiple literary genres from the Nara period we find frequent references to continental-style rites and tropes related to immortals and deities from the popular and elite cultic traditions in China. Broadly speaking, these references have elicited two types of response from Japanese scholars of the period. For many years the widespread presumption of the essentially "native" character of popular *kami* worship led many to simply dismiss explicit references in early Japanese texts to immortals and Chinese deities as affectations of courtiers seeking to demonstrate their familiarity with continental literary tropes. This position is seriously undermined, however, by the existence of cultic centers across the Japanese islands that were dedicated to the worship of just such figures.

A second approach, championed most forcefully by Fukunaga Mitsuji, has argued that such references indicate the presence of extensive Taoist influence within the Japanese islands during the period.[2] Such claims, however, are open to a number of objections, one of the most important being that spirit-quieting, the pursuit of immortality, and the manipulation of *yin* and *yang*, far from being exclusively Taoist phenomena, were part of the basic fabric of Chinese popular religious life of the period. The Chinese festival calendar contained numerous rites and legends related to astral deities, immortals, and, of course, the pacification of demons. Fukunaga's methodology therefore carries significant risks, as any approach that focuses on the textually based Taoist tradition will tend to focus not upon popular cults and deities, but on the small circle of literate figures at court. As we have repeatedly seen in Chapters 1 and 2, however, rulers and courtiers during the period were not only producers of political and religious ideology but also consumers as they sought to grapple with the profound transformations that were sweeping across Japan.

A second methodological risk inherent in drawing a straight line from continental texts to Japanese cultic practices of the seventh and eighth centuries is that important historical and religious differences between the realities of the Japanese islands and the ideals of ancient Chinese sources tend to become blurred. Several of the most pronounced differences concern the role of gender as it related to issues of lineage and political authority. As Shimode Sekiyo has pointed out in another context, one important example can be seen in the fact that the number of female immortals in literature from the Nara and early Heian periods dwarfs that of male immortals. This contrasts sharply with Chinese sources, which, with notable exceptions, tend to be dominated by narratives centered on male protagonists.[3] These discrepancies highlight a crucial difference regarding the cultic status of women within the lineal structures of China and Japan. Whereas lineages remained resolutely male in China, distaff lineages and female ancestors played a major role in the cultic life of the Japanese islands. Indeed, the dissemination of continental cults and legends across Japan was facilitated by the cults of several female immortals who were claimed as founding ancestors by local lineages. These female immortals thus represent vital nodes of intersection between supposedly "foreign" religious modes from the continent and local cultic practices and beliefs that should not be ignored.[4]

In this chapter I propose to investigate this confluence of issues relating to gender, kingship, and immortality in two parts. In the first, I focus on a series of cultic interactions that took place in Yoshino, a region of Yamato province that was connected by the Yoshino river to the Kii peninsula and the Inland Sea.[5] This rather large region appears prominently throughout the literature of the period as a locus for cults and lineages that appear to have roots in the Korean peninsula.[6] In addition, this area was from an early date a prominent center for those who wished to pursue immortality through the performance of austerities and the consumption of drugs as prescribed in various Chinese medical and cultic traditions. It was also a focal point of both early Buddhist narratives and the royal mythologies spelled out in the court chronicles. My purpose is not to untangle this web of practices and beliefs, but to examine their interplay with other regions across the Japanese islands. In doing so I focus on the cultic activities of a small cluster of lineages that controlled much of the coastal regions of the Kii peninsula and Kyūshū and that are also known to have been active in the importation of continental rites and technologies related to healing and the pursuit of immortality. We shall see that such lineages played a major role in the formation of foundational narratives of both Buddhist and royal traditions that related to Yoshino.

In the second section, I examine the surprising degree to which similar legends involving local ancestors and cultic centers can be found in Nara- and early Heian-period sources. After detailing a broad range of narratives concerning female immortals, or "Heavenly Maidens," who were worshipped not only at court, but also at cultic centers across Japan, I then discuss in greater detail the figures of Uranoshimako and Toyouke Hime, two Tamba deities who were explicitly represented as continental-style immortals. Since the Heavenly Maiden Toyouke Hime was installed as the chief deity at the outer shrine of Ise, I also argue that, to a surprising degree, the prominence of rites and beliefs related to the pursuit of immortality within court ritual and narratives reflected not only the inventions of literate courtiers, but also, and crucially, the appropriation of cultic practices and tropes established in other regions throughout the Japanese islands.

Cultic Interactions in Yoshino

Medicine Hunts and Yoshino

Probably the best indication of the degree to which the Yoshino region was associated with Chinese medical techniques and the promise of immortality can be seen in a set of references in the Suiko and Tenji chapters of the *Nihon shoki* to annual medicine hunts (*kusagari*) in the region. These hunts are said to have taken place in the regions of Uda and Yoshino and are presumed to have been searches for herbs that Chinese medical texts asserted would allow a practitioner to attain longevity and even immortality.[7] One notable characteristic of the *Nihon shoki*'s depiction of these medicine hunts is that they were undertaken on the third day of the third lunar month or the fifth day of the fifth lunar month. Both dates were key nodal points in the Chinese calendar, which marked important shifts in the relative balance of *yin* and *yang*. As Wada Atsumu has noted, the editors of the *Nihon shoki* apparently wished to highlight this aspect of the medicine hunts, so much so, in fact, that they altered their customary way of logging entries in order to emphasize the point.[8]

By explicitly linking the acquisition of herbs with specific dates in the Chinese calendar, the editors thus signaled that rulers of the Japanese islands embraced a closely integrated network of beliefs and practices related to medicine, ritual, and astronomy that was commonly held across East Asia. The *Samguk sagi*, for example, the oldest historical chronicle from the Korean peninsula, states that by the end of the sixth century the court of the Korean kingdom of Koguryō regularly engaged in similar activities on the third day of the third month.[9] Such practices, however, were not unique to this kingdom and can be traced back in China as far as the *Li chi*.[10]

Although we have little information regarding the specific nature of the activities undertaken by the Yamato court on such nodal days, numerous examples from Chinese sources suggest that the acquisition of herbs on these particular dates was rooted in conceptions of medicine that were closely intertwined with rites of spirit pacification. Thus the *Ching ch'u sui shih chi*, a record of ritual activity in southern China compiled at virtually the same time as Suiko's reign, states that on the fifth day of the fifth month images of human figures made from *moxa* (mugwort) were hung on gates or worn in the hair in order to disperse noxious spirits and vapors.[11] The text further quotes from the *Rites of Chou* and commentaries on the

Book of Odes to the effect that during the third day of the third month female shamans bathed themselves with medicines and scented water in preparation both for banquets and for rites of purification and spirit-calling (C: *chao hun hsü p'o*) at rivers.[12]

The prominent role played by female shamans in rites of the third day of the third month and fifth day of the fifth month in turn lent itself to further associations with concurrent elements in the Chinese festival calendar. The third day of the third month, for instance, also saw the beginning of a series of rites performed by women that involved feeding mulberry leaves to silkworms. The fifth day of the fifth month similarly marked a new phase in sericulture when women would begin gathering cocoons. From an early date woven items were also worn around the waist or chest on these days in order to forestall the arrival of hostile spirits. These rites, it should be noted, were not simply elements in court ritual of the period, but appear to have been undertaken by the populace at large. Thus Tu Kung-shan's commentary on the *Ching ch'u sui shih chi*'s entry for the fifth day of the fifth month states:

> Five colored strings are tied to the shoulder. This is called "avoiding [*pi*] the armies [of demons]" and will prevent disease. They also exchange presents of bracelets and woven items. . . .
>
> At mid-summer cocoons begin to appear and women spin and dye, with everyone working. They make patterns of the sun, moon, and constellations, birds and animals, embroider with golden thread and offer them to those whom they admire. One is named the "pattern of long life," one is named "the pattern of continuing life," one is called "the pattern of avoiding armies (of demons)," and one is called "vermilion thread." Such names are extremely numerous. Red, green, white, and black are used for the four directions while yellow is put in the center. This is called the "method of avoidance [*pi fang*]." These [amulets] are hung in front of the chest and show one's wife's achievements with silkworms.[13]

This text, suggesting as it does that colored strings and astrological symbols could be used both to prevent disease and to bring about prosperity in the form of silkworms, highlights both the importance of astrological and directional cults across a wide range of practices within the Chinese festival calendar and the highly gendered nature of weaving and sericulture cults. We shall see that this confluence of rites and beliefs related to female shamans and weaver maidens apparently helped spur the development of numerous legends and even cults of female immortals in the Japanese islands.

Although we have no way of knowing what actually occurred during the medicine hunts that are said to have occurred during the Suiko court, one entry from the final year of the life of Tenmu *tennō* states that a Paekche monk named Hōzō and a lay devotee named Konshō were sent to the mountains of Mino province to find life-saving herbs for the dying Tenmu. The entry strongly suggests that the conceptual horizon implied by such practices was already present at court during the final decades of the seventh century.[14] Six weeks later, on a date that was carefully coordinated with the winter solstice and the ascendance of the life-giving *yang* element, the text states that Hōzō gave the ailing ruler an elixir that was presumably made from herbs he had collected in Mino.[15]

Crucially, the text also states that on the same day a rite of "spirit-calling," (J. *shōkon*, Ch. *chao hun*) was performed for the ailing ruler. Although the text does not elaborate upon what was actually done during the rite, later commentators have assumed that this was an early instance of the well-known Rite of Spirit-quieting (J. *chinkonsai*). By the time of the composition of the Taihō Law Code in 701, this rite was probably already an established element of court ritual. By the early Heian period, the Chinkonsai was understood to be a re-enactment of the Heavenly Grotto myth that is recorded in both the *Kojiki* and the *Nihon shoki*. In this legend the royal ancestor and sun deity Amaterasu secludes herself in a cave and thereby plunges the world into darkness, only to be drawn out again when another female deity performs a ritual dance.[16]

For our purposes, however, it is far more important that the rite performed for Tenmu was closely coordinated with the Chinese festival calendar and clearly done with an expectation of ritual efficacy; Hōzō and Tenmu were clearly trying to restore the ruler to health, not simply to re-enact a mythological moment. As we have already seen with the collection of medicines in the third and fifth months, nodal, or transitional points within the Chinese calendar were heavily ritualized because such times denoted important shifts in the relative balance and movement of the forces of *yin* and *yang*. As the winter solstice marked the beginning of the decline of *yin* and the consequent ascendance of *yang*, Hōzō and Tenmu were almost certainly hoping that such a moment would be especially propitious for stirring, or calling back, the *yang* elements of Tenmu's spirit.

There is ample evidence suggesting that such an approach would have constituted common wisdom both on the continent and in Japan. The text of the *Ching ch'u sui shih chi* just quoted notes that female shamans performed rites of spirit-calling at rivers on the third day of the third month. In China, throughout the premodern period, rites of spirit-calling were regularly performed that featured shaking the clothes of the dead or dying in the hopes that they might thereby revive.[17] Such practices were apparently reflected in a core element of the Chinkonsai, wherein woven items that had been worn by the ruler were folded and placed within a spirit box (*tamabako*) and then shaken.[18] Since the practice of waving scarves or clothing in benediction is well attested in a variety of contexts and genres of literature from even before the Nara period, I suggest that the spirit-calling rite that was performed for Tenmu most likely reflected the extensive degree to which even common ritual practice had become influenced by continental rites of healing and spirit-quieting. Indeed, we could hardly hope for a better illustration of the degree to which the early Japanese Buddhist tradition and early court ritual were intertwined with beliefs and practices from the Chinese medical tradition that were themselves closely linked to and correlated with the Chinese festival calendar.

It would thus appear that by the reign of Tenmu *tennō*, Chinese rites of spirit pacification were closely linked with what was considered best medical practice. In addition, it is particularly worth noting that none of the texts cited above can be considered specifically Taoist or Buddhist. Indeed, the *Ching ch'u sui shih chi* was written not so much as a prescriptive text, but as an account of actual popular practice in southern China during the Sui period. All of this thus suggests that rites of spirit-calling entered the Japanese islands as part of a network of beliefs, rites, and cultic practices rooted in commonly held Chinese conceptions of body and spirit that were reflected in the popular Chinese festival calendar. We shall see that even prior to the Nara period such rites and beliefs were integral elements of both popular religious practice and the royal line. We shall also see that the background legends and beliefs for many of these practices highlighted the role of female shamans and weaving maidens as agents for the pacification of spirits.

Imprinting the Royal Seal at Yoshino

The reigns of Tenmu (reigned 673–686) and Jitō (reigned 690–697) witnessed a dramatic reformulation and expansion of the rites of the royal cult. As Tenmu and his successors set about constructing the institutions of a new, *tennō*-centered political and religious polity, they introduced numerous ritual innovations designed to amplify the sacrality of the ruler's person. Although this often involved the introduction of new ritual forms with clear roots in continental models, it also frequently consisted of modifying pre-existing ritual forms in order to give them new meanings that had a strong continental coloration.[19]

One example of this process can be seen in changing perceptions of agricultural rites such as the Tamai (literally, Rice Field Dance), a dance that was apparently originally performed in the hopes of ensuring a bountiful harvest. An entry in the *Nihon shoki* from the reign of Tenmu's predecessor, Tenji, states that the dance was performed at court on the fifth day of the fifth month of 671 in the presence of Tenji, Tenji's crown prince, and the assembled ministers at court.[20] It would thus appear that even prior to Tenmu's reign the rite had already taken on a political character, as the ability to propitiate *kami* and effect control over the forces of nature had come to be seen as a defining attribute of kingship in the Japanese islands.[21] It would also appear, given the date of performance, that the court had begun aligning at least some of its rites with nodal days in the Chinese festival calendar.

Although the Tamai was never abandoned by the court, Tenmu is believed to have instituted a new ritual dance known as the Gosechimai, or Dance of the Five Nodes.[22] In so doing, Tenmu appears to have drawn upon continental legends in which female immortals appear to rulers on important nodal days within the Chinese calendar. One female deity in the Chinese classics who was ubiquitous in this regard was the Queen Mother of the West; she was said to have visited such sage rulers as King Mu of the Chou and Emperor Han Wu-ti on the seventh day of the seventh month in order to present them with the fruits of immortality.[23] By the end of the seventh century, these and other such legends from the continent appear to have helped stimulate the formation of a corpus of legends in which female immortals appeared before Yamato rulers at Yoshino. Thus in the *Kojiki* we find an account of a beautiful young girl who danced like a divinity before the Yamato ruler Yūryaku at Yoshino.[24]

During the reign of Tenmu's chief consort and successor Jitō *tennō*, the court's involvement with Yoshino persisted and may even have intensified. Although Jitō is generally thought to have been an extremely consequential ruler, who worked to extend and deepen many of the cultic and institutional innovations that were begun by Tenmu and his predecessor Tenji, her ascension to the throne was in many ways an improvised response to the early death of her son and heir apparent, the Crown Prince Kusakabe.[25] Without an obvious candidate to replace Kusakabe, Jitō assumed the throne for seven years until her young grandson Prince Karu reached maturity and was able to assume the throne. Jitō's reign thus commenced in the aftermath of a substantial amount of turmoil. Jitō had devoted her energies during Kusakabe's lifetime to ensuring his succession rather than preparing for her own. This had included eliminating popular rivals of Kusakabe such as Tenmu's son Prince Ōtsu. It had also been less than twenty years since Tenmu had seized power in a war that resulted in the death of Tenji's own choice for the throne and the execution of a number of Tenji's highest ranking ministers.

Intriguingly, within this context, Jitō made thirty-one journeys to Yoshino following Tenmu's death. Most explanations for Jitō's behavior turn on the fact that the Yoshino area seems to have held special significance for Tenmu. Tenmu is depicted in the *Nihon shoki* as fleeing during a moment of great peril from the court in Ōtsu to the Yoshino mountains, where he is said to have taken the tonsure and resolved to leave political life. Tenmu's subsequent decision to fight for the throne was apparently made at Yoshino, and from there he and a small band of supporters—including Jitō—first set out on the campaign that eventually led to their victory in the Jinshin war and Tenmu's installment as ruler. Tenmu also famously required his own as well as Tenji's offspring to swear an oath of loyalty at Yoshino and pledge never to rebel. By repeatedly bringing the court to Yoshino, Jitō may have been reminding the Tenmu and Tenji factions at court of Tenmu's victory as well as of the Yoshino vow.[26]

Yet even before Tenmu first raised his banner at Yoshino, Yoshino already occupied an important place in the Yamato imaginary. Much as the *Kojiki* commemorated Yūryaku's encounter with a maiden at Yoshino who played the *koto* and danced like a goddess, Jitō's desire to inscribe her own presence on the Yoshino landscape may have been related to legends from the *Kojiki* and *Nihon shoki* that suggest that the region and its deities played a profoundly important role in the evolving mythologies of the ruling house. One Yoshino deity of utmost importance in this regard was the Nihu kami, or Nihu deity, one of the pre-eminent rainmaking deities throughout the Nara and Heian periods.[27] The Nihu Kawakami shrine, which was located at the source of the Yoshino river, was throughout the Nara and Heian periods a major cultic center for the royal house. Since, as we have already seen in Chapter 2, rites of rainmaking appear to have been an essential element in the cult of kingship in Yamato, the Nihu cult was of obvious importance for the royal cult.[28]

In the court chronicles, however, there are several indications that the importance of the Nihu deity in particular and the Yoshino region in general held an even greater ritual significance for the court. In the Jinmu chapters of the *Nihon shoki* and *Kojiki*, for instance, the Nihu river is depicted as a key site for the ruling line's military and cultic conquest of Yamato.

Having traveled from Kyūshū to Yoshino, Jinmu's army is said to have been stymied in its efforts to enter the Yamato plain. At Yoshino, Jinmu is guided by one Michi no Omi no Mikoto, the founding ancestor of the Ōtomo, an important military kinship group. In order to break the impasse, Michi no Omi no Mikoto prepares ritual implements for Jinmu to use in effecting the conquest of Yamato:

> At this the *tennō* was greatly pleased and taking this clay, had eighty platters, eighty small plates and eighty sacred jars made, went up the Nihu river and used them as he made offerings to the gods of Heaven and Earth. . . .[29]
>
> Again, he made a vow [*ukehi*], saying: I will now take these ritual jars and submerge them in the Nihu river. If the fish, whether great or small, are all carried drunk [downstream] like the *maki* leaves float [along the river], then may I without fail rule this land. If this does not occur, then may all be for naught. He then submerged the jars in the river with their mouths facing down. After a while the fish all came floating up [to the surface] with their mouths gaping as they floated downstream. The *tennō* was greatly delighted and, taking one of the abundant *sakaki* trees that grew upstream of the Nihu river, he worshipped the various gods of the area. This was the beginning of the [practice] of setting the sacred jars.[30]

This legend contains several clues as to the nature of the court's relationship to the Yoshino region. At one level, the text explicitly explains the special ritual uses of the clay from this region in the rituals of the royal cult. Only slightly less obviously, the text also depicts Yoshino as a point of entry for people, goods, and gods into the Yamato plain; having traveled with his army from Kyūshū, Jinmu must conquer resistance at Yoshino before he can claim rulership of the Yamato plain. This is significant for two reasons. First, the editors of the *Nihon shoki* apparently took it for granted that control of Yoshino and waterways such as the Nihu river were of crucial importance for Yamato rulers. Second, and crucially, much of this network of waterways, as well as much of the Kii peninsula, was located in the main base area of the Ōtomo kinship group. As we shall see repeatedly throughout this book, the Ōtomo, as well as a number of immigrant lineages in the coastal provinces of Izumi and Kii, appear to have played a major role in the diffusion of continental culture and technology throughout the Japanese islands.

The legend also reflects two important political and religious dynamics during the period. Because one of Tenmu's most important generals during the Jinshin war was one Ōtomo Muraji Fukei, the prominent place given to an Ōtomo ancestor in this legend of royal conquest mirrors the political and military realities of the post-Tenmu court. Further evidence for this can be seen from the fact that Jinmu himself appears to have been the focus of special ritual interest to Tenmu *tennō* and his line. Within the Tenmu chapters of the *Nihon shoki*, for instance, Tenmu's forces in the Jinshin war are said to receive divine assistance, after which the text is careful to mention that Tenmu had offerings made at Jinmu's tomb.[31]

All of this thus suggests that the cults and deities in Yoshino are best understood within a broader network of political and cultic relations that extended from the court all the way to Kyūshū and beyond. Indeed, the account of a member of the Ōtomo guiding a royal ancestor from Kyūshū into the Yamato plain appears to be emblematic of a broader historical process in which lineages from the coastal regions near Yoshino guided a series of deities from distant regions across the Japanese islands into the royal cult.[32]

Buddhist Practice and the Good Earth

Equally important, the legend also underscores the importance of the topographical characteristics of Yoshino for the royal cult. The effectiveness of the ritual implements used to subdue Jinmu's enemies is attributed specifically to the red clay from the area. Since the term "Nihu" itself contains the character for "red," Wada Atsumu has suggested that the coloration of the earth, along with the medicinal properties associated with it, were of immediate consequence for the clay's perceived ritual efficacy. Wada also notes that red dyes produced from red Nihu earth have been found on funerary figurines (*haniwa*), which suggests that the red pigmentation was considered especially efficacious for spirit-quieting.[33]

The red clay of Yoshino is also of crucial importance for understanding the setting of medicine hunts in the area of Uda and Yoshino. The setting was almost certainly related to the red earth at Yoshino, which is rich in cinnabar, a fundamental element in many approaches to immortality in the Chinese medical tradition.[34] As Wada has noted, directly ingesting such drugs was extremely dangerous and could easily be fatal. By collecting herbs and fish from the environment nurtured by that soil, however, the Japanese appear to have been following a strategy of indirectly ingesting safer quantities of cinnabar.[35]

All of this thus suggests that a wide spectrum of practices in Yoshino, whether they involved the manufacture of ritual vessels or the pursuit of medicinal herbs, may have been directly related to the red earth that typified the region. Not only was this cinnabar-laden ground thought to be the home of numerous female immortals, it would also appear that beliefs and practices related to continental notions of medicine and immortality had already begun to influence the construction of local cultic lore.[36]

Perhaps not surprisingly, these same topographic and cultic characteristics also appear to have strongly influenced the formation of Buddhist practices and legends in and around Yoshino. One indication of the degree to which both the court and the general populace associated the region with the quest for immortality can be seen in a series of legends concerning the region in the *Nihon ryōiki*, a Buddhist apologetic text composed sometime before 824. Consider the following legend concerning the practice of a monk on Mount Ohoniho (Hōkiyama), a mountain on the border between Yoshino and the Takechi district of Yamato province that, as we have already seen, housed both a shrine to the female Nihu deity and a temple supposedly built by the Soga kinship group during the reign of the Yamato ruler Kōgyoku:

> In the reign of Jitō *tennō*, there was a *dhyana* master of Paekche whose name was Tajō. He lived a life of strict discipline in Hōkiyamadera in Takechi district and made it his chief concern to cure diseases. The dying were restored to health by his miraculous works. Whenever he recited formulas for the sick, there was a miraculous event. . . . The *tennō* respected him and made offerings to him, and the people put faith in him and revered him.[37]

From an early date Yoshino was apparently famed as a training ground for numerous Buddhist ascetics, who chanted spells and practiced austerities in the pursuit of immortality and superhuman powers. The most famous such ascetic, known to later generations as En no Gyōja, later served as the paradigmatic figure of the *shūgendō* movement in Japan. The nature of En's practice as it is described in the *Nihon ryōiki* makes clear that En was believed to have had as his primary focus the use of herbs and the pursuit of immortality:

> His greatest desire was to fly on a five-colored cloud beyond the sky and play in the garden of eternity with the guests at the immortals' palace, lying in the flowering garden and sucking the vital force out of the haze to nourish his nature.
>
> Accordingly, in his late forties he went to live in a cave, wore clothing made of vines, drank the dewdrops on pine needles, bathed

in pure spring water to rinse away the filth of the world of desire, and learned the formula of the Peacock to attain extraordinary power. Thus he could employ spirits and kami at his command. Once he summoned them all and ordered them, "Make a bridge between Kane-no-take [in Yoshino] and Kazuraki-no-take." . . . At the end of the Taihō era, he . . . approached the capital, finally becoming an immortal (*hijiri*) flying to heaven.[38]

This passage, with its explicit statement that En's greatest wish was to attain supernatural powers and immortality through the practice of austerities and the consumption of drugs, aptly illustrates the degree to which the pursuit of such powers was associated with Buddhist practice at Yoshino. Numerous legends concerning En and other ascetics in the Yoshino mountains in turn served as the inspiration for countless later generations of practitioners, who sought immortality and supernormal powers amidst the region's red clay.[39]

During the Nara period Yoshino was also a major center for the practice of the Gumonjihō, a rite involving the propitiation of the Buddha Kokūzō. Among the many prominent court-sponsored monks who are known to have practiced this rite are a number of Hata monks such as Dōshō, Gomyō, and Gonsō, all of whom reached the upper reaches of the ecclesial hierarchy. In addition to this, however, the practice of the Gumonjihō rite at Yoshino is of immediate note for our purposes for two other reasons. First, the cult of Kokūzō—literally, the Space Storehouse Bodhisattva—appears to have been closely identified from its inception with Buddhist astrological thought. By the time the Kokūzō cult arrived in the Japanese islands, Kokūzō was already widely associated with the morning star in the east.[40] It thus appears that by the reign of Shōmu *tennō*, Buddhist monks who had at least a rudimentary familiarity with continental astrology were arriving at Yoshino in pursuit of special powers. Perhaps the best indication that such monks were conscious of the astrological dimension of the rite can be seen in the monk Kūkai's account of his own enlightenment experience in 791, in which he cited the appearance of the morning star at the climactic moment following his performance of the Gumonjihō:

At eighteen I entered the college in the capital and studied diligently. Meanwhile a Buddhist monk showed me a scripture called the *Kokūzō gumonji no hō*. In that work it is stated that if one recites the mystic verse one million times according to the proper method, one will be able to memorize passages and understand the meaning of any scripture. Believing what the Buddha says to be true, I recited the verse incessantly, as if I were rubbing one piece of wood against another to make fire, all the while earnestly hoping to achieve this result. I climbed Mount Tairyū in Awa Province and meditated at Muroto Cape in Tosa. The valley reverberated to the sound of my voice as I recited, and the planet Venus appeared in the sky.[41]

The fact that such rites were performed at Yoshino by prominent monks most likely also reflects one further aspect of Buddhist practice in the region: from the early Nara period several of the largest temples in the Japanese islands, including Kōfukuji and Daianji, began building mountain temples at which affiliated monks could stay as they engaged in their practices. Although monks in state-sponsored temples were expected to devote themselves to the study of Buddhist texts and the performance of rites for the benefit of the state, several of the most popular texts promised great spiritual and material benefits for the practitioner who engaged in the performance of austerities or rites that were more easily undertaken in the mountains. The development of Buddhist institutions in Yoshino thus appears to have emerged not in opposition to the more scholastically oriented temples of the Nara plain, but rather in tandem with them. As a result, by the early Heian period the Yoshino region housed a network of temples such as Hisodera (also known as Yoshinodera), Hasedera, Murōji, Tsubosakadera, and Kojimadera, all of which in turn helped shape the character of mountain asceticism for centuries to come.[42]

Yoshino and the Politics of the Local

Because Yoshino came to serve as a site where the most recent Buddhist texts and practices from the continent could be put into practice, its importance for the fledgling Japanese Buddhist tradition only increased over time. One prominent indication of this can be seen in Yoshino's special place in the lore surrounding the transmission of the Buddhist tradition to the Japanese islands. In the *Nihon shoki*, for instance, we are told that the first Buddhist images to be made in the Japanese islands were produced during the reign of the Yamato ruler Kinmei from wood that miraculously appeared off the coast of Izumi province and were then installed in Yoshinodera (Hisodera).[43] In the *Nihon ryōiki* we find an even stronger emphasis on Yoshino in its account of the transmission of the Buddhist tradition to the Japanese islands:

> According to a record, in the reign of Bidatsu *tennō*, sounds of musical instruments were heard off the coast of Izumi province. . . . Lord

Ōtomo no Yasunoko no Muraji heard this tale and reported it to the *tennō*, who did not believe it and remained silent. When he reported it to the queen consort, however, she ordered him to investigate. He went to the seaside himself and found it exactly as reported. While there he found a camphor log which had been struck by thunder. On his return, he said to the queen consort, "I have found a camphor log on the beach of Takaashi. I humbly request permission to make Buddha images out of it." The queen consort gave permission, saying, "Your wish is granted."

Yasunoko was very happy and announced the royal decree to Shima no Ohoomi [Soga no Umako] who, in great joy, commissioned Ikebe no atae Hita to carve three bodhisattvas. They were consecrated in the hall in Toyoura to inspire awe and reverence in the people. However, Lord Mononobe no Yuge no Moriya no Ohomuraji addressed the empress saying, "No Buddha images should be kept in this country. They must be thrown away." . . . He rebuked Yasunoko, saying, "The cause of our present disaster lies in keeping pagan images sent from a neighboring country. Give them up and throw them into the current which flows toward Korea." . . . He was at last overthrown in the reign of Yōmei *tennō*, and the Buddhist images were brought into the open to be kept for posterity. The image of Amida is now enshrined at Hisodera in Yoshino.[44]

In addition to its obvious stress on the importance of Yoshino as the cradle of the Japanese Buddhist tradition, this legend contains several further clues concerning Yoshino's role as an important node in a broader network of cultic and political relations that extended from the Yamato court across the Japanese islands to the Korean peninsula. Here the arrival of miraculous objects to the Japanese islands is said to have occurred in the coastal province of Izumi on the Kii peninsula. Because the protagonist of the tale is also a member of the Ōtomo, the legend again highlights the importance of this lineage for the region; just as the legend of Jinmu's conquest featured an Ōtomo ancestor guiding the would-be conqueror into the Yamato plain, here, too, we see an Ōtomo ancestor both figuratively and literally guiding a new divinity into the Japanese islands.

Because the figure of Ōtomo no Yasunoko appears nowhere in the court chronicles or other accounts of the founding legend of Japanese Buddhism, it would appear that the *Nihon ryōiki* account of the legend drew upon Ōtomo-related sources from the Yoshino region. Further evidence for the primacy of local concerns can be seen at several points in the text.

Whereas the *Nihon shoki* version of the legend, for instance, states that the first Buddhist image in the Japanese islands was presented to the Yamato court by an envoy from the Korean kingdom of Paekche, here we are told that the materials for the icon floated onto the beach at Takaashi. Similarly, whereas the founding legend of Japanese Buddhism culminates with Prince Shōtoku destroying Mononobe no Moriya and building Shitennōji temple in Naniwa, here the destruction of the Mononobe leads to the installation of Buddhist images at Hisodera in Yoshino.

The emphasis on local heroes and temples in the *Nihon ryōiki* account can also be seen in what happens afterward: Ōtomo no Yasunoko meets his former lord Shōtoku in the underworld shortly before the prince receives an elixir of immortality from the famed monk Gyōki.[45] This encounter is of immediate note not only because it once again suggests a strong interest in the pursuit of immortality, but also because it is excellent evidence that the early cult of Gyōki enjoyed widespread support in Izumi province. According to the *Gyōki nenpu*, not only was Gyōki born in Izumi, but he and his followers also built no less than six temples in the Ōtori district of Izumi between 724 and 727.[46] Dated sutra dedications from the 730s in Izumi that list the names of over 700 devotees of Gyōki's movement both testify to his popularity and provide us with further insight into the earliest supporters of Gyōki's movement.

One figure of special note was Kusakabe no Obito Maro, who was both the leader of one of the largest sutra-copying movements and the district chieftain.[47] The prominence of the local Kusakabe in this movement is in turn of interest because, in addition to having been active in the cults of Gyōki and Shōtoku, the Kusakabe and a cluster of collateral immigrant lineages are also believed to have been principal sponsors of the Crown Prince Kusakabe, the designated heir of Tenmu and Jitō. Although Prince Kusakabe died before assuming the throne, his descendants produced several rulers, including his son Monmu *tennō* (reigned 697–707), his daughter Genmei *tennō* (reigned 707–715), his grandson Shōmu *tennō* (reigned 724–749), and his great-granddaughter Kōken *tennō* (reigned 749–758 and 764–770).[48] All of this thus suggests that kinship groups such as the Ōtomo and Kusakabe would have been well placed to influence the construction of foundational narratives that highlighted the importance of Yoshino for both the early Buddhist tradition and the royal line.

Ōtomo and Kusakabe Ancestors

Further evidence concerning the role of the Ōtomo at Yoshino can be seen in numerous entries in the *Nihon shoki* during the sixth century, when the Ōtomo were at the forefront of military and diplomatic interactions with the Korean peninsula. Textual sources suggest that the Ōtomo not only gained firsthand exposure to continental culture, they also brought numerous artisans and workers from the Korean peninsula back to the Japanese islands. These immigrants often appear to have been subsequently organized into service group lineages under the jurisdiction of the Ōtomo.[49]

One particularly noteworthy kinship group, the Yamato Kusushi, is discussed in the *Shinsen shōjiroku*, an early ninth-century genealogical compendium. The text states that one Ōtomo no Sadehiko was sent by the Yamato court to the Korean kingdom of Paekche in the late sixth century. Upon his return Sadehiko is said to have brought back the founder of the Yamato Kusushi kinship group, who were then settled in the Uda district of Yamato province. In light of the fact that the term for "medicine" (*kusushi*) was used as the name for this service group, it appears that by the time of the composition of the *Shinsen shōjiroku*, both the Yamato Kusushi and the Ōtomo were closely associated with the introduction of Chinese medical techniques to the Japanese islands in general and the Uda/Yoshino region in particular.[50]

Further evidence for this can be found in the *Hizen fudoki*, which recounts the story of how Sadehiko arrived in the Matsuura district of Hizen province in Kyūshū, while en route to the Korean peninsula. There, the text informs us, he fell in love with and married the Kusakabe ancestor Shinohara no Otohihimeko. The text continues:

> Scarf Waving Peak. When Ōtomo Sadehiko boarded his ship and crossed over to Mimana, Otohihimeko climbed up to here and, taking her scarf, waved it [towards Sadehiko]. Thus it is called Scarf Waving Peak.[51]

This legend is notable not only for the fact that it associates a local place name in Hizen with the joining of Kusakabe and Ōtomo ancestors, but also for its depiction of Shinohara no Otome waving her scarf in benediction, much as Takakara Megami was said to shake her sleeves five times when she appeared before Tenmu at Yoshino. Elsewhere in the *Hizen fudoki* Otohihimeko is also portrayed in terms that suggest the influence of continental weaving cults.[52] Since, as we have already seen in Chapter 2, this region was also home to a vengeful weaving goddess who demanded offerings in the form of weaving implements, it is entirely possible that such resonances reflect a high degree of penetration of such motifs within the local cultic landscape.

All of this is of note because the text also highlights the importance of Matsuura as an important node for traffic going to and from the Korean peninsula. This conjunction of weaving cults and the Kusakabe and Ōtomo ancestral legends in the Matsuura district of Hizen, when read together with the *Shinsen shōjiroku* statement that Ōtomo Sadehiko settled the Yamato Kusushi in Uda upon his return from the Korean peninsula, aptly illustrates the means by which lineages such as the Kusakabe and the Ōtomo could have facilitated the transmission of both cults and technologies from the Korean peninsula to Yamato. As Kusakabe and Ōtomo ancestors came to be inscribed in the local landscapes along important transmission routes within the Japanese islands, legends of weaving deities and female immortals also appear to have taken up residence at sites of major interest to rulers seeking to control the lineages and spirits of the realm.

Female Immortals

Although Yoshino was closely associated with female immortals and the pursuit of superhuman powers, there is extremely good evidence suggesting that lineages such as the Kusakabe promoted similar cults elsewhere. Consider, for instance, the well-known legend cycle of Uranoshimako, a Kusakabe ancestor that was worshipped in a number of cultic centers in Tamba province. Versions of the Uranoshimako legend may be found not only in a brief account in the Yūryaku chapter of the *Nihon shoki*, but also in the *Manyōshū* and the *Tango fudoki*.[53] The general outline of the legend may be summarized as follows:

1. Uranoshimako is a fisherman from the village of Hioki in the Osa district of Tango province. He is an ancestor of the Kusakabe no Obito, who reside in the district.
2. Once, after being out at sea for three days and nights without catching a single fish, he catches a five-colored turtle that magically transforms itself into a beautiful maiden.
3. The maiden announces that she is an immortal and that she wishes to marry Uranoshimako and take him to P'eng lai, a land of immortals in Chinese mythology.
4. Uranoshimako agrees and the two plunge under the sea, where they go to the land of immortals.
5. After three years in P'eng lai, Uranoshimako suddenly longs to return to his native village and see his parents.
6. The turtle maiden gives Uranoshimako a spirit comb box (*tama kushige*) and tells him that he must keep it but never open it if he wishes to return to P'eng lai.

7. Uranoshimako returns to his native village, only to discover that three hundred years have passed and that all is strange there.
8. Uranoshimako forgets his promise to his wife and opens the spirit box.
9. The box immediately flies away, leaving Uranoshimako without any means of rejoining his wife in P'eng lai.
10. Uranoshimako composes a song lamenting his separation from his love.

Because this legend is filled from start to finish with motifs from Chinese cults and legends of immortality, there can be little doubt of continental influences on the legend. The protagonist is explicitly said to travel to Peng lai, an island of immortals in Chinese mythology, after encountering and marrying a female immortal. In the *Tango fudoki* account, which is by far the most elaborate version, we are even told that Uranoshimako's wife is a Chinese astral deity.[54] There is, however, equally strong evidence suggesting that the legend was well within the mainstream of local cultic practices. Much as a spirit box was used in the Chinkonsai to shake the spirit of the ruler, here Uranoshimako is given a spirit comb box (*tama kushige*) so that he may re-enter the land of immortals. Because the term "*kushi*," rendered here as "comb" was homophonous both with a term for wooden tablets that were used as receptacles for spirits at shrines and for medicines, magic combs as well as divine elixirs are featured prominently in a number of myths and legends from the period.[55] In addition, there is also strong evidence that the figure of Uranoshimako was widely worshipped in Tamba province—several shrines to the hapless fisherman are listed in the *Engishiki* and other early Heian-period texts.[56]

Several hints as to the roots of the Uranoshimako cult can also be found in the basic structure of the legend—a fisherman captures and marries a celestial female immortal, only in the end to be separated forever. This structure appears to be broadly in line with continental narratives related to sericulture, medicine, and the attainment of immortality. One of the earliest forerunners of these legends can be found in the *Huai nan tzu*. This work recounts the paradigmatic myth of the archer Yi, who is given the elixir of immortality by the Queen Mother of the West after he shoots nine suns from the celestial mulberry tree. Before Yi can drink the elixir, however, his wife Ch'ang o steals and drinks the potion and then flies away to the moon. There she remains, accompanied by a rabbit that continuously produces more of the elixir of immortality under a mulberry tree.[57] Other such legends feature female immortals who descended to earth in magical garments that allow them to fly. One typical example can be seen in the *Sou shen chi*, a fourth-century tale collection:

> In Yü chang District, Shin yü County, there was a man who saw six or seven women, all wearing feathered clothes, in the rice paddies. He did not know that they were [in fact] birds. Crouching low, he crawled towards them and took the garments that one of the women had removed and hid them. He then approached the birds, who all flew away, save for the one bird that alone could not leave. The man took her and made her his wife, and she gave birth to three daughters.
>
> Later, the mother sent one of her daughters to ask her father [where he had hid the clothes]. When [the mother] learned that they were under a stack of sheaves, she took them, put them on, and flew away. Later she returned for the three daughters, who also flew away.[58]

By the advent of the Nara period a substantial corpus of legends concerning female immortals who marry mortals before flying away had developed in the Japanese islands as well. One from pre-Nara Japan may be found in a remnant from the *Suruga fudoki*, a gazetteer submitted to the Nara court sometime around 713:

> Long ago there was a divine maiden who descended from heaven and hung her feathered garment on the branch of a pine tree to dry. When a fisherman gathered up the garment and examined it, [he found] it was light and supple beyond words. Whether it was a *rokushu* garment or something that was woven at the loom of the Weaver Maiden [he could not tell].[59] The divine maiden begged the fisherman to return the garment, but he refused. Although the divine maiden wished to fly back to heaven, she did not have the garment, and therefore she had no choice but to become the wife of the fisherman. Later, one day the maiden took the feathered robe and rode off on the clouds. The fisherman also became an immortal and flew up to heaven.[60]

This legend, with its explicit reference to the Weaver Maiden and the central motif of the Heavenly Maiden/immortal who is captured at a body of water, once again suggests roots in continental legends related to sericulture and female immortals. The legend also bears a broad structural resemblance to the Uranoshimako legend, with the important difference that the object permitting travel between the heavenly and earthly realms is not a comb, or medicine, box, but a woven item. Such motifs can be found in a broad range of similar legends that appear in provincial gazetteers and poetry collections from the period. Consider, for instance, the following legend from the *Ōmi fudoki*:

> Iga stream. According to the elders, there is a stream to the south of the village of Yogo in Iga District. Eight sky women transformed themselves into white birds and descended from the sky to the ford to the south of the stream, where they then bathed. At that time, a man named Iga Tomi was on the mountain to the west. When he viewed the birds, it was clear that their appearance was very unusual. Suspecting that they might be divine beings, he went to look, and saw that they were indeed divine. At this, Iga Tomi immediately fell in love and he could not [bear to] leave them. He surreptitiously sent his white dog to steal the heavenly garments, and after obtaining the garment of the youngest maiden, he hid it. When the sky maidens realized [he was there], the seven older sisters flew off to Heaven, leaving only the youngest sister, who was unable to fly away. With the path back to Heaven closed to her for a long while, she finally became an earthly human.
>
> The bay where the Heavenly Maidens bathed is now called the "Divine Bay." Iga Tomi married the Heavenly Maiden and lived here, where she eventually gave birth to two boys and two girls. . . . These are the ancestors of the Iga Muraji. Later, the mother found her Heavenly winged garment, put it on and flew off to Heaven. Iga Tomi could only [live out his days] in empty loneliness, sighing and regretting endlessly.[61]

As with the legends of Uranoshimako and the *Suruga fudoki*, this story again features a female immortal who is captured by a male human at a waterway. We are explicitly told that it is a woven garment that allows the immortal to fly to Heaven. But perhaps most important, this text, composed barely ten years after Jitō *tennō* undertook her last sojourn in Yoshino, once again demonstrates that even before the Nara period female immortals had already become integrated into the ancestral cults of local lineages that ranked far below the inner circles of the court.[62]

All of this matters because, as we noted above, within Nara-period poetry we find numerous poems featuring female transcendents who attained immortality through the consumption of herbs that had grown wild in the red earth of the region. One such figure, known as Nurihime, was the subject of a poem by no less a figure than Fujiwara Fuhito, the second scion of the Fujiwara lineage and a key advisor to several rulers.[63] Although we can tell little about this figure from Fuhito's poem, the *Nihon ryōiki* contains the following account of one Nuribe no Hime from the region:

> In the village of Nuribe, Uda district, Yamato province, there lived an extraordinary woman, who was married to Nuribe no Miyatsuko Maro. Innately pure and straightforward in upholding what was right, she gave birth to seven children, but she was too poor to feed them since she had no one to depend on. . . . Every day she purified herself in a bath and clothed herself in rags. She would gather edible herbs in the fields, and devoted herself to staying at home and cleaning the house. When she cooked the herbs, she called her children, sat up straight, and ate the food, all the while smiling, talking cheerfully, and being grateful. This constant discipline in mind and body made her spirit resemble that of a "guest from heaven."
>
> In the fifth year of the Hakuchi era . . . heavenly beings [immortals] communicated with her, and she ate special herbs gathered in the field in springtime and flew about in the heavens.[64]

This legend, highlighting as it does a common woman from a local lineage in Uda, underscores the importance of female figures such as Nuribe no Hime, Takakara Megami, and the Heavenly Maidens of Suruga and Iga for local cults and legends across the Japanese islands. Perhaps even more striking is the fact that this legend from a Buddhist apologetical text simply takes for granted the belief that medicinal herbs from the Uda region of Yamato could bestow immortality. All of this again suggests the region's close association with immortality, as well as the high degree to which Chinese immortality beliefs had penetrated popular tale literature of the period.[65]

One further indication of the degree to which continental tropes related to sericulture and immortality had penetrated into the literary and cultic discourses of the period can be seen from the fact that not all poetic references to female immortals at Yoshino were composed in Chinese-style verse. In the *Manyōshū*, for instance, we find one poem in particular that is suggestive of the means by which such beliefs proliferated in Yamato. The text of the poem and its accompanying note are as follows:

> Where the hail comes down
> On the heights of Kishimi

> The climb is steep:
> I lose my grip on the grasses,
> I grasp the hand of my girl.

Concerning the above poem, it is also stated that it is a poem given to the Immortal Mulberry-Branch Maiden by Umashine, a man of Yoshino. But an inspection of *The Mulberry-Branch Legend* fails to reveal such a poem.[66]

This text is of immediate interest not so much for the content of the poem, but for the note's reference to an apparently well-known legend involving a man who succeeds in catching the Immortal Mulberry-branch Maiden and making her his lover.[67] The fact that this immortal is named after the mulberry tree, the leaves of which were used for feeding silkworms, also strongly suggests that this figure was associated with continental conceptions of weaver maidens as female shamans/immortals. Perhaps most important, however, the reference to the now-lost *Mulberry-branch Maiden* once again suggests that even prior to the Nara period the configuration of Yoshino as a site frequented by female immortals was a commonplace in the literature of the period.[68]

Several important clues concerning the process by which figures such as the Immortal Mulberry-branch Maiden were constructed can be found in yet another account from the *Hizen fudoki*. This text describes the context for a popular song sung by young men and women during courting festivals each spring in the Kishima district of the province:

> Kishima District. Two leagues south of the district is a solitary mountain. It has three peaks in a line from southwest to northeast. Its name is Kishima. . . . Every year the young men and women from the villages, carrying wine and cithern, climb up hand in hand and gaze out over the valley. They play music, drink, sing, and dance, and when the songs are over they go home. The words of [one of their] songs go:
>
>> Where the hail comes down
>> On the heights of Kishima
>> The climb is steep:
>> I lose my grip on the grasses,
>> I grip the hand of my girl.
>
> This is a Kishima measure.[69]

This text is of immediate interest because it is virtually identical with the song that was presented in the *Manyōshū* as referring to the Immortal Mulberry-branch Maiden. Here, however, the text clearly asserts that the song is of a distinctive type that originated in the Kishima district in Hizen province in Kyūshū. As we have seen repeatedly, this region was a major gateway for people, technology, and ideas from the Korean peninsula into the Japanese islands. The region was home to the Kusakabe and the purported point of entry for Ōtomo Sadehiko when he transported the Yamato Kusushi from Paekche to Yoshino/Uda. It was also a major center for the cults of Akaru Hime, the Munakata deities, and the Sumiyoshi deities, all of whom by the advent of the Nara period had made their way to Yamato and formed an integral part of the royal cult.[70] All of this suggests that the Immortal Mulberry-branch Maiden may have been yet another deity with roots in the Korean peninsula who was transported from Kyūshū to Yamato prior to the Nara period. It would also appear that the Immortal Mulberry-branch Maiden yet again illustrates a primary cultic dynamic of the period, in which deities associated with continental technologies such as sericulture and medicine moved from Kyūshū into the Yamato plain.[71]

Toyouke Hime and Uranoshimako

One female immortal who was also associated with both the Uda/Yoshino region and Tamba province was the Heavenly Maiden Toyouke Hime no Mikoto. According to the *Toyuke no miya gishikichō*, a record from the Ise shrine that was composed in 804, prior to taking up residence in Ise the goddess was worshipped at a shrine in Uda, the home of Nuribe Hime, as well as at various cultic centers across Tamba province, the home of Uranoshimako on the coast of the Japan/Eastern Sea.[72] Crucially, Toyouke Hime no Mikoto, much like the Immortal Mulberry-branch Maiden, the Heavenly Maiden of Iga, and the bride of Uranoshimako, appears in the literature of the period as a female immortal who is captured by a human mortal and forced to remain in the human realm. Fortunately, a lengthy account of the mythic origins of this deity's cult can be seen in the following remnant from the *Tango fudoki*:

> Tango Province, Tamba District. Northwest of the district headquarters is the township of Hiji. There is a wellspring on the summit of Mount Hiji in this township. It is named Manai [True Well]. It has now become a marsh.
>
> Eight sky women came down to bathe in this spring. At this time there was an old couple; they were called the Old Man of Wanasa and

the Old Woman of Wanasa. These old people came to the wellspring and stealthily took the clothing of one of the sky women and hid it. Directly, all the maidens who had their clothes flew up into the sky; only the one without clothes remained behind, staying hidden in the water, alone and ashamed.

Hereupon the old man said to the sky woman, "We have no child. Heavenly Maiden, please be our child." . . .

She accompanied them home, where they lived together for over ten years. There the sky woman used her skill to brew *sake*. To drink one cup was enough to dispel the ten thousand ills. Cartloads of treasure were sent as the price of a single cup. In time the house overflowed with abundance, and the muddy bottoms [*hijikata*] prospered. Hence the township was called Hijikata. . . .

Later the old man and his wife spoke to the sky woman, saying, "You are not our child. You have temporarily lived with us, that is all. Now be off with you."

At this the sky woman looked up at heaven and wept in grief, looked down at the earth and moaned in sorrow. . . . When she had gone beyond the gate, she spoke to the villagers, saying, "For a long time I have been sunken among humankind, and now I cannot return to the sky." . . .

At last she went away. Arriving at the village of Arashio, she told the villagers "When I think of what that old man and woman are really like, my heart is a raging tide [*arashio*]." Thus they called the place the village of Arashio in the township of Hiji. Again, she arrived in Nakiki. . . .

Once more, arriving in the village of Nagu, in Funaki Township, Takano District, she told the villagers, "Here my heart has become tranquil [*nagushiku nirinu*]." [*Nagushi* is the old word for "tranquil."] And she stayed on in this village. She is the goddess known as Toyoukanome no Mikoto residing in the Nagu Shrine in Takano District.[73]

Because this *Tango fudoki* account of Toyouke no Hime is so much more developed than the poetic references to female immortals in the *Manyoshū* and the *Kaifūsō*, it provides several invaluable clues concerning the nature of Nara-period conceptions of such figures. Here, the importance of medicine and immortality for Toyouke Hime no Mikoto's cultic identity is clearly suggested by the text's depiction of the goddess as a producer of *sake*, or *kusushi*, that can be used as a medicine for healing any illness. In addition to this, the figure of Toyouke Hime no Mikoto is also of immediate interest because she is credited in the *Nihon shoki* as being the source of sericulture and other technologies that were transmitted to the Japanese islands from the Korean peninsula during the Asuka and Nara periods.[74] Most likely due to her close association with continental technologies and rites, later texts from the Kamakura period also state that Toyouke Hime no Mikoto had mastered techniques for effecting her own resurrection and subsequent immortality.[75]

One further clue as to the nature of the early cult of Toyouke Hime no Mikoto can be found in the geography of the cultic centers in the areas of Tamba province that she is said to have visited. She and her seven sisters are said to have descended to earth in Hiji township near the heart of the Uranoshimako cult. Since the Uranoshimako narrative also involves a female immortal who bestows a medicine spirit box (*tama kushige*) upon a mortal fisherman after she has been captured in the human realm, I suggest that the Toyouke narrative, in which she sells a magical elixir after being captured, is broadly reflective of the cultic orientations of the Kusakabe in general and the region in particular. The multiple shrines in the region dedicated to Toyouke no Hime and Uranoshimako strongly suggest that the motifs of weaving, *kusushi*, and immortality associated with the Immortal Mulberry-branch Maiden and Toyouke no Hime were not simply literary tropes but common elements in popular cultic practice along the coast of the Japan/Eastern seas.[76] Simply put, there is extremely good evidence that even prior to the Nara period, cults of female immortals and medicine deities had put down roots not only in such coastal provinces as Tamba and Hizen, but also in Uda and Yoshino. Given the influence of the Kusakabe and Ōtomo at court, their prominence in Hizen and in the coastal provinces along the Inland and Japan/Eastern seas, and the prominence of their ancestors in foundational narratives of both the royal line and the Buddhist tradition, it appears that these lineages played a major role in the transmission of the cults of female immortals and medicine deities into the mainstream of Yamato religion.

The Gosechimai, Princess Abe, and Toyouke

One indication of the importance of female immortals for the Nara court in general can be seen in subsequent development in the uses of the Gosechimai—the court dance attributed to Tenmu that appears in the cult of Toyouke Hime. One particularly revealing incident concerning the status of the Gosechimai at court occurred in 743, some five years after Shōmu *tennō* had taken the unprecedented step of naming his daughter, the Princess Abe, as his successor. Opposition to the Fujiwara at court, combined with the fact that the title of *taishi*, usually translated as "crown prince," had never been given to a woman, meant that Princess Abe's position remained precarious.[77] Apparently in response to these concerns, on the 5th day of the 5th month of 743, the crown princess famously performed the Gosechimai in the Daigokuden, the main ceremonial hall for the court. In attendance for the event were her father Shōmu, her grandmother the retired ruler Genshō, and the assembled ministers of the court. Lest anyone at court fail to grasp the significance of the event, Genshō praised the princess's dance as being not simply an act of entertainment, but also a means devised by the "sage king" Tenmu to ensure that hierarchies of rank were kept in good order and that ministers understood their proper relationship with their ruler.[78]

As Joan Piggott has noted in another context, one key element of this performance was almost certainly Abe's relationship with her father, Shōmu *tennō*. In dancing for her father, the princess highlighted both her filial piety and her lineal claim to the throne.[79] I would also submit, however, that Genshō's reference to Tenmu as a "sage"—a term loaded with connotations of immortality—suggests that an important subtext for the dance may also have been related to Tenmu's special involvement with continental notions of immortality and Yoshino.[80] Just as Jitō had reminded the court of her connection with Tenmu by undertaking no less than thirty-one pilgrimages to Yoshino, Princess Abe appears to have utilized the Gosechimai to remind the court of her own lineal connections with the "sage king" who had refashioned so much of court ritual with motifs drawn from legends of female immortals and the Chinese festival calendar.

In light of the close relationship between the Dance of the Five Nodes and the mythic tropes of the Chinese festival calendar, it is perhaps fitting that the Gosechimai later came to be used in conjunction with the worship of Toyouke Hime, the Heavenly Maiden and medicine goddess from Tamba and Uda, who, as we saw earlier, was also credited with giving birth to the products of sericulture within the Japanese islands. By the advent of the Heian period the meteoric rise of this Heavenly Maiden within the royal cult had culminated with the enshrinement of Toyouke as the chief deity of the outer shrine at Ise, where she was worshipped for centuries along with Amaterasu by a consecrated princess in residence near the shrine.[81] Because Toyouke Hime later became the focal object of the religious movement later known as Ise Shintō, the importance of her cult for the history of Japanese religion was enormous.[82] By the time of the completion of the *Toyuke no miya gishikichō* in 804, the exalted status of both this deity and the Gosechimai had been codified within the royal cult. Henceforth, the Gosechimai was to be performed only by a consort of the *tennō*, either in his presence at the Festival of the Tasting of the First Fruits

(Niinamesai), or at the outer shrine of Ise, for the enjoyment of none other than Toyouke Hime.[83]

In light of the importance of Toyouke Hime no Mikoto for the royal cult, it is easy to overlook the fact that the origins of her cult lay not with court intellectuals, but with local lineages that populated coastal regions and were among the first to absorb continental cultural and technological influences. Such roots are important, for they suggest that, far from being the source for such conceptions, the court appears to have absorbed continental beliefs and practices as part of its appropriation of the cultic resources of the Kusakabe, Ōtomo, and other immigrant lineages. It would appear that during the Nara period, cults and legends associated with medicine, sericulture, and immortality did not simply radiate out from the Yamato court to the provinces. Rather, to a surprising degree, such elements were transmitted to the court by lineages in Tamba, Hizen, and Yoshino such as the Ōtomo, Kusakabe, and others.

Conclusion

As Chinese medical and calendrical beliefs spread at court and in the countryside during the middle decades of the seventh century, they engendered a cultic and conceptual revolution that helped transform the political and religious landscape of the Japanese islands. One remarkable by-product of this process was the ideal of the female immortal with control over the processes of life and death. By the advent of the Nara period this ideal, along with Chinese conceptions of medicine and immortality, had emerged as a central element in the mythic vocabulary of numerous ancestral cults across the land.

One region closely associated with this process was Yoshino. With its high altitude and red earth, this area was believed to be particularly productive of herbs and plants that, if consumed properly, could produce health and eventually immortality. As a result, even prior to the Nara period, the Yoshino region had become a central locale in the founding legends of the royal house as well as of the Japanese Buddhist tradition. Even the legendary royal ancestor Jinmu was depicted as pacifying his enemies at Yoshino with special vessels made from the region's red clay, and temples such as Hisodera claimed to be the recipients of the first Buddhist icons to arrive in the Japanese islands.

The importance of Yoshino for both the royal cult and the formative Japanese Buddhist tradition was also almost certainly related to such kinship groups as the Ōtomo, Kusakabe, and Hata, all of which were deeply involved with the affairs of the Korean peninsula on the one hand and the development of court ritual on the other. Each of these groups appears to have absorbed from an extremely early date Chinese conceptions of medicine and immortality into their own ancestral cults and legends. As a result, even before the Nara period legends of female ancestors who were immortals could be found not only at Yoshino, but even in the farthest reaches of the Japanese islands. By the end of the Nara period, as the cults and legends of figures such as Nuribe no Hime, the Immortal Mulberry-branch Maiden, Takakara Megami, and, most spectacularly, Toyouke no Hime were absorbed into the very heart of the emerging royal mythology, these and other such figures played a major role in shaping both the royal cult and the nascent Japanese Buddhist tradition.

The very fact that the construction of Yoshino as a site of immortals was related to the topographical and geographic importance of the region should alert us to an additional set of issues concerning the development of the Japanese Buddhist tradition and the importance of ancestors as *hijiri*. For most of the sixth century, Yoshino was also a major base of the Mononobe, perhaps the most powerful kinship group in the land prior to the reign of Suiko. Not surprisingly, some of the most important lineages to emerge from the Mononobe orbit following their demise in 587 were local lineages associated with Yoshino. Two of these—the Kusakabe and Kamo—went on to play a major role in the construction of the cult of Prince Shōtoku, a royal ancestor who was also the purported sponsor of both the Chinese festival calendar and Buddhist tradition in Japan. Because Shōtoku was also credited with the destruction of the Mononobe, the next chapter will consider how these lineages, using the politics of violence, spirit propitiation, and the Chinese festival calendar helped to inscribe the founding legend of Japanese Buddhism with cultic elements drawn not from Buddhist scriptures, but from the cult of the Queen Mother of the West, the ruler of the land of the immortals and the benefactor of sage rulers.

CHAPTER 4

The Queen Mother of the West and the Ghosts of the Buddhist Tradition

> Reckoning with ghosts is not like deciding to read a book: you cannot simply choose the ghosts with which you engage. . . . To be haunted is to be tied to historical and social effects.
> —Avery Gordon, *Ghostly Matters*[1]

ONE AFTERNOON EARLY in the seventh month of 587, so the story goes, the political and cultic landscape of the Japanese islands was profoundly transformed as an army of pro-Buddhist princes and lineages led by the Soga kinship group overcame the forces of their powerful Mononobe opponents and established a new, pro-Buddhist regime within the Japanese islands. The birth of the new order, however, was also apparently drenched in blood, as the victors hunted down the members of the main Mononobe line and confiscated the lands of their allies. After installing a new ruler, Suiko, upon the throne, the Soga and allies such as Prince Kamitsumiya (Shōtoku) are then said to have set about augmenting the power of the throne through the promotion of continental political, religious, and technological forms.

Although, as is so often the case, this account cannot be considered an accurate rendering of historical reality, the legend was clearly a cornerstone of the early Japanese Buddhist tradition's understanding of its own origins. In addition to the account of the battle and its aftermath that is provided in the *Nihon shoki*, for instance, similar versions of the legend are recounted in the *Hōryūji garan engi narabi ni ruki shizaichō* and the *Gangōji garan engi narabi ni ruki shizaichō*, two of only three extant temple records from the Nara period. The legend is also recounted in the *Jōgū Shōtoku hōō teisetsu*, an early hagiographical text, parts of which are thought to predate the *Nihon shoki*, as well as in the *Nihon ryōiki*, which, as we have already noted, is the oldest collection of Buddhist legends in the Japanese islands. The pervasiveness of this legend across so many different texts and genres testifies to its central place in the earliest Buddhist literature of the Japanese islands.²

The undoubted importance of this legend and the figure of Shōtoku for the early Buddhist tradition, however, should not blind us to the fact that the prince of legend was also depicted in such texts as the *Nihon shoki* as a paragon of continental culture and learning. Within the text Shōtoku is also said to have been a master of non-Buddhist learning, who composed the first historical chronicle in the Japanese islands, promulgated a constitution for the court, and constructed the first continental-style system of ranks for the court. Shōtoku's association with written continental culture can thus be seen in numerous legends depicting the prince as a sage, exegete, judge, lawgiver, and immortal.³

As we have already seen in Chapter 2, the *Nihon shoki* also depicts the Suiko court as the era in which Chinese astrological and divinatory texts were first promulgated at court. There is, further, good reason to believe that continental rites and cults associated with such texts were promoted by immigrant kinship groups such as those at the forefront of the early cult of Prince Shōtoku. In this chapter I therefore propose to explore the nature and uses of Chinese rites of spirit pacification in Nara Japan as they related to the formation of the founding legend of Japanese Buddhism. Because this legend is presented even in primary sources in terms of resistance to the introduction of the "foreign" Buddhist tradition, it is also an ideal vehicle through which to examine in greater depth how the rites of the Chinese festival calendar influenced the development of Buddhist and local cultic traditions of Nara Japan.

This involves venturing into relatively uncharted territory. Although a wide spectrum of Chinese cults and deities informed religious life in the Japanese islands, my focus will be on the influence of the cult of the Queen Mother of the West, an ancient figure in the Chinese pantheon with deep roots in the Chinese calendar, immortality beliefs, and weaving cults. We shall see that the cult of the Queen Mother played a prominent role in the legends and cultic practices of a cluster of influential kinship groups associated with both the Mononobe and the early Shōtoku cult. We shall also see that to a surprising degree the founding legend of Japanese Buddhism itself appears to be structured in terms of ritual gestures and motifs derived not only from Buddhist scriptures, but also from specific rites and dates that were commonly observed in the yearly festival cycle.

The chapter focuses on a series of interlocking issues that are of central importance for understanding both the religion and politics of Nara Japan. Most generally, given their prominent role in the construction of the political and religious worlds of pre-Nara Japan, I suggest that an understanding of the cultic orientations of the Mononobe and their affiliated lineages is essential for even a basic understanding of the cultic practices of the age. Once we focus on the role of lineages affiliated with the Mononobe in the often sanguinary politics of the period, the crucial role of political violence as a catalyst for the proliferation of continental cultic practices becomes readily apparent. In addition to their intrinsic interest, however, these issues also have immediate relevance for our understanding of the founding legend of Japanese Buddhism, in which the tradition is represented as deeply rooted in political violence. Reading the founding legend of Japanese Buddhism in light of rites and legends of lineages associated with the Mononobe thus promises to shed light both on the early Buddhist tradition in Japan and its relationship with such Chinese deities as the Queen Mother of the West. Perhaps most important, however, because this legend specifically paints the Mononobe as champions of native cultic practices, the founding legend of Japanese Buddhism also promises to shed light upon the degree to which rites and beliefs associated with the Chinese ritual calendar were understood by the editors of the *Nihon shoki* to be an integral part of the cultic landscape of the Japanese islands.

The Founding Legend of Japanese Buddhism and the Atsumori Effect

Although composed several hundred years after such texts as the *Nihon shoki*, one of the most compelling depictions of the connections between violence, cult, and spirit-quieting in classical Japanese literature can be found in the Atsumori chapter from the *Heike monogatari*, a thirteenth-century martial romance. In this text the rough, experienced eastern warrior Kumagae easily overcomes the aristocratic youth Atsumori in individual combat, only to be impressed with the youth's aristocratic bearing. Kumagae is eventually forced to kill the youth in order to prevent a more painful execution by other warriors.[4] In Zeami's eponymous Nō play based upon this episode, Kumagae returns to the scene of the battle and once again encounters Atsumori, now a hungry ghost unable to overcome the powerful karma associated with violent death, anger, and the desire for revenge. Throughout, the play focuses on the dramatic tensions resulting not only from Kumagae's encounter with Atsumori's ghost, but also from the more figurative ghosts created by Kumagae's regret at having killed the boy. Eventually both types of ghost find peace as Kumagae, now a monk, prays for the spirit of Atsumori.[5]

Without claiming any direct connection between the Atsumori story and the founding legend of Japanese Buddhism, I suggest that it can help illuminate several important features of that founding legend. Much of the Atsumori story's emotional appeal stems from the fact that the relationship between the two characters begins with a tragic encounter and execution. Whereas Western tragedy often ends with the violent death of one protagonist at the hands of another with whom he or she is intimately connected, here we may say that the relationship between the two men stems from the execution itself. Indeed, rather than saying that the two form a bond in spite of the awkward fact that one kills the other, it is more accurate to say that the two form a relationship precisely because one kills the other.

Although this dialectic of violence producing passions and therefore karmic bonds among antagonists has long been a recognized staple of Japanese drama, there has to date been little or no discussion of the degree to which continental conceptions of violence, spirits, and their pacification were implicated in the need of the Buddhist tradition to confront literal and figurative ghosts from its own past. Such ghosts, however, pervade the *Nihon shoki* account of its founding legend. At the heart of this legend is the violent conflict between the pro-Buddhist forces, led by the Soga kinship group, and the anti-Buddhist forces led by the Mononobe kinship group. As a result of destroying the main branch of the Mononobe, the earliest proponents of the Buddhist tradition had to deal with the Mononobe and their ghosts, which profoundly influenced how Japanese Buddhist tradition depicted its origins and subsequent trajectory. I suggest that while the Mononobe lost the (literal) battle, they won the (figurative) war, as did Atsumori. We might even say that *because* the Mononobe lost the literal battle they—and the Chinese rites of spirit pacification with which they were associated—were able to exert a lasting influence on Japanese religion in general and the Japanese Buddhist tradition in particular.

Building a Foundation

In order to understand this process it is necessary to begin at the beginning, at least as it was later configured by the Japanese Buddhist tradition. Although the narrative is quite long, we may summarize the points of commonality in virtually all of the early sources as follows:

1. During the reign of the Yamato ruler Kimmei, the king of the Korean kingdom of Paekche sends a Buddhist statue to the Yamato court and recommends worship of this new deity, who is more efficacious than all other gods. The king adds that this new

deity is worshipped throughout the rest of Asia. He concludes with a request for military assistance against the Korean kingdom of Koguryō, which has been encroaching on Paekche's territory.
2. A debate breaks out at the Yamato court over whether to accept and worship the new god. The Mononobe, one of the two most powerful kinship groups at court, oppose worship of the statue, arguing that the gods of Japan would be angered by worship of the new deity.
3. The Soga, rivals to the Mononobe and leaders of a cluster of immigrant kinship groups from Paekche, urge worship of the deity.
4. It is agreed that the Soga shall worship the image, even if others do not.
5. A plague breaks out and many die.
6. Mononobe no Yuge Moriya, leader of the Mononobe, seizes the statue and throws it into the canal in Naniwa.
7. Years later the leader of the Soga falls ill and a divination expert declares the reason to be that he has failed to continue worshipping the Buddhist statue.
8. The statue is dredged up from the Naniwa canal, and the Soga resume worship of the statue.
9. The Soga create a league of princes opposed to the Mononobe. Among them is a young prince named Kamitsumiya (Shōtoku), who is of Soga descent.
10. Battle breaks out between the Mononobe and the Soga coalitions. As the forces of the Soga are about to be defeated, Prince Shōtoku makes images of the Four Heavenly Kings (*shitennō*) of Buddhism out of branches from a *nuride* tree. He vows to build a temple to the Four Heavenly Kings and spread the Buddhist tradition if the Soga are granted victory. Soga no Umako, the head of the Soga, makes a similar vow. Shōtoku then places the images of the Four Heavenly Kings in his hair prior to entering battle.
11. The Soga coalition emerges triumphant, after Mononobe no Yuge Moriya is killed in battle.
12. Kamitsumiya is given half of all Mononobe lands and laborers, which he uses to build Shitennōji (Four Heavenly Kings Temple) in Naniwa. The Soga also build their kinship group temple Asukadera.
13. Shōtoku and the Soga then take over the reins of government and usher in a new program of support for the Buddhist tradition and the centralization of the power of Yamato rulers.

Embedded in this legend are several important points regarding the role of Chinese rites of spirit pacification in Nara Japan. Among the most important are the following: (1) At the center of the legend is Prince Shōtoku, whom later texts closely associate with the adoption of Chinese ritual practice by the Suiko court. (2) The legend concludes with the construction of Shitennōji, suggesting that kinship groups associated with that temple would have had an important role in the legend's construction. (3) Following the defeat of the Mononobe, several kinship groups formerly allied with the Mononobe came to be closely associated with the Shōtoku cult and Shitennōji. (4) The construction of Shitennōji itself was made possible by the appropriation of Mononobe lands and labor. (5) Although the text attributes the victory of the pro-Buddhist forces to Shōtoku's worship of the Four Heavenly Kings, Shōtoku's method of propitiation (the placing of images of the Four Heavenly Kings in his hair) does not appear related to any known Buddhist practices from the day.

Winners, Losers, and the Construction of Tradition

Before analyzing the narrative further, it is worth remembering that history is generally written from the perspective of the victors. This judgment, though understandable, seldom goes beyond the fairly obvious observation that the sources with which we reconstruct the past have been biased by the political realities of the age in which they were written. It would perhaps be more to the point to note that the most interesting figures for historians tend to be those who have grasped the power to effect dramatic changes in society and culture. This has been the almost universal tendency with regard to scholarship devoted to the founding legend of Japanese Buddhism. The victory of the Soga is generally understood as important because it ushered in a period of unrivaled hegemony for pro-Buddhist figures intent upon transforming Japanese society.[6] Such a view of the Soga victory naturally leads to a set of questions centered on Prince Kamitsumiya and the Soga. What were Kamitsumiya's relations with the Soga leadership really like? How did they seek to usher in a new age in Japanese history? What did they want to do, and to what degree did they succeed in doing it?

One corollary of focusing on the victors and their agenda has been a comparative neglect of the role played by the Mononobe in the construction of the Japanese Buddhist tradition. The *Nihon shoki* account, upon which most discussions are based, presents the Mononobe as reactionaries who fear that acceptance of the "foreign" Buddhist tradition will disturb the local gods and the status quo. As a result, the Mononobe are almost always portrayed in scholarly literature as a conservative force notable mainly for being opposed to change if not to Buddhism altogether. Thus the Mononobe tend to have been defined primarily in anti-Buddhist terms rather than in terms of their own cultic practices.

I, however, proceed from the premise that the Buddhist tradition was shaped not only by the period's executioners, but also by the victims. We shall see that just as Atsumori's relationship with Kumagae was rooted in the fact that Kumagae killed him, so too did the destruction of the main Mononobe line allow them to achieve a position of influence over Kamitsumiya, the Soga, and the cultic movements that the Soga promoted. Precisely because they were defeated in battle by the forces credited with ushering in the Buddhist tradition, the figurative and literal ghosts of the Mononobe lingered into the new age.[7]

Violence and Its Cultic Consequences

Several clues as to why the defeat of the Mononobe may have increased their influence over subsequent cultic developments can be found in the immediate aftermath of their defeat. As the Soga moved to occupy the geographic and cultic niches previously held by the Mononobe and their affiliated lineages, the Soga were forced to confront or propitiate local deities and ancestors that had previously been aligned with their recent foes. In addition, the absorption of lineages previously aligned with the Mononobe into the new Soga-dominated power structure appears to have facilitated the absorption of rites and deities that had been associated with the Mononobe. Finally, I suggest that destruction of the main line of the Mononobe would have created a large number of spirits and ancestors that would have required immediate and extensive propitiation.[8]

If the consequences of victory were the increased cultic involvement of the victors with the cults of the vanquished, it was also the case that changes in the nature of warfare associated with the Mononobe's period of ascendancy may have accelerated this trend. Among the most important of such political/military developments had been the rise of blocs of kinship groups under the control of kinship group leaders with the titles of Ōmuraji and Ōomi, who both organized laborers on royal estates and served as the military arm for Yamato rulers. According to the *Nihon shoki*, the designation of Ōmuraji was given to the leader of the Mononobe during the reign of the Yamato paramount Yūryaku during the latter half of the fifth century.[9] Mononobe power appears to have continued uninterrupted thereafter until their defeat at the hands of the Soga in 587.

As Yamato rulers during the fifth and sixth centuries sought to extend the breadth and depth of their reach across the Japanese islands and into the Korean peninsula, the Mononobe appear to have become a prominent force across not only the main island of Honshū, but also over much of Kyūshū as well.[10] Because of this, it appears that a large number of kinship groups and newly formed service-group lineages with roots in the Korean peninsula found it prudent to call themselves Mononobe and worship Mononobe ancestors. These groups appear to have frequently been situated near important nodes of transport, which in turn were often the sites of royal estates constructed both to enrich the Yamato rulers and to maintain a tight grip on strategic areas. Although we can only speculate on this point, it seems reasonable to assume that the absorption of immigrant lineages into the Mononobe would also have facilitated Mononobe involvement with immigrant deities.

One key area of overlap between cultic and geopolitical concerns lay in the development of rites of spirit propitiation at the intersections (*chimata*) of strategic roads and waterways across Yamato. By the late sixth century kinship groups such as the Mononobe apparently sought control of such nodes of traffic not only for their economic and military importance but also for the cultic control that they promised over any given region.[11] Thus in the *Nihon shoki* and *Kojiki* we find numerous references to rites at major crossroads and borders designed to bring about the subjugation of both spiritual and military enemies of the Yamato court.[12] By the time of the composition of the Taihō law codes in 701, such practices had been codified within the royal cult in such rites as the Michiae no Matsuri, which involved the propitiation of disease-causing spirits along the roadsides with offerings of animal hides along the roadsides.

Given the wide variety of kinship groups that claimed descent from Mononobe ancestors, it is important to remember that the Mononobe were not a single, monolithic unit in terms of origins or cultic practice. Nor should the Mononobe—or any kinship group from the period—be understood in any "natural" or biological sense. Rather, the Mononobe were a socially constructed phenomenon that arose in response to the political realities of the age. This meant that the cohesiveness of these constructed lineages was most likely enhanced by the worship of common ancestors, but that the cultic flexibility inherent in such as system meant that political upheavals could generate widespread cultic realignments. This dynamic ensured that the absorption and dispersal of the immigrant kinship groups aligned with the Mononobe would result in profound consequences for the development of cultic practices in the Japanese islands.

Among the most important kinship groups, for our purposes, were those that both claimed descent from Mononobe ancestors and were associated with strategic crossroads (*chimata*). One such lineage was the Kusakabe, a kinship group that, as we saw in Chapter 3, was prominent in Kyūshū as well as in Harima and several other coastal provinces along the Inland and Japan/Eastern seas. The Kusakabe apparently followed a pattern common to several kinship groups affiliated with the Mononobe in the wake of the Soga victory. Even as Mononobe lands in Harima province and Naniwa were given to Prince Kamitsumiya, the Kusakabe came to be closely connected with Shitennōji, the very temple that Kamitsumiya is said to have constructed following the defeat of the Mononobe.[13] Other kinship groups that followed this pattern included the Inabe, an immigrant kinship group from Silla that was prominent in the Naniwa area, and the Fumi no Obito, another immigrant kinship group centered in Kawachi province close to the Ega *chimata*.[14]

Among the most important *chimata* in regions controlled by the Mononobe were the Isonokami *chimata* at the intersection of the Upper Lateral Highway and the Yamada Abe Highway in eastern Yamato, the Kataoka *chimata* in the Ikoma mountains of Yamato province, and the Ega *chimata* in Kawachi province.[15] Evidence for Mononobe involvement in *chimata* rites can be seen in legends in early Nara-period provincial gazetteers that depict members of the Mononobe pacifying vengeful deities at roadsides even in distant Kyūshū.[16] Following the defeat of the Mononobe, control of these *chimata* appears to have in most cases fallen to Kamitsumiya and the Soga, who continued to use them as ritual centers for the pacification of spirits and the subjugation of enemies. As kinship groups such as the Kusakabe, the Inabe, and the Fumi no Obito were thereby absorbed into the Soga power structure, they continued to play a major role in the proliferation of Chinese cults of spirit pacification in Yamato. Because these same lineages were later at the forefront of the early cult of Prince Shōtoku, they also represent a crucial cultic link between the prince and the very lineage that he is said to have destroyed.

The Mononobe and Spirit Pacification

Although the Mononobe are depicted in the founding legend of Japanese Buddhism as defenders of "native" religious traditions in the face of the introduction of the "foreign" Buddhist tradition, there is a great deal of evidence suggesting that the Mononobe were closely involved both in the formation of court rites of spirit pacification and the introduction of cultic elements from the Korean peninsula to the Yamato court. As Okada Seishi has noted, within the *Nihon shoki* the Mononobe are said to have reached the pinnacle of power sometime during the late fifth century, when a series of rulers such as "Great King" Wakateru made their capitals in the Kawachi region of central Japan. One indication of the Mononobe's role as ritual specialists can be seen in their name; the suffix "*-be*" indicates a service group, and the term "*mono*" clearly means not "thing," as it would in modern Japanese, but "spirit" or "demon" (as in "*mononoke*"). Thus it would appear that for much of the sixth century the Mononobe were in name and fact a spirit service group. In a similar vein, Matsumae Takeshi has noted that evidence for Mononobe involvement with the peninsula can be seen not only in the semihistorical accounts of the *Nihon shoki*, but also in the fact that several prominent Mononobe bore titles from the Korean kingdom of Paekche.[17]

Further evidence of Mononobe involvement in rites of spirit propitiation can be seen in the *Sendai kuji hongi,* an early Heian-period mytho-historical text thought to have been compiled by a member of the Mononobe.[18] In the following passage the Mononobe ancestor Umashimaji no Mikoto is credited with instructing the first Yamato ruler, Jinmu, in the performance of the Chinkonsai (Mitama Shizume Matsuri), a rite of spirit pacification that, as we saw in Chapter 3, was performed by the court during the New Year. After performing a rite of blessing and pacification (*kotohoki*) Umashimaji no Mikoto relates a Mononobe spell of resurrection:

> The heavenly deity instructed that if there were an area [of the body] in pain, [one should] use these ten regalia, saying "One, two, three, four, five, six, seven, eight, nine, ten, *furu be, yura yura to furube.*" Done in this way, the dead will come back to life. This is the origin of the Spell of Furu. The origins of the Chinkonsai are to be found here.[19]

Although few contemporary scholars would accept this text's assertion that the Chinkonsai was derived from Mononobe rites, the fact that such an assertion could be plausibly made suggests that even in the early ninth century the Mononobe were closely associated with such practices. More important from our perspective, however, the above text and other passages in the *Sendai kujihongi* strongly suggest that the Mononobe practiced their own version of rites of spirit pacification and resurrection at the Isonokami shrine.[20]

Chimata, Hokai, and the Queen Mother

By the time the Mononobe reached the peak of their power in the final quarter of the sixth century, Mononobe cultic centers and *chimata* were apparently so deeply inscribed into the cultic landscape of the Japanese islands that they were able to shape to a considerable degree the cultic terrain in which the Japanese Buddhist tradition developed. One example of how this process unfolded can be seen from the history of the strategic crossroads near the village of Nagano in the Ega district of Kawachi province. In the *Nihon shoki* we are told that during the reign of Yūryaku this area was ceded to the Mononobe at a ceremony that took place at the base of a *tachibana* (Japanese orange) tree in Ega.[21] When the Mononobe established a major base in the adjacent Wakae district of Kawachi, they also extended their influence over local lineages such as the Fumi no Obito, an immigrant kinship group based in the village of Nagano in Ega. Following the demise of the Mononobe, the Fumi no Obito built their kinship group temple Fujiidera in Nagano, which later became a center for the cult of the Mononobe's nemesis, Prince Shōtoku. Thus were any number of Buddhist institutions and narratives in Japan rooted in ground prepared by pre-existing cultic centers, as kinship groups such as the Fumi no Obito first came under the sway of the Mononobe only to later be absorbed into the orbit of Prince Kamitsumiya and the Soga.[22]

The Fumi no Imiki are also known to have played an important role in court-sponsored rites of pacification at the Naniwa canal. According to the *Jingiryō*, a set of regulations in the Taihō law codes governing the court's ritual activities, the Fumi no Obito were designated by the court to read a liturgy using Chinese pronunciations as part of the Rite of Great Purification (Ōharae), one of the most important rites on the Japanese ritual calendar. This rite, which was most likely first performed in this form in 703, was carried out by the sea at Naniwa.[23] Although the *Jingiryō* does not, unfortunately, provide us with the text of the invocation, the *Engishiki*, an early-tenth-century court compendium that contains many older materials, gives the text as follows:

> We humbly beseech the Supreme Ruler of Heaven, the (Six) Great Lords of the Three Terraces, the sun, the moon, the stars, and the planets, the hosts of gods in eight directions, the arbiters of human destiny and the keepers of records, the Father King of the East on the left, the Mother Queen of the West on the right, the five rulers of the five directions, the four climates of the four seasons, as we humbly present these silver effigies [*hitogata*], we beseech ye, free us from calamities. As we humbly present the golden sword, we beseech ye, prolong the reign of our Sovereign. We pronounce the charm: To the east as far as Fusō, to the west as far as Yu yen, to the south as far as the burning tropics, to the north as far as the arctic [weak waters], to a thousand cities, a hundred countries, let the eternal reign extend. Banzai! Banzai![24]

This liturgy is remarkable not only for the fact that it was to be read with Chinese pronunciations, but also for its close correlation with rites of spirit pacification rooted in Chinese astrological and calendrical notions.[25] Not only is the text dedicated to the Supreme Lord of Heaven, it also continues with an extensive petition of astral spirits, seasonal deities, and directional gods from Chinese mythology, such as the Queen Mother of the West and her counterpart, the King Father of the East. The text is also notable in that it refers to Japan as "Fusō," an island of the immortals in Taoist mythology, and for its reference to the "weak waters," a term frequently associated with the Queen Mother.[26] Finally, this rite illustrates how spells were used in conjunction with scapegoat dolls, or *hitogata*, to absorb impurities from the body of the ruler before they were disposed of in the sea at Naniwa.[27]

Further clues as to the nature of the Ōharae can be found in its location in the court's ritual calendar. According to the *Jingiryō*, the Ōharae was performed on the last day of the year and on the final day of the sixth month.[28] The Ōharae was thus both a rite of purification and a major part of the rites of world renewal that took place at the New Year. The pairing of these dates again reflects the court's close adherence to the Chinese ritual calendar, in which the first and seventh months were closely connected.[29] Perhaps even more important for our purposes, the start of the New Year and the seventh month were also the periods of the Chinese ritual calendar most closely associated with the Queen Mother of the West.[30] All of this thus suggests that as kinship groups such as the Fumi no Obito were assimilated into the Soga power structure, continental rites of spirit pacification originally associated with the Mononobe and their followers were absorbed into the mainstream of court ritual practice.

This in turn is of immediate relevance for understanding the foundational legend of Japanese Buddhism, for the Ōharae rite in many ways bears a close resemblance to the *Nihon shoki*'s account of how Moriya disposed of the Buddhist image from Paekche prior to the battle between the Soga and Mononobe. Moriya is said to go to Naniwa from Wakae to rid the land of what he believes to be a disease-causing spirit. There he throws the image of the Buddha into the sea. In the Ōharae, the Fumi no Obito, who were also based in Wakae, perform a rite of exorcism in Naniwa in which they use metal *hitogata* to absorb impurities that might bring disease to the ruler and the capital. These, too, were then thrown into the sea.

All of this suggests that lineages such as the Fumi no Obito that were originally affiliated with the Mononobe played an important role not only in the composition of the founding legend of Japanese Buddhism, but also in court-sponsored liturgies such as the Ōharae. More broadly, the prominence of Mononobe-affiliated lineages also calls into question the common characterization of the Mononobe and their allies opposing the introduction of "foreign" gods and cults. Indeed, once we abandon the premise that the Mononobe were simply conservative xenophobes, it becomes possible to read their actions in the founding legend of Japanese Buddhism almost entirely in terms of rites of spirit pacification rooted at least in part in Chinese ritual and mythic traditions. Far from being a simple legend about the superior efficacy of the "foreign" Buddhist tradition, the text shows Moriya performing a ritual closely resembling practices associated with the Queen Mother of the West and Chinese astrological cults.

I suggest, therefore, that far from being reactionary nativists, the Mononobe may have been prominent ritualists who actively engaged in the development of new ritual systems based on the rites and beliefs of the Chinese ritual calendar. In light of the text's explicit statement that Moriya's actions were undertaken in defense of "native" cultic practice, the legend would appear to suggest that Chinese rites of spirit pacification had already become woven into the basic fabric of Japanese cultic life during the period of the Mononobe's ascendancy.

The Queen Mother of the West in China and Japan

To what degree had the cult of the Queen Mother of the West and other Chinese ritual tropes penetrated the Japanese islands in the wake of the Mononobe? Was the influence of such cults limited to one or two court liturgies, or was it more widespread? And if the cult of the Queen Mother of the West was by that time an important element in the religious life of the Japanese islands, in what ways did it influence the founding legend of Japanese Buddhism? I propose to address these issues by delineating the Queen Mother's most prominent cultic attributes and then examining to what degree they can be found in the cults and legends associated with lineages at the forefront of the early Shōtoku cult.

One of the earliest, most complete descriptions of the Queen Mother in classical Chinese sources comes from the *Shan hai ching*, which describes the Queen Mother's appearance as follows:

> South of the western lake, by the shores of the flowing sands, behind the Red River and before the Black River there is a great mountain called "the heights of K'un lun." There are spirits there with human faces and the bodies of tigers, striped and with tails, white in all cases. Below, there are the depths of the Juo river [Weak Waters] that encircle

the spot. Without, there is the mountain of the flaming fire, and when an object is cast therein it is immediately burnt. There is a person who wears a [weaving implement known as a] *sheng* on her head, with the teeth of a tiger and the tail of a leopard; she dwells in a cave and is named Queen Mother of the West. On this mountain there are found all manner of living creatures.[31]

In the *Po wu chih* we also find a depiction of the Queen Mother in the context of her famed visit to the Emperor Han Wu-ti:

Han Wu ti loved the ways of the immortal beings and he used to worship famous mountains and great lakes so as to seek the ways of those holy ones. Once upon a time the Queen Mother of the West sent her messenger riding upon a white stag to tell the emperor that she was coming; so he furnished the Hall of the Nine Flowery Delights with curtains to await her visit. On the seventh day of the seventh month, at the seventh division of the clock, the Queen Mother arrived at the west side of the hall, riding in her carriage of purple clouds. Being on the south [sic] side she faced east; on her head she carried the seven-fold energies of new growth, pulsating like clouds. Three green birds, as large as crows, waited in attendance at her side; and at the given moment the lamp of nine lights was set up.

The emperor was on the east side, facing west. The Queen Mother produced seven peaches, the size of pellets; five she gave to the emperor, two she ate herself. When the emperor had eaten his fruit, he straightway laid the pips in front of his knees. "What shall you do with the peach stones you have taken?" asked the Queen. "The peaches are so sweet and excellent that I should like to plant them," replied the emperor. With a smile the Queen Mother told him that the peach trees would bear fruit only once in every 3,000 years.[32]

These passages suggest several important elements of early Chinese representations of the Queen Mother. Of particular note are the birds said to serve as her messengers, which often appear to one side of the Queen in early Chinese iconography. These three birds "as large as crows" are also frequently depicted individually as an animal known as the Three-legged Crow, which was often shown against the background of an aureole representing the sun.[33]

The *Shan hai ching* passage also establishes the Queen Mother as the ruler of Mount Kunlun, the abode to which spirits go after leaving the world of the living. For this reason the Queen Mother was frequently represented in Han and Six Dynasties tomb paintings in China. The degree to which the Queen Mother was associated with the afterlife and the pacification of spirits is suggested in the famed Ma wang tui tapestry from Han dynasty China. In the tapestry the Queen Mother is depicted escorting the soul of the deceased to her Western Paradise.[34] At the upper left-hand corner is the Three-legged Crow against an aureole of the sun. Flanking this on the upper right-hand corner is the rabbit in the moon preparing the elixir of immortality.[35]

This motif of the Queen Mother guiding spirits of the dead to her paradise involved more, however, than simply providing for the post-mortem bliss of the departed. From ancient times a primary goal of Chinese death rituals has been to guide the spirit of the deceased to a ritually appropriate locale where it can then receive offerings. Thus an essential element of such rites was the "calling back" (C: *chao hun*, J: *shōkon*) of the spirit. As we saw in Chapter 2 when discussing the *shōkon* rite that was performed for Tenmu shortly before his death, this involved initial attempts to revive the dying individual by reuniting the spirit with the body. If these failed, the soul was then guided to an appropriate ritual center and resting place.[36] Failure to do so left confused and angry spirits prone to wandering on the roadsides and wreaking havoc among the living.[37]

Iconography of the Queen Mother

By the time of the composition of the *Po wu chih* in the mid-third century C.E. it is also clear that the Queen Mother had also become an authenticator of the virtue of rulers. Various texts record meetings between the Queen Mother and such sage rulers as King Mu of the Chou, and the mythic ruler Huang ti.[38] The Queen Mother's association with sage kingship is perhaps most clearly seen, however, in a series of texts depicting her meeting with the Han Emperor Wu-ti. The nature of the Queen's relationship with this ruler can be seen not only in the *Po wu chih* passage cited above, but also in a series of texts that depict the Queen Mother offering peaches of immortality to Han Wu-ti along with exhortations to virtue. Implicit in this and other such narratives is the Queen Mother's role as guide to the land of immortals and authenticator of the sage virtue of kings.[39]

The peaches given Emperor Han Wu-ti highlight one further element in the Queen's cultic identity. As is so often the case in East Asian religion, these symbols of immortality also functioned as implements of spirit-quieting. By the Han dynasty peaches and peach wood were believed to be efficacious in the pacification of demons, and the association of peaches with spirit pacification continued for centuries. The *Ching ch'u sui shih chi*, for instance, notes that during the New Year amulets of peaches were pasted on the doorframes of houses, along with images of chickens, because "the hundred demons fear this."[40]

There is ample textual evidence that such conceptions were well understood in pre-Nara Japan. The *Nihon shoki*, in depicting the god Izanagi's flight from the land of the dead, has him hurling peaches to fend off the thunder spirits that pursue him:

> Now at that time on the side of the road was a large peach tree. Izanagi therefore hid himself at the foot of the tree and took its fruit and threw it at the thunder [spirits], which all ran away. This is the origin of [the practice] of using peaches to keep away demons.[41]

This passage highlights the degree to which Chinese motifs of spirit pacification could permeate even supposedly indigenous myths in the court chronicles. The assertion on the part of the editors of the *Nihon shoki* that this is the "origin of the practice of keeping off evil spirits by means of peaches" also suggests that they assumed such practices were commonly understood by their intended readership at court. For reasons that are far from clear, however, this understanding of the ritual efficacies of peaches also came to be associated with a type of Japanese orange known as the *tachibana*, for by the Nara period it was common practice for people to place *tachibana* instead of peaches above the doorframes of their houses at the New Year.[42]

Perhaps the most distinctive element in the Queen Mother's iconographic representations, however, lay in her headdress, which early texts such as the *Po wu chih* passage cited above consistently refer to as a weaving implement known as a "*sheng*." The association of the Queen Mother with a weaving implement probably reflects the fact that from an early date the cult of the Queen Mother was associated with the seventh day of the seventh month, which was also the festival day for the cult of the Weaving Maiden and the Cowherd. Evidence for this can be found not only in the Queen Mother's iconography, but also from texts such as the *Po wu chih* passage cited above and the broader Han Wu-ti legend corpus, in which the ruler is said to have met the Queen Mother on this day. Thus from a very early date the Queen Mother came to be associated both with the festival of the Weaving Maiden on the seventh day of the seventh month and the rites of world renewal that occurred during the first weeks of the New Year.[43]

These two periods in the Chinese festival calendar were also characterized by heightened ritual interactions between the living and the spirits of the dead. During the first fifteen days of the New Year, spirits and ancestors were thought to be able to return to the realm of the living—recall, for instance, the *Nihon ryōiki* narrative in which a spirit tells the monk Dōtō's assistant that only on the eve of the New Year was it possible for spirits to return and thank the living for their offerings. The first fifteen days of the seventh month were also closely identified with propitiation of deceased ancestors and spirits. Perhaps the best indication of this can be seen from the Buddhist appropriation of the fifteenth day of the seventh month as the culminating date of the ghost festival.[44]

In addition to its obvious associations with weaving cults and sericulture, Kominami Ichirō has also suggested that the *sheng* was closely linked with efforts to "call back the spirits" (*chao hun*) of the recently deceased. In support of this claim Kominami notes that the two days in the Chinese festival calendar most closely associated with the Queen Mother were the seventh day of the first month and the seventh day of the seventh month. Both days, as we have just seen, were midpoints during periods of heightened ritual interactions with the spirits of the dead. Kominami also notes that the Queen Mother's association with these dates was also expressed in the *Po wu chih* and other texts by having the Queen Mother wearing not one, but seven *sheng* in her headdress. Although we can only speculate as to the ritual significance of the seven *sheng*, Kominami notes that sets of seven paper dolls that have been unearthed in tombs in Turfan are shaped remarkably like seven *sheng*. In light of the fact that these dolls bear inscriptions reading "*chao hun*," Kominami argues that these paper dolls, and perhaps the *sheng* as well, served as ritual implements for controlling the spirits of the dead.[45]

The Three-legged Crow and the *Hakuji*

The Queen Mother's close association with the Three-legged Crow, the *sheng, tachibana*, and rites of spirit pacification provide us a road map for tracing the influences of her cult in Nara Japan. Once we look for these elements in the cultic practices and ancestral legends of the immigrant kinship groups most closely affiliated with the early Shōtoku cult, it becomes possible to see how and why the early Buddhist tradition turned to the Queen Mother for help in dealing with the ghosts in its past.

Among the most important sources of information we have about the role of the cult of the Queen Mother in early Japan can be found in the *Nihon shoki* and the *Shoku nihongi*, both of which record various omens and anomalies that attracted the attention of the court.[46]

Perhaps the most revealing instance is a lengthy account in the *Nihon shoki* concerning a white pheasant, or *hakuji*, that the story was presented by Kusakabe Muraji Shikibu to the court of the Yamato ruler Kōtoku in 645. As we have seen repeatedly, the Kusakabe were a Mononobe-affiliated lineage that played a prominent role in the transmission of continental cultic practices to the Japanese islands. Because the *Nihon shoki* provides an extremely detailed account of how the pheasant was received at Kōtoku's court, this incident provides an unusually good snapshot of how omens and divination were understood by the editors of the *Nihon shoki*. According to the text the court was unsure about how to interpret the omen and therefore asked numerous figures to interpret its significance in the light of historical precedent. A typical response is attributed to the eminent monk Dōtō, who is said to have stated:

> Long ago Koguryŏ wished to build a temple, and there was no place that went unexamined. Then in one place a white deer [was seen] slowly moving about, and eventually a temple named the Temple of the Garden of the White Deer was built at the site for the establishment of the Buddhist Law there. Also, [when] a white sparrow was seen on the estate of one temple, the people of the land all said that it was an auspicious omen. Also an ambassador who was sent from the Great T'ang [once] brought with him a dead three-legged crow. The people of the land again said that this was an auspicious omen. Although these are all but small things, they are still said to be auspicious items. How much more so is a white pheasant.[47]

The text continues by stating that the *hakuji* was officially presented to the court at ceremonies marking the advent of the following New Year. We are also told that the court proclaimed the start of a new reign era, bearing the name Hakuji, along with rites marking the beginning of the new era.

Regardless of the historical validity of the *Nihon shoki* account, it is significant that the editors felt that even a dead, imported fowl could plausibly be construed as a good omen. This heightened awareness of omens and symbols such as the Three-legged Crow meshes well with recent archeological discoveries in Korea and Japan. The presence of both the Three-legged Crow and the cult of the Queen Mother in tomb paintings dated to the fifth century in Koguryŏ suggests that the cult of the Queen Mother was well established on the Korean peninsula by Dōtō's time.[48] In Japan, similarly, an image of the Three-legged Crow set against the aureole of the sun can be seen in the Tamamushi shrine at Hōryuji.[49] All of this strongly suggests that the Queen Mother and her emissary were part of a complex of rites and symbols transmitted to the Japanese islands along with the Chinese ritual calendar and Chinese divinatory texts.

Further evidence for the importance of this complex can be seen in the eleventh year of Tenmu's reign, when we are told that a three-legged peacock was presented to the court. Then during the New Year ceremonies of 701, a flag bearing an image of a crow was planted squarely at the main gate of the court's main ceremonial hall, flanked on all sides by images of zodiacal symbols of the four cardinal directions.[50] Archeological remains as well as accounts of such animals in subsequent court ritual manuals confirm that they were an important part of court rites throughout the Nara and Heian periods.[51] All of this thus strongly suggests that even before the Nara period crows and three-legged birds had become firmly established elements in the symbolic vocabulary of the court.

The *Nihon shoki* depiction of the presentation of the *hakuji* thus appears to be emblematic of an important turning point in the politicization of the Chinese ritual calendar; even before the Nara period, rulers of the Japanese islands had begun proclaiming changes in era names in order to mark the appearance of auspicious omens. Indeed, the presentation of auspicious omens soon became an established part of New Year's rites designed to purify the capital and promote the most optimal conditions for the coming year. Because the ritual patterns and practices of the first fifteen days of the New Year were thought to determine the character of subsequent events during the coming year, the crowding of auspicious omens into this period also testifies to the court's growing sophistication in using the ritual calendar. In marking the appearance of auspicious omens in this way, the Yamato court thus placed itself squarely in the mainstream of what was then current practice throughout East Asia. In 690, for example, the *Yu yang tsa tsu* records that Empress Wu was presented with a Three-legged Crow that she interpreted as validating her "restoration" of the Chou dynasty.[52]

One further manifestation of the importance of auspicious crows for Japanese rulers can be found in a series of legends focusing on the Yatagarasu, a mythic crow that was claimed as the founding ancestor of the Kamo kinship group in Yamashiro province.[53]

The figure of the Yatagarasu has drawn the attention of Japanese scholars because of its prominence in the *Nihon shoki* and *Kojiki* accounts of the conquest of the Japanese islands by the legendary royal ancestor Jinmu. In the *Nihon shoki* the Yatagarasu, after appearing to Jinmu in a dream, comes actually to Jinmu at Uda/Yoshino, a region that, as we saw in Chapter 3, served as an important nodal point for the transmission of continental rites and beliefs associated with immortality.

At that time Amaterasu no Ōmikami instructed the *tennō* in a dream, saying: "I will now send [to you] the Yatagarasu. Use it as a guide across the land." Then the Yatagarasu did in fact appear flying down from the sky. The *tennō* said "This crow's arrival has been granted [in accordance with] the auspicious dream. How great, how magnificent! My royal ancestor Amaterasu no Ōmikami wishes to aid me in establishing the royal line!"

At this time Hi no Omi no Mikoto, the distant ancestor of the Ōtomo, taking Ōkume with him as commander of a great army, went up to an opening in the mountains. Looking up and following after the crow, they finally arrived in the lower district of Uda.[54]

Although at no point does the *Nihon shoki* explicitly link the Three-legged Crow with the Yatagarasu, Shinkawa has noted solid evidence suggesting sustained interest on the part of the court in the Yatagarasu and the Three-legged Crow throughout the late Nara and early Heian periods. In 780, for instance, the court established a Yatagarasu shrine in the Uda district of Yamato.[55] By the time of the accession rites of Junna *tennō* in 823, the Yatagarasu was explicitly identified with the Three-legged Crow.[56] The prominence of this Kamo ancestor could only have increased dramatically following the court's adoption of the Kamo shrine as the chief ritual center of the capital in 810.

The Kamo and Hata, however, were by no means the only devotees of the Shōtoku cult to appropriate the symbols of the Queen Mother for their own ancestral legends. One of the clearest examples of Shōtoku devotees depicting their ancestors against the background of the cult of the Queen Mother can be seen in the following legend concerning Tajima Mori, an ancestor of the Miyake Muraji. The Miyake Muraji were yet another immigrant kinship group based along the coast of the Japan/Eastern Sea that were closely associated with Shitennōji and the early Shōtoku cult. The legend as found in the *Nihon shoki* reads as follows:

90th year, Spring, 2nd month, 1st day. The *tennō* commanded Tajima Mori to go to *tokoyo* to search for the fruit that is everlastingly fragrant. This is now called the *tachibana*.[57]

99th year, Spring, the 3rd month. Thereupon Tajima Mori returned from *tokoyo* bearing the fruit that is everlastingly fragrant. . . .

Tajima Mori was filled with grief and wept, saying, "Having received an order from the Heavenly court, I have gone to a distant land, crossing over ten thousand *ri* of waves and the distant weak waters.

This land of *tokoyo* is where the immortals conceal themselves, and ordinary mortals cannot go there. Thus in the course of this voyage ten years passed. How could I have thought that all alone I could withstand the high waves and return to my native land? Yet depending on the spirits of the Sage Kings, I have barely managed to return. [But] now the *tennō* is already dead and I cannot make my report. Although I remain alive, what would it profit me? He then went and wailed before the *tennō*'s tomb and then himself died. When the ministers and people heard of this, they were all moved to tears.[58]

Several factors strongly suggest linkages with the cult of the Queen Mother. Among the most important are the reference to "weak waters," a term often used to identify the waters surrounding the Queen Mother's abode on Mount Kunlun, and the motif of the fruit of immortality. The special nature of Tajima Mori himself is suggested by his declaration that he has been able to go "where the immortals conceal themselves, and ordinary mortals cannot go." Thus the Miyake claimed as an ancestor an immortal capable of traveling back and forth between Kunlun and the Japanese islands.

The language of the text also suggests a close correlation with rites associated with the Mononobe and their retainers. "Weak waters," for instance, directly echoes the reference to the "weak waters" in the Ōharae liturgy read by the Fumi no Obito from Kawachi. Further resonances with the Fumi no Obito's cultic practices can be seen in the narrative's assertion that the fruit of immortality attained by Tajima Mori was none other than the Japanese *tachibana*.

The Queen Mother and Shōtoku

Long before the Yamato court adopted the Chinese ritual calendar, rites of spirit pacification associated with the Queen Mother had come to permeate ritual in China both at court and among the populace. Further evidence of the influence of such rites can be seen in the Taoist ritual calendar, in which the fifteenth day of the first, seventh, and tenth months were said to be the dates when the Queen Mother and members of the Taoist pantheon were believed to order the affairs of both the living and the dead. These dates, known collectively as the *san yuan*, were in turn preceded ritually by the *san hui*, the seventh day of the first and seventh months and the fifth day of the tenth month, during which devotees would assemble for the performance of special rites.[59]

Such Taoist practices had been built upon longstanding popular religious practices involving rites of spirit pacification and animal sacrifice on these days. Thus on the first day of the New Year's period it was customary to sacrifice a rooster and spread its blood on one's gate in order to ward off evil spirits. Native commentators from as early as the Han dynasty explained this practice both in connection with the cock's crow ushering in the New Year as well as the efficacy of the blood of *yang* animals such as roosters and dogs in repelling disease-bearing *yin* spirits.[60]

By the sixth century, however, the sacrifice of live animals in China had been widely replaced or supplemented by the manipulation of ritual effigies, amulets, herbs, and even fruits, many of which were often mounted on gates. The roots of these practices are explained in a remnant from the *Ching ch'u sui shih chi*, which states that on the New Year, "Images of chickens are pasted on doors. Above them they hang braided reeds and insert peach wood amulets in the sides. The hundred demons fear this."[61] The *Ching ch'u sui shih chi* continues by detailing rites performed on the seventh day of the New Year, which was known as the "day of humans" (*jen jih*). As we have already noted, the *jen jih* was paired ritually with its counterpart sixth months later at the midpoint of the Chinese ritual cycle.[62] That date, of course, was none other than the seventh day of the seventh month, a date dedicated to the cults of the Queen Mother of the West and the Weaver Maiden and the Cowherd. Not surprisingly, rites related to the Queen Mother and spirit pacification appear prominently on this day. The *Ching ch'u sui shih chi* states that across southern China the custom on this day was as follows:

> The seventh day of the first month is known as the day of humans (*jen jih*). Gruel is made with seven types of vegetables. Cloth is cut in the shape of human figures. Some people carve the shape of human figures into foil and stick them on screens or wear them in their hair. Some make flower headdresses (*sheng*) and exchange them. [People also] climb to high [ground] and compose poetry.
>
> The [custom of making and exchanging] *sheng* began during the Chin. See the entry regarding Chia Ch'ung's wife Madame Li [in the *History of Chin*], which says that they "should be made like auspicious drawings in the shape of a golden *sheng*." They also represent the headdress of the Queen Mother of the West.[63]

As the interlinear notes to the text make clear, these rites and the symbol of the *sheng* were understood within the context of the age-old project of protecting the household from armies of demons:

> The seventh day of the first month is the day of humans, thus it is called "*jen jih.*" The cloth that is cut and the foil that is carved all are made into the shape of humans. All signify humanity. It is the same as putting images of chickens on the gate.[64]

By highlighting the fact that human images and paper dolls were used in China to represent the Queen Mother's headdress, the text makes clear that such rites were not limited to elite elements of the population, but had penetrated into popular cultic practice. By the sixth century C.E., representations of the Queen Mother's headdress as well as paper dolls could be found in tombs across China, from Turfan in the northeast and on doorframes across southern China.

Because similar practices were well established in the Japanese islands even prior to the Nara period, it is extremely likely that the Nara court was familiar with the significance of both the Queen Mother's headdress and her role in keeping at bay spirits that would destroy the good fortune in store at the start of the year. These rites, in turn, were part of a much broader cultic movement across the Japanese islands that relied upon the use of scapegoat dolls and spells to protect the living from vengeful spirits of gods and the dead. Because, as we saw in Chapter 2, weaving implements in the shape of the Queen Mother's *sheng* were also being offered across the Japanese islands to vengeful deities such as Akaru Hime, it appears highly likely that lineages close to both the Mononobe and the early Shōtoku cult were using such implements in rites of propitiation and pacification. It is also clear that lineages at the forefront of the early Shōtoku cult had incorporated elements from the Queen Mother of the West into their own ancestral legend cycles.

All of this brings us back to Shōtoku's gesture at the climactic moment of the founding legend of Japanese Buddhism. Shōtoku is said to have performed this gesture at the advent of the seventh month—a period closely associated with the Queen Mother of the West. Without claiming a direct linkage between the flowers/dolls used during the *jen jih* and the branches/images ascribed to the prince, it is nonetheless clear that the climactic moment in the founding legend of Japanese Buddhism, in which Shōtoku propitiates the Four Heavenly Kings by placing their images in his hair, was rooted not so much in Buddhist ritual, but in a cultic milieu in which people would "carve the shape of human figures and . . . wear them in their hair" in order to keep spirits at bay. Here as elsewhere throughout the founding legend of Japanese Buddhism, the struggle between the Soga and Mononobe reads in large part as a cultic competition in which both sides sought to utilize such rites to pacify their enemies. Long before the Nara period, violence and victory, even for the forces of Buddhism, occurred on a conceptual battlefield shaped by rites and conceptions from the Chinese ritual calendar.

Conclusion

In light of the prominence of Chinese-style rites of spirit pacification within the ostensibly "native" religious practices championed by the Mononobe, the common characterization of a struggle between forces of nativism versus advocates of a "foreign" religion no longer appears tenable. Instead, throughout the narrative both the Mononobe and Shōtoku behave within a common ritual framework determined by the widespread currency of Chinese ritual elements that were rooted neither in any Buddhist textual tradition nor in any "native" Japanese tradition. Ironically, as the editors of the *Nihon shoki* sought to portray the initial encounter of the Buddhist tradition with the indigenous traditions of the Japanese islands, they codified a narrative in which the practices of the most xenophobic advocates of resistance were deeply colored by Chinese rites of spirit pacification and the Chinese ritual calendar.

The sheer pervasiveness of Chinese rites of spirit pacification throughout the founding legend of Japanese Buddhism also suggests that the image of the paradigmatic Buddhist sage Shōtoku was constructed to a surprisingly large degree in terms of these same rites of spirit pacification. The prominence of motifs such as the *tachibana*, the Three-legged Crow, and even the Queen Mother's *sheng* in a variety of legends and liturgies further testifies to the widely felt need in Nara Japan to develop ritual means of coping with violence and disease. For this reason Chinese conceptions of the afterlife and ritual elements involving *chimata* and the use of *hitogata* were from an extremely early date incorporated into the Shōtoku legend corpus as well as the nascent Buddhist tradition.

The themes of violence and spirit pacification that permeate the founding legend of Japanese Buddhism also suggest that an Atsumori effect played a major role in determining the nature of cultic practice in early Japan. In the final analysis Kamitsumiya's rise to power and all that he accomplished were in large part rooted in the violent destruction of the Mononobe and the appropriation of their lands, laborers, and cultic resources. Materially this meant that the construction of temples such as Hōryūji and Shitennōji was made possible by the appropriation of Mononobe lands. Cultically, the absorption of kinship groups such as the Kusakabe and the Fumi no Obito into the Soga power structure provided the Soga and those who followed them with the ritual means and vocabulary to pacify the spirits of their vanquished foes.

Although it is tempting to simply conclude from all this that the earliest roots of the Japanese Buddhist tradition were closely bound up with notions of purity, violence, disease, and spirit pacification, I would suggest that there are other, broader lessons to be learned here as well. Most notably, the founding legend of Japanese Buddhism took shape at a time when the cult of the royal ancestor Amaterasu and the core rites and legends of the royal cult were also undergoing rapid development. In the chapters that follow we shall repeatedly encounter not only the same motifs involving rulers and spirits, but also, to a surprising degree, the very same lineages as we explore the mythology of the royal cult and the development of such rites as the Chinkonsai (Rite of Spirit-quieting) and the Ōharae (the Great Purification). We will begin this process in Chapter 5 as we trace the origins and development of the legend of the Heavenly Grandchild during the peak of the Mononobe and Ōtomo ascendancy.

CHAPTER 5

Shamanesses, Lavatories, and the Magic of Silk

> Never leave your night soil for someone else's field.
> —Chinese proverb

IN THE STORY of *Rumpelstiltskin*, every western child knows that the mysterious forest dweller's ability to spin straw into gold helped a young maiden become queen of a kingdom. The basic elements of this legend would probably have been intelligible to people across Asia by the sixth century C.E. Indeed, triangles of kings, weavers, and spirits have been ubiquitous elements in East Asian myths and legends since at least the second century C.E. These legends were not rooted, however, in the fanciful premise that straw could be turned into gold. Rather, they focused on something at once more real and more magical, the transmutation of the cocoons of voracious silkworms into the garments of courtiers and kings.

Because sericulture constituted something both miraculous and essential, cults and legends of weavers represent an important intersection of economic, political, and cultic concerns in premodern China, Korea, and Japan. In ancient China the cultivation of silkworms and the production of silk involved not only economic considerations related to the use of land and labor, but also the development and diffusion of ritual systems based upon early conceptions of *yin* and *yang*, astronomy, popular myths, and cultic practices. Thus from the Chou dynasty onward, rites concerned with weaving and sericulture were a primary ritual concern for rulers and commoners alike.

As we saw in Chapter 4, among the most prominent mythological figures related to sericulture and weaving in ancient China was the Queen Mother of the West, who was believed to control the fates of the spirits of the dead and who was depicted wearing a weaving implement as a headdress. Closely related to her cult was that of the Weaving Maiden and the Cowherd, which combined disparate elements from Chinese astronomy with agricultural rites focusing on the attainment of fertility and prosperity. Because the cults of the Queen Mother of the West and the Weaving Maiden and Cowherd are known to have traveled to the Japanese islands by the reign of Tenmu *tennō* (673–686) at the latest, they also represent an important cultic link between the ritual and material culture of China and that of the emerging *tennō*-centered polity of the Nara and Heian periods.

Weaving cults in China also formed part of a larger complex of rites related to the specialization of both agricultural and household functions. Even at the time of the composition of the *Li chi*, or *Book of Rites*, over 2,000 years ago, regularized rites for the gods of household functions were already an established part of the Chinese ritual landscape. Because the dominant paradigm for power relations in early China was the family structure, rites of the household were also deeply implicated in the construction of rank and political authority. Rites closely associated with the household therefore served to pattern not only ritual behavior, but also modes of social organization as well as agricultural and material production. As a result, household deities such as the gods of the gate, kitchen, and the lavatory emerged as major cultic figures even in public cultic life. And because agricultural societies depend heavily on night soil for fertilizer, the deity of the lavatory in particular occupied an important place in each household's aspirations for wealth.[1]

One further set of deities directly related to sericulture in ancient China were the numerous silkworm goddesses who offered prosperity to those who made offerings to them. The nature of such cults can be seen in the following legend from the *Hsü chi chieh chi*, a late fifth- or early sixth-century Chinese compendium of tales and legends:

> Chang Ch'eng of the Wu district awoke one night and suddenly saw a lady standing at the southeast corner of his residence. She raised her hand and gestured for Ch'eng to come and see her. Ch'eng went to her and the lady said: "This place is your silkworm house. I am the god of this place. Tomorrow is the middle of the first month [1.15]. Prepare white rice gruel that is thick as paste and offer it to me. Your silkworms and mulberries will without fail increase a hundred-fold." When she had finished speaking, she disappeared. Ch'eng prepared rice gruel in accordance with her instructions and thereafter obtained a great many silkworms. This is the origin of the practice of offering white rice gruel in the middle of the first month.[2]

Such rites and legends endured for millennia in China. By the Sui dynasty (581–618) there was a virtual identification of silkworms with wealth in China, and silkworm deities were thoroughly integrated into household cults. Texts such as the *Ching ch'u sui shih chi*, a sixth-century gazetteer from southern China, further suggest that a complex of silkworm rites was closely integrated both with the ritual mapping of households and with the lavatory goddess, who was regularly worshipped on the fifteenth day of the first month. As we shall see in Chapter 6, this day, which was known as the first of the *san yuan*, or "days of origin," was specifically associated in the Chinese festival calendar with the lunar cult, female deities, and, to a lesser degree, spirit pacification.[3]

Because household deities were often closely related to gender-specific activities in China, these cults also had an enormous influence on the construction of identities for shamanesses and goddesses across East Asia. Thus we find in the *Book of Rites* that each year on the first day of the third month, one of the emperor's consorts was to be selected by lot and required to enter a ritual enclosure and feed mulberry leaves to silkworms in order to assure an abundant supply of silk during the year.[4] Elsewhere the *Book of Rites* reports that Confucius was filled with scorn for a male individual who worshipped the kitchen stove deity.[5] Silkworm cults appear to have entered the Japanese islands at an early date; in the *Nihon shoki* we are told of a massive millennial movement in 644 in which believers were assured that long life, youth, and riches would be theirs if they but worshipped an insect that "in appearance entirely resembles the silkworm."[6]

As we have already seen, excellent textual and archeological evidence suggests that the gender-specific nature of both weaving and weaving cults carried over to Japan; recall, for instance, Akaru Hime, the vengeful deity of the Himegoso shrine, who represented herself in the form of weaving implements when she demanded worship. However, the significance of weaving cults and implements for gender and cultic discourses was by no means limited to instances involving the propitiation of vengeful goddesses.[7] Just as the wrath (*tatari*) of female deities could be dissipated with offerings of weaving implements, the wrath of male deities was frequently dissipated with offerings of *miko* (female shamans) as brides. All of this suggests that well before the completion of the first court chronicle, weaving rites played an important role in mediating interactions between *kami* and humans, informing not only the means of propitiation, but also the construction of the identities of both the objects and subjects of ritual performance.

I propose to examine how such cults influenced early representations of female shamans, or *miko*, in the Japanese islands. This will involve discussion of two closely related social/political phenomena: the formation of weaving service groups during the fifth century C.E. and the emergence of ancestral myths of weaving maidens in the royal mythologies of the *Kojiki* and the *Nihon shoki*. By taking both the influence and gender-specific nature of weaving and weaving cults seriously, I not only emphasize the importance of continental rites for the myths and legends of the royal cult, but also shed new light upon the role of female shamans in the formation of the political and ritual dynamics that eventually led to the creation of the Nara state.

My focus is on a number of sacerdotal and service lineages that are prominently represented in the court chronicles of a series of rulers who established their palaces in Kawachi during the late fifth and early sixth centuries. As we have seen, this period witnessed not only the ascendancy of the Mononobe and Ōtomo, but also the influx of large numbers of immigrants from the Korean peninsula. Since there is excellent reason to believe that both the Mononobe and Ōtomo were closely involved in the importation of continental technologies and cultic practices, I argue that it is highly likely that even before Tenmu *tennō* proclaimed himself a heavenly sovereign, beliefs and cultic practices from the Chinese festival calendar were already an established part of the cultic life of the Japanese islands. Indeed, it would also appear that as the court appropriated the cultic centers of these lineages into the royal cult, these rites may have exerted considerable influence upon the development of the royal mythologies.

I have divided this chapter into two distinct though closely related sections. The first explores the means by which tropes concerning weaving maidens and spirit pacification came to be intertwined with the ancestral legends of the ruling house. Here I examine a series of legends related to the descent of the "Heavenly Grandchild," Ninigi no Mikoto, from the Heavenly Plain to the land of Kyūshū. We shall see that by focusing on the distaff ancestors of a series of service groups closely associated with the propagation of weaving technologies, it is possible to see how these lineages and the tropes of the Chinese festival calendar helped define the character and content of this and other royal ancestral narratives.

In the second section I examine the founding narratives of the Kamo, Miwa, and Izushi shrines—three major cultic centers for the court that nonetheless featured founding legends based on sacred marriages between weaving maiden ancestors and vengeful deities beyond the court's control. I suggest that each of these legends was constructed against a set of background legends from the Chinese festival calendar related to the worship of the lavatory goddess at the close of the New Year's rites on the fifteenth day of the first month. Because even during the Heian period these shrines were central nodes in the network of shrines and deities that constituted the fabric of the royal cult, they amply illustrate the degree to which the royal cult was imbued with cultic elements with roots that stretched beyond Kyūshū and even Korea into the distant Chinese past. They also illustrate the depth, breadth, and, most crucially, persistence of such beliefs during centuries of political and religious turbulence.

Weaving, Cult, and Social Structure

Although woven items are known to have existed in the Japanese islands over 2,000 years ago, archeological discoveries along the coast of the Japan/Eastern Sea suggest that sericulture and weaving experienced dramatic leaps in both quantity and quality beginning in the fifth century C.E.[8] This corresponds with entries from the *Nihon shoki*, which state that weavers from China and the Korean peninsula were sent to the Japanese islands at roughly this time. The text further states that weaving maidens were housed in such cultic centers as the Munakata shrine in Chikuzen province in Kyūshū and the Miwa shrine on the Yamato plain.[9]

The introduction of new weaving technologies into Yamato appears to have affected cultic practices and beliefs in several registers. From a very early date woven materials played an essential role in interactions between humans and *kami* as the sheer value of woven garments and weaving implements made them both appropriate and then necessary elements of any propitiatory offerings. In conjunction with these developments, at some point yearly rites involving the "marriage" of weaving maidens to ancestral deities also came to pervade the Japanese islands.[10]

Accompanying the transformation of Yamato material culture was the introduction of new systems of knowledge related to, among other things, the manufacture of clothing, the spinning of material, and the raising of silkworms. These in turn required mastery of new techniques for organizing people and manufacturing processes. It is thus probably no accident that the development of crafts such as weaving and metalworking came to permeate the Japanese islands during the same period in which writing, record-keeping, and rudimentary bureaucratic institutions took root at the Yamato court. By the middle of the sixth century, service groups specializing in these technologies already appear to have been formed across the Japanese islands, so it would hardly be surprising if, as changes in the material culture of Yamato stimulated new modes of production and new forms of social organization, they also played an important role in the development of the cultic and ritual practices.

One area of particular note in this process was the emergence of a small number of kinship groups that specialized in managing estates, overseeing production, and running cultic centers dedicated to gods associated with sericulture. These administrators were often closely identified with the Korean peninsula, most likely because their tasks required mastery of various systems of knowledge associated with writing and estate management as well as ritual and mythic systems rooted in the Chinese festival calendar. By mastering such disparate systems of knowledge these newly constituted kinship groups appear to have accumulated power and formed lineal identities on a register markedly different from that of other lineages at the Yamato court.

These developments had far-reaching effects on religious praxis from court to countryside. Increased specialization of labor in the production of handicrafts was accompanied by increased specialization in sacerdotal functions related to everything from ancestral worship to rites of kingship. Further, and crucially, the new crafts, production techniques, and their associated cultic and mythic resources were deeply implicated in the formation of kinship structures. During this period knowledge and ritual were shaped to serve the needs of lineage, as ancestors were re-visioned in the light of new technological and material realities. As a result, rites and myths associated with weaving and sericulture came to be blended with ancestral cults and deities that were defined in terms of both craft and kingship.

Several hints about the political/sacerdotal role of such kinship groups can be found in the *Nihon shoki*, which appears to be particularly concerned to link kinship groups associated with weaving with the figure referred to in the court chronicles as "Wakateru" and commonly known today by the Chinese-style name Yūryaku.[11] Although very little solid historical information remains about this Yamato ruler, he is credited in the *Nihon shoki* and *Kojiki* with the formation of several service groups that played a key role in the development of weaving cults in early Yamato. These same lineages, in turn, appear to have played a major role in shaping the image of Yūryaku that remains with us in the court chronicles.

Weaving Lineages and Wakateru

What little solid information we have about Wakateru's reign suggests that it may have been an important turning point in the history of the Japanese islands. Chinese historical sources indicate that Wakateru sent diplomatic missions to southern China, and during his reign continental forms of kingship appear to have gained prominence.[12] Wakateru may also have been the first Yamato ruler to style himself as a "Great King," in imitation of the title adopted by rulers of the Korean kingdom of Koguryŏ. These changes appear to have come in the midst of a great deal of turmoil and conflict. Yūryaku's reign as it is depicted in the court chronicles was even more sanguinary than usual, as he appears to have been concerned with the destruction of prominent kinship groups that could have challenged his growing authority.

Katō Kenkichi has recently suggested that one clue concerning Wakateru's relationship to weaving lineages can be found in accounts in the court chronicles that state that Yūryaku destroyed a group of powerful lineages in the area of Kazuraki. This area is known to have had extensive contacts with the Korean peninsula, and large immigrant communities from the Korean peninsula are known to have resided there. Katō has proposed that the Hata, who were apparently settled in Kazuraki by local paramounts, came into the orbit of the Yamato court at this time.[13] Perhaps as a result of this, in the Yūryaku chapters of the court chronicles we find several references to weaving rites as well as shrines that were administered by the Hata and other immigrant lineages.

The destruction of powerful local paramounts in Kazuraki and elsewhere was also accompanied by the formation of service groups known as *be*. These groups, which specialized in the production of specific commodities for the court, were organized lineally as kinship groups.[14] Such groups were essential in the formation of royal estates and the creation of specialized labor that enabled Yamato rulers to extend their authority to increasingly distant regions. Although virtually all the specifics of this process have been lost in the mists of time, the cultic consequences appear to have been enormous: lineages required ancestors, and ancestors required ancestral legends, tombs, and cultic centers for the performance of ancestral rites. Perhaps as a result of this, the figure of Yūryaku came to be closely identified in the court chronicles with religious practices and concepts that developed in close conjunction with the adoption of continental technologies and the formation of new lineages. These in turn were heavily influenced by rites associated with sericulture and household functions in China.

Not surprisingly, the interest that Yamato rulers such as Wakateru took in affairs on the Korean peninsula appears to have been motivated in good measure by a desire to import recent cultural and technological developments. The strength of the linkages between weaving technologies, lineal formation, and the centralization of power are reflected in the following account of the restoration of the Hata kinship group, which the *Nihon shoki* presents as the single most important kinship group in Yamato for the production of silk and clothing:

> The Hata people were dispersed and the various Omi and Muraji all used them as they wished and would not leave them to the Hata no Miyatsuko. Because of this, Hata no Miyatsuko Sake was greatly aggrieved, and he went into the service of the *tennō*. He became a favorite of the *tennō*, who ordered that the Hata people all be assembled and given to Hata no Sake no Kimi. [Sake no] Kimi thus led 180 kinds of *suguri* service groups and presented [so many] fine silks for taxes that [when they were] piled up they filled the courtyard. For this he was given the title of "Uzumasa." *One book says "Uzumorimasa"—piled up to overflowing.*[15]
>
> . . . .
>
> 16th year, Autumn, 7th month. A royal edict was issued that mulberry trees be planted in suitable provinces and districts. The Hata people were dispersed [to these places] and made to present service taxes.[16]

Although few scholars would accept this account as historically accurate, it aptly illustrates one of the central dynamics in the politics of lineal formation in early Yamato; by "assembling" lineages such as the Hata, rulers such as Wakateru were able to appropriate technological and bureaucratic skills that resulted over time in the development of new agricultural and tax systems and the extension of centralized authority.

The Yūryaku chapter of the *Nihon shoki* also suggests that other kinship groups closely related to the Hata played a major role in this process. One such kinship group was the Chiisakobe, who are credited in the *Shinsen shōjiroku* with gathering together the scattered Hata kinship group in Hyūga province.[17] Several legends from the *Nihon shoki* concerning the formation of the Chiisakobe kinship group suggest that they, too, were closely involved with sericulture rites and the Chinese festival calendar:

> Yūryaku 6.3.7. The *tennō* [Yūryaku] wished to make his consorts plant mulberry trees with their own hands in order to encourage sericulture. So he ordered Sugaru [Sugaru is a personal name] to gather silkworms [*ko*] throughout the land. Now Sugaru misunderstood and gathered babies [*wagako*], which he presented to the *tennō*. The *tennō* laughed greatly and gave the babies to Sugaru, saying, "You raise them." Sugaru thus raised the orphans by the wall of the palace. He was therefore given a title and made "Chiisakobe no Muraji."[18]

This legend, though doubtless apocryphal, once again exemplifies the close relationship between the formation of service groups (*be*), the importation of new technologies, and the propagation of cultic practices from the Chinese festival calendar. Here Yūryaku is portrayed in terms that are almost certainly derived from Chinese court practices that required the ruler's consorts to personally engage in the planting of mulberries and the feeding of silkworms at the start of the third month. Legends such as these thus strongly suggest that continental technologies not only facilitated the expansion of the ruler's wealth and power, they also resulted in the adoption of continental modes of representing kingship. Fostering continental technologies thus required propagating the ritual forms of the Chinese calendar and the ideologies of kingship and centralized government embedded within them for centuries. One further by-product was the establishment of lineages knowledgeable in the performance of rites for silkworm deities and weaving goddesses.

These rites in turn helped promote a broader sacerdotal transformation within the Japanese islands. Several hints as to how this process unfolded can be seen in other legends involving the Chiisakobe and rites of spirit pacification. Consider the following legend from the *Nihon shoki*:

> The *tennō* commanded Chiisakobe no Muraji Sugaru, saying: "I wish to see the form of the god on Mount Mimuro. *Some books say the god of this mountain is Ōmononushi no kami. Others say it is the god of Sumisaka in Uda.* You are a man of exceeding strength. Go and seize [the god] and bring it back." Sugaru said "I shall attempt to go and seize him." He then climbed Mount Mimuro and seized a large snake, which he showed to the *tennō*. The *tennō*, [however] had not observed any taboos, so the snake's thunder sounded and its eyeballs flashed. The *tennō* was terrified and covered his eyes and did not look [at it]. He then fled into the palace and had [the snake] released on a hill. They accordingly gave [the god] a new name, calling it Ikazuchi [thunder].[19]

This legend, depicting Sugaru as a ritualist capable of taming a volatile thunder god, associates the Chiisakobe not only with sericulture, but also with the propitiation of hostile deities. Two points of particular note in this regard are (1) the deity in question is none other than Ōmononushi, the main deity at the Miwa shrine and a principal object of worship of Yamato rulers during the fourth and fifth centuries, and (2) Yūryaku is portrayed here as singularly unqualified to deal with the god.[20] In contrast to Sugaru's strength and determination, Yūryaku can only cower in the inner precincts of his palace.

This depiction of Yūryaku's fear most probably reflects several important political and cultic realities of seventh- and eighth-century Japan. As we have seen in Chapter 1, there is ample reason to believe that Japanese rulers frequently felt intimidated and bullied by wrathful local *kami*; recall that the *Nihon shoki* itself hints that no fewer than three rulers were killed by angry spirits, including two in the final decades of the seventh century.[21] During this period rulers often turned to lineages familiar with continental rites of spirit pacification for protection from wrathful gods. One by-product of this process appears to have been the emergence of a cluster of legends in which the founding ancestor of a sacerdotal lineage is depicted as the child of a weaving maiden and a vengeful deity beyond the control of the ruler of Yamato.

These developments within the royal cult were deeply implicated in the larger geopolitical dynamics of the age, which were driven in good part by the Yamato court's continued dependence on the Korean peninsula for continental technological and cultic forms. As Yamato rulers such as Wakateru and his successors sought to preserve access to the technological and cultural developments of the Korean peninsula, their involvement in local affairs in Kyūshū, the main conduit of transfer during the period, appears to have greatly increased. According to the *Nihon shoki*, shortly after Yūryaku's reign the Yamato court moved in force to suppress breakaway elements in the area in a bloody conflict. This resulted in greater control by the Yamato court and in greater contact between the Yamato rulers and local cults from the region.[22] One of the most important cultic centers in the region to receive the attention of the Yamato court during this period was that of the Munakata shrine. As we have already seen, the *Nihon shoki* states that weaving maidens sent as "tribute" by the Korean kingdom of Paekche during Yūryaku's reign were offered to the deities of both the Miwa and Munakata shrines. In addition to extensive archeological evidence documenting the court's involvement in the Munakata cult, the close ties between Yamato rulers and the shrine can be seen from the fact that Ōmononushi, the deity of the Miwa shrine and a chief object of court worship during Wakateru's era, was said to have been married to Okitsushima Hime no Mikoto, one of the female deities of the Munakata shrine.[23] Wakateru's linkages with the Munakata shrine are of particular note because archeological findings have demonstrated that the Munakata deities were not only female, they were also regularly propitiated with weaving implements. In light of the fact that Akaru Hime, the deity of the Himegoso shrine in the Ki district of Hizen was also represented with weaving implements, it appears highly likely that not only weaving technologies but also weaving cults had been transmitted to this region of the Japanese islands during the sixth century.

Miko, Ancestors, and One-Night Stands

Since a large number of immigrant or Kyūshū deities persisted at the core of the royal cult for centuries, the significance of the early adoption of the Munakata shrine and other cultic centers in Kyūshū appears to have been far more than a simple augmentation of the number of deities propitiated by the court. As the power of Yamato rulers expanded in conjunction with the importation of continental rites and conceptions of kingship, the construction of an ancestral lineage for what eventually came to be known as the Japanese ruling house became a major political and religious concern. Several important hints as to the role played by weaving cults in the formation of the early royal cult can be found in the *Nihon shoki* and *Kojiki* accounts of the Heavenly Grandchild Niningi's descent from heaven and the subsequent conquest of the Japanese islands by his heirs. Because this legend cycle is most commonly seen as an ideological tool used to justify a Yamato hegemony over the Japanese islands, academic discourse to date has been framed predominantly in terms of the narrative's male characters and primarily from the perspective of the royal line.[24] Especially notable in this regard has been the work of Kōnoshi Takamitsu, who has compellingly argued that divergent accounts of the legend in the *Kojiki* and *Nihon shoki* reflect substantially divergent ideologies of kingship that most likely emerged in the late seventh century.[25]

In contrast to Kōnoshi, however, my concern with the many accounts of this legend will be for what they can tell us about the mythic resources that the court chroniclers appropriated and transformed. Rather than focus on the (primarily male) royal ancestors in the legend, I will discuss the role of the female shamans, consorts, and goddesses that appear throughout these narratives. Because these figures also appear as female ancestors of prominent court lineages and as figures of worship at sites across the Japanese islands, they help reveal not only the plurality of voices and agendas that existed in each of the court chronicles, but also the remarkable degree to which continental rites and beliefs concerning everything from sericulture to household deities were intertwined with the ancestral legends of some of the most important sacerdotal and military lineages in ancient Japan.

Just how such influences served as a catalyst for the formation of the allegedly native conceptions of kings and *kami* in Yamato can be seen once we consider the female figures that are closest to Ninigi no Mikoto. As Mishina Shōei noted long ago, the basic structure of legend of the Heavenly

Grandchild closely mirrors that of the nation-founding narratives of the Korean kingdoms, in all of which a child of a divinity is sent down from heaven to claim his kingdom by his mother, who for protection wraps him in cloth that she has woven for him. Wandering about in search of his kingdom, the divine child is tested, marries, and eventually establishes the ruling dynasty of his kingdom.[26] Evidence suggesting that elements from the Chinese festival calendar had also been adopted within the Korean kingdoms can be seen in tomb paintings in Koguryŏ, which have definitively established the presence of the cult of the Weaver and Cowherd by the fifth century.[27] Entries from the *Samguk sagi*, the oldest historical chronicle in Korea, similarly suggest that by this time weaving rites were part of the Koguryŏ court's ritual calendar.[28]

As Ōbayashi and others have noted, much of the structure of the nation-founding legends of the Korean kingdoms is replicated in the *Nihon shoki*, which contains several versions of the myth in which Ninigi no Mikoto, the son of Takami Musubi's daughter Amayorozu Takuhata Chihata Hime (Princess Heavenly Myriad of Thousands and Thousands of Weaving Looms) is sent down to Hyūga province in Kyūshū wrapped in a protective garment.[29] As Ninigi no Mikoto navigates his way through the region with a local deity for a guide, he encounters and marries a pair of sisters, both of whom are depicted as weaving maidens tending their looms by a ritual enclosure:

> Ninigi no Mikoto asked "Whose children are these [maidens] who have built on the crest of the waves an eight-furlong palace, and whose bracelets jangle as they tend to their loom." [The god] answered "They are the children of Ōyamatsumi no Kami. The elder one is named Iwanaga Hime. The younger one is named Konohana Sakuya Hime, [though she is] also known as Toyoatatsu Hime." . . . Ninigi no Mikoto then visited Toyoatatsu Hime, and she became pregnant in a single night.[30]

One obvious indication that weaving rites and tropes had penetrated this portion of the founding legend of the ruling house can be seen in the fact that every female figure is explicitly represented as a weaver maiden. The mother of Ninigi no Mikoto is listed in the *Nihon shoki* as Princess Heavenly Myriad of Thousands and Thousands of Weaving Looms. As if to eliminate any doubt about the nature of Ninigi no Mikoto's brides Konohana Sakuya Hime and her sister Iwanaga Hime, the text explicitly presents them seated by a river and weaving at looms.[31]

Perhaps even more revealing are the narrative means used to depict these women as progenitors of both royal ancestors and deities of special import for the royal line. Consider, for instance, the following account of Ninigi no Mikoto's reaction after Konohana Sakuya Hime announces that she has become pregnant after a single night with Ninigi:

> Ninigi no Mikoto said "Even though I am a Heavenly deity, how could I have impregnated you in a single night? It could not be my child." Konohana Sakuya Hime [on hearing this] was extremely ashamed and angry. She thus made a doorless ritual enclosure [*muro*] and vowed, "If I have conceived the child of another deity, may it without fail meet with misfortune. If it is truly the child of Ninigi no Mikoto, may it without fail be born safely." She then entered the enclosure and set it on fire. When the flames began to rise, a child was born named Ho no Suseri no Mikoto. Next as the fire grew higher, a child was born named Ho no Akari no Mikoto. Next a child was born who was called Hiko Hoho Demi no Mikoto.[32]

This legend replicates a common mythic structure in Nara-period literature that includes all or part of the following motifs: (1) a weaving maiden with a loom encounters a male deity in or by a body of water; (2) a ritual enclosure (*muro*) is built in order to welcome the deity, who has come to the area from afar; (3) prior to his arrival, the god is given special clothing that aids him in his journey; (4) the maiden receives the god in a *muro*, a temporary ritual chamber used in rites involving motifs of life, death, and resurrection; and (5) the product of the union is then a god whose birth symbolizes the fostering of life and abundance.[33]

As Hirabayashi has noted, this structure closely parallels annual rites in which a female shamaness, or *miko*, would be joined with a local deity in a "sacred marriage" that was ritually consummated in a single night in a *muro*. He also notes that this structure maps closely the basic structure of the cult of Weaver and the Cowherd, in which: (1) the Weaver Maiden waits on the edge of the Milky Way for her lover, the Cowherd deity; (2) the Milky Way is understood to be a river that can be crossed once a year; (3) the Cowherd is able to cross the river after he is given special protective clothing made from the hide of a cow; (4) the Cowherd visits the Weaver Maiden for only one night; (5) the union of the two lovers allows for the *yin* and *yang* elements of the universe to remain in equilibrium, thereby assuring fertility and abundance for the following year.

Perhaps because legends organized around the motif of impregnation of a (weaving) maiden in a single night served as important devices for defining lineal affiliations, they also contain a great deal of information concerning the nature and uses of continental religious tropes in the ancestral legends of nonroyal lineages. Thus, for our purposes, the legend of the miraculous birth of Konohana Sakuya Hime's three children is notable not only as an ancestral legend for the royal line, which traced its descent from Ninigi through the third child, Hiko Hoho Demi no Mikoto, but also for a series of lineages such as the Owari Muraji and the Kusakabe, which claimed descent from Konohana Sakuya Hime's second child, Ama no Hoakari no Mikoto.[34] As we shall see in Chapter 7, the cult of Ama no Hoakari no Mikoto appears to have also been fundamentally connected to the emergence of the cult of the royal ancestor Amaterasu, who is also presented in the court chronicles as a weaver maiden in a ritual enclosure preparing clothing for a religious festival.

The following legend from the Jinmu chapter of the *Kojiki* provides us with important genealogical information related to a series of lineages that were charged with the worship of the Miwa deity Ōmononushi:

Isukeyori Hime was at her home above the Sai River. The *tennō* [Jinmu] went to visit her, and slept with her for one night. . . . The children that were then born were Hikoyai no Mikoto, Kamuyaimimi no Mikoto, and Kamununakawamimi no Mikoto. Three children in all.[35]

Here, as in the legend of the Heavenly Grandchild, we are told of a royal ancestor who visits a daughter of a deity for a single night, and this union results in the birth of three sons. As in the Heavenly Grandchild myth, this legend is of particular interest for the genealogical linkages that are established through the mother and child. Particularly notable is the text's assertion that Kamuyaimimi no Mikoto is the grandson of the Miwa deity Ōmononushi. Because Kamuyaimimi no Mikoto is none other than the founding ancestor of the Chiisakobe kinship group, this genealogy was almost certainly an important background element for a series of legends in the *Nihon shoki* and the *Nihon ryōiki* in which a Chiisakobe ancestor is called upon to pacify the deity Ōmononushi on Mount Miwa.[36]

Perhaps the best indication that legends centering upon a deity's fruitful union with a weaving maiden for a single night were not the exclusive provenance of the royal house, however, can be seen in the following local legend from Matsuura district of Hizen province. As we saw in Chapter 3, Matsuura was a major transit point for traffic to and from the Korean peninsula and the site where the Ōtomo ancestor Sadehiko was said to have parted with his lover, the Kusakabe ancestor Shinohara no Otohihimeko. The following account from the *Hizen fudoki*, a gazetteer composed sometime around 713, relates what happened after Sadehiko's departure:

When Otohihimeko and Sadehiko Muraji had been separated for five days, someone came to Otohihimeko every night to sleep with her, leaving each time early in the morning. His face and shape were like Sadehiko's. The girl thought that very strange, so without doing anything sudden, she secretly tied a thread to her visitor's sleeve. When she went out to trace the thread, she discovered a snake sleeping by the side of a pond at this peak. Its body was that of a man's, and submerged in the pond. The head was lying on the bank of the pond. [The god] suddenly stood up and sang:

> Shinohara no Otohihimeko!
> Though we were together but one night
> Now you shall never return home!

At that time Otohihimeko's serving girl ran back to tell her family what had happened, and when she brought back many of her relatives to look for Otohihimeko, neither the snake nor the girl could be found. Then at the bottom of the pond they found a single human corpse, which all say are Otohihimeko's remains. They built a tomb to the south of the peak, where they interred her. The tomb survives to this day.[37]

Although the *Hizen fudoki* was a work commissioned by the court, I believe that this legend offers several invaluable clues concerning the nature and range of uses for this motif of a divine union within a single night in a region distant from the Yamato court. Most obviously, we again are told of a maiden who is impregnated by a god in a single evening. One indication of the power of this metaphor can be seen in the fact that the song sung by the deity explicitly refers to their one night of conjugal relations, even though the body of the text states that he came to her on five consecutive evenings. Moreover, although the *Hizen fudoki* was composed at the command of the Nara court, no members of the royal line appear in this legend. There is no reason to doubt this legend's stated purpose of explaining the existence of a local ancestral tomb and cultic center in a province far from the Yamato plain. The legend also broadly reflects other legends related to other deities from the region, such as the vengeful weaving deity Akaru Hime and the Munakata deities. Recall, for instance, the legend of the pacification of Akaru Hime discussed in Chapter 2. Just as the Mononobe ancestor Azeko determined the identity of Akaru Hime through the use of weaving implements, here we find Otohihimeko using needle and thread to determine the identity of the cruel deity that has become her lover. As we saw in Chapter 3, legends of female immortals from Matsuura appear to have directly influenced the formation of legends about such figures as the Immortal Mulberry Maiden at Yoshino and in the Yamato plain. We also noted that two lineages prominent in Matsuura were the Kusakabe and Ōtomo and that both appear to have been instrumental in transmitting continental technologies and cultic forms to the Japanese islands. In addition, Shinohara no Otohihimeko, the unfortunate maiden depicted in this legend, is explicitly described as a member of the Kusakabe and the lover of Ōtomo no Sadehiko. I therefore suggest that legends such as these may have played an important role in the formation of the royal ancestral legends. Legends such as these could also be used to link sacerdotal lineages not only to royal ancestors but also to violent deities that were thought to endanger the local populace (Akaru Hime) or rulers and the court (Ōmononushi). By claiming descent from such deities and building cultic centers dedicated to their worship, lineages such as the Kusakabe and the Chiisakobe could claim to be uniquely qualified to pacify violent spirits that would otherwise have been beyond the control of the court. Finally, and crucially, these texts frequently employed terms associated with weaving maidens in the Chinese festival calendar—whether in their names (Princess of Thousands of Looms), in the way they are introduced into the narrative (seated at a river jangling bracelets while tending a loom), or in their actions (tracing the identity of a god with a needle and thread).

Weaving and Binding in the Yamato Plain

The diffusion of rites and legends associated with the Chinese festival calendar was not limited to the appropriation of elements from the Weaving Maiden and the Cowherd; nor was their influence limited to the Yamato plain. Several legends within the court chronicles and *fudoki* suggest that rites and legends related to the lavatory goddess—one of the most important female deities in the Chinese pantheon—helped shape the founding legends of several lineages in charge of prominent shrines in the royal cult. The lavatory goddess was the household deity closely associated with the acquisition of wealth. She was most prominently worshipped on the fifteenth day of the first month at the conclusion of the New Year's rites designed to establish a peaceful and prosperous basis for the coming year. This day was also marked by rites related to the lunar cult, female deities, and, to a lesser degree, spirit pacification.

One of the best examples of the process by which rites and legends associated with the lavatory goddess came to influence the mythology of the Japanese islands can be seen in the founding legends of the upper and lower Kamo shrines in the Kadono district of Yamashiro province. As we saw in Chapter 1, by the early Heian period these cultic centers had been absorbed into the heart of the royal cult and Heian paradigms of political/ religious authority. The importance of these shrines for the ruling house, however, was apparent even prior to the Nara period. Because the lower Kamo shrine was situated at a strategic node for both land and water traffic between such major ports on the Japan/Eastern Sea as Tsunoga, Tamba, and Izushi and the court in Yamato, it played a major role in the diffusion of cultic influences from these areas both to the court and across the Japanese islands. Because each of these ports directly faced the Korean peninsula and contained large immigrant populations from the Korean kingdoms of Koguryō and Silla, the Kamo shrines appear to have occupied an ideal spot for the transmission of cultic practices and mythic tropes associated with immigrant cults and deities.[38]

This location was not, most likely, a product of mere chance, for the Kadono waterway was apparently part of a large network of canals and waterways built by groups such as the Hata throughout Yamato. This constructed geography affected cultic practice at the Kamo shrine in at least two senses: first, the Hata appear to have changed the physical topography surrounding the shrine, transforming it into a cultic center at a *chimata*-type waterway that was ideally suited for rites of purification and spirit pacification. The degree to which the shrine eventually came to be associated with such rites can be seen most dramatically in the early Heian period, when rites of purification for the capital were performed there on a monthly basis.[39]

Even more important, the network of waterways that the Hata created linked not only major ports on the coast of the Inland and Japan/Eastern seas, but also prominent shrines and cultic centers. Over time deities at several of these shrines came to be closely associated with the Hata. By the time the *Nihon shoki* was composed in 720, for instance, the Hata or affiliated immigrant lineages were worshipping the deities at such major cultic centers as the Munakata shrine in Chikuzen, the Izushi shrine in Tajima province, and the Kehi shrine in Tsunoga. It would thus appear that even as the Hata helped to literally transform the physical and cultic landscape of early Yamato, their cultic identity came to be defined by that transformation.

The construction of canals and roadways also greatly aided the expansion of the authority of Yamato rulers into areas hitherto only nominally under their control. The expansion of Yamato power, however, had important secondary consequences for cultic practice in the Japanese islands.

Among the most important of these were the unprecedented levels of traffic among both humans and gods between the archipelago's center and its periphery. As we saw in Chapter 1, local gods from the periphery are depicted in the *Nihon shoki* and elsewhere as being frequently hostile to Yamato rulers. As the Yamato court sought for the means to propitiate vengeful deities from Kyūshū and elsewhere, it turned for help to kinship groups such as the Hata, Miwa, Chiisakobe, and others with special lineal claims and sacerdotal expertise. The increasingly large role played by these groups in the construction of ancestral cults for the Yamato rulers in turn facilitated the absorption of cultic practices associated with weaving and spirit pacification into the fabric of the royal cult.

The following remnant from the *Yamashiro fudoki* describes the rites and legends of the upper Kamo shrine as follows:

> Tamayori Hiko is the ancestor of the Kamo Agatanushi. On his festival day there is horse-riding. [The origins of this custom go back to] the reign of the *tennō* who reigned at Shikishima [Kinmei], when there were tremendous winds and rain and the people suffered greatly.
> At that time, Wakahiko of the Iki Urabe was commanded to perform a divination. He determined that [the troubles] were the vengeance (*tatari*) of the Kamo deity. At this they held a festival on an auspicious day during the fourth month, where they hung bells on horses as men rode the horses wearing boar's masks. They performed horse-riding and offered up their prayers, the five grains ripened, and peace slowly came back to the world. [The Kamo festival's] horse-riding was begun at this time.[40]

This account is notable not only for its depiction of Tamayori Hiko as a wrathful deity in need of propitiation, but also for the strong influences from the continent that are manifest in the rites themselves; horses, animal masks, and arrows were considered strongly *yang* elements, and they were used frequently in the Chinese festival calendar as a means of pacifying dangerous *yin* spirits.[41] This text is also noteworthy for its reference to a diviner from the Iki Urabe lineage. Because, as their name suggests, the Iki Urabe were a sacerdotal lineage that was originally based in Kyūshū, the text again suggests a significant degree of cultic interchange between regions such as Yamashiro and Kyūshū.

In contrast to the male deity in the upper Kamo shrine, the lower Kamo shrine housed a female deity claimed by both the Hata and Kamo lineages. As we saw in Chapter 1, the *Hatashi honkeichō* explains this as follows:

In the beginning there was a Hata woman who came to the Kadono river to wash clothes. At that time an arrow came floating down from upstream. The girl took the arrow and returned home, where she stuck the arrow above the door [of her house]. At this the girl became pregnant without any husband, and she subsequently gave birth to a boy. Her parents thought this strange, and asked her [how this could have happened]. The girl replied that she did not know. They asked her several times, but even after several months she still said she did not know. Her parents said, "Even though she had no husband, a child could not have been born without a father. The father must be from among family and relatives or neighbors that frequent our house." They therefore prepared a feast and invited a great crowd of people. They then ordered the boy to take a cup and offer it to the man that he believed was his father.

At this the boy did not indicate anyone in the gathering, but instead he gazed over to the arrow above the door. He was then transformed into a thunder god, and he burst through the roof of the building as he flew off into the sky. Therefore the [god of the] Upper Kamo Shrine is called Wake no Ikazuchi no Kami. The [god of the] Lower Kamo Shrine is called Mioya no Kami. The arrow above the door is the Matsuno'o Daimyōjin. Thus the Hata worship the gods in these three places.[42]

As numerous commentators have noted, this legend, recounting as it does the birth of Wake no Ikazuchi no Kami (Young Thunder), suggests that the Kamo cult was deeply involved in the pacification of volatile thunder deities. Equally notable, however, is the prominence given to the young god's distaff lineage. Throughout the legend it is the maternal grandfather who determines the setting and timing of events. It is also the maternal grandfather who constructs the *muro* and arranges the offerings. Perhaps most important, here it is the maternal grandfather who bestows the new name, and therefore identity, upon the young god. This focus on distaff lineages almost certainly relates to the text's explicit assertions that the maiden is from the Hata kinship group and that the young god's father is none other than the (Hata) deity of the Matsuno'o shrine.

Kamo and Miwa

The Kamo legend cycle's emphasis upon young maidens and distaff lineages also highlights a remarkable set of continuities with other royal cultic centers. Just as the Chiisakobe depicted their founding ancestor pacifying Ōmononushi (Ikazuchi), the thunder deity at the Miwa shrine, here the origins of the Kamo cult are rooted in the birth of the thunder deity Wake no Ikazuchi.[43] Even more compelling evidence of linkages between the Kamo, Chiisakobe, and Miwa cults can be seen in a series of legends concerning other female ancestors of Chiisakobe and Miwa kinship groups. Consider, for instance, the following legend from the *Kojiki* concerning the Miwa ancestor Seyatadera Hime:

> When [the Yamato ruler Jinmu] sought for a beautiful woman to be his chief consort, Ōkume no Mikoto said: "There is a beautiful maiden here who is said to be the child of a god. The reason she is said to be the child of a god is that the daughter of Mishima no Mizokuhi, who was named Seyatadera Hime, was extremely beautiful. Ōmononushi, [the god] of Miwa was struck by her beauty. When she went to defecate, he transformed himself into a red arrow and, coming down the river where she was defecating, he penetrated her private parts. Startled by this, she stood up and ran away in haste. She then took the arrow and set it by her bed, where it transformed into a handsome man. He then wed the maiden, who gave birth to a child named Hototatara Isusuki Hime.[44]

As in the legend of the birth of the Kamo deity Wake no Ikazuchi, again we have a legend involving a maiden who is approached at a river by a thunder god in the shape of a red arrow. In both legends the maiden takes the arrow home and is impregnated in the space of a single night.

These similarities are all the more intriguing in light of the *Nihon shoki*'s assertion that the maiden Seyatadera was the mother of Isukeyori Hime (referred to in the text as Isusuki Hime). This is of immediate note because, as we have just seen, Isukeyori Hime herself was said to have given birth to Kamu no Yaimimi no Mikoto, the founding ancestor of the Chiisakobe kinship group, after she was impregnated in a single night.[45] Although no one would take such statements as historical truth, the similarities in the legends very probably relate to the fact that the Chiisakobe claimed common ancestry with the Miwa.[46] Legends such as these illustrate how connections between lineages such as the Hata, Chiisakobe, and Miwa could be important mechanisms for the transmission of cultic influences from northern Kyūshū to the Miwa and Kamo cults. They also suggest that the route by which continental weaving and sericulture technologies entered the Japanese islands correlated closely with the transmission for weaving and sericulture cults.

Further evidence suggesting that close linkages in the ancestral legends of these lineages had developed at an early date can be seen in yet other Miwa ancestral legends. Consider, for instance, these entries from the *Nihon shoki*:

> Autumn, 8th month, 7th day. Yamato Tohaya Kamuasajihara Maguhashi Hime, Ōminakuchi no Sukune, a distant ancestor of the Hozumi no Omi, and Ise no Ami no Kimi all three reported [to the throne]: "Last night we [each] had a dream in which a noble man said to us: 'If you give Ōtataneko no Mikoto charge of the worship of Ōmononushi no Ōkami . . . [then] the land will without question be at peace." When the *tennō* learned the words of the dream he was more and more delighted in his heart. He issued a proclamation seeking for Ōtataneko, who was then found in the village of Sue, in the district of Chinu, and sent to the Emperor. [Sujin] asked Ōtataneko, saying: "Of whom are you child?" Ōtataneko answered, saying: "My father is called Ōmononushi no Ōkami. My mother is called Ikutamayori Hime, the daughter of Suetsu mimi."
>
> . . . .
>
> 11th month. . . . Ōtataneko was given charge of the worship of Ōmononushi. . . . Thereupon the pestilence first ceased, the country was increasingly quiet, the five kinds of grain were produced, and the peasantry prospered.[47]

Because this legend concludes with a justification for the Miwa being invested with control of the cult of Ōmononushi, Wada Atsumu and others have argued that it could only have been created after Yamato rulers began delegating responsibility for worship of Ōmononushi to the Miwa. Wada dates this shift to the early sixth century, when archeological evidence suggests that a dramatic change took place in the cultic practice at the Miwa shrine.[48] Among the most important evidence for such a shift was the profusion of ritual implements that have been dated to this period and that appear to have been made in the Korean kingdom of Silla. Discoveries of virtually identical implements and a kiln in the Ōtori district of the region, formerly known as Chinu, have tended to corroborate this view.[49]

Equally important, however, the cultic geography of this legend suggests the possibility that it originated in a cultic context strongly influenced by lineages from Kyūshū as well as the coastal regions along the Inland Sea. As we saw in Chapter 3, the Chinu district of Izumi province, which was located on the Inland Sea in close proximity to the Kii peninsula, appears to have been a major port of entry for immigrants from the Korean peninsula. We also saw that during the Nara period the lead kinship group of this district was the Kusakabe, the very lineage that claimed Shinohara no Otohime as one of their ancestors. Thus the fact that this legend tells us that the Miwa ancestor Ōtataneko was "found" in just this area, coupled with the fact that his mother's name Suetsu Mimi, which may be rendered as "abundant pottery," once again underlines the importance of these regions for the transmission of ritual implements from the Korean peninsula to the Japanese islands during the very same period that witnessed the formation of service groups such as the Kusakabe, Chiisakobe, Hata, and others.[50]

Equally importantly, legends of Hizen deities such as the Kusakabe ancestor Shinohara no Otohime exhibit a high degree of correlation with legends from the Miwa cult in other ways as well. Consider the *Nihon shoki* account of the birth of Ōtataneko's mother, Seyatadera:

> The reason why the man called Ōtataneko is known to have been the son of a god is that the above-mentioned Ikutamayori Hime, who was extremely beautiful, was visited suddenly in the middle of the night by a handsome man who was moved by her incomparable beauty. Thus they loved each other, and after they had wed and lived together but a short while, the maiden was pregnant. Then her father and mother marveled at her being pregnant, and they asked their daughter "You are now pregnant. [Yet] without a man what could have caused this pregnancy?" She answered saying "I have been naturally impregnated by a beautiful man, whose name I do not know, who comes every night to stay with me." At this the parents, wanting to know the man's [identity], instructed their daughter, saying: "Spread red earth before your bed, pass a skein of thread through a needle and pierce his garment with it." She therefore did as she had been instructed, and when they looked the next morning, the hemp that had been put in the needle had come out through the hole in the door hook with only three loops [*miwa*] left. Then, knowing that he had gone out through the hole in the door hook, they followed the thread all the way up to the shrine on Mount Miwa, where it stopped. Thus they knew that the child was the child of a god. Because the thread had remained in three loops [*miwa*], this place was called Miwa.[51]

The similarities between this legend and that of Shinohara Otohime are so great as to hardly bear elaborating. Here again we find a mysterious deity visiting a maiden only at night, only to have his identity revealed when the maiden uses a needle and thread to trace the god back to his lair. As in the Shinohara Otohime legend cycle, the god is said to have been ashamed to be seen in his natural form as a snake, with the net result being that the maiden dies a violent, unhappy death because of the god's anger. Again the text concludes with the construction of a tomb/cultic center for the lineage.

This legend also appears to reflect several other legends involving continental-style immortals. In Chapter 3 we saw the cultic significance of red earth for the female immortals and deities of Yoshino, and here we find Seyatadera's parents commanding her to spread red earth before her bed upon the god's arrival. As the Miwa, Kamo, and others incorporated weaving-maiden motifs into the legend cycles of their own female ancestral deities, I would therefore suggest that two further shifts also occurred: first, as cults and female deities from Kyūshū and the coastal areas of the Japan/Eastern Sea streamed into the Yamato plain, the conceptual vocabulary surrounding shamanesses and female ancestors became colored by terminology related to sericulture and weaving technologies.[52] Second, as lineages such as the Kamo, Hata, Chiisakobe, and Miwa achieved prominence at court, their shrines and their ancestors helped establish this vocabulary at the very heart of the royal cult.

None of this, of course, need be seen as part of any grand design to promote a certain worldview or religious orientation. It does suggest, however, that as lineages rose to prominence they may have utilized mythic and ritual tropes from the continent to create or amplify genealogical linkages and political accommodation. It would also appear that genealogical unions were often achieved or at least manifested through legends concerning female ancestors who were represented in the vocabulary of continental legends concerning weaving maidens, goddesses, and female immortals.

Izushi Otome and the Lavatory Goddess

Further evidence concerning the mechanisms driving this process can be found in the area of Izushi in Tajima, a coastal province that faced the Korean kingdom of Silla. The Izushi shrine was home to the Silla immigrant cowherd deity Ame no Hiboko, who is said to have come to the Japanese islands in search of his wife, the vengeful weaving goddess Akaru Hime. Several Ame no Hiboko shrines are known to have existed in Hizen, Chikuzen, and Buzen provinces, often in areas such as Matsuura where the Kusakabe are also known to have had a strong presence. This region is of immediate interest because both textual sources and *mokkan* from the area suggest that even before the Nara period the most powerful kinship groups in the region were the Kusakabe and the Miwa. As we have seen repeatedly in Chapters 3 and 4, the Kusakabe were actively involved in the importation of continental-style immortality cults. In addition to all this, Izushi also appears to have been a major center for the production of woven goods and an important point of entry for elements of continental culture.[53]

It is perhaps not surprising, therefore, that archeologists have uncovered tens of thousands of ritual implements from the Nara and early Heian periods in extremely close proximity to the former provincial administrative offices and to the Izushi shrine. Among the most important discoveries have been large numbers of clay vessels, animal figurines, and *hitogata*, many of which bear spells from Chinese ritual manuals calling upon deities from the Chinese pantheon to subdue disease-causing spirits. Given both the nature and sheer volume of artifacts, it appears highly likely that Izushi was a major center for continental-style rites of spirit pacification.[54]

Crucially for our purposes, the deity of the Izushi shrine was none other than Ame no Hiboko. We have encountered this deity as an immigrant cowherd deity from Silla who was married to the vengeful weaving goddess Akaru Hime. Ame no Hiboko was also said to have been the father of Izushi Hime, yet another weaving goddess whose story correlates closely with the Miwa and Kamo legend cycles:

> This deity [Ame no Hiboko] had a daughter by the name of Izushi Otome no Kami. Although many gods wished to have her, none were able to wed her. At this, there were two gods, an older brother, who was named Akiyama Shitabi no Mikoto, and a younger brother, who was a young man named Haruyama Kasu no Mikoto. So the older brother said to the younger brother, "Although I have pleaded with Izushi Otome, I still cannot have her as a wife. Would you be able to obtain this maiden?" The younger brother replied "I could have her easily." Then the older brother said "If you can have her, I will remove my upper and lower garments, brew for you *sake* in a jar equal to your height, and I will prepare for you all the things of the mountains and rivers [as payment for winning this] wager.
>
> Then the younger brother told his mother everything that the older brother had said. She then took [hemp made from] wisteria vines (*fuji no kazura*) and, in a single night, she wove and sewed an over garment (*kinu hakama*) and trousers and socks. She also made a bow and arrow. She then had him wear the garments and take the bow and arrow and sent him to the maiden's house, where the clothes and the bow and arrow all turned into wisteria flowers. At this Haruyama no

Mikoto took the bow and arrow and fastened them to the maiden's lavatory. Now Izushi Otome thought these flowers were very strange. When she brought them home, [Haruyama no Mikoto] followed behind her, entered her room and wed her. They thus gave birth to a child. Then he announced to his brother, "I have obtained Izushi Otome."[55]

Because this legend brings together elements from virtually all of the legends that we have considered so far, it provides invaluable evidence suggesting how and to what degree cultic influences from Kyūshū came to penetrate the early royal cult. Here, as in the Kamo legend cycle, Izushi Otome is impregnated in one night after bringing home an arrow that she has found near the water and that has been placed upon a doorframe. As in the legend cycle of the Heavenly Grandchild Nininigi no Mikoto, the narrative also features the protagonist's mother, who in the space of a single night, weaves for him clothing that allows him to attain his goal.[56] Perhaps most intriguing of all, however, are the legend's resonances with the legend of Ōmononushi and Seyatadera. Whereas Ōmononushi, after assuming the form of an arrow impregnates Seyatadera while she is defecating, Izushi Otome is impregnated after bringing home an arrow that has been placed on the doorframe of her lavatory.

Although Japanese scholars have almost invariably passed over this final aspect of the Seyatadera legend in embarrassed silence, I suggest that this detail most likely reflects the longstanding importance of lavatory goddesses in the popular religious practice of China.[57] Since lavatory goddesses in China were also often associated with weaving cults and the creation of wealth, the association of two prominent female ancestors with the lavatory should hardly be surprising. I suggest, therefore, that the association of both Seyatadera and Izushi Otome with the lavatory is actually another indicator of continental influences in the formation of two core legends of the supposedly native Japanese tradition.

Perhaps most important of all, however, the Izushi Otome legend illustrates the degree to which both the Miwa and Kamo cults drew upon the resources of weaving deities situated in Kyūshū and along the coast of the Inland Sea. Here we find that the founding legends of both the Kamo and Miwa shrines closely reflect a legend of yet another immigrant deity closely associated with the Kusakabe and the Chinese festival calendar. To consider the closeness of this set of legends, consider Table 2.

There can be little doubt that the founding myths of the Izushi, Kamo, and Miwa shrines not only overlap significantly, but also a number of their traits suggest strong influences from the Chinese festival calendar. The

Table 2 Arrows and Divine Pregnancies in the Court Chronicles

KAMO SHRINE	MIWA SHRINE	IZUSHI SHRINE
Maiden finds god as arrow	Maiden approached by god as arrow	Maiden finds god as arrow
Maiden finds god at river	Maiden meets god at river while defecating	Maiden meets god at lavatory
Maiden brings arrow home	Maiden brings arrow home	Maiden brings arrow home
Maiden becomes pregnant	Maiden becomes pregnant in one night	Maiden "is wed to" god in one night

extensive overlap was almost certainly related to close political, lineal, and geographic linkages among the Hata, Kamo, Chiisakobe, Kusakabe, and Miwa, making it apparent that the diffusion of sericulture and weaving technologies went hand in hand with a cultic revolution in which newly formed lineages created ancestral legends centering on young maidens married to volatile deities in need of frequent pacification.

All of this also suggests that the genealogies of such supposedly native cultic practices and legends extended all the way back from the Japanese shores to the cults and practices of ancient China. As lineages such as the Hata, Kamo, Kusakabe, and Miwa rose to prominence at court, these cultic roots nourished the emerging royal cult. By the Nara period, concern with sericulture deities and spirit pacification topped the cultic agenda both at court and in the countryside

By the advent of the Heian period, the process had culminated in the emergence of the Kamo, Miwa, and Izushi shrines as central nodes in a series of ritual centers that surrounded the ruler's person and court with concentric rings of ritual purity and abundance. At the center of this network was the lower Kamo shrine, the cultic center adopted by Saga *tennō* in 810 as he sought the assistance of the Kamo deities in putting down the Kusuko uprising. For the next 500 years following Saga's establishment of the Kamo priestess, young women from the royal line serving as officiants at the shrine presided at the apex of the court's most important ritual network. Thus did matters come full circle as the royal lineage moved from delegating ritual authority to kinship groups such as the Hata and their weaving-maiden daughters to a royal embrace of the weaving maiden/*miko* paradigm. Henceforth distaff members of the royal lineage would receive the Kamo deity Wake Ikazuchi in the fourth month of each year. Throughout the Heian period it was female members of the ruling line who were charged with purifying the capital and propitiating a powerful network of mostly immigrant deities in order to protect the body and spirit of the ruler.

Conclusion

The transmission of sericulture and weaving technologies to the Japanese islands occurred within the context of broader political and economic transformations, for new modes of material production (estates) helped spur the creation of new modes of social organization (service groups). As the lineages most closely associated with these transformations rose to prominence, they created ancestral cults and legends that appropriated tropes and practices embedded in the Chinese festival calendar and the cultic technologies that were entering the Japanese islands from the continent. In the process these groups also developed claims of special sacerdotal efficacy at major cultic centers and came to fill the role of cultic specialists in the service of Yamato rulers.

Accompanying this specialization of labor was the formation of ancestral legends centered upon volatile deities who required their descendents to perform rites of pacification. As we have seen repeatedly, an unexpected by-product of Yamato expansion into areas such as Hizen and Chikuzen was that the rulers were forced to confront hostile deities there. Moreover these areas were also populated by female deities, weaving deities such as Konohana Sakuya Hime, Akaru Hime, Shinohara Otohihimeko, and the Munakata deities, who soon penetrated not only royal mythology but also the major cultic centers of central Japan. By the Nara period sacred marriages between weaving maidens and vengeful gods were core elements of annual rites across the Japanese islands, and major cultic centers such as the Munakata, Himegoso, Izushi, Matsuno'o, Kamo, and Miwa shrines all traced their origins to weaving maiden/*miko* and the wrathful gods that they propitiated.

This thus highlights yet again the degree to which continental technologies and ritual tropes informed the construction of gender roles and ritual power. Just as we saw in the case of female immortals in Chapter 3, here we find that one of the root tropes for the configuration of female shamans cum ancestors was the figure of the weaving maiden. In the next chapter we shall examine the role of such tropes in depictions of royal consorts in the court chronicles before examining in the final chapter their role in the construction of the pre-eminent figure in nativist discourse—the weaving maiden and silkworm goddess Amaterasu no Ōmikami.

CHAPTER 6

Silkworms and Consorts

IN 608 A delegation from the court of the Chinese ruler Sui Yang-ti arrived on the shores of the Japanese islands with the goal of establishing amicable relations with Yamato in advance of a planned invasion of the Sui's nemesis, the Korean kingdom of Koguryŏ. Although geopolitical concerns almost certainly were foremost in the minds of the Sui envoys, the cultural and cultic effects of their arrival reverberated across the Japanese islands long after the Sui dynasty itself had ceased to exist. Because diplomatic contact with the Sui required participation in diplomatic protocols that were deeply rooted in Chinese conceptions of kingship and ritual, the arrival of the Sui envoys marked for the Yamato court an important moment of engagement with not only the Sui government, but also continental political and cultic norms.

In the *Nihon shoki* there are several indications that even before the arrival of the envoys the Yamato court began a program of emulating Chinese court ritual practices. Just a few years before the arrival of the envoys, for instance, we are told that the court instituted a new system of court ranks that appears to have been based upon continental models.[1] Similarly, accounts of ministers presenting memorials to the throne from this time reflect a change in court etiquette. We are also told that in 604 Prince Kamitsumiya, known to later generations as Shōtoku, composed the well-known Seventeen Article Constitution, a list of admonitions concerning proper relations between ruler and minister that argues that ritual should be the basis of government.[2]

While very few scholars today would take the *Nihon shoki* account at face value, there is substantial evidence that with the intensification of diplomatic contacts with successive Chinese dynasties, as well as with the kingdoms of the Korean peninsula, the Yamato court was increasingly adopting and propagating Chinese court ritual forms as well as the Chinese festival calendar. Nishimoto Masahiro notes that a similar process seems to have occurred on the Korean peninsula, with the Korean kingdom of Silla fully adopting Chinese court ritual in 651.[3] In the preface of the *Kaifūsō*, a poetic anthology completed in 751, we are told that during the Suiko court Prince Kamitsumiya "established the ranks and offices at court and began the ordering of ritual," while the Yamato ruler Tenchi "established the five rites" some forty years later.[4] Perhaps the best evidence suggesting that the Suiko court was familiar with the Chinese festival calendar, however, can be seen in the *Sui shu*, an official history of the Sui dynasty completed by 656. Here we are told that, with the exception of New Year's rites, observances on the nodal days of the calendar were close to those practiced in China.[5]

All of this suggests several important points concerning the role of both Chinese court ritual and the Chinese festival calendar in seventh-century Yamato. First, it would appear that the Yamato court's embrace of Chinese court ritual forms was not a discrete historical event, but rather an extended process that most likely began early in the seventh century but came to fruition during the reign of Tenchi, more than fifty years after the arrival of the first Sui envoys and over a decade after the last Korean kingdom had completed a similar transition. Second, the adoption of Chinese court ritual was almost certainly promoted by Yamato rulers intent upon transforming the status of the throne and the realm. From ritual flowed authority and then power.

The consequences of this transformation were enormous. Although scholars of Japanese religion have long focused on the proliferation of Buddhist icons, temples, and priests in the Japanese islands when discussing religious developments at the start of the seventh century, the adoption by the court of the Yamato ruler Suiko (reigned 592–628) of rudimentary Chinese court ritual forms as well as basic elements from the Chinese festival calendar heralded a shift in cultic practice that may have been no less momentous. As Yamato rulers increasingly adopted the ritual practices and festivals of the Chinese ritual cycle as their own, Chinese myths, legends, and cosmological visions came to pervade the basic means by which political, cultic, and even natural events were organized and categorized. Few if any aspects of court life remained untouched by these changes.[6]

Long before the compilation of the *Sui shu*, Chinese rites tended to fall on specific days that were closely correlated with Chinese numerology—thus the pre-eminence of festivals on the first day of the year, the third day of the third month, the fifth day of the fifth month, and so forth—and the agricultural cycle—thus festivals on the solar and lunar equinoxes, the midautumn festival, and so forth. By adopting the Chinese festival calendar the Yamato court thus embraced an entire worldview that integrated political, ritual, and even astronomical events into a single, coherent whole that promised to harmonize relationships among the various elements of the cosmos even as it helped transform the hearts and minds of its participants.

On a more mundane level, however, rites associated with the production of manufactured goods such as silks and woven fabrics were also given fixed dates throughout the year. Thus women prayed for silkworms on the fifteenth day of the first month and skill in weaving on the seventh day of the seventh month. During the fourth month a variety of taboos related to silkworms were observed, while much of the tenth month was taken up with offerings of thanks to the silkworm goddess.[7] Other rites related to agriculture, metalworking, and medicine were also ubiquitous throughout the year.

Although seldom discussed as such, the diffusion of continental ritual forms was also of immediate consequence for the proliferation of continental textual traditions and narratives. Not only did the calendar provide new patterns for organizing cultic life, it also facilitated the diffusion of continental historical and poetic tropes that were closely connected with the ritual calendar. Thus court-sponsored historical narratives such as the *Nihon shoki* not only utilized the new chronicle genre, but they also constructed a new past conceived in large part in terms of continental norms and conceptions of kingship. Because much of the poetry of the age was composed to commemorate occasions at court, the adoption of stock poetic allusions from continental literature also required extensive familiarity with the legends and practices associated with the Chinese festival calendar.

It is not surprising then that one of the best sources we have for studying the introduction of weaving cults into the Japanese islands is the poetry of the period, much of it composed on occasions such as the Tanabata festival marking the reunion of the Weaver Maiden and Cowherd deities. The corpus of *tanabata* poetry in the *Manyōshū* and *Kaifūsō*, two collections composed during the Nara period, is surprisingly large. Several such poems, including a well-known cycle composed by Kakinomoto Hitomaro, demonstrate that the observance of the Tanabata festival predated the Nara period.[8]

References to weaving maidens and immortality were by no means limited to poetry; as we have seen repeatedly, we also find goddesses, shamanesses (*miko*), and female immortals represented as weaving maidens in court chronicles and local gazetteers. While these figures are of enormous interest in their own right, their narratives are especially significant for two further reasons. First, as we saw in Chapter 5, the use of continental tropes to represent female ancestors and deities appears to have been an important moment in the reformulation of gender identities in the cultic life of the period. Second, given the fundamentally allusive nature of much of the literature of the period, these texts can also tell us much about the horizon of reception against which these deities developed.

The continued influence of prewar nationalist paradigms has meant that until recently historians of Japanese religion have viewed cults and legends rooted in Chinese mythology as peripheral elements in the religion of the period. Scholars of Japanese literature have also long assumed that allusions to Chinese legends in the poetry of the period merely reflect the heavy dependence of Japanese intellectuals on Chinese models for the composition of Chinese prose and verse.[9]

In what follows I propose to explore a small set of poems and legends that feature royal emissaries who prostrate themselves and crawl as they call out to women with whom rulers have become enamored.[10] Because the motifs of crawling and "calling out" appear related to rites of calling to the spirits of the recently deceased, these legends offer a small glimpse into the means by which the myths and legends associated with the Chinese festival calendar came to inform even apparently native cultic practices and literature. Although no one would mistake these texts for historical reality, their very constructed nature provides us with invaluable information concerning the means by which continental cults and practices associated with weaving and sericulture informed gender paradigms across the cultic and literary spectrum of Nara Japan.

Once we analyze the sources used in the construction of these legends, three salient features involving Chinese rites of sericulture become apparent. First, these legends of crawling and calling out, and the poetry associated with them, amply illustrate the degree to which motifs from Chinese legends of weaving and sericulture informed the literature of the period. Second, the immigrant kinship groups that transmitted the technologies associated with sericulture to the Japanese islands were also likely sources for the diffusion of such weaving cults and legends. Finally, the silkworm's ability to "die" within its cocoon, only to re-emerge as a moth capable of flight, meant that rites of sericulture in Japan were associated not only with the acquisition of wealth, but also with resurrection and immortality.

Of Weavers, Worms, and Kings

Although the rites of the Chinese festival calendar are frequently discussed in terms of the Confucian agenda of harmonizing relations between ruler and ruled, ritual during the period was far more than simply politics by other means. Balancing the *yin* and *yang* elements in the cosmos was necessary to ensure proper rainfall and abundant crops. Similarly, the profusion of rites related to sericulture and weaving reflected not only the importance of those activities for the court, but also the necessity of such rites for the successful production of silks and fabrics.

The adoption of the Chinese festival calendar in Japan was thus inextricably linked with the development of technologies related to weaving and metalworking. As we saw in Chapter 5, the diffusion of these technologies was greatly facilitated by immigrant kinship groups from the Korean peninsula, who were coming to the Japanese islands in large numbers in the mid-fifth century. The transformations that they engendered in terms of social organization and economic productivity increased the wealth of the Yamato court and thus helped make possible the expansion of Yamato power and the subsequent formation of the Ritsuryō law codes, which typified government during the Nara period.

Several clues as to the economic dimensions of this process can be seen in this legend recounting the formation of the Hata, one of the largest and most powerful immigrant kinship groups:

> In the days of the Emperor who reigned at the Asakura Palace in Hatsuse, the members of the Hata family became dependent on other families unrelated to their original house. The Emperor, however, graciously favoring the Hata chieftain, Sake no Kimi, who served at the court, was pleased to gather again all the scattered members of that family and place them under the control of Sake no Kimi, who with 180 excellent workmen, presented taxes to the court of fine silks, with which he filled the palace courtyard. . . . These taxed soft silks when worn are very pleasing to the skin, and so the family name Hata, or Hada, meaning "skin" originated. With these same silks they covered the hilt of the sacred sword when worshipping at the Shinto shrine, and that ancient custom still remains unchanged. Thus we see how the silk weaving industry was originated by the Hata family in Japan.[11]

This legend, though doubtless apocryphal, highlights two central social and economic facts regarding the diffusion of sericulture and weaving rites. First, fabrics and silks were not simply one type of valued commodity among many. Rather, they were a central medium of exchange throughout the period. The degree to which silks and fabrics served as the lifeblood of both economic and administrative activity in premodern Japan can be seen in the tax codes and registers of the Nara and Heian periods, which consistently suggest that the vast majority of materials collected by the court as taxes came in the form of rice, fabrics, and silks.[12] Stipends to courtiers and officials were paid predominantly in fabrics. Thus throughout this period the production of silks and woven fabrics closely approximated the production of money itself.

This legend highlights once again the degree to which the introduction and diffusion of technologies related to weaving and sericulture was related to the immigration of kinship groups such as the Hata. This is suggested not only by the high degree of familiarity with continental modes of culture and technology that such groups possessed, but also by contemporaneous sources themselves, which frequently refer explicitly to immigrant kinship groups in conjunction with the dissemination of weaving technologies.[13]

As we have seen repeatedly, one further element of enormous consequence for the development of rites and legends associated with weaving was the highly gendered division of labor that accompanied the diffusion of sericulture. In Japan as elsewhere in Asia, only women operated the looms that made fabric. Women also appear to have been responsible for the extremely labor-intensive practice of feeding mulberry leaves to the silkworms. Women thus occupied a central position in the production of wealth in many households.

Not surprisingly, these social and economic realities were reflected across a wide spectrum of myth and cultic practice. By the start of the Nara period the most common offerings to deities were woven items, weaving implements, and weaving maidens. Perhaps the best illustration of the degree to which weaving motifs penetrated religious discourse at court can be seen in the well-known Heavenly Grotto myth in the *Nihon shoki*. Here even the sun goddess and royal ancestor Amaterasu is depicted in a ritual weaving chamber working at her loom prior to her encounter with her violent brother Susanoo and her seclusion within the Heavenly Grotto.[14]

These tropes were not limited, however, to accounts of the land's mythic origins; as we saw in Chapter 5, the court chronicles were also at pains to portray rulers and their consorts in terms of Chinese sericulture rites. In the *Nihon shoki*, for instance, we are told that the Yamato ruler Yūryaku instituted sericulture rites in which a royal consort was required to personally feed mulberry leaves to silkworms at the start of the third month.[15] Such rites were practiced in China even at the time of the composition of the *Nihon shoki*; the *Chiu T'ang shu,* for instance, records that even Empress Wu Tse-t'ien (reigned 690–705) fed silkworms in this manner during the reign of her husband Kao-zu.[16] All of this thus suggests that by the time of the composition of the *Nihon shoki* in 720 the court was well aware of the special association of royal consorts and even empresses with silkworms and sericulture within Chinese court ritual. As such ritual associations came to inform even legends of courtship among rulers and their consorts, the tropes and legends from the Chinese festival calendar came to pervade even the purportedly native poetry and legends of the period.

One example of the degree to which technological processes and cosmological concerns were intertwined can be seen in an entry in the *Rites of Chou* that states that the Chou banned the "double cultivation" of silkworm cocoons during a single year.[17] The reasons for this interdiction are discussed in the *Sou shen chi*, a Chinese tale collection from the fifth century:

> The Book of Silkworms says, "When the moon is in the position of great fire, then [fire] pervades its nature. The silkworm and the horse are of the same character." In the *Rites of Chou* it is written that the Master of the Horse Stables "forbade the double cultivation of silkworms." The note says, "Two things [within the same classificatory group] cannot predominate [at the same time]. The double cultivation of silkworms was forbidden because this would harm horses."[18]

This rather remarkable text illustrates the degree to which technical knowledge concerning the raising of silkworms was implicated in broader cosmological and cultic systems. Here we find that double cultivation of silkworms was conceived of in terms of astral cults and five phases (*wu hsing*) thought. Such concerns were so established in China that they persisted for centuries after the court of Suiko began to integrate such beliefs into the daily rhythms of life in the Japanese islands.

This broader cosmological framework is of central importance for understanding the cultic effects of the transmission of sericulture. Although, given modern prejudices, it is perhaps natural to view production processes almost exclusively in terms of technology, the above text demonstrates that sericulture during the period involved much more than proper techniques for using land, cultivating mulberry trees, and raising silkworms. It also required knowledge of deities, rites, and legends, not only those associated with weaving and silkworms, and their relationships to all other elements of the cosmos.

Silkworms and Immortality

It is therefore not surprising that the court's preoccupation with sericulture appears to have been matched by an equally powerful interest in silkworm cults among the populace. Indeed, silkworms were the object of considerable cultic attention in both China and Japan throughout the premodern period. As silkworms were the source of silk and, by extension, prosperity, this ritual focus is perhaps not surprising. Evidence of one such cult can be found in the Kaiko no Yashiro (Silkworm shrine), a Hata cultic center in Yamashiro province that housed a silkworm deity.[19]

The life cycle of silkworms, exhibiting as it did a three-stage process of birth, "death" within the cocoon, and "rebirth" as a moth, also presented a powerful metaphor for immortality and resurrection. One of the earliest indications that such associations were widespread in the Japanese islands can be found in a *Nihon shoki* entry:

> A man from the eastern lands in the area of the Fuji river named Ōfube no Ōshi encouraged the people in the villages to worship an insect, saying "This is the god of the everlasting world [*tokoyo no kami*]. If you worship this god, it will bring you wealth and long life." Shamans pretended to receive oracles saying, "If [they] worship the *tokoyo no kami*, the poor will become wealthy and the old will return to youth." They thus increasingly encouraged the people to throw away their household valuables, and line up *sake*, vegetables, and the six domestic animals by the roadsides. They also had them cry out, "The new wealth is coming!" People in the capital and the countryside took the *tokoyo* insect and installed it on sanctified platforms. They sang and danced for wealth and threw away their treasures without obtaining any benefit. The loss and waste were extreme.
>
> At this Hata no Miyatsuko no Kawakatsu from Kadono, hating to see the people so deluded, killed Ōfube no Ōshi. The shamans were frightened by this and ceased encouraging the cult. The people of the time thus made a song, singing:
>
>> "It's a god, a god!"
>> So came its fame resounding
>> But Uzumasa
>> Has struck down and punished it
>> That god of the Everworld [*tokoyo*].
>
> This insect usually breeds on the *tachibana* (Japanese orange) or *hosoki* trees. It is over four inches in length and its thickness is about that of a thumb. It is green colored with black spots and in every way resembles a silkworm.[20]

This passage is notable not only for the expectation that the god of immortality will appear in a form that "in every way resembles a silkworm," but also for the fact that the lone description in the court chronicles of a mass religious movement suggests a strong popular awareness of silkworm cults and deities. It would thus appear that one by-product of the introduction of sericulture into the Japanese islands was a powerful awareness of silkworm deities and a widespread linkage of the silkworm with popular aspirations for both prosperity and eternal life. All of this thus once again suggests that long before the completion of the *Nihon shoki* in 720, continental material culture had already produced dramatic changes in the popular religious imagination.

The linkage between sericulture and immortality may also be seen in the pervasive literary motif of the female immortal who appears on earth in the form of a weaving maiden. As we saw in Chapter 3, one of the best-known such figures was Tsuminoe no Hijiri Hime (literally: Immortal Mulberry-branch Maiden), a female immortal from Yoshino who is repeatedly referenced in the poetry of the period. This maiden was said to have assumed the form of a mulberry branch floating in a mountain stream in Yoshino, only to be forced to marry a human male who had discovered the magic garment that allowed her to fly between heaven and earth. Because Tsuminoe no Hijiri Hime is said to have ultimately recovered her cloak and returned to heaven, the legend, as told from the point of view of the husband, featured prominently in poetry expressing regret over lost love.[21]

One example of how motifs drawn from legends of figures such as Tsuminoe no Hijiri Hime came to pervade the poetic vocabulary of the period can be seen in the following poem attributed in the *Nihon shoki* to the ruler Nintoku. The poem is set within the context of a legend in which Nintoku seeks to repair relations with his estranged chief consort, Iwa no Hime:

The Emperor launched on the river and betook himself to Yamashiro.
Just then a mulberry branch floated by. The Emperor saw the mulberry branch and sang:

> Vine-swarming
> Rock Princess Iwa no Hime
> Not indifferently
> Will hear of you
> Leafy mulberry tree:
> You shouldn't go near them

> All those bending river bends
> But you round them every one
> Leafy mulberry tree.[22]

This poem, which somewhat improbably posits a relationship between Iwa no Hime and a mulberry branch floating in a river, brings to mind the following poem from the *Manyōshū*, in which Tsuminoe no Hijiri Hime's benighted husband is said to recollect Tsuminoe no Hijiri Hime's first appearance on earth as a mulberry branch in a river at Yoshino:

> If this evening
> A branch of wild mulberry
> Should come floating by,
> I've set no traps to catch it in,
> And it might get away.[23]

Given the thematic similarities between these two poems, it would appear either that the two poems were unrelated, in which case they serve to illustrate the widespread degree to which continental tropes concerning women and sericulture had penetrated the poetic imagination of the age, or the editors of the *Nihon shoki* consciously utilized a poem rooted in the Tsuminoe no Hijiri Hime legend cycle in order to evoke Nintoku's regret at his separation from his wife. If this is in fact the case, then the use of such imagery suggests that by the time of its composition the *Nihon shoki*'s editors could be confident that the Tsuminoe no Hijiri Hime legend cycle would be well known to their readers. This is especially important because, unlike the legend concerning Yūryaku's establishment of Chinese-based rites of sericulture, Nintoku's poem is based upon references to a female immortal who was a fixture of indigenous legends.

Crawling and Calling Out

These allusions to female immortals in the depiction of Iwa no Hime are especially important because of a series of poems and legends recounting episodes from the stormy relationship between Nintoku and Iwa no Hime that feature the following rite of prostration and calling out:

> As Kuchiko sang his song, a great rain began to fall. Without trying to avoid the rain, he prostrated himself before the front door of the hall. The queen consort [then] went out to the back door. He went and

prostrated himself before the back door of the hall, and she went back out to the front. As he crawled back and forth and prostrated himself in the courtyard, the water came up to his waist. At the time, the Omi was wearing a red sash with a green garment. As the water reached the sash, the green all turned red.

Now Kuchiko's younger sister Kuchihime was in the service of the queen consort. Kuchihime thus made a song, saying:

> My lord and elder brother,
> Calling out [*mono mōsu*] in the palace
> At Tsutsuki in Yamashiro.
> Is on the verge of tears.[24]

This unusual legend again illustrates the degree to which the transformation in court ritual in the Suiko period was reflected in royal ancestral legends by the advent of the Nara period. Here Kuchiko's prostration before the queen consort appears to be a direct reflection of the adoption of Chinese court ritual, which would have required this expression of reverence before a queen consort. A more subtle suggestion of the influence of the new court decorum can also be found in the text's depiction of Kuchiko's attire; the envoy's green robes and red sash correspond precisely with the prescribed coloring for the ritual garb for *onmyōdō* ritualists at both the T'ang and Nara courts.[25] Details such as these thus suggest that this legend was composed after the penetration of the ritual practices and legends associated with the Chinese calendar into the Japanese islands in the first quarter of the seventh century.

Other elements of Kuchiko's behavior, however, cannot be accounted for simply in terms of continental forms of court etiquette. The text's assertion that Kuchiko actually crawled back and forth in Iwa no Hime's courtyard, for instance, appears unrelated to the court decorum adopted by Suiko. Such crawling resonates strongly, however, with indigenous funerary practices before the body or tomb of a recently deceased figure. Shinkawa suggests, therefore, that Kuchiko's actions may also have been related to ritual gestures associated with death and resurrection.[26]

Several clues as to how Kuchiko's crawling might have been related to early death rituals can be seen in the legend of the death and resurrection of yet another Wani ancestor, the prince Yamato Takeru. Because the *Nihon shoki* version of this legend shows the prince achieving resurrection in terms closely resembling those in legends of Chinese immortals, this legend is also often cited as a prime example of Taoist influences in early

Japanese religion.[27] Of particular note is the *Kojiki*'s account of the reaction of Yamato Takeru's family to his death:

> Thereupon his consorts who lived in Yamato, and all his children, came down and made him a tomb. Crawling around in the muddy paddies, they cried and sang:
>
> > In the sticky fields
> > In among the stalks of rice,
> > Among the rice stalks,
> > We crawl around and around
> > Creepers of wild yam . . .
>
> These four songs were all sung at his funeral. Thus even unto today they sing these songs at an Emperor's funeral.[28]

This text is notable for its assertion that the songs calling back the spirit of the deceased were an established part of royal funerary rites by the early Nara period. Shinkawa notes that one of the best-known examples of this practice can be found in the *Nihon shoki* account of the origins of death, in which the deity Izanagi crawls about the head and feet of his deceased wife Izanami before he undertakes to bring her back from the underworld:[29]

> When it was time for the fire god Kagutsuchi to be born, his mother Izanami was burned and died. Izanagi no Mikoto said bitterly: "[I have] exchanged the sister that I love for just one child!" He then crawled about at her head and feet, wailing and shedding tears.[30]

When read against legends such as these, the legend of Kuchiko's crawling about the queen consort's courtyard in *onmyōdō* ritual garb in order to call out the queen consort Iwa no Hime, suggests the intriguing possibility that ritual/literary tropes for calling to the spirits of the dead may have come to influence even the tales of courtship between rulers and consorts that dot the pages of the court chronicles.

Silkworms, Weavers, and Calling Out

Fortunately, several clues as to the nature and role of such tropes can be seen in two further legends from the court chronicles that feature the motif of a ritualist/envoy seeking to call out an imperial consort. The most developed of these concerns the efforts of the royal envoy Nakatomi no Ikatsu, who is sent by the ruler Ingyō to summon Sotōri Iratsume (Otohime), the sister of Ingyō's chief consort. Otohime, fearful of her sister's jealousy, is at first reluctant to appear before the ruler:

> Hereupon Ikatsu no Omi, having received his orders, retired. Hiding provisions in his clothing, he went to Sakata and prostrated himself in Otohime's courtyard, saying, "By command of the Emperor, I call you." Otohime answered, "How could I not reverentially receive the command of the Emperor? I but wish to not harm the feelings of the queen consort. [Therefore] even though it cost me my life, I will not go back [to the Emperor].
>
> At this Ikatsu no Omi replied "Your servant has already received a royal command—I must bring you back. If you do not come, I will surely be judged to be guilty [of negligence]. Rather than returning and being executed, I would rather die prostrate in this courtyard." At this he then lay prostrate in the courtyard for seven days, and though they offered him food and drink, he did not partake. [Instead] he secretly ate from the provisions that he had concealed.
>
> At this Otohime thought "Due to the queen consort's jealousy I have already disobeyed the Emperor's command, and my lord, who is a faithful minister, will die. This too will be my fault." She therefore decided to go back with Ikatsu.[31]

This legend closely resembles that in which the envoy Kuchiko calls out the Queen Consort Iwa no Hime.[32] Further thematic similarities can be seen elsewhere in the legend cycle of Ingyō and Otohime/Sotōri's courtship, where we again find what appear to be references to Chinese rites and practices related to sericulture. Consider, for instance, the following passage from the *Nihon shoki*:

> In the eighth year, spring, the second month, he [the Emperor] went to Fujiwara and secretly observed the demeanor of Lady Sotōri. That evening Lady Sotōri was alone, yearning for the Emperor. Unaware that the Emperor had come, she composed a song, saying:
>
>> Tonight is the night
>> My young love will come to me:
>> Little bamboo crab
>> Spider's antics make it clear,
>> Oh, very clear tonight!

The Emperor was moved on hearing this song, and composed a song of his own:

> Fine-patterned
> Sashes of brocade undone,
> Lying at our ease,
> Many times we have not slept—
> Only for a single night.[33]

Although the editors of the Nihon koten bungaku taikei edition of the *Nihon shoki* gloss Sotōri Itatsume's poem as referring somewhat incongruously to a spider web on an umbrella, Hirabayashi has suggested that it refers to a common divination practice performed on the evening of the *tanabata* festival.[34] This practice is described in the *Ching ch'u sui shih chi*, a late sixth-century text detailing the popular ritual calendar of southern China:

> On this evening housewives tie colored threads [with which] they thread needles with seven holes, some of which are made of gold, silver, or precious stones. They place fruits in the courtyard and pray for skill [in weaving]. They are happy if a spider weaves a web on the fruit, which they interpret as an [auspicious] sign.[35]

Because the *Ching ch'u sui shih chi* was composed only slightly before the Suiko court adopted the Chinese festival calendar, the court was almost certainly aware of such rites. Further evidence for this can be seen in physical items from the period: sets of just such colored balls of yarn and ritual needles preserved in the Shōsōin storehouse in Nara demonstrate that such rites were performed in Japan as well as in China.[36]

Further allusions to *tanabata* motifs centering on the annual meeting of the Weaver Maiden and Cowherd can be found within other poems from the Otohime/Sotōri poem cycle. Although we are told in the text that Otohime is unaware that Ingyō is near, in the poem she declares, "This is the night my husband will come." Ingyō's reference to a meeting of lovers for "but one night only" is also inexplicable outside of the context of the *tanabata* rites, which celebrate the annual meeting of the Weaver and Cowherd for a single night. All of this thus again highlights the importance of Chinese weaving cults and myths for the text's horizon of reception, for once again the editors of the *Nihon shoki* appear to be quoting a widely known Chinese tradition of ritual and legend in order to convey both the expectation and sorrow felt by this royal ancestor and his newly acquired consort.

Perhaps the most conclusive evidence that this legend cycle was conceived in terms related to sericulture and weaving cults, however, can be found in the following poem, in which Iwa no Hime refers explicitly to herself and her rival as silkworms:

> Summer crawlers,
> Silkworms that make double clothes:
> Wearing two layers,
> Sleeping snug and bundled up—
> Oh, no, that can't be right![37]

Although this legend is usually glossed as a protest against Nintoku's keeping two lovers, there can be no doubt that rites and practices associated with sericulture were essential background elements. One important clue may be found in the allusion to the insect "wearing double garments." Assuming that this indicates a silkworm in its cocoon, the text's protest against double garments would suggest some connection with the Chinese interdiction of the double cultivation of silkworms.[38]

These references, when taken together, suggest that the editors of the *Nihon shoki* deliberately highlighted Chinese tropes derived from weaving and sericulture as they set down a cluster of legends centered upon the calling out of royal consorts. Although the limited scope and nature of these sources allows for few definitive conclusions, the familiarity with Chinese cultic practices that these allusions demonstrate strongly suggests that the adoption of the Chinese festival calendar had by the Nara period given rise to a broader poetic and ritual vocabulary that informed even the supposedly native legends and rites of the period.

Nurinomi and the "Insect of the Three Transformations"

Fortunately, much more solid evidence concerning the nature and extent of the court's interest in Chinese silkworm cults can be found in the conclusion to the *Kojiki* account of the Wani ancestor Kuchiko's attempt to call out the Queen Consort Iwa no Hime from the home of one Nurinomi, an immigrant woman from the Korean peninsula who raises silkworms:

> Then Kuchiko no Omi, his younger sister Kuchi Hime and Nurinomi discussed [the situation] all three [together], and sent word to the Emperor saying "The reason for the queen consort's journey is [to

be found] in some insects that Nurinomi is rearing. These marvelous insects at one time are crawling insects, at one time are cocoons, and one time become [like] flying birds—[they are] marvelous insects of three transformations and colors. She has come here simply to see these insects. She has no strange intentions." When they had made this report, the Emperor said, "If that is the case, then I wish to go and see these [insects], as I think they [must be] strange and marvelous."[39]

Set in the Tsutsuki district of Yamashiro province, a stronghold of both the Wani and the Hata kinship groups, this text displays several familiar literary tropes. The image of an immigrant from the Korean peninsula introducing members of the court to the process of raising silkworms appears emblematic of the broader process by which sericulture came to be introduced into the Japanese islands.

More concretely, however, the passage also suggests how and why Chinese silkworm cults came to be related to the legends of calling out. Here the text explicitly pairs the motif of the Wani ancestor calling out a queen consort with an image of a queen consort shut in an enclosure watching silkworms. Since we have already seen that the Nara court was keenly aware of Chinese court rituals that required the queen consort to perform just this role, this text is almost certainly yet another instance of the Nara court representing itself and its ancestors on the basis of Chinese ritual paradigms related to sericulture.

Even more important than the content of the legend, however, are the textual sources upon which it is based; this legend demonstrates an awareness on the part of the Nara court of popular Chinese silkworm cults that cannot be traced to classical poetic sources. Here Nurinomi is not depicted in the vocabulary of the *Book of Rites* "encouraging the silk industry"; rather, she is extolling the silkworm's strange and wondrous powers to die and then be reborn. Especially notable in this regard is Nurinomi's use of the phrase "transformations in three colors" in reference to the silkworm. This phrase appears closely related to a passage from the *Po wu chih*, a third-century Chinese gazetteer that also refers to the silkworm as the insect of "three transformations."[40] Although the legend may have little basis as historical fact, it strongly suggests that the editors of the *Nihon shoki* were familiar with popular conceptions of silkworms in China. If we assume that such allusions formed part of a broader conceptual vocabulary familiar to the text's readers, then it would appear that the miraculous ability of the silkworms to "die" within cocoons only to be reborn was a cause for wonder not only among millennial movements in the countryside, but also among the literate members of the court.

Crucially, this motif of the silkworm as the insect of "three transformations" was enshrined prominently in the popular Chinese festival calendar on the fifteenth day of the first month of the year. This date, which marked the ritual end of the New Year, was a period when the spirits of the dead were thought to be capable of returning to visit the living. Known as the first of the "three origins" (Ch. *san yuan*), it was also thought to mark a major turning point from which events of the coming year were thought to flow. As a result, on this day, as throughout the New Year's period, rites of divination for the following year were performed along with rites for the spirits of ancestors and other household deities.[41]

Because the fifteenth day of the first month of the year also marked the first full moon of the year, this date was also closely associated with the lunar cult and women. In China these resonances eventually led to a bifurcation of ritual along gender lines, with woman participating in cultic activities on the fifteenth day of the first month and men participating in cultic activities for the stove god in the twelfth month.[42] In the midst of this confluence of rites of gender, divination, and spirit worship, was a series of rites designed to call out the spirits of female deities associated with silkworms. According to the *Ching ch'u sui shih chi,* these began during the day with a rite that called out mice, which were perceived to be the enemy of the "silkworm which ages three times."[43]

These rites were followed with a further set designed to call out a lavatory/sericulture goddess, one of the most important female deities in China during the period in question. As we saw in Chapter 5, motifs related to this deity appear to have been embedded in the ancestral legends of several lineages at court. Equally important, much as Iwa no Hime and Sotōri Iratsuhime were called out by Nakatomi and Wani ancestors dressed in T'ang ritual garb, popular Chinese cultic practices on the evening of the fifteenth day of the first month centered upon the calling out of the spirit of the lavatory goddess for the purpose of divining the year's yield of silk:

> On this evening they welcome Tzu-ku, and divine [the amount of] their future silks and other affairs. According to Lui Ching-shu's *Yi yuan*, Tzu-ku was originally somebody's concubine. The first wife was jealous of her. On the fifteenth day of the first month, she died from grief and humiliation. For this reason people make images of her and receive her, saying a spell. . . . If [the doll] becomes heavy, then the goddess has come.[44]

In light of the fact that the *Ching ch'u sui shih chi* was composed at virtually the same time that the Suiko court was first receiving envoys from the Sui court, it should not be surprising that rites associated with sericulture that were performed on one of the most important days in the Chinese yearly ritual cycle may have influenced the mythic and ritual life in the Japanese islands in the decades that led to the composition of the court chronicles. On these days women across China not only performed rites of divination designed to maximize the number of silkworms that would come to them during the coming year, they also called out of an enclosure the spirit of a silkworm goddess. By the Nara period, such motifs were part of the basic conceptual vocabulary in terms of which past rulers such as Yūryaku and Ingyō as well as their consorts were represented in the newly minted chronicles of the court.

None of this is to say that figures such as Iwa no Hime or Nurinome exercised great influence over the development of the religious institutions of Nara Japan. Rather, these and other such figures are of interest for what they reveal about the sources for the construction of the tropes of kingship and courtship during the period. By the Nara period, the trope of the weaver maiden/consort feeding mulberry leaves to the "insect of three transformations" had penetrated not only the Chinese-style poetry of court intellectuals, but also the verse and narratives recording local legends and courtly romances from a past that never was. As the mysterious silkworm fascinated not only silk-clad courtiers but also the desperate followers of millennial movements, sericulture rites and tropes from the continent became fixtures in the conceptual universe that shaped the pillars of Nara Japan.

Conclusion

The adoption of the Chinese festival calendar was part of a broader cultural and political transformation that saw not only the expansion of the power of the rulers of the Yamato plain, but also a transformation in the means by which that power was understood and represented. Among the most important elements allowing for the expansion of the wealth and power of these rulers was the introduction of manufacturing technologies from the continent. These technologies, central to political and economic life in both China and the Japanese islands, were also heavily represented in the rites and legends associated with the Chinese calendar. As a result, many of the cultic practices adopted by the Suiko court were built not only upon conceptions of *yin* and *yang* and so forth, but also upon what at the time was considered best practice in the crafts and industries that made courtly life possible. Thus as the Yamato court adopted the Chinese festival calendar, it not only promoted new modes of governance, it also furthered the ritual program associated with the crafts and industries that formed a major part of its economic foundation.

Among the many by-products of this confluence of influences in ritual, craft, and poetry was a transformation in the way women were represented by both poets and chroniclers. Thus throughout the court chronicles as well as in the poetry of the age we find repeated references to women as weaving maidens, immortals, or even, as we have seen, as mulberry branches and silkworms. One further corollary of this process involved envoys sent to call out royal consorts and queen consorts from ritual enclosures where they claimed, among other things, to be tending silkworms.

These legends of calling out are immediately relevant to the question of how continental motifs of immortality and resurrection came to occupy such a large place in the literature of the period. Although it would be foolish to draw firm conclusions based on such a small sampling of texts, the above poems and legends suggest that the horizon of reception for the poems and legends of the age was substantially influenced by the diffusion of sericulture and the adoption of the Chinese festival calendar. Thus even as the metaphor of the silkworm undergoing three transformations resonated among members of the mass millennial cult of Ōfube no Ōshi, so too did figures such as Tsuminoe no Hijiri Hime and Tzu-ku come to haunt the poetic and mythic vocabulary of the Nara court. As a result, a new template for the formation of purportedly native rites and legends pervaded the Land of Eight Islands.

By the advent of the Nara period this process had become so advanced as to fundamentally reshape many of the most important institutions of early Japanese religion. In the following chapter we examine how the material and technological revolution that swept the Japanese islands directly influenced the formation of the cult of Amaterasu, the principal ancestor of the royal line.

CHAPTER 7

Silkworm Cults in the Heavenly Grotto
Amaterasu and the Children of Ama no Hoakari

IN THE DECADES following the Suiko court's decision to actively promulgate continentally inspired court ritual and the Chinese festival calendar, successive rulers worked at expanding an extensive program of bureaucratic and ritual innovations that were in large part rooted in continental conceptions of divination, spirit pacification, and sage kingship. By the reign of Tenmu *tennō*, one important element was the development of ancestral rites and legends for the freshly minted *tennō* at the apex of the newly constituted organs of government. Accompanying this shift was an increased focus within the royal cult on the Ise shrine and the figure of Amaterasu, who was promoted aggressively by Tenmu and his descendants as the main royal ancestor.[1]

Although there is a great deal of debate as to when and why the figure of Amaterasu came to occupy an important position in the royal cult, there can be little doubt that Tenmu and his successors were determined to underscore her importance as the chief ancestor of the ruling line. In the *Nihon shoki* we are told that Tenmu revived the custom of sending a consecrated princess to reside at Ise after a lapse of fifty years. Similarly, Tenmu's consort and successor, Jitō, is said to have taken the unprecedented step of personally visiting the Ise shrine. Not long after Tenmu's death, the status of Amaterasu as paramount royal ancestor was manifested institutionally by the Department of Rites (Jingikan), which oversaw a yearly cycle of rites for the court that were heavily focused on the connection between the *tennō* and the royal ancestor at Ise. All of this suggests that representations of Amaterasu in court ritual and the court chronicles were being constructed and modified at a time when the court was also actively embracing legends of female immortals and continental conceptions of astrology.

Given the importance of the Ise cult for Tenmu, whose reign in many ways appears to have been a political and cultic watershed in the history of the Japanese islands, it is perhaps not surprising that scholarship of early *kami* worship in the Japanese islands has been heavily oriented towards the study of the royal cult in general and the Ise shrine in particular. While it would be unfair to say that local lineages and cults have been completely ignored, it is nonetheless the case that local or nonroyal cultic concerns during the period tend to be discussed mainly in terms of how they shed light upon the development of Ise and the royal cult.

In this chapter I propose to reverse this orientation. Although cultic influence is often assumed to have emanated from the court out towards the periphery, I argue that the cult of Amaterasu and court rites (*jingi*) of the period can in many ways be viewed as epiphenomena rooted in deeper cultic movements that were sweeping across the Japanese islands even prior to Tenmu's reign. As we have seen repeatedly, many of the most important cultic developments of the age were stimulated by cultural and political contacts with the Korean peninsula and by the activities of immigrant lineages that took up residence in the Japanese islands. Although, given the nature of the textual sources available to us, it is not possible to ignore the cultic activities of the court, I take the rites and legends associated with Amaterasu and the Ise shrine as a point of departure, not an endpoint for my inquiry. One central premise in this approach is the belief that the *jingi* rites and mythic paradigms of the post-Tenmu court were not created ex nihilo, but through the appropriation and transformation of pre-existing mythic and ritual resources. In the pages that follow, I examine this process through a discussion of the well-known myth of the Heavenly Grotto and its relationship to the Chinkonsai and the Ōharae, two of the most important rites of the post-Tenmu court.[2]

Isolating important moments of cultic appropriation in the court-sponsored textual corpus requires simultaneously pursuing several distinct, though closely related tracks. Much of this chapter focuses on three lineages that appear to have retained distinct cultic and mythic traditions even as they enjoyed close relations with the Yamato rulers during the sixth century. One lineage, the Owari Muraji, claimed descent from the god Ama no Hoakari no Mikoto, a deity whose cult appears to have been closely related to the nascent cults of Amaterasu and of Yamato Takeru, an ancestor of considerable mythic importance by the time of the Tenmu court. The legend cycle of Yamato Takeru is of particular interest not only for its intimate connection with Ise mythology, but also because it prominently features the motifs of death and resurrection that also appear in the legend of the Heavenly Grotto. There is also extensive evidence that both the Ise cult and the cult of Yamato Takeru experienced rapid development in the latter half of the seventh century.

I also focus on the cultic activities of the Wani, another lineage that claimed descent from Ama no Hoakari no Mikoto. As in the case of the Owari Muraji, in both the *Kojiki* and the *Nihon shoki* the Wani are said to have provided consorts for several rulers during the fifth and sixth centuries, when successive monarchs located their courts in the region of Kawachi province. As we saw in Chapter 6, Wani consorts also appear in several legends of rulers calling out consorts in terms derived from continental legends related to weaving and sericulture. The Wani also feature prominently in our discussion because Prince Yamato Takeru himself was said to be the child of a Wani mother, and because the Wani appear to have repeatedly incorporated continental-style motifs of death and resurrection into their ancestral legends.

Finally, a great deal of this chapter involves discussion of the cultic practices of the Mononobe, a lineage that we have already encountered in a variety of contexts ranging from the founding legend of Japanese Buddhism to the mythic origins of the Miwa shrine. The Mononobe make an ideal subject of study for several reasons. As we have already seen, they are known to have played a major role in the political and military life of the Yamato court from at least the time of the Yamato ruler Wakateru until the demise of the main Mononobe line at the hands of the Soga in 584. There is also ample evidence that by the sixth century the Mononobe had developed their own distinctive cultic and mythic traditions and that they played a prominent role in the cultic life of the sixth, seventh, and eighth centuries. Because there exist from the Nara and early Heian periods a substantial number of legends and documents related to the Mononobe, it is also possible to speak with greater confidence about the cultic practices of the Mononobe than for most other lineages.

In addition, during the sixth century the Mononobe are known to have played an important role in the turbulent relations between the Yamato court and the Korean peninsula, and they appear to have been closely connected with numerous immigrant lineages that claimed to descend from Mononobe ancestors. The Mononobe thus appear to have been ideally placed to serve as a conduit for the diffusion of cultic influences from the Korean peninsula to the royal cult and across the Japanese islands. Some of the most powerful of these cultic influences were rooted in continental rites and legends concerned with resurrection, spirit-quieting, and the origins of sericulture. These cults and legends served as important pillars not only for major *jingi* rites such as the Chinkonsai and the Ōharae, but also for the cults of the main deities of the inner and outer Ise shrines.

The Heavenly Grotto Myth and the Post-Tenmu Royal Cult

In the pages that follow much of my discussion will focus on questions concerning how and to what degree rites and legends related to spirit-quieting, sun deities, and resurrection from across the Japanese islands may have helped shape the well-known legend of the Heavenly Grotto, in which the sun goddess Amaterasu hides herself in a cave, only to be lured out by a multitude of deities who are urgently seeking to bring the light of the sun back into the world. Because this legend served as an emphatic statement of Amaterasu no Ōmikami's paramount status among the gods, there is a general consensus that it most likely took final shape around Tenmu's reign, as Amaterasu came to be a central focus within the royal cult.

Although I have referred to the Heavenly Grotto myth as a single entity, it is important to note that the legend is rather long and appears in several variants in the *Kojiki* and *Nihon shoki*. As a careful discussion of each variant is well beyond the parameters of this book, I shall restrict my discussion to the following elements, each of which appears in several—though not necessarily all—of the variants. Again my purpose is not to try to combine these elements to determine one basic outlook for the court, but rather to situate these mythic and ritual tropes within a broader context of practices and beliefs associated with lineages and cultic centers throughout the Japanese islands:

1. The deity Susanoo storms up to the Heavenly Plain to see his sister, the sun deity Amaterasu. Unsure of her brother's intentions, Amaterasu puts on a suit of armor and awaits her brother, weapons in hand.
2. Susanoo no Mikoto challenges Amaterasu to a contest in which each seeks to produce more children than the other. Amaterasu produces three, while Susanoo produces five.
3. Susanoo unilaterally claims victory in the contest and goes on a rampage in which he commits various depredations, including filling in ditches and destroying ridges in the fields.
4. Amaterasu, in contrast to her brother's antisocial behavior, is depicted as preparing for the Niinamesai, a harvest rite and one of the most important events in the court's ritual calendar. As part of this preparation, Amaterasu enters a ritual weaving chamber where she sits at a loom and begins making special woven items to be used as offerings in the Niiname rites.

5. Susanoo, still on a rampage, throws feces into the weaving chamber, thereby defiling it. He also flays a piebald horse "in the reverse direction" and throws the carcass into the weaving chamber.
6. In some versions of the legend, Amaterasu, outraged, impales herself upon her shuttle. Her spirit enters the Heavenly Grotto, and perpetual night settles over the earth.[3]
7. The other gods seek to lure Amaterasu out by hanging ritual implements such as special woven cloth (*shidori*), clay implements, jewels, and mirrors outside of the cave.
8. The ancestral deities of important ritual lineages at Ise make ritual offerings. The goddess leaves the cave, however, only after she hears the other gods laughing as the goddess Uzume Hime performs a lewd dance near the cave.[4]
9. The other gods then seize Susanoo, perform a rite of purification (*harae*), and banish him to the underworld.[5]

For many years the dominant approach to this and virtually every other myth in the court chronicles was that of scholars such as Okada Seishi, who viewed the Heavenly Grotto myth as the origin of such court rituals as the Ōharae (Rite of Great Purification) and the Chinkonsai (Rite of Spirit-quieting). Most likely due to a tacit assumption that court texts such as the *Kojiki* and *Nihon shoki* represented two examples of a single, unified royal ideology, Okada often either glossed over important discrepancies between the texts of the *Nihon shoki* and the *Kojiki* or treated them as simply reflecting different stages in the development of royal myth. This approach has been criticized by scholars such as Kōnoshi Takamitsu, who has argued forcefully that Okada fundamentally misunderstand not only the distinct ideological agenda of each text, but also their relationship to the development of court rituals such as the Ōharae and the Chinkonsai. Rather than treat differences between the texts as markers of historical development, Kōnoshi argues that they are best understood as indications of divergent ideological agendas.[6]

Somewhat more controversially, Kōnoshi has also argued against seeking the roots of such rites as the Ōharae and Chinkonsai in the myths and legends of the court chronicles. He writes:

> The *Kojiki* recounts the establishment of the existing world order, beginning with the formation of the world, while the ritsuryō rituals attempt to guarantee the orderly procession of the seasons. Until now, all of these (*Kojiki*, *Nihon shoki*, and norito) were seen as part of a

single, preexisting mythology, but a single, unified mythology was created only *after* the writing of the *Kojiki* and the *Nihon shoki*....

These various elements—as represented by the *Kojiki*, the *Nihon shoki*, and actual ritual practice—formed more or less independently, possessing characteristics that could not be completely reconciled with each other.[7]

Regardless of whether Kōnoshi is correct in asserting that the ideological agendas of the *Kojiki, Nihon shoki,* and the *jingi* rites of the court formed independently and in the service of different agendas, it is far more important for our purposes that each element developed against a horizon in which numerous lineages and shrines at court and across the Japanese islands engaged in rites of purification (*harae*), spirit-quieting (*chinkon*) and spirit-shaking (*tama furi*). As we shall see, the ancestral legends of several of these lineages involved motifs of resurrection and the worship of sun deities. Thus, rather than simply asserting that the ideological agenda of the *Nihon shoki* differed from that of the *Kojiki*, which may or may not have been so, I focus on the multiple voices, conflicts, and redundancies that exist in each of these texts and between them.

Much of my discussion also centers on the relationship between the mythologies of the *Nihon shoki* and *Kojiki* on the one hand and court rituals such as the Ōharae and the Chinkonsai on the other. Addressing such connections is essential if for no other reason than the fact that several of the most important of the royal myths, including the myth of the Heavenly Grotto, make explicit reference to court rituals. Consider, for instance, the following passage from the *Kojiki*, which states that rites of "great purification" (*ōharae*) were ordered across the land after the Yamato ruler Chūai was struck down by wrathful deities in northern Kyūshū:

> Taking up sacred objects [*ōnusa*], they performed a rite of great purification [*ōharae*] [after first] seeking out [instances of] such sins as flaying [animals] alive, flaying backwards, destroying boundary ridges and filling in ditches in the fields, defilement through defecation, illicit relations between parent and child, and marriages to horses, cows, and chickens and dogs.[8]

As numerous scholars have noted, the sins addressed in this liturgy closely match the actions of Susanoo in the Heavenly Grotto myth—so much so, in fact, that the text is simply not comprehensible without reference to the Heavenly Grotto legend.[9]

In contrast to the explicit references to the Niinamesai and rites of "great purification," the first use of the term "Chinkonsai," or "Rite of Spirit-quieting" is thought to have been not in the *Kojiki* or the *Nihon shoki*, but in the Taihō law codes, which were composed in 701. In the *Nihon shoki*, however, we do find reference to a "Rite of Spirit-calling" (Shōkonsai) that was performed by the monk Hōzō for the ailing ruler Tenmu. There is thus a great deal of room for interpretation concerning purpose and origins. Matsumae, for instance, notes that the *Ryō no gige*, a commentary on the Taihō and Yōrō law codes that was completed in 833, states that the purpose of the Chinkonsai was to ensure the health of the ruler by reviving his spirit and recalling it to his body should it start to wander.[10] Others, such as Watanabe Katsuyoshi, have seen the rite as an important ceremony of kingship, in which the spirits of former rulers would be quieted.[11] Fortunately, given the mythic and ritual complexities associated with the Chinkonsai, it is not necessary for our purposes to try to isolate the "real" meaning of the rite. Indeed, in light of the extensive historical layering in both the ritual and the legend, it is extremely doubtful that any single meaning for the ritual can be adduced.[12]

I shall therefore restrict much of my discussion of the Heavenly Grotto myth to one aspect that has received considerable attention from Matsumae Takeshi, who argues that in a least some variants Amaterasu is clearly represented as having died and then come back to life. In support of this view, Matsumae notes that this is the position of the earliest commentaries that we have on the Chinkonsai and that the expression *"iwa gakuri,"* used in the *Nihon shoki* for the goddess's entry into the cave, is also used in the *Manyōshū* as a euphemism for death.[13] Matsumae also notes that the timing of the Chinkonsai in the court's ritual calendar corresponds precisely with the rite of spirit-calling that was performed by the monk Hōzō just prior to Tenmu's death. In addition, there is excellent textual evidence suggesting that the Mononobe also practiced a *chinkon* rite that was explicitly concerned with "shaking" or reviving the spirit of the ruler and thereby restoring health and life.

These observations underscore the fact that neither the many variants of the Heavenly Grotto myth nor such rites as the Ōharae and the Chinkonsai were created in isolation. Indeed, as we shall see repeatedly, there is powerful evidence that the Heavenly Grotto myth and the Ōharae and the Chinkonsai developed in conjunction with, and in response to, similar cultic beliefs and practices of kinship groups throughout the Japanese islands. When viewed as sites of appropriation and contestation, these and other rites and legends of the court thus promise to help us glimpse, albeit indirectly, powerful cultic concerns and influences that resonated from Kyūshū all the way to the Yamato plain.

Takami Musubi, Ama no Hoakari, and Early Sun Cults

An ideal way to approach the Heavenly Grotto myth is to observe that there was not one but many sun cults in ancient Japan.[14] One such deity that we have already encountered in Chapter 2 was the Silla immigrant deity Ame no Hiboko, or Heavenly Sun Spear. This god is represented in the *Nihon shoki* and *Kojiki* as a cowherd who marries Akaru Hime, a daughter of the sun, who demands offerings of weaving implements.

Just as Ame no Hiboko and Akaru Hime were said to have entered the Japanese islands in Kyūshū and from there moved closer to the Yamato plain, so, too, did other sun deities from Kyūshū come to be worshipped by the Yamato court. One example can be found in the Kenzō chapter of the *Nihon shoki*:

> A sun god possessed someone and said to Abe no Omi Kotoshiro:
> "Take rice fields from Iware and offer them to my forebear Takami Musubi no Mikoto." Kotoshiro thereupon reported this [to the court].
> Just as the god requested, forty-four *chō* of rice fields were offered.
> The Tsushima Shimoagata no Atai was charged with worship there.[15]

Although this text does not state which sun god asked Kotoshiro for the consecration of the rice fields, the founding ancestor of the Tsushima Shimoagata no atai, as Senda Minoru has noted, was a deity named Ama no Higami no Mikoto—literally, the Heavenly Sun God.[16] Figures such as Ama no Higami no Mikoto are of immediate interest because they illustrate the simple fact that not one but many sun deities existed in the Japanese islands. Long before the composition of the court chronicles, sun gods were worshipped by lineages and local paramounts across the Japanese islands. This particular legend, which appears to have been designed to explain how the cult of one sun deity from Kyūshū penetrated the Yamato region well before the Nara period, offers us an invaluable reminder that the goddess Amaterasu of the Ise shrine was but one of a number of sun deities prior to her adoption by the court.

Further clues concerning the nature of such sun cults can also be found in the main cultic center of the Tsushima Shimoagata no Atai in Kyūshū. Intriguingly, the name of this shrine was Amateru Jinja. Since, as we shall see momentarily, the *Nihon shoki* legend continues with the moon deity (and Amaterasu Ōmikami's brother) Tsukiyomi no Mikoto appearing before Kotoshiro, it would also appear that the Amateru Jinja in Tsushima may have in some way been related to the court's appropriation of the Amaterasu cult at Ise.

One further clue concerning this process can also be found in the fact that the main deity at the Amateru shrine in Tsushima was not Ama no Higami no Mikoto, but rather Ama no Hoakari no Mikoto. As we saw in Chapter 5, this deity appears in the court chronicles as the eldest son of the Heavenly Grandchild and the weaving maiden Konohana Sakuya Hime and as the grandson of Takuhata Chichi Hime, the Princess of Thousands and Thousands of Looms. Equally important, however, Ama no Hoakari was also claimed as a founding ancestor by several lineages that appear to have played an important role in the formation of early court mythology. In the *Kojiki*, *Nihon shoki*, and the *Shinsen shōjiroku* we are told that Ama no Hoakari no Mikoto was the founding ancestor of the Owari Muraji, while the *Sendai kuji hongi* states that he was also none other than the founding Mononobe ancestor Nigihayahi no Mikoto. Both of these lineages are known to have been present in numerous areas in Kyūshū as well as in the coastal regions between Kyūshū and Ise province.

Further clues concerning the cults of early sun deities can also be gathered from another legend concerning Abe no Omi Kotoshiro in the *Nihon shoki*:

> Abe no Omi Kotoshiro, having received an order, went to Mimana as an envoy. There the moon god took possession of someone and said: "My forebear Takami Musubi no Mikoto performed meritorious service in conjunction with the creation of Heaven and Earth. Dedicate people and lands to the moon god. If you offer to me as I have instructed, you will enjoy prosperity." At this Kotoshiro returned to the capital and reported everything and the Utaarasu rice fields were dedicated [to the moon god]. [*The Utaarasu rice fields are in the Kadono district of Yamashiro province.*] Oshimi no Sukune, the ancestor of the Iki Agatanushi, was appointed to officiate [at the shrine].[17]

As befits a moon deity, he sheds indirect light in this legend on two central aspects of the development of sun cults in the Japanese islands. Much as we saw in the case of the Tsushima Shimoagatanushi no Atai, the Iki Agatanushi were originally based on the island of Iki between Kyūshū and the Korean peninsula. Just as the legend of the sun deity appearing to Abe no Omi Kotoshiro appears to have been designed to explain the dedication of rice fields in Yamato to a Kyūshū deity, here we have a legend that explains the consecration of rice fields in Yamashiro province to Amaterasu's brother, the moon deity Tsukiyomi no Mikoto. Tellingly, however, here we are also told that the moon deity appeared to Kotoshiro not in Kyūshū, but in the kingdom of Mimana on the Korean peninsula.

The location of Tsukiyomi no Mikoto's shrine in the Kadono district of Yamashiro province is also of note because this district was the main base of the Hata, the immigrant kinship group who played such a major role in the introduction of continental political and religious forms to the Japanese islands. Perhaps not surprisingly, by the late Nara period, this cultic center had come to be a subshrine of the Matsuno'o shrine, one of a network of Hata shrines in Yamashiro province that, as we saw in Chapter 1, were so important in the formation of the early Heian royal cult. Furthermore, the Utaarasu fields were in close proximity to yet another Hata shrine in the Kadono district, known as the Konoshima ni masu Amaterasu Mitama Jinja. This shrine, which is attested in entries from the *Shoku Nihongi* for the pre-Nara period, is of note not only because it appears to represent a deliberate pairing of an Amaterasu cultic center with one dedicated to the moon god Tsukiyomi no Mikoto, but also because the shrine later came to be referred to as Kaiko Jinja (Silkworm shrine).[18] This clustering thus offers an important example of how cultic centers dedicated to sericulture, local Amateru shrines, and deities from the royal cult could literally be rooted in the same terrain. It also suggests that sacerdotal lineages with roots both in the Korean peninsula and Kyūshū may also have been an important factor in the emergence of Amaterasu at the pinnacle of the royal cult.

One further legend of note in this regard concerns another member of the Abe kinship group and one Takuhata Hime, a princess sent by the Yamato ruler Yūryaku to be chief priestess (*saiō*) at the Ise shrine:

> Yūryaku 3.4. Abe no Kunimi slandered Princess Takuhata and her personal attendant[19] Ihoibe no Muraji Takehiko, saying: "Takehiko has violated the princess and made her pregnant." . . . Takehiko's father Kikoyu heard of this and fearing disaster, called Takehiko to the Ihoki river. There, like a cormorant diving for fish in the water, Kikoyu caught Takehiko unawares and killed him. The *tennō*, hearing of this, sent an envoy to the princess and asked her of the affair. The princess replied, "I do not know [anything about this]." Then, suddenly, the princess took the sacred mirror and went to the Isuzu river and, seeking out a place where people seldom go, she buried the mirror and strangled herself. The *tennō*, wondering at the absence of the princess, searched for her constantly both east and west. Then, above the river something

like a rainbow appeared that was four or five *jō* [high].[20] When they dug at the source of the rainbow, they recovered the mirror. Not far from that place, they found the body of the princess. When they cut open her abdomen, there was a watery object [inside]. Within the water was a stone. Kikoyu was thus able to prove his son's innocence, and he regretted having killed him. He wished to kill Kunimi for revenge, but [Kunimi] fled to the Isonokami shrine and hid himself there.[21]

In this rather grisly story we find several highly suggestive elements. Most obviously, the text is written as if the custom of sending a royal princess to be priestess at the Ise shrine had already been established during Yūryaku's time. Although the historical accuracy of such a depiction is wide open to question, the text is consistent with later traditions that locate several important developments in the Ise cult within the time frame of Yūryaku's reign.

The figure of Takuhata Hime is also of interest because her name appears to have been constructed as a direct reflection of Takuhata Chichi Hime, the mother of the Heavenly Grandchild Ninigi no Mikoto. Since, as Okada Seishi has noted, Takuhata Chichi Hime was also worshipped within the Ise shrine alongside Amaterasu, it is highly unlikely that the overlap of names was purely accidental. It is also of note that, as we saw in Chapter 5, Takuhata Chichi Hime is not only explicitly identified in the text with looms (*hata*) and weaving, but her son Niningi is said in several variants to have descended to the Japanese islands after having been given a cloth coverlet. As we have seen in Chapter 5, the motif of a nation founder receiving a piece of cloth from his mother prior to his departure for the land he is destined to rule is a common trope in the nation-founding legends of the kingdoms of the Korean peninsula.[22] Thus Princess Takuhata Hime's name not only explicitly identifies her as a weaving maiden, but it also suggests an important trope from the royal founding narratives that in turn appears to reflect influence from the Korean peninsula.

Further clues concerning the origins of this legend also appear in the story's resolution. Although the text does not elaborate on this point, the stone within the princess's stomach appears to have been taken as proof that Takuhata Hime was pregnant not with a human child, but with the child of a sun deity.[23] This trope of a young woman impregnated by a sun god giving birth to a stone can also be seen in the birth narrative of the vengeful weaving deity Akaru Hime, who was said to have been born in the Korean kingdom of Silla as a red stone after the sun deity impregnated her mother at a pond. Thus this legend, in which the chief priestess was said to have been pregnant with a child of a (presumably male) sun deity, would again indicate that the early Ise cult and early Yamato sun worship were constructed within the context of background legends from the Korean peninsula.

Further evidence of such connections can also be seen when we examine the genealogical connections of the figures in the legend. Abe no Kunimi, for instance, appears to have been created in conjunction with his putative kinsman Abe no Omi Kotoshiro. Because, as we have just seen, Kotoshiro was purportedly visited by the moon deity Tsukiyomi no Mikoto in the Korean kingdom of Mimana, it would appear that the sources for these legends were interested with linking the royal cult with deities and practices that had roots in the continent. Takuhata Hime's links with the Korean peninsula are suggested even more immediately in the name of her putative mother, Karu Hime, whose name may be rendered literally into English as "Korean princess."

These apparent links with cults and legends from the Korean peninsula also highlight another ubiquitous motif from early Yamato mythology; namely, the prominent violence against women in legends related to the Ise cult. This can be seen not only in the death of the Ise priestess Takuhata Hime, but also in the apparent suicide of Amaterasu in some variants of the Heavenly Grotto legend, and, as we shall see shortly, in yet another legend from the court chronicles in which the moon deity Tsukiyomi no Mikoto is said to have murdered Toyouke Hime, the goddess of Ise's outer shrine. Although seldom commented upon, I suggest that the violence against female shamans and deities is of note for three reasons. First, the fact that such legends appear as a recurring element in the court chronicles suggests that they played an important role in early royal mythologies. Second, such legends also appear to have been directly related to rites of spirit-calling and spirit-shaking that were performed by female shamans, who were often represented in association with looms and in vocabulary from weaving cults. Finally, such legends also suggest possible connections with a corpus of continental myths and legends that highlight sericulture motifs and women/female shamans who die violent deaths. These legends, as we shall see shortly, also frequently discuss measures to quiet the spirits of the newly dead.

Takuhata and Ise

Perhaps the best place to begin unraveling these issues is to return to the apparent connection between the Ise priestess Takuhata Hime and Takuhata Chichi Hime, the mother of the Heavenly Grandchild. Crucially, Takuhata Chichi Hime was also enshrined in the main hall in the inner shrine at Ise, where, along with a third deity named Techikarao, Takuhata Chichi Hime was propitiated daily together with Amaterasu. As Okada Seishi has noted, this pairing is extremely odd in that it groups Amaterasu with her daughter-in-law, but omits Amaterasu's son. Since Amaterasu and Takuhata Chichi Hime have no other apparent connection, Okada suggests that when Takuhata Chichi Hime was installed in the shrine, the mythic background for these deities must have been different. Noting Takuhata Hime's role as priestess at Ise, Okada speculates that the main deity at the shrine was originally the male sun god Takami Musubi no Mikoto, and that his priestess, to whom he would have been "married," was eventually deified and joined him as an object of worship. Okada therefore argues that the name Takuhata Chichi Hime or Princess of Thousands and Thousands of Looms would have been either a generic term for a female shaman or at the very least a name that highlighted an essential characteristic of *miko* from the period.[24]

In light of Amaterasu's appearance in the myth of the Heavenly Grotto as a weaving maiden who is preparing offerings for the Niinamesai, Okada also suggests that Amaterasu and Takuhata Chichi Hime were both products of the same process of euhemerization. He speculates that Takami Musubi must have first been worshipped in tandem with his consort deity Takuhata Chichi Hime, but when, for still poorly understood reasons, Amaterasu eventually replaced Takami Musubi at Ise, she was simply paired with Takuhata Chichi Hime, who was already established there.

As Okada himself notes, there is an important corollary to this view. This suggests that the legend of the descent of the Heavenly Grandchild would originally have had a much simpler structure. As we saw in Chapter 5, this legend appears to have incorporated several generations in part to give an important role to both Takami Musubi and Amaterasu. Prior to the emergence of Amaterasu, however, Okada argues, the Heavenly Grandchild was most likely seen as the son of Takuhata Chichi Hime and Takami Musubi.[25] The structure of such an earlier legend would closely reflect the nation-founding legends of the Korean peninsula, in which the son of a male sun deity is given a woven cloth by his mother prior to descending to the human realm to establish his kingdom. Although Okada does not pursue this point, it is perhaps equally important for our purposes that in such a scheme Takuhata Chichi Hime's eldest grandson would have been none other than Ama no Hoakari no Mikoto.

Mononobe Legends of Ancestral Descent

One further piece of evidence suggesting Ama no Hoakari's connections with the cult of Amaterasu can be seen in the *Nihon shoki*, which also refers to Ama no Hoakari as Amateru Kuniteru Hiko Ama no Hoakari. Ama no Hoakari is also featured prominently in the *Sendai kuji hongi*, an ostensibly seventh-century text that is generally thought to have been composed sometime in the ninth century by a member of the Mononobe. In the *Sendai kuji hongi*, Ama no Hoakari is explicitly identified with the Mononobe ancestor Nigihayahi no Mikoto, who is referred to by the improbably long name Amateru Kuniteru Hiko Ama no Hoakari Nigihayahi.[26]

In the *Sendai kuji hongi* we also find an elaborate recounting of the descent of Nigihayahi no Mikoto to the Japanese islands. Several hints as to the existence of a set of legends centering upon Nigihayahi's descent can also be found in the *Nihon shoki* and *Kojiki*. In the *Nihon shoki* we find the following essential elements concerning the founding Mononobe ancestor:

1. Nigihayahi descends from the Heavenly Plain to the top of a mountain in Ikaruga, in Kawachi province.
2. Nigihayahi, the child of a heavenly deity, is said to be preparing to build a capital in Yamato, suggesting that he intends to be ruler of the land.
3. Upon meeting Jinmu, Nigihayahi's descendant Nagasunebiko shows Jinmu weapons, a quiver and arrow, as proof of his own divine descent.
4. Nagasunebiko then secures victory for Jinmu's army at Yoshino and leads his forces into the Yamato.
5. In the *Nihon shoki* we even find a note saying that the land of Yamato is known as "the land that was seen from the sky" because Nigihayahi, the "Son of the Heavenly Deity" had descended from Heaven in a stone boat there.[27]

In the *Sendai kuji hongi*, this story is amplified to include the following details:

1. Nigihayahi's son, Umashimaji, teaches the rite of the Chinkonsai to Jinmu and his consort. At the heart of this rite is a spell of spirit-shaking (*furu no kotohoki*).
2. This rite is not only said to be the origins of the Chinkonsai, but its intent is also explicitly stated to be to revive the sick and even the dead.
3. The means by which spirits are to be revived or resurrected involve ten regalia that are said to have been bestowed upon Umashimaji, as well as the spell of spirit-shaking (*tama furi*).

4. Accompanying Nigihayahi in his descent are twenty-five deities who are said to be ancestors of collateral Mononobe lineages.
5. These twenty-five deities are said to have been grouped into five groups of five.
6. Several of these Mononobe sublineages bear names that clearly mark them as immigrant lineages from the Korean peninsula.
7. Upon his death, Nigihayahi is said to have been taken back up to Heaven for burial. As Ōbayashi has noted, this trope is also found in nation-founding myths of the Korean kingdoms.[28]

Because the provenance and dating of the *Sendai kuji hongi* are still very much in dispute, very few scholars believe that it can be used as a reliable guide to pre-Tenmu mythology. Fortunately, however, a considerable amount of the listed material can also be found in other sources from the period. The title Amateru Kuniteru Hiko Ama no Hoakari, for instance, appears in the *Nihon shoki* itself. The ten regalia brought down by Nigihayahi as well as the Mononobe resurrection spell are referred to in late-Nara or early-Heian-period sources.[29] As Matsumae Takeshi has also noted, further evidence suggesting the influence of spirit-quieting rituals at the Isonokami shrine can also be seen in early Chinkonsai liturgies from the Ise shrine, which make explicit reference to the sword deity Futsunushi no Mikoto who was reverenced at the Isonokami shrine.[30]

Perhaps the most significant aspect of these accounts may simply be that they suggest that Mononobe rites and legend cycles may have developed separately from those of the royal house.[31] As Ōbayashi Taryō has pointed out, the *Nihon shoki*, the *Kojiki,* and the *Sendai kuji hongi* all present the myth of the descent of Nigihayahi no Mikoto in ways that suggest profound influence from the nation-founding legends of the Korean kingdoms. Evidence of such influences can be seen not only in the general trope of the ancestor who descends from Heaven to a mountain peak, but also in the types of weapons Nigihayahi and his son Imashimaji no Mikoto are said to bear. As Ōbayashi notes, in both the *Kojiki* and *Nihon shoki* these weapons are offered as proof of Nigihayahi's heavenly descent and are accepted as valid even by the would-be Yamato ruler Jinmu.[32] Motifs such as the organization of collateral descent units in groups of five, as well as the inclusion of numerous lineages with clear roots in the Korean peninsula, further suggest that Mononobe legends of the descent of Nigihayahi no Mikoto were profoundly affected by cults and legends from the Korean peninsula.[33]

Mononobe Spirit-Shaking Rites

There is also good evidence from numerous sources that the Mononobe practiced their own version of a *chinkonsai*, or spirit-shaking rite. One indication can be seen in the name of the main deity of Isonokami shrine, who was none other than Futsunushi no Mikoto (Master Shaker). This god appears in the court chronicles as a military figure who pacifies for the court the spirits of rebellious local deities.[34] Direct evidence that the Mononobe were associated with *chinkon* rites can be found in later court histories such as the *Nihon kōki*, which records the performance of such a rite at the Isonokami shrine for the ailing Kanmu *tennō* in 805.[35] Since this rite was performed at roughly the time most scholars believe the *Sendai kuji hongi* was being composed, the account also suggests that the *Sendai kuji hongi* depiction of the Chinkonsai as a rite involving Mononobe regalia was not simply a literary invention, but most likely rooted in actual cultic practice at the Isonokami shrine.[36]

All of this in turn sheds further light on the role of the Mononobe in the *Nihon shoki* and *Kojiki* accounts of the Yamato ruler Jinmu's conquest of Yamato. Consider the following account from the *Kojiki*, which recounts how the Isonokami deity, referred to here as Futsunushi no Mitama, saved Jinmu and his army after a local diety had brought them to the brink of death:

> At this Kamu Yamato Iware Hiko [Jinmu] suddenly became ill, and his army also became ill and fell prostrate. At this time, Kumano no Takakuraji . . . took a broad sword and went and offered it to the prostrate child of the heavenly deity [Jinmu], who revived and said, "I must have had a long sleep." He himself then took the sword and cut down all the wild deities of the Kumano mountains. . . .
> *This sword is called the Sashi Futsu deity. . . . It also has the name of Futsunushi Mitama. This sword is enshrined in the Isonokami Shrine.*[37]

Not only does this legend link the Mononobe again with the geographical regions most closely associated with Yamato rulers such as Great King Bu, but it also again clearly depicts the Mononobe deity Futsunushi no Mikoto as the embodiment of a sword that is capable of both quieting the spirits of the land and reviving the spirit of a Yamato ruler. The connection between Futsunushi no Mikoto and spirit shaking is also of immediate note because shrines bearing the name of this deity are known to have existed in coastal provinces stretching from Okinoshima off the coast of Kyūshū all the way to the Inland Sea near Ise. It would thus appear that the Mononobe and the cult of Futsunushi no Mikoto were well established along the same routes that were used to transmit cultic practices and sericulture technologies from the Korean peninsula across the Japanese islands.

The Isonokami Shrine

Additional evidence concerning Mononobe cultic practices can be seen in a series of legends in the court chronicles related to the main Mononobe cultic center, the Isonokami shrine. One indication of its importance is its designation not simply as a "shrine" (*jinja, yashiro*) but as a "*jingū*," a title given in the ancient period only to the Ise, Izumo, and Isonokami shrines. This term most likely derived from royal ancestral cultic centers in the Korean kingdom of Silla.[38] Further evidence of the remarkable role of the Isonokami shrine can be seen in the fact that the court used the shrine to store the regalia of lineages throughout the Japanese islands that had submitted to Yamato's ruler. It is generally assumed that this practice stemmed from a belief that control over sources of cultic power served to guarantee political control as well. Thus the *chinkon* rites at Isonokami may have served both to guarantee the political authority of rulers and to pacify the spirits of the numerous submitting lineages.[39] The shrine also appears to have been used by the court as a major storehouse for weapons.

Both the *Kojiki* and the *Nihon shoki* make clear that the shrine's role as a storehouse of both weapons and regalia was intimately connected with the political and military role of the Mononobe. Not only are Mononobe figures shown at various points appropriating regalia for the court, they also appear at the conclusion of the shrine's foundational legend. This legend traces the shrine's origins to the Yamato ruler Suinin, who commanded his son Inishiki Irihiko to create a thousand swords to be used as ritual implements, and these were subsequently stored in the Isonokami shrine. But in the text we find several hints that Inishiki Irihiko was closely connected with the Mononobe. Prior to creating the swords, Inishiki Irihiko is said to have built a pond in Tomi, the base of a major Mononobe sublineage and the site of the tomb of Nigihayahi no Mikoto, the first Mononobe ancestor, who is said to have descended from Heaven to Central Japan. Later the text also explains the origins of Mononobe involvement at Isonokami:

> In one writing it is said that when Prince Inishiki was residing above the Utogawa no Kawakami in Chinu, he made 1,000 swords, to which he gave the name "Kawakami." . . . The 1,000 swords were first stored

in the village of Osaka. Later they were moved from Osaka to the Isonokami shrine. At that time, the god [of the shrine] said: "Have a member of the Kasuga Omi named Ichikawa placed in charge." Ichikawa was accordingly given charge [of the shrine]. He was the founding ancestor of the Mononobe Obito.[40]

This legend is of immediate note both for its explanation of the origins of ritual implements at the Isonokami shrine and for the information that is encoded in the genealogical affiliations of the legend's main actors. We saw how in addition to being the first officiant at the Isonokami shrine, Inishiki Irihiko is also of note because he is said to have been not only the son of Hibasu Hime no Mikoto, the chief consort of the Yamato ruler Suinin, but also the grandson of Tamba no Michi Nushi, the founding ancestor of the Kusakabe kinship group and a descendant of Ama no Hoakari no Mikoto. He is also said to have been the brother of Yamato Hime, the legendary first chief priestess of the Ise shrine.[41]

Ancestral legends of lineages such as the Mononobe and the Wani reflect strong influences of continental cultic and mythic forms. Although we can only speculate on this point, they also appear to reflect the political and geographic realities during the Mononobe's ascendancy in the sixth century, when the Mononobe are believed to have dominated much of the Great Northern Lateral Highway that extended across Central Japan from Isonokami through the main Wani base near the foot of Mount Miwa towards the Heguri mountains and the port of Naniwa. This geographic proximity undoubtedly facilitated the creation of genealogical links as well as legends in which Mononobe ancestors are shown defending the interests of Wani consorts at court. All of this suggests that well before the composition of the *Sendai kuji hongi*, the Mononobe were most likely closely associated with the deity Ama no Hoakari no Mikoto and his numerous putative descendents.[42]

Yamato Takeru and the Ise Priestess

All of this has direct relevance for understanding the cult of Yamato Takeru, a royal ancestor who was a major focus for Tenmu *tennō* and his successors. Crucially, the court chronicles and even gazetteers of the period show female ancestors of such lineages as the Mononobe, Owari Muraji, and Wani play a major role in the legend cycle of this prince who, perhaps more than any other figure from the period, was closely associated with both the Ise shrine and resurrection. One female figure of particular note in this regard is the prince's aunt Yamato Hime no Mikoto, the legendary first consecrated princess (*saiō*) to serve at the Ise shrine. In the court chronicles Yamato Takeru is said to have made repeated visits to Yamato Hime prior to embarking upon military campaigns. During these visits he receives from his aunt such implements as the famed Kusanagi sword. As Naoki Kōjirō has argued, such legends appear to have been designed to connect the Ise cult with the figure of Yamato Takeru and, by extension, the court's conquest of the distant reaches of the realm.[43] Since the *Nihon shoki* and even sources from Ise tell us that the practice of sending a royal princess to Ise was revived by Tenmu after a hiatus of fifty years, it seems fair to speculate that such legends also reflected the interest of Tenmu and his successors in the institution of the *saiō* and the Ise shrine.[44]

As we have noted, Yamato Hime is said to have been the daughter of Suinin, a Yamato ruler who purportedly established his palace in Isonokami and whose maternal grandmother is said to have been a member of the Mononobe kinship group.[45] Even more revealing, however, are Yamato Hime's distaff relations. Both the *Kojiki* and the *Nihon shoki* state that her mother was Suinin's chief consort Hibasu Hime, whose father was none other than Tamba no Michi Nushi, the purported founding ancestor of the Kusakabe kinship group. These genealogical links are also suggestive of further possible connections between the figure of Ama no Hoakari no Mikoto and the Ise cult because yet another local deity from Tamba, Toyouke Hime, was installed as the main deity of the outer shrine at Ise, and because Tamba no Michi Nushi was himself said to have been the child of a Wani mother and a descendant of Ama no Hoakari no Mikoto.[46]

We noted in Chapter 4 that the figure of Hibasu Hime also appears to have been closely associated with early legends concerning funerary practices and the pursuit of immortality. In the *Nihon shoki*, for instance, her death is said to have been the occasion for the establishment of funerary lineages that specialized in burial rites and the production of clay figurines surrounding tombs.[47] Even more intriguing, the *Kojiki* contains an account of how Tajima Mori, a descendant of the Silla prince Ame no Hiboko and an ancestor of the immigrant Miyake Muraji lineage, left before Hibasu Hime and Suinin's tombs the fruit of immortality from the realm of the Queen Mother of the West.[48]

Such background legends appear to have played an important role in shaping early understandings of Yamato Takeru and the post-Tenmu Ise cult. As we have noted earlier, the first apparent reference we have to the Rite of Spirit-quieting comes in the Tenmu chapter of the *Nihon shoki*, where the monk Hōzō performs a rite of "spirit calling" (J. *shōkon*, Ch. *chao hun*) for Tenmu on the winter solstice just weeks before the monarch's death. One crucial clue for understanding the conceptual background for the performance of this rite is that Tenmu's final illness was not ascribed to mere chance, but rather to the anger of the Kusanagi sword, the very weapon given to Yamato Takeru by Yamato Hime.[49]

By Tenmu's time the Kusanangi sword was housed in the Atsuta shrine in Owari province, where it was worshipped by the Owari Muraji, a prominent lineage that the *Nihon shoki* and the *Shinsen shōjiroku* list as a main line of descendants from the god Ama no Hoakari. If the court chronicles may be believed, the Owari Muraji had at several times during the fifth and sixth centuries provided consorts for Yamato rulers. Genealogical information given in the *Sendai kuji hongi* and *Nihon shoki* also suggests substantial intermarriage with members of the Kazuraki Omi, a powerful kinship group thought to have settled numerous immigrant lineages such as the Hata within its domain prior to its destruction at the hands of Yūryaku and the Mononobe towards the end of the fifth century.[50] Such links are important because, when taken together with the presence of villages such as Taka Owari sato in Kawachi province, they suggest that the Owari Muraji, much like the Mononobe and the Hata, were from a very early date connected not only with Kawachi rulers such as Yūryaku, but they were also an important point of entry for immigrant culture and technologies.[51]

Although we have no way of knowing why the Kusanagi sword was blamed for Tenmu's illness, scholars such as Yokota Ken'ichi have speculated that Tenmu may have felt a special connection to the Owari Muraji and the Atsuta shrine due to his own lineal affiliations. Yokota notes that prior to ascending the throne, Tenmu was known as Prince Ōama and suggests that the prince was most likely raised by the Ama, a lineage located in coastal regions in Tamba and Owari provinces as well as in numerous areas of Kyūshū. Like the Owari Muraji, the Ama claimed descent from Ama no Hoakari no Mikoto, and in the *Nihon shoki* one Ōama Hime is explicitly stated to be an ancestor of the Owari Muraji.[52] One further indication that the Ama may have been influenced by the Atsuta cult is the fact that the Ama district of Owari province is located immediately adjacent to the Owari shrine. Perhaps the best indication that the strength of Tenmu's links to the Ama carried over to the Owari Muraji can be seen in the *Nihon shoki* account of Tenmu's funerary rites, which states that the first eulogy for the deceased ruler was given by Ama Sukune Arakama.[53]

Further evidence suggesting that Tenmu and his successors associated the Ise cult with conceptions of resurrection and long life can also be seen in yet another passage from the Suinin chapter of the *Nihon shoki*:

In one writing it is said that the *tennō* [Suinin] offered Yamato Hime no Mikoto as a medium to Amaterasu no Ōmikami, and Yamato Hime no Mikoto enshrined the goddess in a sacred tree in Shiki and worshipped her there. On the *kōshi* day of the 11th month of the 26th year, [the goddess was] moved to the Watarai palace in Ise province.

At this time Yamato no Ōkami possessed Ōminakuchi no Sukune, a distant ancestor of the Hozumi no Omi and spoke, saying: "At the beginning [of the world] I swore 'Amaterasu no Ōmikami shall rule over the Heavenly Plain, and my royal descendants shall rule the multitudinous gods of the Middle Realm. I [Yamato no Ōkami] shall govern the gods of the Earth.' . . . During the time of Sujin *tennō*, although the gods of Heaven and Earth were worshipped, their root was not [comprehended] to the deepest and most detailed degree, and they stopped at the vulgar leaves and branches. Thus that *tennō* had but a short lifespan. Now that you the current ruler, regretting that [Sujun] did not reach [the longevity of former rulers], are carefully worshipping, you shall attain long life and all under Heaven shall again enjoy great peace."[54]

This passage is notable for a number of reasons. Most obviously, the text serves to explain both the means by which Amaterasu came to reside in Ise and the origins of the institution of the Ise priestess. As we have already noted, the custom of sending a royal princess to Ise to serve as a priestess was apparently revived after a long period of neglect during Tenmu's reign. Seen in this light, the god's statement that such a ritual program would guarantee long life for Yamato rulers would appear to have been constructed with the ritual agenda of the Tenmu court in mind. This agenda, in turn, appears to have linked sun worship and the Ise cult with the mythic longevity of ancient rulers; just as the monk Hōzō sought to revive the dying Tenmu with a spirit-calling rite that was held in conjunction with the winter solstice and the "rebirth" of the sun, here we are told that the institution of the Ise priestess and proper worship of the sun goddess would extend the life span of rulers by hundreds of years.

It is also of note that the text highlights not only Yamato Takeru's aunt Yamato Hime, but also Ōminakuchi Sukune, a Mononobe ancestor who is also said to have received oracles from the Miwa deities as well. I suggest that the prominence of a Mononobe ancestor in this text not only indicates that Mononobe cultic traditions continued to exert sacerdotal influence on the emerging cultic program of the Tenmu court, but also that the court may also have been highly conscious of the Mononobe *chinkon* rites at the

Isonokami shrine that could revive the sick and even bring the dead back to life.

One clear indication that Yamato Takeru was also closely associated with the motif of resurrection can be found in the *Nihon shoki* account of the events immediately following the prince's burial:

> At this time Yamato Takeru no Mikoto was transformed into a white bird, whereupon he left his tomb (*misasagi*) and flew off in the direction of Yamato. When the ministers opened the coffin and looked [within], all that was left was his empty funerary clothing without the corpse. Messengers were then sent to follow the bird. . . . However, in the end it flew high up to Heaven and only his clothing and his court cap were buried.[55]

As numerous commentators have observed, this depiction of Yamato Takeru's resurrection appears to have been directly rooted in continental legends of immortals who, having attained "liberation from the corpse," leave behind an article of clothing after they depart from their tomb. It is worth noting that although this motif is frequently labeled as "Taoist," such legends circulated in a wide variety of contexts in Chinese literature, many of them directly related to the realm of immortality ruled by the Queen Mother of the West.[56] By the time Tenmu began his reign in 673, such legends had become thoroughly integrated into popular Chinese religious and literary discourse. Seen in the context of such immortals as Uranoshimako, Takakara Megami, and Toyouke Hime, the legend of Yamato Takeru's liberation from the corpse again highlights the degree to which continental beliefs and cultic practices related to death and immortality had come to influence legend cycles not just at court but also across the Japanese islands. It also suggests that lineages such as the Mononobe, Owari Muraji, and Wani may have played an important role in the diffusion of such conceptions.

Women and Resurrection in the Yamato Takeru Legend Cycle

As is so often the case, several further clues related to the diffusion of continental immortality beliefs and the origins and formation of the legend of Yamato Takeru's resurrection can be found in the background context provided by his consorts and affinal relations. In Nara-period literature we find a series of legends related to Yamato Takeru's mother, Waki no Iratsume, his aunt, the Ise priestess Yamato Hime, and two consorts, Oto Tachibana

Hime and Miyazu Hime. In the court chronicles we are told that Waki no Iratsume was born into the Wani kinship group, while Oto Tachibana Hime is said to have been the daughter of the founder of the Hozumi Muraji, one of the most important branches of the Mononobe kinship group. Miyazu Hime is said to have been a member of the Owari Muraji and a priestess at the Atsuta shrine. It would thus appear that the three women most closely associated with Yamato Takeru were all from prominent lineages that were closely associated with the god Ama no Hoakari no Mikoto.

How the cultic inclinations of these lineages may have been related to the legend of Yamato Takeru's liberation from the corpse can be found in a reference in the *Nihon shoki* to the founding ancestor of the Mononobe as Kushitama Ninigi no Mikoto, literally, Jade-combed Ninigi no Mikoto.[57] The term "*kushitama*," a commonly used prefix for a number of deities, is generally thought to have been associated with wooden tablets (*kushi*) that were used as receptacles for descending spirits, while the term *tama* is understood to indicate a spirit. Both of these terms, however, were homophonous with a number of terms in ancient Japanese. Thus "*tama*" was often rendered with the character for jade, while "*kushi*" was homophonous with the term for comb (櫛, *kushi*) as well as the term for medicine (薬, 酒, *kusushi, kushi*).

As we saw in Chapter 3, legends relating to medicine and immortality can be found in numerous Nara and early-Heian sources.[58] In addition, a surprising number of legends in the literature of the period suggest that combs were used to represent the attainment of life after death as well as power over the forces of the underworld. Thus the god Izanagi is said in the *Kojiki* and *Nihon shoki* to have repelled spirits of the underworld with light that emanated from his burning comb, while in the Luck of the Sea legend Ama no Hoakari no Mikoto's brother Ho no Suseri no Mikoto inadvertently drives off Ikutamayori Hime, his wife from beneath the sea, when he lights a comb in her birthing chamber.[59]

In Nara-period sources combs were also closely associated with female immortals and entry into the land of eternal life (*tokoyo*) beneath the sea. In the Luck of the Sea narrative we are also told that Ho no Suseri no Mikoto enters *tokoyo* by plunging into the sea in a basket made from bamboo that has sprung from earth touched by a magical comb.[60] There he is greeted by a sea god who welcomes him upon "eight thicknesses of mats," and eventually allows his daughter Tama Yori Hime to be wed to Ho no Suseri no Mikoto.[61] The Kusakabe ancestor Uranoshimako is similarly said to have received a spirit comb box (*tama kushige*) from a female immortal whom he has wed during his stay in *tokoyo* beneath the sea.[62]

In other legends combs appear to have a function similar to that of the robe left behind in Yamato Takeru's tomb. We find legends in which combs are enshrined as substitute foci of worship for women believed to have entered the land of the immortals beneath the sea. Consider, for example, the following legend concerning the death of Yamato Takeru's Mononobe consort Oto Tachibana Hime:

> When he went in from there and was crossing a place where the sea flowed in a swift current, the god of the crossing raised waves and spun the boat around so that it was unable to proceed. Thereupon his consort, whose name was Oto Tachibana Hime no Mikoto, spoke and said, "I shall take the place of the Prince and go into the sea. Let the Prince fulfill his charge of government and return to make his report." And when she was about to go into the sea, they spread eight thicknesses of sedge mats, eight thicknesses of skin mat, and eight thicknesses of silk mats on the waves, and she went down and sat upon them. . . .
>
> Now, after seven days his consort's comb washed ashore. And they took her comb and made a grave and placed it in the mound.[63]

Several markers in this legend suggest at least a family resemblance with the Luck of the Sea narrative. There Ama no Hoakari's brother enters the land of immortals beneath the sea in a basket prepared with a magical comb and is greeted by the sea god seated upon eight thicknesses of sedge; here Ama no Hoakari's descendant Oto Tachibana Hime plunges into the sea upon eight mattresses of sedge and disappears from the human realm, while her comb is entombed in her stead. Important evidence suggesting that Oto Tachibana Hime was believed to have attained some sort of life after death can be seen in the number of shrines dedicated to her that bear names such as Kushitama Jinja.[64]

The motif of the installation of a comb as a substitute body for a female who has traveled to *tokoyo* beneath the sea is also found in the death account of Yamato Takeru's mother, Waki no Iratsume.[65] Consider the following text from the *Harima fudoki*, a gazetteer that was prepared for the court sometime around 714:

> After some years Waki no Iratsume died at this palace. They thus built a tomb at Hioka to bury her. As they transported her corpse down the Inami river, a whirlwind blew from under the river, and the corpse was submerged in the middle of the river. Though they looked [for her remains]

they could find nothing but her comb box and scarf. So they buried these two items in the tomb, which is called *hire haka* [scarf tomb].[66]

All of this suggests that the motif of death and resurrection may have been a recurring element in legends related to Yamato Takeru; not only is Yamato Takeru said to have left behind a robe before bursting forth from his tomb, but legends have the combs of his consort and his mother enshrined and worshipped following their deaths and (presumed) entry into *tokoyo*.

One further example of liberation from the corpse occurs in the legend of Prince Shōtoku's encounter with a beggar on the road to Kataoka. As in the story of Yamato Takeru, the motif of liberation from the corpse is explicitly highlighted. As told in the *Nihon shoki* the legend concludes:

> The crown prince called one of his personal attendants and said to him, "The starving man we saw lying by the road several days ago was no ordinary man. He must certainly have been an immortal (*hijiri*)." So he sent [another] messenger to look [at the tomb]. The messenger returned and said, "When I arrived at the tomb, [the earth] was firm and had not moved. [Yet] when I opened it and looked inside the corpse had already disappeared. There was only the clothing folded above the casket."[67]

Although the beggar is never given a name, his appearance in the Shōtoku legend corpus strongly suggests that kinship groups such as the Hata and Kusakabe that were at the forefront of the early Shōtoku cult may have been associated with this legend. One hint as to how and why this motif may have entered the Shōtoku legend corpus can be seen from this legend's geography: Kataoka, the site of the prince's encounter with the beggar, was located on the Northern Great Lateral Highway just to the west of the main Wani base near the foot of Mount Miwa, which was located just to the west of the Isonokami shrine, the main cultic center of the Mononobe.[68]

All of this suggests that during the time Amaterasu was rising to preeminence in the royal cult, a cluster of lineages had fashioned ancestral legends in which motifs of resurrection or liberation from the corpse were prominent elements. Although our sources provide only a limited number of cases, the information seems to indicate a strong correlation between such legends and lineages claiming descent from Ama no Hoakari no Mikoto. To see the closeness of this correlation, consider Table 3, in which four of the five figures listed were claimed as ancestors by lineages that traced their descent from Ama no Hoakari no Mikoto.

Table 3 Legends of Resurrection and Liberation from the Corpse

NAME	ITEMS LEFT BEHIND	TYPE OF LIFE AFTER DEATH	LINEAL AFFILIATION
Yamato Takeru	clothes/cap	liberation from corpse	Wani
Oto Tachibana Hime	comb	*tokoyo*	Wani/ Mononobe
Waki no Iratsume	comb, scarf	*tokoyo*	Wani
Uranoshimako	comb box	*tokoyo*	Kusakabe
Kataoka beggar	robe	liberation from corpse	?

Since these legends appear in such varied sources as the *Nihon shoki*, the *Kojiki*, provincial gazetteers, the *Manyōshū*, and the *Nihon ryōiki*, it appears that they represented a cultic trend that extended beyond the parameters of the royal cult. Equally important, there is very good evidence that these legends commanded the attention of Tenmu and his successors. A brief examination of Table 3 suggests that these legends and their associated lineages were closely related to the cults of Yamato Takeru and Prince Shōtoku, two figures of unquestionable importance for the post-Tenmu court. It would hardly be surprising, therefore, if lineages associated with the cults of these two royal ancestors influenced the development of the cult of Amaterasu, the legend of the Heavenly Grotto, and the Chinkonsai. We have already seen at least two Ama no Hoakari no Mikoto cultic centers that contained the term "Amateru" in their names, which again strongly suggests that Ama no Hoakari lineages both propagated legends of resurrection and played an important role in the formation of the cult of Amaterasu.

Ama no Hoakari and Amaterasu

How and why was Ama no Hoakari related to Amaterasu? Unfortunately, little about Ama no Hoakari is known beyond his birth narrative in the legend of the descent of the Heavenly Grandchild. As we saw in Chapter 5, Ama no Hoakari no Mikoto first appears in the *Nihon shoki* when the weaving maiden Konohana Sakuya Hime encloses herself in a *muro*, or ritual shelter, in order to prove that her children have been conceived by the Heavenly Grandchild in a single evening.

The overall structure of Ama no Hoakari's birth narrative bears a strong thematic resemblance to that of the Heavenly Grotto myth; in the birth narrative, Konohana Sakuya Hime first appears weaving at a loom, becomes pregnant with three children, encloses herself within a *muro*, immolates herself, and then re-emerges alive. In the Heavenly Grotto myth, Amaterasu produces three children with her brother Susanoo, encloses herself within a *muro*, impales herself while weaving at a loom, and then re-emerges alive. It thus appears that the legend of the Heavenly Grotto was not simply a fabrication dating from Tenmu's reign, but an extensive series of appropriations from cultic traditions related to the Mononobe, Owari Muraji, and other lineages that traced their descent to Ama no Hoakari no Mikoto.

This in turn suggests that the roots of the Ama no Hoakari and Amaterasu cults may be found not only at court, but also in local cultic centers affiliated with lineages that claimed descent from Ama no Hoakari. Fortunately, the existence of such shrines can be verified by a simple survey of the local cultic centers listed in such texts as the *Engishiki*, which provides cursory information on court-sponsored shrines throughout Japanese islands. As Table 4 illustrates, cultic centers with names such as the Amateru Jinja in Tsushima and the Konoshima ni masu Amateru Jinja in Yamashiro province were surprisingly common in ancient Japan; indeed, at least ten such shrines are known to have existed during the period.[69] Crucially, these Amateru shrines were closely correlated with the worship of Ama no Hoakari no Mikoto. No fewer than seven are known to have housed this god as their main deity. Given this overlap, I propose that there can be little doubt that the cult of Amaterasu was in some profound way linked to the cult of Ama no Hoakari and his descendants.

Tables 3 and 4 suggest several important conclusions concerning the nature and origins of the Ise cult, that of Yamato Takeru, and the legend of the Heavenly Grotto. First, because Ama no Hoakari no Mikoto was claimed as an ancestral deity by several lineages that were also closely associated with the royal ancestor Yamato Takeru, it appears likely that the influence of these lineages on the early royal cult was both multifaceted and extensive. Many of the legends propagated by these lineages highlighted their female ancestors, who were frequently represented in terms of continental tropes related to continental sericulture and weaving cults. The influence of these lineages is particularly pronounced in a series of legends that linked the figure of Yamato Takeru with the Kusanagi sword and the Ise shrine. In light of Tenmu *tennō*'s personal relationship with the Kusanagi sword and the Owari Muraji, it would appear that the influence of these cults continued through the Tenmu era and beyond.

Several of the most prominent lineages claiming descent from Ama no Hoakari no Mikoto fashioned legends involving motifs of resurrection or liberation from the corpse that were rooted in tropes from continental

Table 4 Amaterasu Shrines Outside of Ise

SHRINE NAME/PROVINCE	AFFILIATED LINEAGE	ANCESTRAL/SHRINE GOD
Konoshima ni masu Amateru mitama Jinja (Yamashiro province)	Hata	Amateru Kuniteru Hiko Ama no Hoakari
Minushi ni masu Amateru mitama Jinja (Yamashiro province)	Minushi Atae	Ama no Hoakari
Osada ni masu Amateru mitama Jinja (Yamato province, Shikinokami district)	?	Ama no Hoakari
Kagamizukuri ni masu Amateru mitama Jinja (Yamato province, Shikinoshimo district)	?	Ama no Hoakari
Niiya ni masu Amateru mitama Jinja (Settsu province, Shimashimo district)	Kure no tsuguri (?)	Ama no Hoakari
Iibo ni masu Amateru Jinja (Harima province, Iibo district)	Owari Muraji	Ama no Hoakari
Amaterasu Ōmikami Takakura Jinja (Kawachi province, Takayasu district)	Hata	Amaterasu Ōmikami (also Takami Musubi)
Ise Amaterasu mitama Jinja (Chikugo province)	?	Ise Amaterasu Ōmikami
Amateru Jinja (Tsushima province, Shimoagata district)	Tsushima Shimoagata no Atai	Ama no Hoakari
Amateru Tama no Mikoto Jinja (Tamba province, Amata district)	Owari Muraji	Ama no Hoakari

tales of immortals. Since the legend of the Heavenly Grotto also features this motif in the death and resurrection of Amaterasu, it appears highly likely that the lineages played an important role in introducing continental conceptions of the body and the afterlife into the legend of the Heavenly Grotto, the Chinkonsai, and the cult of Amaterasu.[70]

From a very early date lineages like the Mononobe, the Owari Muraji, and the Wani also appear to have absorbed cultic influences from the Korean peninsula into their own ancestral legends, a process almost certainly facilitated by the large number of Mononobe shrines and deities such as the "Master Shaker" Futsunushi no Mikoto that were situated along the main routes of technological and cultural transmission from the Korean peninsula to Oki no Shima off the coast of Kyūshū to the port of Naniwa and beyond.

Sericulture, Cult, and Gender

There is also evidence suggesting that other lineages and cultic concerns may have also played an important role in the formation of the legend of the Heavenly Grotto and the cult of Amaterasu. In Table 3, for instance, we see that while four of the five figures listed belonged to lineages that claimed descent from Ama no Hoakari, the final figure was also clearly associated with the cult of Prince Shōtoku. Similarly, in Table 4 we find that while seven out of ten shrines were associated with Ama no Hoakari lineages, two were cultic centers of the Hata, an immigrant weaving lineage that was also at the forefront of the early Shōtoku cult. One further shrine, the Niiya ni masu Amateru mitama Jinja, appears to have been a cultic center of the Kure no Tsuguri, yet another immigrant lineage that traced its ancestry to a group of weavers purportedly sent to Yamato from southern China during the reign of the Yamato ruler Ōjin.[71] Not only do Mononobe and Wani ancestral legends highlight weaving motifs, but so do immigrant weaving lineages such as the Hata.

The association of two immigrant weaving lineages with the Amateru shrines may shed further light on the Ise cult in other ways as well. As we have noted, the basic structure of the legend of the Heavenly Grotto in many ways resembles that of the birth of Ama no Hoakari and the Heavenly Grandchild, in which the weaving maiden Konohana Sakuya Hime enters a ritual chamber while alive, sets it afire, and then re-emerges into the world unscathed. More broadly, however, I suggest that the figure of Amaterasu can also be seen in the Heavenly Grotto legend as undergoing a three-part transformation: at the start she is a weaving maiden preparing for a rite; in the middle she is enclosed in a cave that is identified with *tokoyo*; and at the climax of the legend she triumphantly re-emerges from the land of the dead as the undisputed supreme deity of the pantheon.

Although we can only speculate on this point, at a very general level this tripartite structure resembles early beliefs concerning the miraculous "insect of three transformations" that fascinated both the immigrant sericulturalist Nurinome Hime and the multitudinous worshippers of Ofube no Oshi's *tokoyo* deity that "in every way resembled a silkworm." Since the Konoshima ni masu Amateru Jinja came at some point to be called Kaiko Jinja or the Silkworm shrine, I propose that it is worth asking whether—and

Horses, Purification, and the Death of the Weaver Maiden

A great deal of background information concerning continental rites and legends related to the origins of sericulture, resurrection, and violence against women can be found in classical Chinese sources. Throughout the premodern period women at virtually every level of Chinese society participated in sericulture rites. Women across China prayed for skill in weaving on the seventh day of the seventh month, while rites from the start of the third month involved the empress and the ruler's consorts in gathering mulberry leaves to feed silkworms.[72] We have also repeatedly seen that as this vocabulary came to dominate historical and cultic discourse in the Japanese islands, weaving and sericulture cults helped shape the horizon of reception for the emerging myths and legends of numerous royal ancestors and local female divinities.

One hint as to how such legends may have influenced the development of the Ise cult can be seen in the continental legends related to spirit-quieting rites on nodal days in the Chinese festival calendar. One recurring trope involves the death of young women whose spirits are then propitiated with rites of purification at rivers. Thus in the *Hsü chi chieh chi*, an early-sixth-century Chinese text composed by Wu Chün (469–520), we find the following account of the origin of the court banquets that were held across Asia on the third day of the third month:

> Chin Wu-ti asked the royal secretary Chih Chung-ch'ia, "What is the meaning of the water banquets of the third day of the third month?" [Chung-ch'ia replied] "During the time of Han Chang-ti, in P'ing-yuan, Hsü-chao had three girls born to him at the start of the third month, [but] by the third day all three had died. The entire village thought this strange and went together to the water's edge to purify [themselves] and send wine cups down the river. The origins of the banquets at the river must be here."[73]

Although this text should by no means be taken for historical reality, it amply illustrates the degree to which concerns over purification and attention to spirits of the dead informed Chinese cultic discourse in the sixth century.

Of equal importance, we are told here that the origins of an important rite on a nodal date in the calendar can be traced back to the untimely deaths of three girls.

Further linkage of such motifs with the third day of the third month can be seen in the *Ching ch'u sui shih chi*, which relates popular religious practices on this day to rites of spirit-calling that were performed by female shamans at rivers. The text quotes references to such rites in several classical texts, beginning with the *Han shih,* a noted commentary on the *Book of Songs*:

> The [Han] commentary says, "Now, in the third month, beneath peach blossom water, people's *yin* and *yang* spirits are summoned and extended [Ch: *chao hun hsü p'o*, J: *shōkon zokubaku*] and defilements are purified." . . . Cheng's commentary [on the *Rites of Chou*] states: "It is the same as [what is done] now at the water at the start of the third month."[74]

Passages such as this are of immediate interest for our purposes for several reasons. As we have noted several times, a spirit-calling rite (*shōkonsai*) was performed for Tenmu at the end of his reign; the court is known to have engaged in both medicine hunts and sericulture rites at nodal points such as the third day of the third month in the festival calendar; and royal banquets on this day are mentioned repeatedly throughout the *Nihon shoki*. All of this appears to be of direct relevance for understanding the cultic background of the Heavenly Grotto legend.

How such legends relate to that of the Heavenly Grotto can be seen if we recall that the Heavenly Grotto legend appears to have formed the mythic basis for the liturgy of the Rite of Great Purification, which was listed in the earliest law codes along with the Chinkonsai, as one of the major rites in the court calendar. A core element of the liturgy for the Rite of Great Purification is the confession of a list of sins that have brought pollution upon the court and that need to be removed. These sins appear to map extremely closely with the actions of Susanoo prior to Amaterasu's entry into the cave. One curious aspect about the list, however, is that it juxtaposes bestiality and illicit relations between parent and child with sins such as the removal of agricultural sign posts and the filling in of irrigation ditches. Nowhere in the court chronicles is Susanoo accused of such activities. Since we nowhere find references to anyone else marrying horses or chickens in the literature of the period, it is difficult to believe that such practices were so widespread that they required confession and expiation twice a year. Although we can only speculate on this point, I suggest that since neither the Heavenly Grotto myth nor contemporary social practices appear to have been the source for this element of the rite, it most likely comes from a background legend for the Heavenly Grotto myth.

One indication of what such a legend may have looked like can be found in the fact that the Rite of Great Purification appears to have been heavily influenced by several continental rites and legends. As we saw in Chapter 3, during this rite an invocation was read, with Chinese pronunciation, by members of a sublineage of the Kawachi no Aya, an immigrant lineage that appears to have been under the influence of the Mononobe prior to the destruction of the main Mononobe line in 584. The text, as given in the *Engishiki*, centers on an invocation of numerous astral deities and such popular Chinese cultic figures as the Queen Mother of the West and the King Father of the East. As we saw in Chapter 2, the cult of the Weaver Maiden and Cowherd also appears to have originated in ancient Chinese rites that most likely involved the sacrifice not only of cows, but also of young maidens. Given that the Heavenly Grotto legend features the death of a weaver maiden, it behooves us to ask whether continental legends involving horses, silkworms, and weaving maidens may have influenced such supposedly "native" legends as that of Amaterasu's death and resurrection.

Fortunately, just such a legend recounting the origins of sericulture has been preserved in the *Sou shen chi*, a fourth-century compendium of Chinese legends:

> It is said that of old there was an eminent man who had to journey far away from his home. At his home there was no one else save for his daughter and their stallion, which the girl cared for. Living all alone, and missing her father, the girl jokingly said to the horse, "If you can bring my father back to me, I will marry you." The horse, upon receiving these instructions, broke his reins and traveled until he arrived at the place where the father was. The father was surprised and delighted to see the horse and began to ride him.
>
> The horse looked towards the direction he had come from, and whimpered ceaselessly. The father said, "This horse would not be this way for no reason. Has something happened at my home?" and hurried back.
>
> Because he had shown special sensitivity for an animal, the father rewarded the horse with special fodder. The horse, however, would not eat, and every time he saw the daughter coming and going, he

would become delighted or angry, even to the point where he would kick her. This happened more than once or twice. The father sensed that something strange had happened, and surreptitiously asked his daughter what [had happened]. The daughter told him everything, saying that this must be the reason.

The father said, "Don't tell anyone! [If this gets out], it will ruin our family's reputation. You should not go out for a while." The father then went, secretly prepared a bow and arrow, and then shot and killed the horse. He then hung the horse's hide up in the courtyard.

The father then left, and the daughter, along with a neighbor girl, began playing in the place where the horse's hide was. She kicked the horse's hide and said "You are an animal and you want to take a human for your bride? You brought this skinning upon yourself. How does this feel?" When she had not quite finished, the horse's hide suddenly flew up, wrapped up the girl, and flew away. The neighbor girl was terrified and dared not try to help her. She ran to tell the father. The father returned, looked for her, but could not find a trace.

After several days, they found them in the branches of a great tree. The girl and the horse hide had been completely transformed into silkworms, and there were cocoons all the way up to the top of the tree. Their threads were especially thick and large, unlike ordinary silkworms. The neighbor women took them home and raised the silkworms and obtained many times more silk [than normal]. For this reason that tree is called "mulberry" [Ch. *sang*]. "*Sang*" is the same [homophonous] with *sang* [death]. Because of this the peasants all compete to plant these trees, which they use to raise silkworms even today.[75]

This remarkable assertion that the origins of sericulture can be traced to the tragic, aborted wedding of a young maiden and a horse not only features the by-now familiar themes of the violent death of a maiden and sericulture, but it also explicitly highlights motifs of bestiality as well as a domestic situation in which a father is living alone with his daughter. Intriguingly, the motif of the flayed horse also features prominently in the Heavenly Grotto legend, where we also find that flaying the horse directly precedes the death of the weaver maiden.

Such similarities did not go unnoticed by later generations. Japanese folklorists have long cited the closeness of these two legends as the most likely source of the popular *oshira* cult, in which young girls dressed in horse skins pray for skill in weaving. Although a lack of documentation precludes any speculation as to when the *oshira* cult first came into existence, it continues to be performed today at numerous shrines in northeastern Japan as well as at the Konoshima ni masu Amateru Jinja in Yamashiro province.[76]

Beyond the Grotto: Amaterasu and Sericulture Cults

Yet in spite of the important thematic similarities between the Heavenly Grotto myth and the *Sou shen chi* account of the origins of sericulture, there are important structural differences as well. Most notably, in the *Sou shen chi* account, the violent death of the maiden does not lead to resurrection, but rather to the birth of silkworms and abundance for the community. Crucially, however, this motif also appears in the court chronicles in an additional set of legends that concern Amaterasu's actions following her emergence from the Heavenly Grotto. Among the most important of these for our purposes is told in the following legend, in which the sun goddess sends the moon deity Tsukiyomi no Mikoto to visit the goddess Toyouke Hime (here referred to as Ukemochi no Kami):

> When Amaterasu no Ōmikami was already in Heaven, she said, "I have heard that in the Central Land of the Reed Plain there is the goddess Ukemochi no Kami [Toyouke Hime]. Go and inquire after her." Tsukiyomi no Mikoto received his orders, descended, and went to the place where Ukemochi no Kami was. Ukemochi no Kami turned her head, and when it faced the land, rice came forth from her mouth. When she faced the sea, broad-finned and narrow-finned [fish] came out of her mouth. Again, when she faced the mountains, rough-furred [animals] and fine-furred [animals] came out of her mouth. These things she prepared and piled up for a feast on a hundred tables. At this Tsukiyomi no Mikoto became flushed with anger and said, "How defiling! How disgusting! How dare you offer to me as food things that you have spit out from your mouth!" So he drew his sword, struck, and killed her. He later went back and reported everything. Then Amaterasu no Ōmikami was extremely angry and said, "You are a wicked deity. I will not meet with you [again]." Thus she was separated from Tsukiyomi no Mikoto, and they lived apart, one by day and one by night.[77]

Several clues as to the horizon of reception for this legend can be seen once we consider the cultic geography of each of these deities. As we saw at the beginning of this chapter, a shrine to Tsukiyomi no Mikoto was purportedly established in the Kadono district of Yamashiro province after the moon deity appeared to Abe no Omi Kotoshiro on the Korean peninsula and demanded to be worshipped. We also noted that this shrine was incorporated at an early date as a subshrine of the Matsuno'o shrine, and that it was apparently also paired with the Konoshima ni masu Amateru Jinja, yet another Hata cultic center later known as the Silkworm shrine. In addition, as we saw in Chapter 3, not only did Toyouke Hime come to be worshipped in the outer shrine at Ise, but she was also featured in local legends in Tamba province in which she was depicted as a female immortal and medicine deity. Since this legend highlights the violent death and transformation of Toyouke Hime, it strongly suggests the influence of continental tropes related to sericulture and the violent deaths of young women. Further evidence for continental influences can be seen in the conclusion of the legend, which is none other than a mythic account of the origins of sericulture:

> Amaterasu then later sent Ama no Kumahito to go and see [the situation]. At this time Ukemochi no Kami was truly already dead. However, the top of her head had been transformed into cows and horses. The top of her skull had produced millet, and her eyebrows had produced silkworm cocoons. Grasses were produced from within her eyes, and rice was produced from within her stomach. From her genitals there had been produced barley, large and small beans.[78]

Because this legend depicts the origins of several primary elements of Chinese civilization, it is perhaps not surprising that it once again highlights several familiar themes from Chinese mythology. Not only does the text trace the origins of sericulture to the violent death of a woman, but it also explicitly correlates various parts of Ukemochi's body with the origins of the most essential elements of continental material culture. Even more remarkably, these correspondences all appear to have been based upon phonetic correspondences in ancient Korean between the term for each body part and the term for item produced.[79] These thematic and linguistic linkages once again suggest a fairly direct continental influence on the formation of the legend.

The text also provides compelling evidence that sericulture cults and legends from the Chinese festival calendar were directly related to the figure of Amaterasu:

Ama no Kumahito took all of these things and offered them [to Amaterasu no Ōmikami]. At this time Amaterasu no Ōmikami was delighted and said, "These are the things by which the people of the visible world shall eat and live." She thus took the millet, grasses, barley, and beans to be seeds for the dry fields, and she took the rice as seeds for the irrigated fields. Then she accordingly appointed village headmen in heaven and with the rice seeds began the planting of the narrow fields of heaven and the long fields of heaven. That autumn the ears [of the rice plants] drooping down in abundance, were eight hand spans long and very refreshing [in appearance].

[Amaterasu no Ōmikami] also put the cocoons into her mouth and then drew thread from them. From this the way of raising silkworms began.[80]

It is difficult to imagine a clearer representation of Amaterasu no Ōmikami as a silkworm goddess than this text, which explicitly depicts the goddess drawing threads of silk from her mouth in the manner of a silkworm. Taken together with the myth of the Heavenly Grotto, where Amaterasu is portrayed as a weaving maiden who dies and is resurrected, this legend provides a powerful illustration of the importance of the rites and legends of sericulture for the construction of this deity's identity.

Perhaps even more important, this legend speaks volumes about the nature of the forces that shaped the cultic identity not only of local deities such as Toyouke Hime, but also of the royal lineage itself. In spite of the fact that Amaterasu has long been seen as a pillar of Japanese national identity, it is clear that her cult was deeply rooted in Chinese conceptions of ritual and spirit as well as the technological innovations of sericulture. It is also abundantly clear that such conceptions were in no way peripheral to the construction of her cultic identity. Nor, for that matter, were they peripheral for the ritual program of the post-Tenmu court.

On the contrary, it would appear that such rites and conceptions reflect the depth and power of the technological and cultural forces that transformed the political and material realities of the age even as they redefined the cultic agenda that made the royal house possible. Seen in this light, it should hardly be surprising that the Amaterasu legend cycle—or that of Tsukiyomi no Mikoto, Toyouke Hime, or any other of a host of "native" deities—is simply not intelligible outside of the context of Chinese conceptions of everything from resurrection to horses.

None of this is to suggest that the figure of Amaterasu was "really" Chinese or that her cult was any more or less important for being influenced by immigrant lineages and Chinese cults. But it does clearly show how fundamentally misguided understandings of the "native" in Japanese culture and religion, left over from prewar scholarship, continue to distort our understanding of some of the most basic parameters of the religious traditions of Japanese islands. It also shows how a wider range of issues relating to the construction of gender roles, the creation of wealth, and the proliferation of new conceptions of spirit and resurrection—all rooted in continental culture—served as the template for the construction of so much of what we think of as the foundations of Japanese religion.

Conclusion

This chapter has argued that as the figure of Amaterasu no Ōmikami became implicated in the construction of the royal lineage, she also became entwined with contemporaneous conceptions of ritual, *onmyōdō* thought, and gender that were promulgated by immigrant kinship groups from the Korean peninsula and the Chinese mainland. Understanding this process has required both a heightened awareness of the role of Chinese cultic practices in Asuka and Nara Japan and a re-examination of the usefulness of the categories of "native" and "foreign" for understanding the cultic developments of the Asuka and Nara periods.

Because the cult of Amaterasu no Ōmikami has since at least the Meiji period been treated as a cornerstone of Japanese "native" cultic and political identity, she has been seen by folklorists, historians, and ideologues alike as a core element of a native cultural/religious identity that was defined in opposition to the "foreign" Buddhist tradition. One ironic consequence of this bivalent approach to Japanese religion has been that virtually all non-Buddhist cultic practices have been lumped together in an attempt to create a "native" religious tradition. As a result, legends depicting Amaterasu as a weaver maiden or even as a silkworm goddess have been pressed into the service of Japanese nativist ideologies.

Yet once we consider the figure of Amaterasu no Ōmikami within the much broader framework of popular religious practice in the Asuka and Nara periods, the degree to which the figure of Amaterasu in particular and the royal cult in general were rooted in paradigms from the Chinese festival calendar becomes readily apparent. A close look at Amaterasu and other deities from the Ise cult reveals profound associations with immigrant lineages such as the Hata as well as deep roots in continental sericulture rites. All of this suggests that the cult of Amaterasu underwent rapid development just as continental notions of ritual and spirit pacification were penetrating the Japanese islands. As a result, the premises and practices of the Chinese festival calendar functioned as core elements in the Ise cult as it was configured in the Nara period and thereafter.

These cultic elements appear to have been the result of widespread borrowing on the part of the royal house from popular cults that were themselves thoroughly imbued with Chinese conceptions of spirit, resurrection, immortality, and sericulture. Thus as the Ise cult appropriated popular cultic elements from the cult of the goddess and female immortal Toyouke Hime, the figure of Amaterasu herself came to be deeply colored by Chinese conceptions of resurrection and immortality. Because these conceptions were almost certainly propagated by immigrant kinship groups at the forefront of sericulture and the importation of continental culture, it would also appear that the figure of Amaterasu as we know her, and, for that matter, the royal cult, could not have been what they were without immigrant lineages and the rites of sericulture and spirit pacification that they promoted.

Conclusion

IN THIS BOOK we have examined several key moments in the formation of the Japanese Buddhist tradition, the Japanese royal cult, and popular worship of *kami* in the Japanese islands. We have seen that from at least the time of the Yamato ruler Wakateru down to the Heian period, both the royal cult and popular cultic life were characterized by tremendous ferment, as changes in the technological and material culture of the Japanese islands helped spur dramatic changes in political and cultic orientation both at the Yamato court and in the countryside. As continental cults and deities were inscribed into the landscape of the Japanese islands, they played a major role in the formation of even purportedly native religious practices. I have sought to provide a framework for explaining not only the presence of such continental cults and practices, but also the mechanisms of their transmission and their evolving role in the cultic life of the Japanese islands.

In so doing, I have focused on a series of lineages and cultic centers that to a large degree shaped the cultic and political context in which the royal cult and the Buddhist tradition emerged. Most prominent in this regard have been immigrant lineages such as the Hata and Kawachi no Aya, whose ancestral deities were by definition *karakami*. Given their cultural and cultic prominence not just at court but across the Japanese islands, the cultic practices and deities of the Hata and other such immigrant groups represent perhaps the most immediate means for the transmission of continental cults to the Japanese islands. Crucially, however, we have also seen that even such supposedly xenophobic lineages as the Mononobe and Ōtomo aggressively sought out technological and cultic forms from the Korean peninsula even as sacerdotal and service lineages such as the Kusakabe, Chiisakobe, Kamo, Wani, and Miwa incorporated continental rites and narrative tropes into their own ancestral cults. It is perhaps not surprising that the Nara period drew to a close just a few years before the court settled into a Hata stronghold in Yamashiro province and thereafter sought the protection of Hata-affiliated deities at the Kamo, Matsuno'o, Hiyoshi, and Fushimi Inari shrines.

Location, Location, Location

Because the *kami* were as often as not ancestors in premodern Japan, they frequently migrated along with their descendants. As immigrant lineages such as the Hata, which had a strong presence in the coastal regions along the Inland and Japan/Eastern seas, rose higher and higher at court, and as ancestral *karakami* grew in importance in the royal cult, the court increasingly absorbed continental rites and practices from local cultic centers throughout the domain. By tracking the movements of both lineages and cults—that is, paying attention to where cultic practice *took place*—we have been able to identify and trace the flow of both cults and technologies from the Korean peninsula to Japan's coastal regions and into Yamato. When seen in this light, the influx of technologies, diseases, and deities from Kyūshū to Yamato becomes not only explicable, but also a significant indicator of the appeal that continental practices had for the insecure rulers and courtiers of the age.

One further theme that has become readily apparent is the degree to which fear of disease and vengeful *kami* helped drive the development of both the royal and popular cults. Because both rulers and commoners during the period were frequently overawed by forces beyond their control, they frequently sought new methods to propitiate the spirits that were thought to visit their wrath upon the human realm.

All of this suggests several conclusions not only about the nature of religion in the Japanese islands, but also about the means by which we approach the study of the Nara and Heian periods. I have throughout this book sought to highlight the importance of an integrated approach to the religion of this era that takes into account not only political maneuverings at the court, but also the important developments in the material culture and technological capabilities of the age. This approach stems from a belief that in many ways the expansion of road networks or the diffusion of sericulture may have had a greater impact upon the way spirits were worshipped than the edicts promulgated by the court. In a similar vein, once we see the royal cult as being in constant interaction with local cults across the Japanese islands, the importance of understanding the cults, deities, and lineages in such remote regions as Hizen, Tamba, Suruga, and Yamashiro becomes obvious. By inquiring into the nature and origins of such interactions, I have resisted post-Meiji categories of "native" and "foreign" in order to shed a brighter light on the cultic horizon in terms of which the court's ritual parameters were both defined and transgressed.

None of this, of course, is to deny the importance of the royal cult, nor does it in any way diminish the importance of particular actors and rulers in the development of early Japanese religious forms. Time and again we have seen, however, that these figures drew upon the cultic resources offered by local deities from distant regions and, frequently, the ancestral deities of important service groups and immigrant lineages that were familiar with continental methods of propitiating spirits and bringing prosperity.

More broadly speaking, I have also argued that each of these developments must also be seen in the context of a patterning of narratives and ritual that was codified within the popular Chinese festival calendar. This patterning provided an essential template for the construction not only of the edifice of court ritual and, indeed, governance, but also for the harmonization of innumerable aspects of daily life within a single, overarching context. Because the calendar tracked the waxing and waning of *yin* and *yang* throughout each yearly cycle, it helped make sense of everything from the rhythms of agriculture to the choice of colors for clothing to the encouragement of crafts and industry. If weaving maidens, goddesses, and female immortals played a prominent role in the court-sponsored narratives, it was due not simply to literary fancy, but to the vital importance of these women for the workings of the ritual and economic systems on which the court depended.

In a similar vein we have seen that this same template played a major role in shaping the formation of the early Japanese Buddhist tradition. We have seen this not only in accounts in the *Nihon shoki* and the *Nihon ryōiki* of the founding legend of the Japanese Buddhist tradition, but also in popular narratives concerning the way to propitiate spirits on the roadsides and to escape the reach of Emma, the king of hell. In these narratives it appeared that even in the land of the dead, ancestors and demons understood that events needed to flow within a set calendrical regimen punctuated by nodal points in which contact with the living could be achieved and ritualized.

Future Directions

One of the most important results of this investigation has been to illuminate the profoundly important role played by local cults and deities in shaping the emerging royal cult. It is my hope that this view may serve as an important corrective to the court-oriented biases of much modern scholarship as well as virtually all of our earliest sources. It is telling that although we have only scratched the surface of important cults and deities of the period, the total volume of scholarly attention given to all of the deities mentioned in this book is dwarfed by that given to the royal ancestor Amaterasu. This imbalance appears all the greater when we consider the scholarly research devoted to the Buddhist institutions and practices of the court. Although no one can doubt the influence of Nara-period Buddhism on Japanese religious history, there is nonetheless little evidence that Buddhist cultic practices dominated religious life in the countryside. Indeed, provincial gazetteers composed in 714 scarcely mention the tradition. Much work remains to be done.

I also suggest that we have barely begun to understand how gender helped drive the material, political, and social changes that transformed life in the Japanese islands even before the Nara period. In every chapter of this book we have seen that gender roles played a crucial role in these processes, and that legends of female deities, ancestors, and shamans helped shape not only how royal consorts were represented in court chronicles, but also notions of immortality and the propitiation of spirits. Because of the gender-specific nature of weaving, these figures also represented a major link between the economic and material culture of the Japanese islands and the worship of local *kami*.

Although the bulk of this book has focused on religious developments leading up to and including the Nara period, we have also seen that the considerations under discussion should be of immediate interest for the study of later eras as well. Certainly the end of the Nara period, marked as it was by the ascendancy of the healer-monk Dōkyō, the rule of the female *tennō* Kōken, and the emergence of the Kyūshū deity Hachiman, deserves renewed scrutiny. Given the importance of *karakami* in the system of twenty-two temple-shrine complexes sponsored by the court, it also appears that the importance of immigrant lineages and deities for the court during the Heian period may have been equally great.

There is also good reason to believe that the worship of *karakami* continued to flourish among the populace in the Heian period and beyond. I suggest, for instance, that healer monks, *yin-yang* specialists (*onmyōji*), and popular festivals for the propitiation of *goryō* that burst into prominence in this period were in innumerable ways related to roadside rites of spirit pacification and animal sacrifice that had deep roots in popular cultic practices in China and the Korean peninsula. Such connections are of particular note not only because of their indisputable influence upon the cultic life of both the court and the populace in subsequent periods, but also because they suggest that as continental medical and astrological systems continuously shaped and were in turn shaped by popular religious movements, they served as touchstones for understanding the mysteries of purity, politics, disease, and death for monks, rulers, commoners, and *kami* alike for centuries to come.

Glossary of Names and Terms

Abe no Kunimi This doubtless legendary figure is said to have slandered the chief priestess of the Ise shrine during the reign of Yūryaku. Although few scholars would accept the historicity of virtually any aspect of the account, the legend would appear to once again suggest some connection between the Abe and early sun cults in the Japanese islands.

Abe no Omi Kotoshiro This otherwise unknown figure appears within the Kenzō chapter of the *Nihon shoki*, where he is said to have been possessed first by a sun deity who requests that land be set aside for the worship of Takami Musubi no Mikoto and then by the moon deity Tsukiyomi no Mikoto while in the Korean kingdom of Mimana. Because this latter legend also served as the shrine-founding legend for the Kaiko Yashiro (Silkworm shrine), a Hata cultic center in Yamashiro province, the text also suggests the possibility of some sort of early cooperation between these two kinship groups. Both groups were later closely associated with Shitennōji temple in the port of Naniwa and the early cult of Prince Shōtoku. In addition to the importance of this legend for our understanding of the development of worship of the sun deity Amaterasu, these legends also suggest the possibility that the Abe kinship group may have at one point been associated with spirit possession and the use of mediums.

Akaru Hime Within the *Nihon shoki* and the *Kojiki* this deity is at various points said to be the wife of both Ame no Hiboko and Tsunuga Arashito, two immigrant cowherd deities from the Korean peninsula. Akaru Hime herself is said to have been born as a red stone on the Korean peninsula, after a young girl was impregnated by a ray from the sun. Within the *Hizen fudoki* she is also depicted as a vengeful weaving goddess who demands offerings in the form of woven items. One of several deities from Kyūshū who came to play an important role in the royal cult, within the court chronicles she

197

is said to have resided in the Himegoso shrines in Buzen and Settsu provinces. During the Heian period she also took up residence in the Suminoe shrine.

Ama no Hoakari no Mikoto Although little is written about this deity in the court chronicles, there is good reason to believe that the cult of this deity played a major role in the formation of early royal mythology. Within the *Nihon shoki* and *Kojiki,* Ama no Hoakari no Mikoto appears as one of the children of Konohana Sakuya Hime in the myth of the descent of the Heavenly Grandchild. He was also claimed as an ancestor by a number of cultically and politically influential lineages, including the Owari Muraji, the Wani, and the Kusakabe. Later texts such as the *Sendai kuji hongi* also state that Ama no Hoakari no Mikoto was none other than the founding Mononobe ancestor, Nigihayahi no Mikoto.

Amaterasu As the chief deity of the Ise shrine and the principal ancestor of the royal line, the sun deity Amaterasu occupied a central place in court ritual throughout the Nara period and beyond. Although we have little concrete information concerning this deity's origins, her cult appears to have been intimately connected not only with sun worship, but also with continental legends and kinship groups associated with rites related to sericulture and weaving.

Amayorozu Takuhata Chihata Hime *See* Takuhata Chichi Hime.

Ame no Hiboko Ame no Hiboko appears in both the *Kojiki* and the *Nihon shoki* as a Silla prince who emigrated from the Korean peninsula to the Japanese islands in pursuit of his estranged wife, Akaru Hime. Since he is also presented within these texts in the role of a defender of cows, it would appear that his union with the weaving deity Akaru Hime may have been connected with this image of Ame no Hiboko as a cowherd. Elsewhere in the court chronicles he is said to have been the father of Izushi Hime, an important figure whose legend cycle in several important ways mirrors that of the Miwa and Kamo no Kimi lineages.

Atsumori Atsumori appears within the *Tale of the Heike* as a young Taira warrior with a refined, courtly demeanor that renders him thoroughly unsuited for his final, fatal battle with the experienced Minamoto warrior Kumagae. Later the relationship between these two figures became the subject of a Nō play by Zeami, who depicted a subsequent encounter and final reconciliation between Kumagae and the ghost of his lamented young victim.

Atsuta shrine The Atsuta shrine in Owari province was the kinship group shrine of the Owari Muraji, a prominent regional lineage that purportedly provided several consorts to rulers during the fifth and sixth centuries. The shrine, which plays an important role in the Yamato Takeru legend cycle, also claimed as its main object of worship Yamato Takeru's weapon, the Kusanagi sword. Intriguingly, this sword was also believed to have caused the final illness of Tenmu *tennō*.

Benshō Benshō was a monk from the Hata kinship group that was sent to China for study during the Taihō era (701–704). During his stay in China, Benshō was purportedly well received by the Emperor Hsüan-tsung. Although Benshō died in China, his son, Hata no Asamoto, returned to the Japanese islands and succeeded in marrying his daughters to prominent members of the Fujiwara.

Bu, Great King *See* Yūryaku.

chimata *Chimata* were crossroads or intersections of major roadways. In addition to being of tremendous importance for the military, economic, and political systems of the Japanese islands, *chimata* were also frequently the site of rites of propitiation and pacification of dangerous spirits that were thought to travel the roadways of the Japanese islands. As such, *chimata* represent an important point of intersection between religious practice and political/material developments during the period.

Chinkonsai (Mitama Shizume Matsuri) Chinkonsai is generally thought to have been one of the most important rites in the court's ritual calendar, in which the spirit of the ruler is "shaken" in order to prevent death and assure the ruler's health. Since at least the ninth century the mythic background for the rite was understood to be the legend of the Heavenly Grotto, in which the spirit of the sun goddess entered into a cave and thereby plunged the world into darkness until she was tricked into coming out by deities engaged in a number of ritual activities. It is doubtful, however, that the origins of the rite lay strictly with the royal house, as lineages such as the Mononobe and Wani also appear to have performed rites of spirit-calling and resurrection independently of the royal cult. Within the *Sendai kuji hongi* we are even told that the origins of the royal Chinkonsai are to be found in rites performed at the Isonokami shrine, a major Mononobe cultic center.

Chiisakobe kinship group This lineage, which claimed descent from the royal ancestor and liturgist Kamu Yaimimi no Mikoto, appears to have played an important role in the formation of court rites related to spirit-quieting and sericulture. Within several legends in such sources as the *Nihon shoki, Kojiki,* and the *Nihon ryōiki,* members of the Chisakobe are also closely associated with the Yamato ruler Yūryaku and with the introduction of sericulture to the Japanese islands. Within the *Shinsen shōjiroku,* they are also explicitly singled out as having played a major role in the formation of the Hata, an immigrant lineage from the Korean peninsula that was said to have been the foremost producers of silk during Yūryaku's reign.

Chūai Within the court chronicles, this Yamato ruler is said to have been slain by the Sumiyoshi deities after he scoffed at their suggestion that he invade the Korean kingdom of Silla. Within the *Kojiki* account of his death and its aftermath, we also find the first depiction of the Ōharae, along with an invaluable account in which Chūai's consort and successor Jingū Kōgō serves as a medium for communication with the *kami.* Perhaps because of the prominent role of Silla immigrant lineages in the construction of the Jingū legend cycle, Chūai was, by the early Heian period, identified with the immigrant cowherd deity Tsunoga Arashito.

Daianji Prior to the construction of Tōdaiji and the Great Buddha, Daianji served as the main administrative headquarters for the state's ecclesial bureaucracy. The abbot of temple for most of this period was Dōji, one of the pre-eminent intellectuals of the day and a devotee of the Shōtoku cult. Although the temple in its earliest incarnations appears to have been the kinship group temple of the Nukadabe (Dōji's own lineage), the temple's official account of its origins traces the temple's construction to Shōtoku himself. In addition to the Chinese-educated Dōji, the temple also served for much of the Nara period as a home for the Tao-hsüan, one of the first and most prominent Chinese monks to emigrate to the Japanese islands. The temple was also a primary center for the Gumonjihō, an important rite associated with the Space Buddha Kokūzō.

Dōji One of the most prominent intellectuals of his day, Dōji studied in the Chinese capital at Ch'ang-an for over fifteen years before returning to the Japanese islands in 718. He is credited with playing a major role in the formation of the *kokubunji* system, and he is known to have been instrumental in convincing Shōmu's Queen Consort Kōmyō to help support the rebuilding of Hōryūji after a plague decimated a substantial portion of the court, including four of Kōmyō's brothers. Dōji is also thought to have been related to the proliferation of the Gumonjihō rite and the worship of the bodhisattva Kokūzō.

Dōkyō Few monks in Japanese history have inspired such enduring condemnation as Dōkyō, a monk who purportedly attempted to usurp the throne during the reign of Kōken *tennō* through the manipulation of omens and oracles. Although Dōkyō has been condemned for centuries as a particularly unscrupulous monk whose political entanglements brought about the end of the Nara period, very little is known about the events surrounding his rise and fall and even less is known about his Buddhist practice. What little we do know about Dōkyō, who came to power shortly after healing Kōken of a near-fatal disease, suggests that he utilized Buddhist healing practices recently imported from the continent that had roots in astrological and *onmyōdō* traditions. Intriguingly, Dōkyō was also said to have practiced austerities in the Kazuragi region of Yamato not far from Yoshino and also to have been a member of the Yuge Mononobe lineage.

Dōshō Dōshō was a Hata monk and Gumonjihō practitioner who was also a student of Kūkai. For most of his career he served as the abbot of the Hata kinship-group temple Kōryūji, where in 859 he built a retreat center for the worship of the Space Buddha Kokūzō. He eventually attained the rank of *shosōzu* (junior priest general) and was a confidant of Seiwa *tennō*.

Dōtō Dōtō was a monk from the Ema, an immigrant kinship group from the Korean kingdom of Koguryŏ that was based in Yamashiro province. Although he is referenced only briefly in the *Nihon shoki*, he appears in a legend in the *Nihon ryōiki* concerning a grateful spirit that sought to repay the kindness of Dōtō's servant from beyond the grave. The text also asserts that Dōtō was responsible for constructing the region's famed Uji Bridge.

En no Gyōja Although shrouded in mystery, this legendary mountain ascetic became from an early date a paradigmatic figure for practitioners of mountain asceticism across the Japanese islands. What little we know of En can be found in his biography in the *Shoku Nihongi* and in a legend in the *Nihon ryōiki* concerning his career and his battle with the deity Hitokoto Nushi. Of particular note in this latter account is the text's assertion that En was from a branch of the Kamo no Kimi kinship group. Both accounts stress En's ability to control spirits as well as his pursuit of superhuman powers in the region near Mount Kazuragi and Kane no Take (Mount Yoshino).

Fujiwara no Tanetsugu Fujiwara no Tanetsugu was the son of Fujiwara no Umakai and a daughter of Hata no Asamoto. As the head of the

Shiki branch of the Fujiwara, he played a major role in engineering the accession of Kōnin *tennō* to the throne following the tumultuous reign of Kōken *tennō*. Tanetsugu's line probably reached the apex of its power during the reign of Heizei *tennō* (reigned 806–809), when his daughter Kusuko served as Heizei's chief consort and his son Nakanari served as Heizei's chief advisor.

Fushimi Inari shrine Fushimi Inari shrine, much like the Matsuno'o, Kamo, and other Hata cultic centers in Yamashiro province, enjoyed a surge of royal patronage following the court's arrival in Yamashiro at the start of the Heian period. The Fushimi deity also quickly came to be worshipped within the precincts of Kūkai's temple Tōji and from there across the Japanese islands by practitioners of mountain asceticism.

Futsunushi no Mikoto Futsunushi no Mikoto is depicted in the *Nihon shoki* as a spirit-quieting deity who, along with the *chimata* deity Kunado, pacifies the realm for the Heavenly Grandchild Ninigi no Mikoto. He is also said to have been sent from the Heavenly Plain by the royal ancestor Amaterasu to revitalize the spirit of the Yamato ruler during Jinmu's campaign to conquer Yamato. Futsunushi no Mikoto was also worshipped in the form of a sword at the Isonokami shrine, the most important cultic center of the Mononobe kinship group, and he was claimed as a founding ancestor by the Kasuga no Omi, a major sublineage of the Wani kinship group.

Gomyō Gomyō, a Hata monk, was one of the most prominent members of the powerful Hossō school of Buddhism in the decades following the move of the capital to Heian. He also held several of the highest posts in the court's ecclesial hierarchy, including Sōjō (Supreme Priest). Gomyō is also of note because he was an early practitioner of the Gumonjihō rite and because he took a famously adversarial stance to the Tendai patriarch Saichō.

Gonsō Gonsō was a Hata monk who studied with Dōji's disciple Zengi at Daianji. Much like his fellow Hata monk Gomyō, Gonsō was also a Gumonjihō practitioner who rose to become one of the most prominent monks of the early Heian period. In 827 Gonsō succeeded Gomyō in the position of Sōjō.

Gumonjihō The Gumonjihō is a rite of propitiation of the Space Buddha Kokūzō, which, if performed properly, offers the devotee the promise of the ability to understand any Buddhist scripture. Because of the extremely arduous requirements of the rite, the *Kokūzō bosatsu nōman shogan saishōshin darani gumonji no hō* recommends its performance in remote mountain settings such as are found in Yoshino. During the Nara and early Heian periods the rite was popular among monks seeking superhuman knowledge. Several of the most prominent such practitioners, including such monks as Gomyō, Gonsō, and Dōshō were from the Hata kinship group.

Hachiman Although Hachiman is not mentioned within the *Nihon shoki* and *Kojiki*, this deity from northern Kyūshū became one of the most influential deities in the Japanese islands during the Nara period. Although the reasons for Hachiman's rise are not entirely clear, it appears likely that the deity was given credit for quieting local unrest in Kyūshū during the reign of Shōmu *tennō*. In 752 Hachiman was brought from Kyūshū to Nara and installed at Tōdaiji, apparently as a result of aid that the deity was believed to have given in the creation of the Great Buddha. Hachiman would later play a central role in the downfall of the monk Dōkyō, who was accused of having manufactured an oracle from Hachiman suggesting that Dōkyō be allowed to ascend the throne.

hakuji The *hakuji* was an auspicious white pheasant that was purportedly discovered and presented to the court during the reign of the Yamato ruler Kōtoku by a member of the Kusakabe kinship group.

Hata kinship group As one of the largest immigrant lineages in the Japanese islands, the Hata exerted a powerful and enduring influence upon the formation of the political and religious institutions of the Japanese islands. Although little is known of their origins, it would appear that at least one major branch of this lineage was composed of immigrants from the Korean kingdoms that were settled in the region of Kazuragi in the fourth and fifth centuries by the Kazuragi no Omi, one of the most powerful lineages of that age. Within the court chronicles the Hata appear in prominent cultural and technological roles following the destruction of the main line of the Kazuragi no Omi by the Yamato ruler Yūryaku. Within the *Nihon shoki* we are told that the Hata were instrumental in such activities as building canals and administering royal estates and storehouses. They are referred to as the paramount weavers of the Japanese islands, and they are also shown performing important sacerdotal functions for the court, both as propitiants of *kami* and as worshippers of buddhas. In addition to all this, the Hata are also known to have been at the forefront of the early Shōtoku cult. With the establishment of the Heian capital in the main Hata base of Kadano in Yamashiro province, Hata cultic centers were also absorbed into the heart of the royal cult.

Hata no Asamoto Hata no Asamoto was the son of Benshō, a Hata monk who was sent to China to study during the Taihō era (701–704). Following Asamoto's arrival in the Japanese islands, he succeeded in marrying two of his daughters to sons of Fujiwara no Umakai, the leader of the Shiki Fujiwara, the most powerful branch of the Fujiwara kinship group for much of the Nara period. As a result, Asamoto became the maternal grandfather and great-grandfather of some of the most powerful figures of the late Nara and early Heian periods.

Hata no Shimamaro Although little is known about the background of Hata no Shimamaro, he appears to have been the head of the Hata kinship group in the Kadono district of Yamashiro province during the reign of Shōmu *tennō*. When Shōmu decided to build a new capital in Yamashiro in 740, Shimamaro appears to have provided major economic aid and labor for the project. As a result, Shimamaro was raised to the fourth rank. Shimamaro then married his daughter to Fujiwara no Ogimaro, who became the head of the northern branch of the Fujiwara and perhaps the most influential member at court for much of his life. Evidence of the importance of such links can be seen in the name of Shimamaro's grandson Fujiwara no Kadono, who would later play an active role in moving the court from the Nara capital to the Kadono district.

Heavenly Grotto The legend of the Heavenly Grotto, which is recounted in numerous forms in the *Nihon shoki* and *Kojiki*, served as an essential pillar for the construction of royal myth and ritual during the Nara period and afterward. At the center of the legend is the figure of the royal ancestor Amaterasu, who is engaged in a contest with her brother Susanoo no Mikoto. After Susanoo performs a series of outrageous and defiling acts, Amaterasu enters the Heavenly Grotto, thereby plunging the world into darkness. Following a great deal of ritual activity on the part of the other gods in the Heavenly Plain, Amaterasu re-emerges from the cave. She is then in effect recognized as the supreme deity, while Susanoo is punished. The legend came to be used as the basis for the liturgies of the Chinkonsai and the Ōharae, two of the most important rites in the court's liturgical calendar.

Heavenly Maidens Throughout the literature of the Nara period we find references to female immortals or deities who are apparently based upon continental models related to the Weaver Maiden. Within these narratives a Heavenly Maiden is typically said to descend to earth to bathe, only to have her magical garments stolen by a human male, who forces her to marry him. After she has given birth to one or more children, however, she almost invariably finds the garments or some other device that allows her to fly away and rejoin the immortals.

Hibasu Hime   Within the court chronicles Hibasu Hime is said to have been the daughter of Tamba Nushi no Mikoto, an important figure claimed as an ancestor by the Kusakabe and Wani kinship groups. She is also said to have been the mother of Keikō *tennō*, Yamato Hime, and Inishiki Irihiko. Within the court chronicles her death and funeral are said to have led to the formation of a number of funerary service groups. In addition, Tajima Mori, the Miyake Muraji ancestor who purportedly journeyed to the realm of the Queen Mother of the West, is said to have left fruits of immortality as offerings at her grave upon his return to Yamato.

Hiei, Mount   Although Mount Hiei is most famous as the center of the Saichō's Tendai Buddhist movement, this mountain in Ōmi province was also the site of the Hiyoshi shrines, two important cultic centers that predated Saichō by at least one hundred years.

Himegoso shrines   Located in Buzen and the port of Naniwa in Settsu province, the Himegoso shrines housed the vengeful weaving deity Akaru Hime.

hitogata   *Hitogata* appear to have been used from an extremely early period as effigies in purification rites. Discoveries of *hitogata* from all areas of the Japanese islands that bear inscriptions and spells from continental purification texts have conclusively established the presence of such ritual systems in the Japanese islands from at least the late seventh century.

Hiyoshi shrines   Although the history of the Hiyoshi cultic centers on Mount Hiei in Ōmi province is quite murky, within the *Kojiki* we are told that the deity of the mountain was Ōyamakui no Mikoto, who was also worshipped at the Matsuno'o shrine, an important Hata cultic center in adjacent Yamashiro province. At some point the cultic center devoted to Ōyamakui, which was located at the base of the mountain, came to be referred to as the lower Hiyoshi shrine, in contrast to the upper Hiyoshi shrine, a cultic center higher up the mountain that housed the Miwa deity Ōmononushi. During the Heian period the number of shrines on the mountain continued to proliferate in conjunction with the tremendous growth of the Tendai sect. During the medieval period new understandings of these deities rooted in the Buddhist doctrine of *honji suijaku* led to a recasting of these deities as the figure Sannō Gongen and, eventually, to the formation of the movement known as Sannō Shintō.

hokai   Variously translated as "prayer," "blessing," and even "toast," *hokai* appear to have been spells of a specific type in which the voicing of a wish ("May you . . .") was believed to help effect its actualization. *Hokai* also appear within early sources as a means of divination, following a formula in which a condition is first attached to the content of the *hokai* (If . . . , then may . . .). *Hokai* can be found throughout royal mythology as well as in provincial gazetteers from across the Japanese islands.

Hōryūji   As the kinship group temple of Prince Kamitsumiya (Shōtoku), Hōryūji has for over a thousand years enjoyed a special status among the Buddhist temples in the Japanese islands. Although the temple's fortunes are thought to have gone into decline following the elimination of the main line of Kamitsumiya's lineage and a subsequent fire in 670, much of the temple was rebuilt in the 730s and 740s as the court turned to the figure of the prince for superhuman protection from a series of plagues that ravaged the capital and countryside.

Hōzō   According to the *Nihon shoki*, Hōzō was a monk from Paekche who sought to cure the ailing Tenmu *tennō* of his final illness both with herbal medicine and with a rite of "spirit-calling" (*shōkon*) that was timed to coincide with the winter solstice.

Inishiki Irihiko, Prince   Within the court chronicles Inishiki Irihiko is said to have been the son of Hibasu Hime and the Yamato ruler Suinin and the brother of Yamato Hime, the legendary princess first consecrated to the worship of the royal ancestor Amaterasu. Inishiki Irihiko is also said to have produced over 1,000 weapons and ritual implements that were stored in the Isonokami shrine, the main cultic center of the Mononobe kinship group.

Isonokami shrine   Located near the important Isonokami *chimata* in Yamato province, the Isonokami shrine served for centuries both as the main kinship group shrine of the Mononobe and as one of the most important cultic centers of the royal line. For the Mononobe, the main object of worship at the shrine was their ancestral deity Futsunushi no Mikoto. Although little is known about the type of rites that were performed, there are scattered indications throughout the early literature that the shrine was closely associated with rites of "spirit-shaking." For the court, the shrine was also used to house sacred objects, or regalia, of important lineages from across the Japanese islands. In addition, the shrine appears to have functioned at least partially as a military storehouse in which thousands of weapons could be stored.

Izushi Otome no Kami Within the *Kojiki* we are told that Izushi Otome no Kami was the daughter of Ame no Hiboko, an immigrant cowherd deity from Silla who also had a strong cultic presence in Izushi. Within the text Izushi Otome no Kami is said to have been the object of competition of two brothers, one of whom wins her after she brings home a magic arrow that has been placed above her lavatory.

Jingū Within the court chronicles Jingū is said to have been the chief consort of the Yamato ruler Chūai and the mother of the Yamato ruler Ōjin. Immediately following Chūai's death, which is said to have occurred following his refusal to heed the advice of the Suminoe deities, Jingū is said to have carried out the gods' will by attacking and conquering the Korean kingdom of Silla. Intriguingly, within the court chronicles she is also said to have been a descendant of the Silla prince and immigrant deity Ame no Hiboko.

Jinmu Within the court chronicles Jinmu is said to have been the first member of the royal line to enter into Yamato. The tale of Jinmu's conquest of the Japanese islands highlights the role of the Ōtomo and Mononobe, two kinship groups that were at the peak of their power in the sixth century C.E. Of particular note, for our purposes, is the extensive discussion devoted within both texts to the ritual and political activities of Jinmu and his allies at Yoshino.

Jitō *tennō* Although Jitō *tennō* (reigned 690–697) was the queen consort of Tenmu *tennō* and the daughter of the Yamato ruler Tenchi, she is generally thought to have assumed the throne only as a temporary measure following the death of Prince Kusakabe, her son by Tenmu. Jitō's reign was nonetheless extremely significant for the formation of the political institutions of the Japanese islands, for she consolidated and extended many of the bureaucratic reforms initiated by Tenchi and Tenmu. Cultically, her reign was also notable for her unprecedented visit to the Ise shrine and for her numerous pilgrimages to Yoshino.

Kamitsumiya, Prince *See* Shōtoku.

Kamo Agatanushi kinship group Based in the Kadono district of Yamashiro province, the Kamo Agatanushi are said to have frequently intermarried with the Hata. During the Heian period, the Kamo shrines, which housed Tamayori Hime and Wake no Ikazuchi no Kami, two deities that the Kamo claimed as ancestors, came to be ranked alongside the Ise shrines as among the most important centers in the royal cult. In addition, the Kamo Agatanushi claimed as an ancestor the Yatagarasu, a legendary crow that purportedly guided Jinmu's army during that Yamato ruler's conquest of the Japanese islands.

Kamo no Kimi kinship group Based in the Yoshino region of Yamato province, the Kamo no Kimi appear to have been an important sacerdotal lineage in the fifth and sixth centuries. Along with the Miwa, another major sacerdotal lineage charged with worshipping the deity Ōmononushi on Mount Miwa in Yamato province, the Kamo no Kimi claimed descent from Ōtataneko no Mikoto, a paradigmatic ritualist for the royal line.

Kamo shrines Located in the Kadono district of Yamashiro province, the upper and lower Kamo shrines came to serve as principal foci in the Heian court's ritual program. As early accounts of the shrines diverge on such basic points as the names and character of the gods in residence at the shrines, it would appear that from an early date both cultic centers were contested religious sites. According to the *Yamashiro fudoki* the lower Kamo shrine housed the female deity Tamayori Hime, while the upper Kamo shrine housed her male counterpart Tamayori Hiko. Within the court chronicles, however, we are told that the upper shrine housed Tamayori Hime's child Wake no Ikazuchi no Kami. Making the picture even murkier, according to a remnant of the *Hatashi honkeichō*, the deity of the upper shrine was Wake no Ikazuchi no Kami, while the deity of the lower shrine is referred to only as a "Hata woman" whose name is Mioya Kami (the parent deity). Such multiple claims are most likely indicative of the importance of the Kamo shrines within cultic discourse of the period as well as their disputed status.

karakami The term "*karakami*" (literally "continental deity") appears in conjunction with immigrant deities, such as Ame no Hiboko and Tsunoga Arashito, who were said to have come to the Japanese islands from across the sea. Perhaps not surprisingly, given the large number of immigrant lineages and ancestral cults in the Japanese islands, *karakami* appear in virtually every literary genre from the period.

Kitora Kofun Kitora Kofun, a pre-Nara-period tomb in the Asuka region of ancient Yamato, captured the attention of scholars worldwide when it was discovered in 2001 that its ceiling contained what is thought to be the oldest extant star chart in East Asia. Thanks both to its degree of preservation and its complexity, there can now be little doubt that even before the Nara period there was a substantial interest in and knowledge of continental astrological systems.

Kōgyoku Kōgyoku, the chief consort of Jomei *tennō* and the mother of Tenchi and Tenmu, ascended the throne twice during the middle decades of the seventh century. Within the *Nihon shoki* her death and funeral are depicted in terms that suggest that she was believed to have been killed by a demon in Kyūshū. During her reign, we are also told, her prayers were able to end a drought after sutra readings and even animal sacrifice had failed to bring rain.

Kōken *tennō* Kōken *tennō*, the daughter of Shōmu *tennō* and his Queen Consort Kōmyō, ruled twice, from 749 to 757 and again from 764 to 770. These reigns are remembered as having been marked by numerous upheavals, not the least of which was the rapid rise and even more rapid fall of her counselor, the healer-monk Dōkyō. Following Kōken's death, no woman was allowed upon the throne for several hundred years.

kokubunji The *kokubunji* temple network was created by order of the Shōmu court in the wake of a series of natural and political disasters.

Kokūzō Literally the Space Storehouse Buddha, Kokūzō appears to have been associated with astral beliefs long before his cult arrived in the Japanese islands at the start of the Nara period. During the Nara and early Heian periods, Kokūzō was a popular object of worship among monks seeking enhanced powers of understanding through practice of the Gumonjihō rite in the mountains of Japan. During the Heian period Kokūzō was also widely worshipped by members of the Shingon and Tendai movements.

Kōmyō, Queen Consort As the daughter of the Fujiwara leader Fujiwara Fuhito and the chief consort of Shōmu *tennō*, Queen Consort Kōmyō was among the most influential figures at court throughout the 730s and 740s. A devout Buddhist, Kōmyō provided crucial support for the reconstruction of Hōryūji and the early Shōtoku cult.

Konohana Sakuya Hime Konohana Sakuya Hime appears in the legend of the Heavenly Grandchild as a Weaving Maiden who is the mother of three children by Ninigi no Mikoto, including not only the royal ancestor Hiko Hoho Demi no Mikoto, but also the fire deity, Ama no Hoakari no Mikoto, and Ho no Suseri no Mikoto, purportedly the founding ancestor of the Hayato people of southern Japan.

Konoshima ni masu Amaterasu Mitama Jinja Located in the Kadono district of Yamashiro province, this Hata cultic center appears to have been a shrine dedicated to the sun deity Amaterasu. Intriguingly, the shrine was also located in extremely close proximity to rice fields dedicated to Amaterasu's brother, the moon deity Tsukiyomi no Mikoto. At some point the shrine also came to house a subshrine known as the Kaiko Yashiro (Silkworm shrine).

Kūkai Easily one of the most influential monks in Japanese history, Kūkai is claimed today as a founder by the Shingon sect. Like many other monks from the period, Kūkai in his early years practiced the Gumonjihō rite. After spending a number of years in China, he returned to the Heian court, where he introduced a number of esoteric scriptures into the mainstream of Japanese Buddhist discourse. During his lifetime Kūkai also sought to establish connections with several prominent deities, including the deity of the Fushimi Inari and Nihu shrines.

kusagari Kusagari, or medicine hunts, are first mentioned in the *Nihon shoki* during the reign of Suiko. Although there is no way of knowing if such events did in fact occur, such entries at the very least confirm that by the time of the composition of the *Nihon shoki* in 720, such practices were associated both with nodal days in the Chinese festival calendar and with such mountainous regions as Yoshino.

Kusakabe kinship group The Kusakabe were a service lineage group with significant populations in several coastal regions across the Japanese islands. Although within the court chronicles there are several accounts of the group's origins, within the *Nihon shoki* they are said to have been descended from one Hiko Imasu no Mikoto, the grandfather of Hibasu Hime and a descendant of the fire deity Ama no Hoakari no Mikoto. During the reign of Tenmu *tennō* the Kusakabe appear to have enjoyed a significant rise in status, for Prince Kusakabe, who was apparently raised with the aid of a Kusakabe sublineage, was named crown prince. Although Prince Kusakabe died before ascending the throne, subsequent rulers for virtually the entire Nara period were his descendents.

Kusakabe, Prince The son of Tenmu *tennō* and Jitō *tennō*, Prince Kusakabe was expected to ascend to the throne, but he died an untimely death in 689. As a result Kusakabe's mother Jitō ascended the throne, which she held for some eight years before stepping aside in favor of her grandson Monmu. Although Prince Kusakabe never ascended the throne, rulers for the next eighty years were all either his descendents or consorts of his descendents.

Kusanagi sword The Kusanagi sword, which is the main object of worship at the Atsuta shrine in Owari province, was purportedly the weapon used by Yamato Takeru as he moved to pacify the realm for his father, the Yamato ruler Keikō. Further indications of the importance of the sword for the royal line can be seen from the fact that within the court chronicles we are told that the sword was given to Yamato Takeru by his aunt Yamato Hime, the legendary first chief priestess at the Ise shrine. We are also told that the sword brought about the death of Tenmu *tennō*.

Kusuko incident The Kusuko incident occurred in 810, when the recently retired Heizei *tennō*, against the wishes of the recently installed Saga *tennō* (reigned 809–823), sought to force the court to abandon the Heian capital and return to Nara. In the brief, violent struggle that ensued, Heizei, his consort Fujiwara no Kusuko, and Fujiwara Nakanari were defeated after Saga visited the Kamo shrines and pledged that rulers in perpetuity would send a consecrated princess to worship at the shrines. In the aftermath the Kamo shrines emerged as the primary cultic centers for the capital.

Kwallŭk According to the *Nihon shoki*, Kwallŭk was a monk from the Korean kingdom of Paekche who presented the court of Suiko with books on astrology and divination. He is said to have instructed students at the court in these arts and was later purportedly made the head of an official ecclesial hierarchy that we are told was established by the Suiko court.

Lavatory goddess Within Chinese popular religion the lavatory goddess played an important role both for her association with fertilizer and abundance and as a manifestation of the tendency to localize specific deities within specific household locations and functions. Rites for this deity were performed on the fifteenth day of the first month in the popular Chinese festival calendar. Resonances with the cult of this deity can be seen in the founding ancestral legends of the Miwa, Chiisakobe, and Kamo no Kimi kinship groups.

Matsuno'o shrine This Hata cultic center in Yamashiro province appears to have been closely connected from a very early date with the nearby Kamo shrines. Evidence for this can be seen in numerous edicts from the court addressing the shrines in tandem, and in a remnant from the *Hatashi honkeichō* that asserts that Ōyamakui, the main deity at the Matsuno'o shrine, was the father of Wake no Ikazuchi no Mikoto, the deity of the upper Kamo shrine.

Michiae no Matsuri (Rite of Roadside Offerings) Although a regular part of the court's ritual calendar, the Michiae no Matsuri was also frequently employed as a defense against epidemics. At its core, the rite involved using animal hides to propitiate potentially hostile, disease-causing spirits on the roadsides of the Japanese islands.

Mitoshi no Kami Although the Mitoshi Kami appears only briefly in the court chronicles, he is the subject of a legend in the *Kogoshūi* that recounts the origins of the Toshigoi Matsuri. Within the text he appears incensed at the prospect of meat being consumed by farm workers, with the result that meat offerings are eventually made to the god instead.

Miwa kinship group The Miwa were a sacerdotal lineage dedicated to the worship of the deity Ōmononushi on Mount Miwa. Several legends concerning such Miwa ancestors as Seyatadera, Ōtataneko, Isukeyori Hime, and others can be found in the court chronicles.

Miyake kinship group The Miyake Muraji were an immigrant kinship group that claimed as its founding ancestor the Silla immigrant deity Ame no Hiboko. Other prominent members of the Miyake Muraji included Tajima Mori, a sage figure who is said to have traveled to the land of immortals and brought back the fruit of immortality for his sovereign, the Yamato ruler Sujin.

Mononobe kinship group One of the most powerful kinship groups of the sixth century, the Mononobe were also one of the most important sacerdotal lineages in the Japanese islands. They are perhaps most commonly remembered, however, for their role in the founding narrative of Japanese Buddhism, in which they were portrayed as the greatest antagonists of the new tradition. Far from being xenophobes, however, there is good reason to believe that the Mononobe were actively involved in promoting continental-style rites of spirit-quieting and resurrection within the Japanese islands.

Nara Osa According to the *Shinsen shōjiroku*, the Nara Osa were an immigrant kinship group from the Korean kingdom of Koguryŏ that settled in Yamashiro province during the sixth century.

Nigihayahi no Mikoto The founding ancestor of the Mononobe kinship group, Nigihayahi is said to have descended from the Heavenly Plain in much the same manner as the Heavenly Grandchild Ninigi no Mikoto. Within the *Sendai kuji hongi* Nigihayahi is also identified as the fire deity Ama no Hoakari no Mikoto.

Nintoku Nintoku was a Yamato ruler said to have been the son of the Yamato ruler Ōjin. Within the *Kojiki* we find a series of poems that make heavy use of sericulture imagery and were purportedly composed by Nintoku for his estranged consort Iwa no Hime.

norito   *Norito* is a term given to petitionary prayers spoken in court liturgies. The earliest textual sources for *norito* are in the *Engishiki*, a ritual and administrative compendium composed around 927.

Nunoshiki no Omi Kinume   Nunoshiki no Omi Kinume is the central figure in a narrative from the *Nihon ryōiki* in which a demon from the underworld accepts a bribe in the form of roadside offerings and agrees to seek out a substitute victim to bring back to the king of the dead.

Nuribe Hime   Within the *Nihon ryōiki* Nuribe Hime appears in a narrative recounting her travails as a mother and her eventual attainment of immortality after ingesting herbs from the Uda region of Yamato.

Ōfube no Ōshi   Ōfube no Ōshi appears in the *Nihon shoki* as the leader of a popular millennial movement focused on the imminent arrival of a *tokoyo* deity that was said to resemble in every way a silkworm.

Ōharae   Ōharae was a rite of purification performed on the final evening of the sixth and twelfth months in order to purify the court and the realm at the start of each half of the year. The liturgy for the rite appears to have been closely based upon the legend of the Heavenly Grotto, in which the numerous offenses committed by Susanoo are confessed to as defiling acts that require divine purification.

Ōmononushi   Ōmononushi, the god of Mount Miwa, is believed to have been the chief focus of royal worship for much of Japan's ancient period. At some time during the fifth century, worship of the deity was apparently given over to the Miwa, a sacerdotal lineage that rose to prominence at the Yamato court at roughly this time.

Ōtataneko   Within the court chronicles Ōtataneko—purportedly the founding ancestor of the Miwa and Kamo no Kimi kinship groups—appears in a legend recounting the origins of the court's involvement in the cult of Ōmononushi, the deity of the Miwa shrine. Within these texts Ōtataneko is said to have been the child of Ōmononushi and Ikutamayori Hime.

Owari kinship group   The Owari Muraji were a prominent regional lineage that purportedly provided several consorts to rulers during the fifth and sixth centuries. They are generally associated with Owari province, where their chief cultic center, the Atsuta shrine, was located. The Owari Muraji appear prominently in the legend cycle of Yamato Takeru, and they also appear to have had a special connection with Tenmu *tennō*, who bore the name of a lineage affiliated with the Owari Muraji prior to ascending the throne. In addition, by the time of the composition of the *Shinsen shōjiroku* at the start of the

Heian period, the Owari Muraji were considered to be a main line of descent from their founding ancestor Ama no Hoakari no Mikoto.

Ōyamakui no Mikoto Ōyamakui no Mikoto was the chief object of worship at the Matsuno'o shrine, a Hata cultic center in Yamashiro province, and at the lower Hiyoshi shrine, a cultic center located on Mount Hiei in neighboring Ōmi province. Although he does not appear prominently within the court chronicles, he did play an important role in mythology of the Kamo shrines.

Queen Mother of the West The Queen Mother of the West was one of the most widely venerated deities in the Chinese pantheon. As early as the Warring States period she was believed to reside on Mount Kunlun in western China, where she purportedly ruled over the realm of the immortals. Later she was also seen as the authenticator of sage rulers and an important member of the Taoist pantheon. The appropriation of the cult of the Queen Mother of the West within elite traditions did not, however, preclude popular worship of the goddess. Within the *Han shu* we are told that towards the end of that dynasty a popular millennial movement centering upon the advent of the Queen Mother of the West broke out near the capital. The Queen Mother of the West, whose main iconographic attribute was a weaving implement that served as her headdress, was also closely associated with sericulture and the figure of the Weaver Maiden. Evidence suggesting that the Queen Mother was known in the Japanese islands can be seen in the *Kojiki* account of Tajima Mori's journey to the land of immortals and in legends and prognostications related to the Three-legged Crow, an animal from the Chinese pantheon that was often associated with the Queen Mother.

River Earl The River Earl, another widely venerated deity within the Chinese pantheon, was regularly propitiated across East Asia for his ability to bring rain. The importance of this deity on the Korean peninsula can be seen in the founding legend of Koguryŏ, which states that the River Earl was the maternal father-in-law of the founding ancestor of the royal line. Within the Japanese islands we find references to the River Earl in the court chronicles within the contexts of canal-building and rain-making.

Saga *tennō* Saga *tennō*, the brother of Heizei *tennō* and the son of Kanmu *tennō*, reigned from 809 to 823. During the Kusuko incident of 810, the recently installed Saga petitioned the Kamo deities for assistance in quelling the uprising. In return, Saga pledged that rulers thereafter would send a consecrated princess to the shrines at the start of each reign.

Saichō Although Saichō's Tendai sect came to be the dominant religious institution for much of the Heian period, during his lifetime Saichō's group remained a small, isolated movement on the periphery of the Buddhist establishment. Saichō and his successors not only succeeded in transforming Buddhist doctrinal discourse in the Japanese islands, but they also successfully identified themselves with—and then promoted—the cults of Prince Shōtoku and the deities of the Hiyoshi shrines.

Saimei *See* Kōgyoku.

Seyatadera Hime Seyatadera appears in the court chronicles as the wife of Ōmononushi and the mother of Isukeyori Hime, a maiden who gives birth to three children after being with her husband Jinmu for only a single night. As the mother and grandmother of Kamu Yaimimi no Mikoto, both women were claimed as ancestors by the Miwa and Chiisakobe kinship groups.

Shinohara no Otohihimeko Shinohara no Otohihimeko appears in two legends in the *Hizen fudoki*, a provincial gazetteer that was composed sometime around 713. In the first story she is said to have been the lover of one Ōtomo no Sadehiko, a leader of the Ōtomo kinship group, who was said to have been active on the Korean peninsula during the sixth century. In the second, she is said to have been visited nightly in much the same manner as the unfortunate Miwa ancestor Ikutamayori Hime. Like Ikutamayori Hime, Shinohara no Otohihimeko meets a violent end after discovering her lover's secret identity.

Shōmu *tennō* The son of Monmu *tennō* and a daughter of Fujiwara no Fuhito, Shōmu *tennō* (reigned 727–749) is generally remembered as a patron of the Buddhist tradition whose long and complicated reign left a lasting mark on innumerable aspects of court culture. During his reign Shōmu ordered the formation of the *kokubunji* system of provincial temples dedicated to the protection of the realm. He also committed tremendous resources to the construction of new temples such as Tōdaiji and the creation of icons such as the Great Buddha. During Shōmu's reign much of Hōryūji was also rebuilt, as the cult of Prince Shōtoku flourished. While still on the throne, Shōmu declared that he was a servant of the Three Jewels of Buddhism, and in retirement he took priestly orders. Shōmu's daughter Kōken *tennō* continued this trend, for she became the first monarch in the Japanese islands to take the vows of a Buddhist nun.

Shōtoku (Prince Kamitsumiya)   Although little is known about the historical Prince Kamitsumiya—Prince Shōtoku, as he came to be known in legend—he was widely seen as having played a crucial role in the establishment of the Buddhist tradition in the Japanese islands. Even as the Shōtoku cult continued to grow in importance during the Nara and Heian periods, however, Shōtoku was also closely identified with the importation of continental ritual and literary systems as well. Thus, in addition to his role as a temple-founder and warrior for the Buddhist cause, within the *Nihon shoki* Shōtoku was also said to have composed the first history of the royal line, to have established a comprehensive rank system for the court based upon continental models, and to have cultivated powers of sage-like perception.

Suiko   The reign of Suiko, the first woman to be referred to as "*tennō*" in the court chronicles, is presented within the *Nihon shoki* as having been in many ways a cultural and political watershed for the Japanese islands. Having assumed the throne in the aftermath of the battle for the establishment of Buddhism in the Japanese islands, the Suiko court is presented as opening relations with the Sui empire and aggressively supporting the importation of continental cultural, political, and religious systems. Although the *Nihon shoki* and later hagiography often associate these events with Prince Kamitsumiya (Shōtoku), it appears highly likely that Suiko and her kinsmen in the powerful Soga kinship group were primarily responsible for the affairs of the court.

Sumiyoshi deities   The three Sumiyoshi deities, like many other vengeful gods from Kyūshū, play an important role in the myths and legends of the court chronicles. Most famously, they are said to have killed the Yamato ruler Chūai, after Chūai refused to obey their command to invade the Korean kingdom of Silla. By the early Heian period, there is good reason to believe that the Sumiyoshi cult had merged with the cults of Jingū and Akaru Hime, the wife of Jingū's distaff ancestor, the Silla prince Ame no Hiboko, for both Jingū and Akaru Hime had by then taken up residence in the Sumiyoshi shrine in the port of Naniwa. Yet another legend stating that Sumiyoshi Daijin, an aggregate form of the shrine's deities, flew across Yamato and Kawachi provinces upon a dragon while dressed in continental garb also suggests that the Sumiyoshi cult was closely associated with the Korean peninsula.

Suruga, Heavenly Maiden of   The Heavenly Maiden of Suruga is depicted in the *Suruga fudoki* in terms that make explicit reference to the

Weaver Maiden of Chinese mythology. As is the case in many such legends, this Heavenly Maiden descends to earth to bathe in a pond, only to have her clothes stolen by a human male whom she is forced to marry. Unusually, however, this legend concludes with both the Heavenly Maiden and her husband becoming immortals.

Susanoo no Mikoto The brother of the royal ancestor Amaterasu, Susanoo plays the role of Amaterasu's antagonist in the legend of the Heavenly Grotto, where he is depicted as a volatile, powerful deity who commits a series of defiling acts and is eventually driven from the Heavenly Plain by the other gods. Following his banishment, however, he is depicted in a far more sympathetic light as he travels in the land of Izumo. There are indications within the court chronicles as well as in local gazetteers (*fudoki*) that Susanoo may have been closely associated with the Korean kingdom of Silla.

Tajima Mori Within the court chronicles Tajima Mori appears as a devoted servant of the Yamato ruler Sujin, who travels to the land of the immortals in order to bring back the fruit of immortality for his ailing monarch. Tajima Mori is also said to have been a descendant of Ame no Hiboko, an immigrant cowherd deity from the Korean kingdom of Silla.

Takakara Megami Although virtually nothing is known about this deity, she appears in mid-Heian period texts such as the *Seiji yōryaku* as a goddess whose dance before Tenmu *tennō* at Yoshino inspired the incorporation of the Gosechimai dance into court ritual.

Takamatsuzuka Kofun In 1972 scholars investigating the Takamatsuzuka Kofun in the Asuka region of ancient Yamato were startled to find extremely well-preserved wall paintings illustrating not only the court dress and material culture of the period, but also figures from the Chinese zodiac. The tomb thus stands as an important indication that Chinese astrological beliefs had been incorporated in the cultic practice of the elite in the Japanese islands by the time of the tomb's construction, sometime towards the end of the seventh century.

Takami Musubi no Mikoto Although little is known about the cult of this deity, Takami Musubi no Mikoto plays a central role in what are thought to be the oldest versions of several important royal myths, including the legend of the Heavenly Grandchild. He also appears as a central object of propitiation in the Festival of the Tasting of the First Fruits (Niinamesai) and in royal accession ceremonies. It is therefore widely believed that Takami Musubi no Mikoto may have been the court's chief object of worship prior to the eventual adoption of Amaterasu as the chief ancestor of the royal line.

Takuhata Chichi Hime Also known as Amayorozu Takuhata Chihata Hime, Takuhata Chichi Hime appears in royal mythology as the mother of the Heavenly Grandchild Ninigi no Mikoto. Takuhata Chichi Hime was also from an early date installed in the inner shrine at Ise, alongside the sun deity Amaterasu no Mikoto. Given her name (Princess of Thousands and Thousands of Looms) and the prominent motif of the woven covering that was given to Ninigi prior to his descent from the Heavenly Plain, it would appear that Takuhata was at some point also conceived of as a weaving maiden.

Takuhata Hime Takuhata Hime appears in the Yūryaku chapter of the *Nihon shoki* as a consecrated princess at the Ise shrine who is slandered by one Abe no Kunimi. In the legend Takuhata Hime runs off with a sacred mirror and commits suicide. The legend concludes by stating that after the mirror gave off a miraculous light, her corpse was found, and she was vindicated. Takuhata Hime is also of note because of the close resemblance between her name and that of Takuhata Chichi Hime, the mother of the Heavenly Grandchild and one of the principal deities of the Ise inner shrine. Possible connections between Takuhata Hime and the Korean peninsula are also suggested by her mother's putative name, Karu Hime, which may be rendered in English as "Korean princess."

Tamayori Hime, Tamayori Hiko Within the *Yamashiro fudoki* we are told that these figures were the main deities of the lower and upper Kamo shrines, respectively. Elsewhere, however, we are told that the chief deity of the upper shrine was Tamayori Hime's child Wake no Ikazuchi no Kami. Although Tamayori Hiko does not appear in any other sources from the period, he is depicted within the *Yamashiro fudoki* as a vengeful deity who was propitiated in the annual Kamo Matsuri.

Tamba Michi no Nushi Within the court chronicles Tamba Michi no Nushi appears as a powerful regional paramount from Tamba who offers his daughters as consorts for the Yamato ruler Keikō. He is said to be the father of Hibasu Hime and was claimed as an ancestor by the Wani and Kusakabe kinship groups.

Tenmu *tennō* The brother of the Yamato ruler Tenchi, Tenmu came to power following the Jinshin war of 670. He is credited with accelerating a wide-ranging series of institutional and cultic innovations that led eventually to the creation of the *ritsuryō* state. During Tenmu's reign the importation of continental systems of technology and governance was greatly accelerated. Among the most important developments in this regard were the construction of an astrological observatory, the establishment of a Bureau of Yin and Yang (Onmyōryō), the adoption of the title *"tennō"* for the ruler, and the revival/institution of the practice of appointing a consecrated princess dedicated to the worship of the royal ancestor Amaterasu at Ise. Tenmu was also the first Yamato ruler to be proclaimed a manifest deity, and at the end of his life he had performed a rite of "spirit-calling" that appears to have been a forerunner of the Chinkonsai.

Toyouke Hime   Toyouke Hime is best known as the chief deity of the outer shrine at Ise. She also appears in a *Nihon shoki* account of the origins of sericulture, in which silkworms and other products of human civilization emerge from her body after she is slain by the moon deity Tsukiyomi no Mikoto. Within the *Tango fudoki*, however, Toyouke appears as a Heavenly Maiden who descends to earth and is captured by an elderly couple who force her to live as their daughter. The legend further tells us that while on earth Toyouke makes money for her parents by selling a magical elixir that can cure any illness. The text also refers to several shrines to the deity within Tamba, suggesting that before she was appropriated by the royal cult, Toyouke was an important local deity in the region.

Tsukiyomi no Mikoto   Within the court chronicles Tsukiyomi no Mikoto appears as a moon deity and brother of the sun goddess and royal ancestor Amaterasu. Although we have very little way of knowing much about the origins of Tsukiyomi's cult, we are told in the Kenzō chapter of the *Nihon shoki* that lands and a shrine in the Kadono district of Yamashiro province were dedicated to this god after he appeared to one Abe no Omi Kotoshiro in the Korean kingdom of Mimana. Tsukiyomi no Mikoto also appears in the *Nihon shoki* in an account of the origins of sericulture in which he slays Toyouke Hime, a female immortal and the main object of worship of the Ise outer shrine.

Tsuminoe no Hijiri Hime   Although little is known about this legendary figure, she is referenced in both Chinese and *waka*-style poems from the period. Judging from these poems and one important prefatory note in the *Manyōshū*, she appears to have been a female immortal who descends from Heaven to Yoshino only to be discovered by a human male who forces her to marry him. There is also evidence, however, that Tsuminoe no Hijiri Hime may also have had roots in Hizen province in Kyūshū.

Tsunoga Tsunoga was a port in the region of Koshi on the coast of the Japan/Eastern Sea. Not surprisingly, given its location directly across from the Korean peninsula, Tsunoga appears to have been from an early date a center for immigrants from the Korean kingdoms of Silla and Koguryŏ. The Kehi shrine, the largest cultic center in Tsunoga, was home to the immigrant cowherd deity Tsunoga Arashito.

Umashimaji Purportedly the son of the founding Mononobe ancestor, Nigihayahi no Mikoto, Umashimaji is depicted in the court chronicles as playing an important role in aiding the would-be Yamato ruler Jinmu to enter the Yamato plain. Within the *Sendai kuji hongi* he is also said to have instructed Jinmu on the use of a spell of resurrection related to the early Chinkonsai.

Uranoshimako The legend of Uranoshimako, a fisherman who, having captured and married a female immortal, enters the land *tokoyo* beneath the sea, appears to have been widely circulated even prior to the Nara period. While the legend bears the unmistakable imprint of popular continental conceptions of immortality, Uranoshimako was also worshipped as a local deity at several shrines in Tamba province. He was also claimed as an ancestor by members of the Kusakabe kinship group in Tamba.

Uzume Hime Uzume Hime was claimed as a founding ancestor by the Sarume no Kimi, an important liturgical lineage at the Yamato court. Within the court chronicles she appears in the legend of the Heavenly Grotto, where she draws the royal ancestor Amaterasu out of the cave by performing a lewd dance for the assembled gods. In light of this, Uzume Hime has often been taken as a prototypical representation of female shamanism in the ancient period.

Wake no Ikazuchi no Kami Within the *Hatashi honkeichō* Wake no Ikazuchi no Kami, the main deity of the upper Kamo shrine in Yamashiro province, is said to be the child of a female Hata ancestor and Ōyamakui no Mikoto, the chief deity of the Matsuno'o shrine and lower Hiyoshi shrine. At some point in the mid-Heian period this legend appears to have served as the basis for rites in which Ōyamakui no Mikoto was brought from the Hiyoshi shrine in Ōmi province to the Kamo shrines in Yamashiro, where he was joined with his son and consort.

Waki no Iratsume Within the court chronicles Waki no Iratsume is said to have been a consort of the Yamato ruler Keikō and a member of the Wani kinship group. Within the *Harima fudoki* she is also the subject of a legend that appears to suggest that following her death she attains entry into *tokoyo* beneath the sea. This legend is also notable for its use of motifs that appear to be drawn from continental narratives of immortals that attain "liberation from the corpse."

Wani kinship group   Within the court chronicles, the Wani are said to have provided numerous consorts to Yamato rulers in the fourth, fifth, and sixth centuries. Numerous sublineages of the Wani, such as the Kasuga no Omi, the Kakinomoto, and the Ono appear to have played an active role in the formation of royal mythology and ritual during the seventh century as well. Intriguingly, several legends from the Wani ancestral legend corpus feature themes of death and resurrection.

Weaver Maiden and Cowherd   Going back at least as far as the Warring States period in China, the legend of the Weaver Maiden and the Cowherd appears to have played an important role within both popular and elite religious practice. Within the literature of the Nara and early Heian periods we find such figures as Ame no Hiboko, Tsunuga Arashito, and Mitoshi no Kami in the role of defender of cows. Each of these deities also appears to have had close genealogical associations with deities from the Korean peninsula, including, in the case of Ame no Hiboko and Tsunoga Arashito, the immigrant weaving deity Akaru Hime.

Yamato Hime   Yamato Hime appears prominently within the court chronicles as the legendary first consecrated princess dedicated to the worship of the royal ancestor Amaterasu. She also features prominently in the narrative of Yamato Takeru, the royal prince who purportedly subdued resistance to royal authority across the Japanese islands during the reign of the Yamato ruler Keikō. In addition Yamato Hime appears to have played an important role in supplying genealogical linkages between a number of lineages and their putative founding ancestors. Thus in addition to being an aunt of Yamato Takeru, she is also said to have been the daughter of Hibasu Hime, the sister of Inishiki no Irihiko, and the granddaughter of Tamba no Michi Nushi, who was claimed as an ancestor by both the Wani and Kusakabe kinship groups.

Yamato Takeru   Yamato Takeru is presented in the court chronicles as the son of the Yamato ruler Keikō and Waki no Iratsume, a consort from the Wani kinship group. He is said to have pacified the realm for his father only to eventually be killed by a god on Mount Ibuki on the border between Ōmi and Mino provinces. By the seventh century at the latest, the Yamato Takeru legend cycle appears to have been linked with that of the Ise shrine and the royal ancestor Amaterasu.

Also featuring prominently within the corpus of legends related to this prince are figures from the Wani, Mononobe, and Owari Muraji, three kinship groups that claimed descent from the fire deity Ama no Hoakari no Mikoto. Among the most famous legends associated with the prince takes place after his death and burial, when his spirit was said to burst forth from his tomb in the shape of a white bird, a manner reminiscent of continental narratives of immortals attaining "liberation from the corpse."

Yatagarasu Within the court chronicles the Yatagarasu appears as a crow sent by the royal ancestor Amaterasu to serve as a guide for the would-be Yamato ruler Jinmu during his campaign to subdue the Central Plain of the Japanese islands. The Yatagarasu was also claimed as an ancestor by the Kamo no Agatanushi, a kinship group based in Yamashiro province that claimed the upper and lower Kamo shrines as their kinship group shrines.

Yoshino Yoshino is a region of Yamato known for its red earth, which was believed to be rich in cinnabar, a metal that figured prominently in continental beliefs concerning medicine and the pursuit of immortality. The region appears prominently in such major myths and legends as Jinmu's conquest of the Yamato plain and the founding legend of Japanese Buddhism. It also appears in numerous narratives from the period as a home for (mostly female) immortals and for the practice of mountain asceticism.

Yūryaku (Great King Bu) This Yamato ruler, who during his lifetime was apparently referred to as "Great King Bu," is believed to have come to power at the end of the fifth century. In many ways Bu's reign appears to have been a watershed moment for the formation of political institutions in the Japanese islands, as lineages such as the Mononobe and Ōtomo helped extend both the depth and the reach of the Yamato court's influence over the Japanese islands. Within the court chronicles Yūryaku is said to have destroyed the power of the Kazuragi no Omi, a powerful lineage from the Kazuragi region of Kawachi that appears to have been extremely active in settling immigrant lineages such as the Hata and others within Yamato. During Bu's reign immigrant lineages appear to have played a major role in the formation of institutions of kingship at court as well as the transmission of technologies associated with writing, metal working, weaving, and governance. Perhaps not surprisingly, legends concerning the Hata, Mononobe, and several other such lineages also appear frequently in the Yūryaku chapters of the *Nihon shoki* and *Kojiki*.

Appendix

Notes on Sources

The following notes are intended to provide background information on the primary sources used in this book. For a more complete historiographic account of these and many other Japanese sources, see Joan Piggott et al., eds., *Dictionary of Sources of Classical Japan*. For Chinese sources, see William H. Nienhauser, ed., *Indiana Companion to Traditional Chinese Literature*. For the textual history of the many *Chih kuai*, or "anomaly accounts," that appear below, see Robert Campany, *Strange Writing: Anomaly Accounts in Early Medieval China*.

Japanese Sources

Myth and Chronicle

Kogoshūi. The *Kogoshūi*, a mytho-historical text submitted by Imbe no Hironari to the court in 807, purports to give a history of the role of the Imbe, a liturgical kinship group for the court, from the Age of the Gods down to its date of composition. Hironari utilized a wealth of mytho-historical material to argue for a return to what Hironari believed to be the ancient Imbe ritual prerogatives at court. Although the text may have played an important role in unifying later royal mythology, the text is nonetheless at several points at variance with court chronicles such as the *Nihon shoki* and *Kojiki*. Of particular note for this book is the *Kogoshūi* account of the origins of the Toshigoi Matsuri, which appears to take for granted the practice of offering meat to the *kami*. Along with such texts as the *Tōshi kaden*, the *Sendai kuji hongi*, and the (mostly lost) *Hatashi honkeichō*, the *Kogoshūi* also serves as an important reminder that during the ancient period textual production was undertaken not only for the court, but also, and perhaps primarily, for particular lineages.

Kojiki. Ostensibly a written record of the oral recitations of one Hieda no Are shortly before the Nara period, the *Kojiki* is one of the oldest extant historical accounts in Japanese literature and hence a treasure trove of information concerning the emergence of writing in the Japanese islands, early Japanese historical consciousness, and early Japanese poetic traditions. In addition, because it purports to trace the history of the royal lineage from the Age of the Gods to the reign of the Yamato ruler Suiko, this text also contains a wealth of genealogical information and what appear to be kinship-group narratives from lineages across the Japanese islands. Thus, although highly dubious as an historical document, it can provide an oblique vantage point from which to view a range of mythic and ideological crosscurrents that raged just below the text's unified narrative of royal dominion. Of special interest for this book are the *Kojiki*'s depiction of female ancestors both in the legend of the descent of the Heavenly Grandchild and in later legends of royal consorts.

Nihon shoki. The *Nihon shoki,* which purports to chronicle the history of the royal line from the Age of the Gods through the abdication of Jitō *tennō* at the end of the seventh century, serves for better or worse as the main point of departure for the study of ancient Japan. Although notoriously unreliable for all but perhaps the latest periods it covers, the *Nihon shoki*, unlike the *Kojiki*, provides numerous diverging accounts of individual myths and political events. Although no one doubts that the text was edited to elaborate on the mytho-historical underpinnings for the post-Tenmu court, the *Nihon shoki*'s plurality of voices, as well as its sheer scope and depth, make it a necessary point of departure for understanding not only the historical events it purports to relate, but also the period of its composition. Throughout this book I have treated the *Nihon shoki* as a site of ideological contestation that was shaped by a multitude of competing forces both at court and in local power centers throughout the Japanese islands.

Sendai kuji hongi. The *Sendai kuji hongi* appears to have been composed by a member of the Mononobe kinship group at some point in the ninth century. Much as the *Kogoshūi* served as a mytho-history for the advancement of the interests of the Imbe, this text highlights the role of the Mononobe in court history from the Age of the Gods to the Nara period. Of particular interest to us is the account of the descent of the Heavenly Grandchild, which provides in great detail the independent descent from Heaven of the founding Mononobe ancestor Nigihayahi no Mikoto. Although the *Sendai kuji hongi* differs markedly from the account found in the court chronicles, it does appear to have drawn on sources that are hinted at in the *Nihon shoki* and *Kojiki*. For this study the text's account of the origins of the Chinkonsai as well as the overall cultic orientation of the Mononobe is a basic resource for understanding the role of spirit-quieting in the period.

Shoku Nihongi. The *Shoku Nihongi,* the sequel to the *Nihon shoki,* contains far fewer of the outright fabrications than do the *Kojiki* and the *Nihon shoki.* Because the text records numerous edicts promulgated by the court during times of plague and famine, it often provides the most concrete information we have about the court's ritual responses to crises. Also of immediate interest for this book are the text's biographies of prominent monks such as Dōji and En no Gyōja.

Hagiography and Tale Collections

Denjutsu isshin kaimon. The *Denjutsu isshin kaimon* recounts the life of the Tendai patriarch Saichō and the history of the early Tendai movement. It was composed sometime around 833 by Kōjō, one of Saichō's main disciples. It is one of the earliest accounts we have of Saichō's life and one of the earliest examples of Tendai polemics. For this study the *Denjutsu isshin kaimon* provides an account of Saichō's devotion to the cult of Prince Shōtoku and includes a poem that Saichō is said to have dedicated to the prince while the prince was worshipping at Shitennōji.

Jōgū Shōtoku hōō teisetsu. The *Jōgū Shōtoku hōō teisetsu* is a collection of materials related to Shōtoku (Prince Kamitsumiya), the seventh-century prince who came to be seen as the paradigmatic Buddhist monarch, a fountainhead of continental learning, and a sage immortal. Although the text probably did not reach its final form until sometime in the late tenth or early eleventh century, it is believed to contain a wealth of older material, some of which probably predates the *Nihon shoki* and the *Kojiki*. Much as in the case of the *Hōryūji garan engi narabi ni ruki shizaichō* and the *Daianji garan engi narabi ni ruki shizaichō,* the text appears to reflect the influence of a number of immigrant lineages on the legend corpus of a particular Buddhist temple (Hōryūji), and it amply illustrates the degree to which continental notions of divination and sagehood permeated the story of one of the most important building blocks of the Japanese Buddhist tradition.

Nihon ryōiki. The *Nihon ryōiki,* which was composed by the monk Kyōkai sometime before 824, is the oldest Buddhist tale collection in the Japanese islands. Comprising some 116 stories, the *Nihon ryōiki* provides virtually our only point of entry into popular culture and religious beliefs beyond the purview of the early Heian court. Its influence on the development of Japanese tale literature and Buddhist preaching are believed to be equally great. In this book I frequently use the *Nihon ryōiki* for its references to continental-style ritual practices and for its account of the founding legend of Japanese Buddhism.

Sangō shiiki. The *Sangō shiiki*, which is thought to be the oldest extant literary work of the Shingon patriarch Kūkai, was completed sometime around 797. It is notable both as a rare example of prose literature from this period and for its account of a fictional discussion among three animals on the relative merits of the Confucian, Taoist, and Buddhist traditions. For this study the text is of great interest for its apparently autobiographical preface, in which Kūkai describes his early practice of the Gumonjihō rite of the astral Buddha Kokūzō.

Tōshi kaden. The *Tōshi kaden*, a mid-eighth-century text, contains extended biographies of three of the earliest heads of the Fujiwara lineage. It is believed to have been composed at the direction of Fujiwara no Nakamaro, the highest-ranking official at court in the 750s and 760s. The text is a supplementary historical source for events that occurred during the seventh and early eighth centuries and an example of a nonofficial document with obvious ideological intent. Of special interest for us, the *Tōshi kaden* asserts a connection between the Fujiwara and the immigrant deity Tsunoga Arashito and indicates that Tenchi *tennō* played a major role in establishing continental-style ritual at court. For a recent critical edition of the text see Okamori Takuya et. al., eds., *Tōshi kaden: Kamatari, Jōe, Muchimaro den chūshaku to kenkyū*.

Provincial Gazetteers (*Fudoki*)

Fudoki, which were produced at the order of the court in 713, contain a wealth of information concerning pre-Nara local geography, customs, legends, and cultic practices. Although composed by literate courtiers at the behest of a court seeking to portray itself as the center of a realm that included "all under Heaven," the *fudoki* differ from such texts as the *Nihon shoki* and *Kojiki* in that they were composed in far closer proximity to the regions they describe, and often, apparently, with substantial input from members of local elite. As such they provide a wealth of information about local customs and beliefs across the Japanese islands. Although only five gazetteers exist in full or even partial form, quotations in numerous sources allow us to piece together fragments of others. Notably, while these gazetteers make only sporadic references to Buddhist temples or legends, they contain numerous legends that appear to demonstrate the penetration of continental mythic and cultic tropes into the farthest reaches of the land. Gazetteers from Buzen, Hizen, Ōmi, Suruga, Tango (Tamba), and Yamashiro provinces have been a fruitful source for legends featuring female deities, weaving maidens, and immortals. All extant *fudoki* as well as fragments have been collected and annotated by Uegaki Setsuya in *SNKBZ* 5: *Fudoki*.

Ritual Texts and Law Codes

Engishiki. The *Engishiki* is very large compendium of the ritual and administrative procedures of the court that was completed in 927. Covering virtually all court functions first set out in the Yōrō law codes, the text provides the finest details of court functions and the material culture of the age. Of particular note for the student of Japanese religion are Books 9 and 10, which list and rank all court-sponsored shrines and deities in the Japanese islands. The text also preserves detailed information concerning the material support given to the Ise shrine and the Kamo shrines as well as liturgies and petitionary prayers (*norito*) that were read at specific rites in the court's ritual calendar.

Honchō gatsuryō. Attributed to Koremune no Kinkata, the *Honchō gatsuryō* is believed to have been composed sometime between 930 and 946. Although only a portion remains, it details major ritual activities at court and at important court-sponsored shrines for each month of the year. Due to its extensive citation of other sources, many of which are now lost, the *Honchō gatsuryō* also has considerable historiographical value. Moreover, the text helps identify which sources were considered authoritative by intellectuals during the early to mid-Heian period. The text is of immediate interest because Kinkata and his brother Koremune no Naoto, in addition to being premier intellectuals of their day, authored a number of works that have had a major impact on our understanding of the court's ritual agenda during the Heian period. Since the Koremune kinship group was a sublineage of the Hata, the prominence of these figures also testifies to the continued influence of the Hata into the Heian period. The text has also preserved crucial information from the now-lost *Hatashi honkeichō*, including a series of claims that the Hata regularly intermarried with the Kamo no Kimi lineage in Yamashiro province and performed rites at the Kamo shrines.

Ryō no gige. The *Ryō no gige* is a commentary on the Yōrō law codes. It was composed by court order and completed in 833. Because this work preserves the Yōrō law codes in their entirety, it is of immense value for any student of Japanese history. In addition, its relatively early composition has allowed scholars to trace divergences in commentarial and intellectual traditions at court by comparing the *Ryō no gige* with the slightly later *Ryō no shūge.*

Ryō no shūge. The *Ryō no shūge*, a heavily annotated commentary on the Yōrō law codes, was composed during the mid-tenth century by Koremune no Naoto. In addition to providing a line-by-line exegesis of the law codes, the *Ryō no shūge* also cites a wide range of otherwise lost works concerning all aspects of court procedures and practices. It is therefore a major resource for the study of early court institutions as well as for Japanese intellectual history. Of immediate interest here are the *Ryō no shūge*'s detailed commentaries on ritual performance at court as well as on contemporaneous understandings of the origins and nature of those rites.

Seiji yōryaku. Composed by Koremune no Tadasuke in 1002, the *Seiji yōryaku* seeks to give a comprehensive account of the administrative procedures at court as well as the court's annual ritual cycle. As is true of the *Ryō no shūge* and the *Honchō gatsuryō*, two other notable works composed by members of the Koremune lineage, this text contains a wealth of references to now-lost texts as well as information on the nature and methods of interpretation of ancient sources during the period. Of particular note here is the *Seiji yōryaku*'s account of the origins of the Gosechimai (Dance of the Five Nodes), which it traces to the appearance of a Chinese goddess before Tenmu *tennō* at Yoshino.

Yōrō ritsuryō. The *Yōrō ritsuryō* is a compilation of administrative procedures believed to have been completed during the Yōrō era (717–724), although it was not fully implemented until 757. It is thought to have followed very closely on the Ōmi and Taihō codes, the latter of which was adopted in 701. It is an important resource for understanding the institutional structures and procedures of the court. Although the earlier codes have been lost, the Yōrō code is known to us through the *Ryō no gige.* Of particular note for the scholar of Japanese religion is the text's account of procedures for court ritual (*Jingiryō*) and for Buddhist monks and nuns (*Soniryō*), both of which function as foundational sources for understanding court ritual practice at the start of the Nara period.

Temple and Shrine Sources

In this book we discuss three temple sources from the Nara period: the *Hōryūji garan engi narabi ni ruki shizaichō*, the *Gangōji garan engi narabi ni ruki shizaichō*, and the *Daianji garan engi narabi ni ruki shizaichō*. These texts, which were composed in 747 at the direction of the court, contain the founding narratives as well as accounts of later important events for three of the largest court-sponsored temples of the Nara period. In addition, they contain detailed accounts of each temple's possessions and iconography. As such, they provide information on extant sources and the nature of the court's patronage of Buddhist tradition. Along with the *Jōgū Shōtoku hōō teisetsu*, these records also contain some of the earliest accounts of the emergence of the Japanese Buddhist tradition itself. Of particular note here is the fact that each text in one way or another locates its origins with the figure of Prince Shōtoku, the paradigmatic Buddhist layman and sage. Crucially, however, this prince was also closely identified with the introduction of continental ritual and cultic forms at court.

Toyuke miya gishiki chō. The *Toyuke miya gishiki chō*, which was submitted to the court in 804, details the purported origins, ritual procedures, and material holdings of the outer shrine at Ise. Together with the *Kōtai jingū gishikichō*, it provides information concerning the state of the Ise cult immediately following the demise of the monk Dōkyō and the shift of the capital to Heian. Of particular interest for this study is the figure of Toyouke Hime, the main deity of the outer shrine, originally a Heavenly Maiden with cultic roots in Tamba province, who also attained a continental-style liberation from the corpse.

Yamato Hime Mikoto no seiki. The *Yamato Hime Mikoto no seiki*, generally thought to have been composed in the late Heian or early Kamakura period, recounts the journey of the Yamato Hime, the first royal princess said to have been brought the deity Amaterasu to Ise. The text is of immediate interest not only for its highly elaborated legends concerning the Wani ancestor Yamato Hime, but also for its depiction of the figure of Toyouke Hime, the chief deity of the outer shrine at Ise

Poetry Collections

Kaifūsō. The oldest extant collection of Chinese-style verse (*kanshi*) in the Japanese islands, the *Kaifūsō* contains a preface dating from 751. It constitutes an essential resource for understanding not only the development of Japanese literature, but also intellectual currents at court during the first half of the Nara period. Of particular note here is the view presented of the court of Tenchi, who is hailed as an enlightened ruler who, among other things, instituted continental-style ritual practices at court.

Manyōshū. This massive compendium of some 4,500 Japanese-style poems (*waka*) was most likely completed shortly after 759. In addition to its enormous influence on the development of poetry in the Japanese islands, the text is a treasure trove of information concerning everything from contemporaneous geographic appellations to early understandings of the afterlife. Of particular interest here are several poems that refer to weaving maidens and female immortals.

Other Literary Sources

Atsumori. A Nō play by Zeami, *Atsumori* is based upon the Heike tale of the encounter between young Taira warrior Atsumori and the older Minamoto warrior Kumagae. The Heike tale ends with the death of Atsumori at the hands of Kumagae, but the Nō drama focuses on the relationship between Atsumori's spirit and Kumagae, who, having taken the tonsure, seeks to release Atsumori from his torment. Intriguingly, Zeami claimed—probably spuriously—to have been of Hata descent.

Heike monogatari. This epic work is actually a series of tales related to the House of Taira during the height of their power and then spectacular fall at the end of the Heian period. As the first great warrior romance in the Japanese islands, its influence on later Japanese literature has been enormous. For this study the importance of the work lies in the deep roots it appears to have had in earlier story-telling forms related to Buddhist preaching as well as *onmyōdō* rites of spirit pacification that can be traced back even as far as the reign of Tenmu.

Shinsen shōjiroku. This genealogical compendium, which was composed sometime around 815, contains some 1,182 entries detailing information related to founding ancestors and claims of descent for lineages in residence at the capital and in five surrounding provinces. According to the preface, one of the main objectives of the work was to standardize lineal accounts and thereby discourage immigrant lineages from claiming descent from the gods of the Japanese islands. In this study I frequently refer to information provided about such important lineages as the Mononobe, Ōtomo, Hata, Chiisakobe, Kamo, and Wani kinship groups.

Chinese and Korean Sources

Ching ch'u sui shih chi. The *Ching ch'u sui shih chi* is an account by the literatus Tu Kung-shan of popular festival observances in southern China during the sixth century. It offers an extraordinary snapshot of popular religious practice during the period. Written in an almost anthropological style, Tu Kung-shan first chronicles what customs are observed at each festival and then seeks for textual precedents to explain their origins and provide perspective for their interpretation. The text thus both documents practices related to the festival calendar even as it theorizes about the overarching ritual framework in which each particular festival was situated. For this study the text is particularly valuable because it was completed not long before a mission from the Sui court arrived in the Japanese islands and observed that observances on nodal days in the calendar did not markedly differ from those practiced in China. Of particular note in this regard are the numerous references to sericulture rites, shamanesses, and spirit-quieting.

Chou li. The *Chou li* (*The Rites of Chou*), a text from the Warring States period, purports to present the administrative and ritual procedures of the Chou dynasty of ancient China. Along with the *Li chi* (*Book of Rites*) and the *Yi li* (*Ceremonies and Rituals*), this text has been considered as one of the three classic texts on ritual from at least as far back as the second century C.E. The *Chou li* is of immediate interest for this study because of its account of ritual procedures related to sericulture.

Ch'u tz'u. The *Ch'u tz'u* is an ancient poetic anthology composed of seventeen poems that are thought to have been composed in the southern state of Ch'u between the second and third centuries B.C.E. It was compiled and provided with a commentary by Wang I in the second century C.E. Because the poems appear to have drawn upon shamanistic verses and themes for their inspiration, they offer insight not only into early Chinese poetic forms, but also into early Chinese understandings of spirits and their relationship to humans. Of particular note for this study are three poems entitled "Spirit Summoning" (Ch: Chao hun, J: Shōkon), "The Great Summons," (Ch: Ta chao, J: Daishō), and "Summoning the Recluse" (Ch: Chao Yin, J: Shōinshi), all of which center on the theme of spirit-summoning.

Han Wu ku shih. The *Han Wu ku shih*, which was probably composed during the third century C.E., centers on the relations between the Han

Emperor Wu-ti and members of his court. The text is of note for this study because it features the famed legend of the visit paid to this ruler by the Queen Mother of the West.

Han Wu-ti nei chuan. Much like the *Han Wu ku shih*, the *Han Wu-ti nei chuan* also highlights the legend of the Queen Mother of the West's visit to the Han ruler Wu-ti. Unlike the *Han Wu ku shih*, however, there are strong indications that this text emerged in the context of the Mao Shan tradition of Taoism towards the end of the Six Dynasties period. In the text the Queen Mother bestows not only the peaches of immortality on Wu-ti, but also Taoist texts and talismans.

Hsü ch'i chieh chi. The *Hsü ch'i chieh chi* is a small collection of anomalous tales compiled by Wu Chun (469–520) a prominent literary figure and historian. Although much of the text has been lost, it appears to have exerted considerable influence in the formation of later *chih kuai* literature. Of particular note for this study are the text's frequent references to popular ritual observances on nodal days in the Chinese calendar.

Huai nan zu. The *Huai nan zu*, a compendium of Huang-Lao thought, was commissioned and perhaps edited by Liu An, the ruler of Huai-nan and the grandson of Liu Pang, the founder of the Han dynasty. For this study the chapters on cosmological and astrological thought are of immediate interest.

Lun heng. The *Lun heng* is a collection of rationalist essays from the first century, C.E. In many ways the essays represent an astounding achievement of critical inquiry as the author seeks to dispel numerous notions related to, among other phenomena, the supernatural. The value of the *Lun heng* for this study rests in his presentation of the beliefs that the author seeks to denigrate—in choosing such topics for criticism, he indirectly testifies to their salience in popular thought. Of particular importance here are the author's discussions of popular understandings of death, spirits, and their relationship to the forces of *yin* and *yang*.

Pao p'u tzu. The *Pao p'u tzu* is a work by Ko Hung (283–343) that details innumerable spells, medicines, and alchemical recipes for the pacification of spirits and the pursuit of health, longevity, and immortality. Although Ko Hung is sometimes described as a Taoist, as Nathan Sivin has noted in his article "On the Pao P'u Tzu Nei Pien and the Life of Ko Hong," Ko Hung does not appear to have received any Taoist initiations and was apparently not even aware of the existence of the tradition of the Celestial Masters or any other Taoist sect. While conspicuously failing to reference any communal forms of salvation that were at the center of early Taoist thought and practice, his work is filled with instructions concerning elixirs, spells, and mantic practices. He is thus perhaps a quintessential example of the degree to which such pursuits, far from being the exclusive domain of Taoist recluses, were an essential part of the popular religious landscape of ancient China. Judging from numerous allusions to the *Pao p'u tzu* in such texts as the *Nihon ryōiki*, we can be confident that his work was transmitted to the Japanese islands at an early date and that it exerted influence over Buddhists and non-Buddhists alike.

Po wu chih. The *Po wu chih* consists of ten volumes related to anomalous geographic and culture phenomena across the Chinese empire, and hence the text does not center on the court. The text is of particular note for this study for its account of the appearance of the Queen Mother of the West and its description of the silkworm as an insect of "three transformations."

Samguk sagi. Although the *Samguk sagi* was not completed until 1145, this chronicle stands as our single most important source for understanding the earliest history of the Korean peninsula. Given the text's late date, it is generally thought to be reliable. For this study the text provides information concerning the speed with which weaving cults and the rites of the Chinese festival calendar were adopted on the Korean peninsula.

Shan hai ching. Although the *Shan hai ching* in its current form appears to have taken shape during the late Han or early Six Dynasties periods, much of its material is believed to date from as far back as the Warring States period. It focuses on strange and exotic geographic and cultural phenomena across the Chinese empire. As such, the text is considered the oldest anomaly account in Chinese literature. For this study the text is of immediate interest for its account of the Queen Mother of the West and because it is believed to have served as an important source of inspiration for the Yamato court's decision to order the composition of provincial gazetteers (*fudoki*) in 713.

Sou shen chi. The *Sou shen chi* is a compendium of anomalous and otherworldly stories thought to have been compiled by Kan Pao, a literatus and historian who died in 320. Kan was supposedly inspired to collect the stories after hearing tales of the afterlife told to him by family members who had died and come back to life. Although it would be a mistake to view each tale as a simple transcription of a popular narrative, the over 400 stories constitute a treasure trove of information concerning popular beliefs on the subject during the period. For this study two legends are important because they recount the origins of sericulture and the descent of a Heavenly Weaver Maiden who is forced to marry a human after he steals her cloak of feathers.

Sui shu. The *Sui shu*, the official history of the Sui dynasty, was completed in 636. As with all Chinese dynastic histories, it contains detailed information about the administrative workings of the Sui empire as well as the accomplishments of many of its brightest cultural lights. For this study, however, the most valuable section of the text is the small account of the kingdom of Yamato. Because much information in this section was derived from successive missions from the Sui to the court of Suiko, it offers a perspective on early Japanese society that is not colored by the historical revisionism of the Japanese court.

Yi ching. The *Yi ching*, the most ancient of Chinese divination texts, served as a touchstone for Chinese intellectual and mantic traditions throughout the premodern era. Not surprisingly it appears to have played an important role in the formation of early conceptions of *onmyōdō* in the Japanese islands. Evidence for this can be seen not only because the text was part of the required curriculum for students in training for positions at the Nara court's Bureau of Yin and Yang, but also because of its influence over the *Wu hsing ta yi*, a Sui-dynasty divination manual that appears to have been transmitted to the Japanese islands as early as the seventh century. In the literature of the period we also find references to *Yi ching* practitioners in the *Tōshi kaden*, which asserts that the future ruler Tenchi and Fujiwara Kamatari studied the text with the monk Bin, and in the *Nihon ryōiki*, which makes casual reference to a *Yi ching* diviner in residence at a local shrine.

Yi yuan. The *Yi yuan* is a collection of anomalous anecdotes and stories compiled sometime in the fifth century by one Liu Ching-shu. The text is notable for its accounts of popular beliefs and tales. One indication of its influence can be seen in an entry from the *Ching ch'u sui shih chi*, which cites the text in order to explain popular understandings of rites performed on the fifteenth day of the first month.

Yu yang tsa tsu. The *Yu yang tsa tsu*, a work by Tuan Ch'eng-shih (800–863), consists of brief accounts and reports concerning a wide variety of strange or difficult-to-classify phenomena. Throughout the text Tuan retains a critical outlook, as in the open skepticism with which he describes Wu Tse-t'ien's claims to have been presented with an auspicious three-legged crow.

Buddhist Scriptures

Chin kang po jo po luo mi ching (J: *Kongō hannya haramitsu kyō*). This scripture, one of the most popular in East Asian Buddhism, long served as a primary means for preventing disasters and plague. Evidence for the scripture's popular appeal can also be seen in the *Nihon ryōiki*, which features narratives of spirits requesting the sutra be chanted for their benefit.

Kokūzō bosatsu nōman shōgan saishōshin darani gumonji no hō. This text, which was apparently first brought to the Japanese islands by the monk Dōji in 718, served as the source for the Gumonjihō, a rite of propitiation of the Space Buddha Kokūzō. This rite held out the promise of virtually unlimited understanding of the Buddhist scriptures to all those who performed it correctly.

Kujakuō shukyō. Although little is known about the means by which the *Scripture on the Spell of the Peacock King* was transmitted to the Japanese islands, it appears to have played an important role in the religious history of the Nara period. In addition to the *Nihon ryōiki*'s assertion that the spell was used by En no Gyōja, the spell was also famously used by the monk Dōkyō to heal the ailing Kōken shortly before she moved to retake the throne in 765.

Sukuyōkyō. This scripture is concerned almost exclusively with providing instructions for astral divination and the means by which calamities associated with numerous astral deities could be avoided. Although the famed Central Asian monk Amoghavajra claimed that the text was simply a translation of an Indian Buddhist scripture, he appears to have actually created the work by combining two distinct Indian astrological manuals. During the Heian period and afterward, the text was highly prized by the Shingon school, but it served as a foundational astrological manual for Buddhists of all persuasions.

Notes and Abbreviations

Abbreviations and Citation Methods

CCSSC	Ching ch'u sui shih chi
DNBZ	Dai Nihon Bukkyō zensho
ES	Er shi si shi
GR	Gunsho ruijū
KT	Kokushi taikei
MYS	Manyōshū
NI	Nara ibun
NKBT	Nihon koten bungaku taikei
NSK	Nihon shoki
NST	Nihon shisō taikei
SNG	Shoku Nihongi
SNKBT	Shin Nihon koten bungaku taikei
SNKBZ	Shinpen Nihon koten bungaku zenshū
SSC	Sou shen chi
ST	Shintō taikei
STZ	Shōtoku taishi zenshū
SZKT	Shintei zōhō kokushi taikei
T	Taishō shinshū daizōkyō
ZGR	Zoku gunsho ruijū

Throughout this book references to the *Nihon shoki* (*NSK*) list the reign date followed by the volume and page number in the three-volume edition of the text in the *SNKBZ* series, which had as its chief editor Kojima Noriyuki. For references from the *Shoku Nihongi* (*SNG*), I also use the same reign-date format, followed by a citation from the five-volume *SNKBT* series edition of the text, for which Aoki Kazuo was chief editor. Interlinear notes from these texts are translated in italics. For all references from the Buddhist canon I first cite the Taishō volume and page number followed by the Taishō number of the text under discussion. For romanization of Chinese and Korean terms I use the Wade-Giles and McCune-Reischauer systems, respectively.

Introduction

1. *Nihon shoki* (henceforth *NSK*) Suiko 10.10. *SNKBT* 3:539. Nishimoto Masahiro, *Nihon kodai girei seiritsushi no kenkyū*, 9.

2. For an excellent discussion of continental influences on the trajectory of court ritual during the seventh and eighth centuries, see Shinkawa Tokio, *Nihon kodai girei to hyōgen*; and Nishimoto Masahiro, *Nihon kodai girei seiritsushi no kenkyū*. Other notable works on early court ritual include Miyake Kazuo, *Kodai kokka no jingi to saishi*; and Obinata Katsumi, *Kodai kokka to nenjū gyōji*.

3. I realize that the concept of "immigrant," like race or ethnicity, is socially constructed. In the following pages I will use the term "immigrant kinship group" to refer to any kinship group that claims as its founding ancestor a figure who was said to have come to the Japanese islands from across the sea. I will use the term "immigrant deity" to refer to any god that is explicitly said to have crossed over the sea to the Japanese islands. Similarly, I shall in most cases use the term "Yamato"—an early term for the Japanese islands—in place of "Japan" in order to highlight the fact that "Japan" itself was being constructed at just this time. For convenience and stylistic purposes, however, I have occasionally found it necessary to use the term "Japan." In such instances I do not mean to imply the existence of a unified national entity.

4. In using the term "Chinese" I am emphatically not referring to an essentialized Chinese religious identity to be contrasted with a Japanese one. By "Chinese festival calendar" I am referring not to the intricate astrological and mathematical apparatus involved in the lunar calendrical system, but rather to the broad patterning of rites and festivals that constituted the ritual year for court and populace alike across China. I have therefore relied not only on canonical texts such as the *Book of Rites* and the *Rites of Chou*, but also on texts such as Kan Pao's edition of the *Ching ch'u sui shih chi*, a detailed account of the popular ritual cycle in southern China that was completed in the Sui dynasty shortly before such rites began to proliferate rapidly across the Japanese islands; see Wang Yü-jung, ed., *Ching ch'u sui shih chi*.

5. Because figures labeled as immortals (*hijiri*) were frequently worshipped in shrines and referred to in texts such as the *Nihon shoki* and *Kojiki* as "*kami*," I shall also frequently refer to them as *kami* in this book. Please also note that, in accordance with modern convention, I shall often refer to the title of post-Tenmu rulers as "*tennō*," although there were many possible readings for this term in the ancient period.

6. See, for instance, Fukunaga Mitsuji, *Dōkyō to kodai Nihon* as well as his *Dōkyō to Nihon bunka*. See also Ueda Masaaki, *Kodai no dōkyō*; Takikawa

Masajirō, *Ritsuryō to daijōsai*; Yoshino Hiroko, *In'yō gogyō shisō*; Yoshino Hiroko, *In'yō gogyō to Nihon*.

7. For a sympathetic review of Fukunaga's disputes with his critics, see Bialock, *Eccentric Spaces*, 26–32.

8. For more on these issues, see Kohn, "Taoism in Japan." See also Tim Barrett's thoughtful essay "Shinto and Taoism," which systematically combs through official Chinese sources that might have made an impact on emerging notions of kingship and statecraft in the Japanese islands.

9. See, for instance, the first two essays of Fukunaga's *Dōkyō to Nihon bunka*, in which he repeatedly equates Taoism with "Chinese religious thought" and offers as examples of "Taoist" influence references to such broad-based Chinese religious phenomena as *Yi ching* divination and Chinese pole-star cults. Fukunaga, *Dōkyō to Nihon bunka*, 7–56.

10. Seidel, "Imperial Treasures"; Stein, "Religious Taoism"; Strickmann, "History, Anthropology"; Kleeman, "Licentious Cults"; Sivin, "On the Word 'Taoist.'"

11. Denecke, "'Topic Poetry is All Ours,'" 4.

12. Murayama Shūichi, *Nihon onmyōdōshi sōsetsu*; Shinkawa Tokio, *Nihon kodai girei to hyōgen*; Wada Atsumu, *Nihon kodai no girei to saishi*.

13. This book also owes a great debt to a broad range of western scholars of Japanese religion and history. Scholars such as Gary Ebersole (*Ritual Poetry*), Paul Groner (*Saichō*), and Ryūichi Abe (*Weaving of Mantra*) have transformed our understanding of the religious history of the period, while scholars such as Joan Piggott (*Emergence of Japanese Kingship*) and Wayne Farris (*Population, Disease and Land*) have similarly opened up new avenues of inquiry into the institutional and social history of the Nara period. I have also benefited enormously from the work of Herman Ooms (*Imperial Politics*), who has emphasized the role of *onmyōdō* influences on the formation of the early cult of the *tennō*, as well as from the work of David Bialock (*Eccentric Spaces*), who has demonstrated the extraordinary degree to which *onmyōdō* practices influenced the formation of genres of literature and performance.

14. The divergence of the ideological positions found in such texts as the *Nihon shoki* and *Kojiki* is a theme that is developed at length in Kōnoshi Takamitsu, *Kojiki to Nihon shoki*. For a brief, English-language summary of Kōnoshi's views, see Kōnoshi, "Constructing Imperial Ideology."

15. These texts were first identified as a set in Shinkawa, *Nihon kodai no saishi to hyōgen*, 23–45.

Chapter 1: Immigrant Gods on the Road to Jindō

1. Fukunaga Mitsuji, *Dōkyō to Nihon bunka*; Shinkawa Tokio, *Dōkyō o meguru kōbō*; Herman Ooms, *Imperial Politics*; Bialock, *Eccentric Spaces*.

2. Kuroda Toshio, "Shinto in the History of Japanese Religion"; Mark Teeuwen, "From Jindō to Shintō," 243–247.

3. For a sampling of works on the role of immigrant lineages in the political and cultural discourses of the age, see Ueda Masaaki, *Kikajin*; Hirano Kunio, *Kikajin to kodai kokka*; Mizoguchi Mutsuko, *Kodai shizoku no keifu*; and Katō Kenkichi, *Hatashi to sono tami*.

4. For the background for these events, see Abe Shigeru, *Heian zenki seijishi no kenkyū*, 18–92.

5. This incident is discussed briefly in Mikael Adolphson's *Gates of Power*, 32. For an overview of rites performed at the capital, see Kaneko Hiroyuki, "Miyako o meguru matsuri." See also Emura Hiroyuki, *Ritsuryō tennōsei saishi no kenkyū*, 359–408. For the history of the Kamo shrine in the Nara period, see Okada Seishi, "Nara jidai no Kamo Jinja." For the role of the Kamo priestess in the Heian period, see Uwai Hisayoshi, *Nihon kodai no shinzoku to saishi*, 43–61.

6. The passage is quoted in the *Honchō gatsuryō*, an eleventh-century court document. The text may be found in *ZGR* 4:309–310. All translations are my own unless otherwise indicated.

7. *ZGR* 4:310.

8. These and other immigrant cults are discussed briefly in Ueda Masaaki, *Kodai kokka to shūkyō*, 164–216.

9. Abe argues persuasively and at length that Kūkai's energies were directed to a large degree in redefining not only Buddhist hermeneutics but also Buddhist-*tennō* relations. See Abe Ryūichi, *Weaving of Mantra*, 305–358.

10. See, for example, Kōnoshi, *Kojiki no sekaikan*, 163–171.

11. For a detailed examination of such legends, see Como, *Shōtoku*, 75–92.

12. The original text may be found in Saeki Arikiyo, *Shinsen shōjiroku no kenkyū* 1:145. The translation is from Kiley, "Surnames in Ancient Japan," 178. Kiley concludes by noting: "The *Shinsen shōjiroku* reflects an attitude whereby all persons of acknowledged foreign origin, however thoroughly naturalized in the cultural sense, are equally alien" (ibid., 185).

13. One fundamental means of differentiating ruler and ruled was the fact that although the ruler was the source of surnames, the ruler did not have one. When Saga's brother Heizei revolted in 810, Saga executed Heizei's subordinates and then "granted" his brother a surname, thereby forever eliminating Heizei's line from consideration for the throne.

14. For the early Shōtoku cult, see Como, *Shōtoku;* Hayashi Mikiya, *Taishi shinkō no kenkyū*; Iida Mizuho *Shōtoku taishiden no kenkyū*. I discuss this prince repeatedly throughout the book.

15. For a discussion of the role played by the Hata and others in the construction of the royal ancestral legend cycles and notions of sage kingship in the Asuka period, see Como, "Divination."

16. The translation, with emendations, is from Katō and Hoshino, trans., *Kogoshūi or Gleanings from Ancient Stories*, 38. For the original text, see *ST koten hen* 5: *Kogoshūi*, 35.

17. Although I know of no one who has attempted to do a genealogy of the concept of the "immigrant," or even the purportedly "native," in Japanese history, the contrast here with the *Kojiki*, which blithely states that rulers such as Ōjin and Jingū were descended from the Silla prince Ame no Hiboko, is striking; see *Kojiki*, Ōjin chapter. *SNKBZ* 1:277.

18. For Kanmu, see Inoue Mitsuo, *Kanmu tennō*; and Abe Shigeru, *Heian zenki seijishi no kenkyū*. Kanmu's policies towards shrine worship are also discussed in length in Okada Shōji, "Heian zenki jinja saishi no 'kōsaika.'"

19. Piggott's discussion of the role of Buddhist ideology in the politics of the period can be found in her *Emergence of Japanese Kingship*, 236–280.

20. The classic study of the role of disease in early Japanese history is William Wayne Farris, *Population, Disease and Land*.

21. I have discussed the Hata's role in the early Shōtoku cult extensively in *Shōtoku*.

22. These events are discussed in detail by Ōyama Seiichi in his *Nagaya no ōkimike mokkan to kinsekibun*, 276–281. See also Como, "Of Temples, Horses, and Tombs," 8–10.

23. *NSK* Saimei 7.5.9, 7.7.24, and 7.8.1. In *SNKBZ* 4:242–244.

24. *NSK* Tenmu, Suzuka, 1.6. *SNKBZ* 4:461.

25. I will discuss such rites in greater detail throughout this book. After long neglect, the number of works on the role of *onmyōdō* has recently grown substantially. Among the most important are: Murayama Shūichi et al., ed., *Onmyōdō sōsho*; Hayashi Makoto and Koike Jun'ichi, eds., *Onmyōdō no kōgi*; Bernard Frank, *Kataimi to katatagae*; Suzuki Ikkei, *Onmyōdō*; Murayama Shūichi, *Shūgen, onmyōdō to shaji shiryō*; Murayama Shūichi, *Nihon onmyōdōshi sōsetsu*; Noguchi Tetsurō and Sakai Tatao, eds., *Senshū Dōkyō to Nihon*.

26. *Kojiki* Chūai, part 2. *SNKBZ* 1:243.

27. There is strong, though circumstantial evidence indicating that the Sumiyoshi deities were conceived of in close conjunction with the Korean kingdom of Silla. The *Nihon shoki* records a sighting of a god "with the appearance of a foreigner [*karabito*]" flying over the Yoshino region of Yamato and

then to Suminoe on a dragon before heading westward to the continent. The later pairing of this shrine with a temple named Shiragidera (Silla temple) also suggests strong associations with the Korean peninsula (*NSK* Saimei, Period Prior to Accession. *SNKBZ* 4:203–204). I am therefore inclined to believe that the legend originally centered on the Sumiyoshi gods and that Amaterasu was a much later addition. For more on connections between the figures of Chūai, Jingū (as well as their son Ōjin), and Silla immigrant deities from northern Kyūshū, see Como, *Shōtoku*, 55–74.

28. *NSK* Kimmei, Period Prior to Accession. *SNKBZ* 2:357–359.

29. The text, which is quoted in the *Honchō gatsuryō*, may be found in *GR* 4:305.

30. Relations between the Munakata, the Hata, and the royal house are discussed in Wada Atsumu, "Oki no shima to Yamato ōken."

31. *NSK* Richū 5.3.1. *SNKBZ* 3:90–92. This legend has also been treated briefly in Taketani Hisao, *Kodai shizoku denshō no kenkyū*, 351–354; and Como, *Shōtoku*, 67–69.

32. *SNG* Tempyō Shōhō 1.12.27. *SNKBT* 14:97–98. For the Hachiman cult, see Nakano Hatayoshi, *Hachiman shinkō no kenkyū*; Nakano Hatayoshi, *Hachiman shinkō*; and Nakano Hatayoshi, *Hachiman shinkō to shūgendō*. For Hachiman and Ōjin, see Nakano, *Hachiman shinkō*, 84–99; and Mishina, *Nissen shinwa densetsu no kenkyū*, 96–98. For the early Hachiman cult, see Saigō Nobutaka, "Hachiman kami no hassei."

33. The poem is included in the *Denjutsu isshin kaimon*, which was completed in 834 by Saichō's disciple Kōjō. The text is discussed in Hayashi Mikiya, *Taishi shinkō no kenkyū*, 195; and Wang Yung, *Shōtoku taishi jikū chōetsu*, 380–393.

34. Como, *Shōtoku*, 150–152.

35. Literally, "It is not from overseas." The relationship between the Shōtoku commentaries and the legend of Hui-ssu's incarnation in Japan is discussed in Iida Zuiho, *Shōtoku Taishiden*, 73–109. Wang also cites numerous references to Shōtoku as an incarnation of Hui-ssu in Tendai texts from both China and Japan; see Wang, *Shōtoku taishi jikū chōetsu*, 326–394.

36. *Nihon ryōiki*, 3.39. *SNKBZ* 10:367–371.

37. Asamoto later returned to China, where Hsüan-tsung is said to have granted him an audience and treated him warmly. Benshō, Asamoto, and the Fujiwara are discussed in Nakamura Shūya, *Hatashi to Kamoshi*, 191–199.

38. Thus at the advent of the Heian period, rulers such as Heizei, Saga, and Junna were all descended from Umakai.

39. Hata building projects are discussed in Katō Kenkichi, *Hatashi to sono tami*, 130–144.

40. This event is discussed in Nakamura Shūya, *Hatashi to Kamoshi*, 168–186.

41. For more on the role of Kadono and other Hata-affiliated Fujiwara in the construction of the Heian capital, see ibid., 187–203.

42. For the politics of lineage and the decision to build a new capital, see Ronald Toby's "Why Leave Nara?" Ueda Masaaki and others have also argued that Kanmu would have been attracted to Yamashiro due to his own distaff affiliations with immigrant lineages from the Korean kingdom of Paekche; see Ueda Masaaki, *Ueda Masaaki chosakushū*, 3:209–216.

43. For the archeology of the temple, see Beppu Daigaku Fuzoku Hakubutsukan and Usa-shi Kyōikuiinkai, *Tempyō no Usa*. The temple is also mentioned briefly by Edward Kidder in his discussion of Hōryūji-style temples; *The Lucky Seventh*, 394.

44. I will discuss the worship of Kokūzō and Yoshino in greater detail in Chapter 3.

45. The assertion comes in Kūkai's *Sangō shiiki* (Indications of the goals of the Three Teachings), which has been translated by Hakeda Yoshito in his *Kūkai: Major Works*, 102.

46. Abe Ryūichi, *Weaving of Mantra*, 73–75.

47. The history of Kōryūji is discussed in Katō Kenkichi, *Hatashi to sono tami*, 185–195.

48. Sonoda Kōyū, "Kokūzō shinkō no shiteki tenkai," 144–149.

49. This is discussed briefly in Katō Kenkichi, *Hatashi to sono tami*, 128–129.

50. Ibid., 155–160. Dōji is also known to have brought several Kokūzō scriptures to the court upon his return from China in 718.

51. Gomyō and Gonsō, in fact, played a major role in the careers of both Saichō and Kukai. Gomyō's opposition to Saichō meant that Saichō's career was dogged by conflict with the monastic establishment. In contrast, Kūkai was careful to cultivate good relations with Gomyō, whom he referred to as his teacher and for whom he composed congratulatory birthday poems. Later generations of Shingon monks claimed that Kūkai had been taught the Gumonjihō rite by Gonsō. Although such claims may be spurious, they are most likely rooted in close relations between the two monks: both Gonsō and his student Enmyō, for instance, also served in the post of chief administrator of Tōji. All of this suggests that Hata influence was such that Kūkai found it prudent to cultivate good relations with Hata monks and institutions.

52. The history of cultic centers on Mount Hiei is extremely complex. The *Honchō gatsuryō* notes, however, that Ōyamakui no kami is designated as the deity on Mount Hiei by both the *Kojiki* and the *Senda kuji hongi*,

another liturgical history submitted to the court in the first decades of the ninth century (*ZGR* 4:304).

53. Sagai Tatsuru, *Hiyoshi Taisha to San'ō Gongen*, 157.

54. Uwai, *Nihon kodai no shinzoku to saishi*, 46. For the original text, see *ST* 29: *Jinja hen: Hiyoshi*: 52. Relations between the Hiyoshi, Kamo, and Matsuno'o shrines are discussed at length in Uwai, *Nihon kodai no shinzoku to saishi*, 43–61. Although source materials for the Hiyoshi shrines are distressingly sparse, numerous references to cultic interactions between the Hiyoshi and Kamo shrines can be found in our two earliest sources for Hiyoshi; the *Hiesha negi kudenshō*, a late Heian-period text, and the *Yōtenki*, a text generally thought to have been composed during the eleventh century (*ST* 29: *Jinja hen: Hiyoshi*: 1–6 and 7–96, respectively). These interactions were undoubtedly facilitated by the fact that the Hafuribe liturgical lineage at Hiyoshi claimed common descent with the Kamo. For a dissenting view that questions both the dating of these texts and the lineal connections of the Hafuribe and Kamo, see Okada Seishi "Hiyoshi Jinja to Tenchichō Ōtsumiya," 54–57. Okada's view, however, appears to be compromised by the fact that the Hafuribe are explicitly listed as a sublineage of the Kamo in the *Shinsen shōjiroku*, an early ninth-century genealogical text (Saeki, *Shinsen shōjiroku no kenkyū*, 1:241).

55. The relationship between the Inari shrine and Tōji is discussed in Murayama Shūichi, *Shūgen, onmyōdō to shaji shiryō*, 32–38.

56. The shrine, located close to Suminoe, is said to have been established by Jingū after her conquest of Silla; see *NSK* Jingū 1.2. *SNKBZ* 2:439. In addition, the Hirano shrine, which was closely associated with Kanmu *tennō*'s distaff line, also housed deities that were clearly of continental provenance. This is discussed in Ueda Masaaki, *Ueda Masaaki chosakushū* 3:209–216. Ueda notes that the shrine housed both a hearth deity (Kudo no kami) as well as a deity named Imaki no kami, who was apparently associated with Paekche immigrant lineages that bore the same name.

57. This figure would be much higher if we included deities of immigrant lineages that have fallen out of the purview of this study. There is strong evidence suggesting that the Kitano, Gion, and Hirano shrines were all closely associated with immigrant kinship groups that were prominent in Kanmu's distaff lineage. Katō Kenkichi has provided strong circumstantial evidence suggesting that the Nihu deity was also closely associated with the Hata; see Katō Kenkichi, *Hatashi to sono tami,* 120–130. I will discuss the Nihu deity in greater detail in Chapter 3.

Chapter 2: *Karakami* and Animal Sacrifice

1. As quoted in Kleeman, "Licentious Cults," 190.

2. As I have already noted, in using the term "Chinese festival calendar" I do not wish to associate the deities and rites discussed with any essentially "Chinese" characteristics. I only seek to underscore the fact that understanding such rites requires an examination of their roots in the cultic practices and beliefs of the Chinese mainland. As should already be apparent, a major thesis of this book is that these rites constituted a core element in what later came to be understood as native Japanese religious practice.

3. Thus recently Stuart Picken has stated that "traditionally, death, childbirth, and any occasion where blood is present were sources of pollution" (*Historical Dictionary of Shinto*, 113), while the *Shintō daijiten* defines impurity (*kegare*) in similar terms (Shimonaka Nisaburō, ed., *Shintō daijiten*, 494).

4. For notions of purity and taboo in the Japanese islands, see Okada Shigekiyo, *Imi no sekai*; Okada Shigekiyo, *Kodai no imi*; and Yamamoto Kōji, *Kegare to ōharae*.

5. *SNG* Yōrō 6.7.7 (722), *SNKBT* 13:119–123. *SNG* Tempyō 2.9 (730), *SNKBT* 13:237–239. *SNG* Tempyō 4.7.5 (732), *SNKBT* 13:257–259. *SNG* Tempyō 9.5.19 (737), *SNKBT* 13:321–322. *SNG* Tempyō 13.2.7 (741), *SNKBT* 13:387.

6. *SNG* Tempyō 9.8.2 (737), *SNG* 13:325. *SNG* Tempyō 13.3.24 (741). *SNKBT* 13:387–391.

7. Ueda Masaaki, "Satsu gyūma shinkō no kōsatsu." Nakai Kazuo, "Satsuma girei to sono shūhen," 107–118.

8. *SNG* Enryaku 10.9.16. *SNKBT* 16:507. The editors of the *SNG* also note that yet another edict, recorded in the *Ruijū kokushi* from Enryaku 20.4.8, forbids worship of a "Butcher god" in Echizen province (*SNKBT* 16:625–626, note 40: 92; for the original citation, see *Ruijū kokushi* in *SZKT* 5: 90).

9. Ueda notes the entries in the *SNG* Yōrō 6.7.7. (722), Tempyō 4.7.5 (732), and Tempyō 9.5.19 (737) just cited that the consumption of alcohol and butchering of animals was banned due to drought. Note also that at this time, as we saw in Chapter 1, the court was reeling from revolts, internal divisions, and a series of devastating plagues that had killed large numbers of courtiers only a few years earlier.

10. *SNG* Tempyō 13.2.7 (741). *SNKBT* 13:387.

11. *SZKT* 23:196.

12. *SNG* Tempyō 6.12. *SNKBT* 13:293. We shall see further evidence suggesting popular use of the *Kongō hannya kyō* shortly.

13. *NSK* Kōgyoku 1.7.25 through 1.8.1. *SNKBZ* 4:63–65.

14. This conception of cosmic resonance (*kan ying*) was not only a hallmark of Chinese political philosophy, but pervaded astrological and medical systems as well. I will discuss the importance of continental astral and medical systems later in this chapter and in Chapter 3.

15. The River Earl, in addition to being one of the main water deities in the Chinese pantheon, also appears as a founding ancestor in the legends of kingship in the Korean kingdoms.

16. Such practices were almost certainly related to the fact that markets took place at the intersections of major roads (*chimata*) and that they were therefore important nodes of interaction between intermingling *yin* and *yang* elements. For an extended discussion of the role of *chimata* in early Japanese religion, see Maeda Haruto, *Nihon kodai no michi to chimata*.

17. *SNG* Keiun 2.6. *SNKBT* 12:89.

18. Intriguingly, the *Nihon shoki* contains another passage from virtually the same time as Kōgyoku's purported rain contest with the Soga in which the leaders of a popular millennial cult encourage their followers to "throw away their household valuables, and line up *sake*, vegetables, and the six domestic animals by the roadsides." In light of the fact that the Michiae no Matsuri also involved offerings of animal hides on the roadsides, it is possible that the court's rites reflected popular cultic practice. See *NSK* Kōgyoku 3.7. *SNKBZ* 4:93–95.

19. Not surprisingly, rainmaking was a central cultic concern of the court throughout the Nara and Heian periods. For the history of rainmaking rites in the Japanese islands, see Yabu Motoaki, *Amagoi girei no seiritsu to tenkai*; and Namiki Katsuko, "Heian jidai no amagoi hōbei."

20. See, for instance, Wakamatsu Ryōichi, "Saisei no inori to jinbutsu haniwa"; Segawa Yoshinori, "Umakai shūdan no kami matsuri,"122–130; Tanigawa Ken'ichi, "Torigata doki ni tsuite."

21. Thus an entry in the *SNG* from 706 states: "In many provinces there is plague, and many peasants have died. Begin making earthen cattle [figurines] for a great *tsuina* rite [pacification rite]." *SNG* Keiun 3. *SNKBT* 12:109. In the *Hizen fudoki*, a gazetteer compiled for the court sometime around 713, we also find an entry for the Saga district recounting how two shamanesses used *hitogata* (human figurines) and *umagata* to placate an angry deity and ward off a plague. The text may be found in *Hizen fudoki*, Saga district. *SNKBZ* 5:326–327.

22. For a superb discussion of *hitogata* and related ritual implements, see Wada, *Nihon kodai no girei to saishi* 2:151–214. See also Izumi Takeshi, "Hitogata saishi no kisōteki kōsatsu," 144–191.

23. Murayama Shūichi, *Nihon onmyōdōshi sōsetsu*. See also Kaneko Hiroyuki, "Bukkyō, Dōkyō."

24. Early interest in continental ritual systems was also almost certainly stimulated by the transmission and use of such texts as the *Gogyō taigi*, a Sui-dynasty work that set out a comprehensive framework for understanding the workings of *yin* and *yang* and the five phases within a broad range of phenomena related to governance, cosmology, and medicine. The text may be found in Nakamura Shōhachi, *Gogyō taigi*. See also Nakamura Shōhachi, *Gogyō taigi kisoteki kenkyū*; and Nakamura Shōhachi, *Gogyō taigi zenshaku* 1. It would also appear that the transmission of continental medical texts to the Japanese islands helped reorient early Japanese cultic practice in terms of *yin* and *yang* and the Chinese festival calendar. I will discuss the diffusion of Chinese conceptions of the body and immortality in greater detail in Chapter 3.

25. This is discussed in Yokota Ken'ichi, *Asuka no kamigami*, 97. *Chimata* rites are also a central focus of Maeda Haruto, *Nihon kodai no michi to chimata*. For more on popular disease cults in the Heian period, see Kubota Osamu, *Yasaka jinja no kenkyū*, esp. 59–84; Neil McMullen, "On Placating the Gods"; Sasō Mamoru, "Heian jidai ni okeru ekijinkan no shōsō." See also Shibata Minoru, "Gion Goryōe"; Murayama Shūichi, "Gionsha no goryōjinteki hatten"; and Kikuike Kyōko, "Goryō shinkō no seiritsu to tenkai."

26. *NSK* Suiko 10.10. *SNKBZ* 3:539.

27. *NSK* Suiko 22.4. *SNKBZ* 3:586.

28. See Como, "Divination." See also Tamura Enchō, *Nihon Bukkyōshi* 4: 419–441.

29. *NSK* Tenmu 4.1.5. *SNKBZ* 4:359. For the history of astrology and calendar-making within the Japanese islands, see Hosoi Hiroshi, "Tenmondō to rekidō"; Yamashita Katsuaki, "Tenmon, reki, sukuyōdō," 411–425; and Yamashita Katsuaki, "Onmyōdōryō to onmyōdō." For astrological cults in China, see Edward Schafer, *Pacing the Void*.

30. For the Takamatsuzuka tomb, see Inokuma Kanekatsu and Watanabe Akiyoshi, eds., *Nihon no bijutsu* 217: *Takamatsuzuka kofun*; and Suenaga Masao and Inoue Mitsusada, eds., *Takamatsuzuka kofun to Asuka*. For Kitora, see Nara Bunkazai Kenkyūjo Asuka Shiryōkan, *Kitora kofun to hakkutsu sareta hekigatachi*.

31. Hirabayashi, *Tanabata to sumō no kodaishi*, 232.

32. The text may be found in T'sai Chen-ch'u, ed., *Hsin i: Lun heng tu pen* 2:1143.

33. Ibid., 2:1060.

34. Chinese numerology, while extremely complex, was itself predicated upon the belief that odd numbers were *yang* and even numbers were *yin*. As a result, although there were several systems for recording cycles of time in China, the performance of many of the most important rites of the calendar

was gradually fixed in a regular sequence of odd numbered "nodal" days—that is, the first day of the first month, the third day of the third month, the fifth day of the fifth month, the seventh day of the seventh month, and so on.

35. For a general introduction to the Chinese festival calendar, see Nakamura Takashi, *Chūgoku saijishi no kenkyū*.

36. I will discuss legends concerning the origin of the Gosechimai (Dance of the Five Nodes) at the Yamato court in Chapter 3. Throughout the rest of the book I shall repeatedly make reference to these nodal days.

37. As we shall see in Chapters 3 and 4, Han Wu-ti also became the subject of a number of legends related to the cult of the Queen Mother of the West and the acquisition of immortality.

38. *Lun yü* Book 3, 12. In *Hsin i ssu shu tu pen*, eds. Hsieh Ping-ying et al. For an excellent translation and commentary, see Slingerland, *Analects*, 21.

39. Kleeman, "Licentious Cults," 200–211. Bokenkamp notes that although the earlier Taoists sought to ban sacrifices entirely, the demand for such practices was such that they eventually had to allow for offerings to ancestors on a limited number of days within a prescribed ritual context; Bokenkamp, *Ancestors and Anxiety*, 181–182.

40. Kleeman, "Licentious Cults," 195.

41. For the cult of the Weaver Maiden and Cowherd in China, see Kominami Ichirō, *Seiōbo to tanabata denshō*; and Hung Shu-hui, *Niu lang chih nü yen chiu*. For the Weaver Maiden in Japan, see Alan Miller, "Ame no Miso-Ori Me"; Alan Miller, Of Weavers and Birds"; and Hirabayashi Akihito, *Tanabata to sumō no kodaishi*.

42. *Ching ch'u sui shih chi* (henceforth *CCSSC*), 7.7. Kominami, *Seiōbo to tanabata denshō*, 31.

43. Nakamura Takashi, *Chūgoku saijishi no kenkyū*, 343–344.

44. Ibid., 345. Kominami, *Seiōbo to tanabata denshō*, 228. As we saw earlier, sacrifice to the River Earl was apparently not unknown in the Japanese islands prior to the Nara period.

45. See, for instance, Watase Masatada, "Kakinomoto no Hitomaro."

46. Hirabayashi Akihito, *Tanabata to sumō no kodaishi*, esp. 128–226. Throughout this book we shall see repeated examples of female deities and ancestors represented in Nara-period texts in vocabulary drawn from continental astral and weaving cults. In Chapters 5, 6, and 7, I will discuss the role of the Hata, as well as numerous other immigrant lineages, in the transmission of weaving and sericulture technologies to the Japanese islands.

47. Kaneko Hiroyuki, "Gakki, shuzōgu, bōshokugu." Kaneko also notes that the *Engishiki* mandates that weaving implements be regularly offered to

the Tatsuta shrine, one of the most important shrines for the Tenmu court, while shrine records from the Hiyoshi Taisha, the Kasuga shrine, and the Hayatama shrine in the Kumano region of Wakayama prefecture all also stipulate that weaving implements were to be used as offerings.

48. *Hizen fudoki,* Ki no gun, Himegoso no sato. *SNKBZ* 5:316–317.

49. The figure Azeko, whose lineage in the legend is given charge of worshipping the deity, is from a sub-branch of the Mononobe kinship group, the main lineage that is said to have opposed the entry of Buddhism into the Japanese islands. For more on Azeko and this legend, see Masaki Kisaburō, "Munakata san megami to kiki shinwa," 66–70. I will discuss the Mononobe in detail in Chapter 4. For drawings of ritual weaving implements found in this region of Kyūshū, see Kikuchi Yasuaki, *Ritsuryōsei saishi ronkō,* 488. See also Kaneko Hiroyuki, "Gakki, shūzōgu, hōogu," 156–160.

50. The translation is from Katō Genchi and Hoshino Hikoshiro, trans., *Kogoshūi or Gleanings from Ancient Stories,* 48–49.

51. Yoshie Akiko, *Nihon kodai no saishi to josei,* 185. The legend is also discussed at length in Yokota Ken'ichi, *Asuka no kamigami,* 94–119.

52. *Kojiki,* Age of the Gods. *SNKBZ* 1:97.

53. *Kojiki,* Ōjin chapter. *SNKBZ* 5:275–277. This text's account of the birth of Akaru Hime is notable in one further way as well; although she is clearly represented as a daughter of a sun deity, she was never represented as a child of the royal ancestor and sun divinity Amaterasu. In point of fact there were many sun deities that were worshipped at different sites across the Japanese islands. I shall discuss other such sun deities—and their implications for our understanding of the cult of Amaterasu—in Chapter 7.

54. According to the *Tōshi kaden,* a late Nara-period history produced by the Fujiwara, this deity, located at the port of Tsunoga along the Japan/Eastern Sea, was also claimed by the Fujiwara as a special protector deity. The text may be found in *NI* 3:875–886.

55. See, for instance, Hayashi On and Marui Keiji, ed., *Myōken bosatsu to hoshi mandara,* 377. See also Lucia Dolce, "Introduction."

56. Kaneko Hiroyuki, "Bukkyō, Dōkyō," 180. Throughout the Nara and Heian periods, the court appears to have shown a marked predilection for Buddhist scriptures that were composed in China. Among the most notable were the *Bonmyō kyō,* the *Ninnō-kyō,* and the *Sukuyōkyō.* For a discussion of the reception of this last astrological text in the Heian period, see Yano Michio, "Bukkyō keiten no naka no reki, *Sukuyōkyō.*" See also Yano Michio, *Mikkyō senseijutsu.*

57. *Nihon ryōiki* 1.12. Kyoko Nakamura, *Miraculous Stories,* 123–124. *SNKBZ* 10:60–62.

58. The first reference in the *NSK* to the settling of immigrants highlights the role of the Kishi, an immigrant lineage that is said to have brought Koguryŏ artisans to the village of Nukatasato in the Yamabe district of Yamato (*NSK* Ninken 6. *SNKBZ* 3:261–263). This is thought to be the home village of Dōji, the final editor of the *Nihon shoki* and the head of Daianji, the largest state temple of the day. In Chapter 4 we shall also see that Dōtō is also mentioned within the *Nihon shoki* in the context of interpreting the appearance of an auspicious omen at the court of the Yamato ruler Kōtoku.

59. See, for example, *NSK* Suiko 21. *SNKBZ* 3:569. For the development of early Japanese road networks, see Kinoshita Ryō, *Kodai dōro*.

60. I will discuss this topic briefly in Chapter 3. Disease and economic privation may in fact have increased as a result of the numerous construction projects undertaken by the court during the Nara period. One reference to hardships and death on the roadsides can be found in *SNG* Wadō 5.1.16. *SNKBT* 12:177. For more on the cultic significance of this, see Como, "Horses, Dragons and Disease"; and Yamachika Kumiko, "Michi to matsuri." For the influence of roadside rites on the early Japanese Buddhist tradition, see Como, "Of Temples, Horses, and Tombs."

61. *Nihon ryōiki* 2.25. Kyoko Nakamura, *Miraculous Stories*, 194–196. *SNKBZ* 10194–10197.

62. Although the text does not explicitly say that the food offerings Kinume made involved meat, in light of the fact that offerings of meat and/or animal hides are known to have been made to spirits in the Toshigoi no Matsuri and Michae no Matsuri, I suspect that the text is intended to imply that the food the demons desired was meat. We shall see this made explicit shortly in another legend from the *Nihon ryōiki*.

63. Similar linkages between popular spirit cults and the figure of Emma (Ch: Yen-luo) appear to have occurred in China by the sixth century, and even in the Japanese islands, the figure of Yen lo had from an early date become closely connected with the figure of T'ai Shan Fu Chun, a member of the Chinese pantheon who sat in judgment of the dead. Indeed, T'ai Shan Fu Chun appears as an attendant of Emma in such texts as the *Yen lo wang kung hsing fa tsu ti*, a liturgical manual in use for much of the Heian period. (*T* 1290, 21:374–376). By the tenth century, *yin-yang* masters at the Heian court were petitioning T'ai Shan Fu Chun using virtually the same form as that used by Buddhist priests who petitioned King Emma. For more on this, see Shigeta Shinichi, *Abe no Seimei*, 34–45.

64. *Nihon ryōiki* 2.5. Kyoko Nakamura, *Miraculous Stories*, 164–165. *SNKBZ* 10:131–137.

65. Kaneko, "Bukkyō, Dōkyō," 170.

66. Shinkawa notes that one figure closely associated with this process was none other than Ōtomo no Sadehiko, a figure whom we shall encounter again in Chapters 3 and 5; see Shinkawa, *Nihon kodai no saishi to hyōgen*, 302–303. References to official guest residences for Koguryō emissaries appear in the *Nihon shoki* as early as 570 (Kinmei 31.4. *SNKBZ* 3:457–458). The first reference to the settling of Koguryō immigrants in Yamato highlights the role of the Kishi, an immigrant lineage closely associated with the Hata (*NSK* Ninken 6. *SNKBZ* 3:261–263).

67. Both the Nara Osa and the following legend are discussed at length in Wada, *Nihon kodai no girai to saishi* 2:215–242.

68. *Nihon ryōiki*, 2.25. Kyoko Nakamura, *Miraculous Stories*, 192–194. *SNKBZ* 10:194–197. For the use of the *Kongō hannya haramitsu kyō* among the populace in the early Heian period, see Tachibana Kyōdō, "Wagakuni ni okeru goryō." The Kumarajiva translation of the *Chin kang po jo po luo mi ching* (J: *Kongō hannya haramitsu kyō*) may be found in *T* 235, 8:748–752.

69. Another point worth noting is that Iwashima is said to be traveling on business for Daianji temple. Daianji also appears to have been closely connected with immigrant kinship groups from the Korean kingdom of Silla from an early date. Its connections with the early Shōtoku cult, at which the Hata were at the forefront, can also be clearly seen from the *Daianji engi*, an account of the temple's origins that was submitted to the court in 747. The text claims as the temple's founder none other than Shōtoku. See *NI* 2:366–367.

Chapter 3: Female Rulers and Female Immortals

1. *Pao pu tzu. Nei p'ien,* 15th fascicle. The text may be found in Li Chung-hua's annotated edition *Hsin i: Pao p'u tzu,* 379.

2. Fukunaga's contention that the source of these religious borrowings can be found within the Taoist textual tradition remains extremely controversial. For a brief appraisal of Fukunaga's place in Japanese scholarship on the period, see Bialock, *Eccentric Spaces*, 26–28.

3. Shimode Sekiyo, *Kodai shinsen shisō no kenkyū*, 105.

4. The role of gender and family structures is a topic of vast importance that remains understudied by scholars of Nara-period religion. For a discussion of the advance of patriarchal notions of lineage during the Nara period, see Sekiguchi Hiroko, "The Patriarchical Family Paradigm." See also Yoshie Akiko, *Nihon kodai no uji no kōzō*; Fukutō Sanae, *Ie seiritsushi no kenkyū*; and Yoshie Akiko, *Nihon kodai no saishi to josei*.

5. Today Yoshino remains an administrative unit within Nara prefecture, comprising, along with the Uda district, almost two-thirds of the prefecture's territory.

6. As Wada notes, understandings of Yoshino's borders appear to have shifted over time. Yoshino's physical characteristics as well as its roadways and even bridges are discussed in detail in Wada, *Nihon kodai no girei saishi*, 129–142. Note, however, that my purpose here is not to present a detailed account of religious practices within a fixed geographic site, but to investigate how Yoshino and similar sites were imagined within the cultic discourse of the period.

7. Although Uda and Yoshino constituted two adjacent administrative units within the structures of the early state, they formed one common topographical/botanical region (Wada, *Nihon kodai no girei saishi* 3:131). Throughout this chapter I therefore treat them as one entity.

8. Ibid., 2:99.

9. *Samguk sagi* 4:121.

10. Wada, *Nihon kodai no girei saishi* 2:111–115. Further evidence suggesting that the Yamato court was actively pursuing knowledge of continental medical techniques can also be found in the Yōrō law codes, which stipulate a curriculum of Chinese medical texts that all aspirants for governmental medical posts were required to master (*NST* 5:421). Evidence suggesting that Yoshino was highly valued as a site for the collection of medicinal herbs can also be found in an entry from the *Shoku Nihongi* for the year 699 that refers to both En and one Karakuni Muraji Hirotari practicing austerities in nearby Kazuragi in pursuit of immortality (*SNG* Monmu 3.5.24, *SNKBT* 12:17). Karakuni's existence is attested in several other Nara-period sources, including the *Tōshi kaden*, which lists him as one of the notable medical figures of the age (*Tōshi kaden*, 111).

11. *CCSSC* 5.5. The text may also be found in Wang Yü-jung's annotated edition, *Ching ch'u sui shih chi*, 156–157. See also Moriya Mitsuo, *Keiso saijiki*, 123. Note that the *CCSSC* has been transmitted to us along with a commentary composed by Tu Kung-shan sometime between 605 and 619, which is to say, during Suiko's reign.

12. Quoted in *CCSSC* 5.5; Wang Yü-jung, ed., 156–157. I shall discuss this further in Chapter 7.

13. *CCSSC* 5.5. Moriya, *Keiso saijiki*, 136. *CCSSC* Wang Yü-jung, ed., 170–173. The *CCSSC* also goes on to cite Ke Hung's discussion of amulets used on the fifth day of the fifth month in his *Pao p'u tzu, Nei pien,* 15th fascicle. The text may be found in Li Chung-hua's annotated edition *Hsin i: Pao p'u tzu*, 374–375.

14. *NSK* Tenmu 14.10.8. *SNKBZ* 4:452.

15. This event is discussed in detail in Shinkawa Tokio, *Dōkyō o meguru kōbō*, 67–100. See also Bialock, *Eccentric Spaces*, 80–84; and Ooms, *Imperial Politics*, 156–163.

16. I will discuss this rite further in Chapter 7.

17. For rites of spirit-calling and clothing, see Yü Ying-shih, "O Soul, Come Back!" For examples of scarves and clothing being waved within the context of funerary rites or benedictions, see Hitomaro's ode to his deceased wife in *MYS*, Book 2, no. 207. *SNKBT* 1:252–253. The text has also been translated in Ebersole, *Ritual Poetry*, 192–194. I will discuss the Kusakabe ancestor Shinohara Otohihimeko in greater detail in Chapter 5. I will discuss rites of resurrection in greater detail in Chapter 7.

18. I will discuss this rite in greater detail in Chapter 7.

19. Many scholars also believe that it was during this period that the court began to emphasize the cult of Amaterasu. Tenmu, for instance, is said to have sent a female member of his line to serve as priestess (*saigū*) at Ise after a fifty-year hiatus during which this custom was not observed. Tenmu's consort and successor Jitō, similarly, made the first visit to the shrine by a ruler. I will discuss Amaterasu and the *chinkonsai* in greater detail in Chapter 7.

20. *NSK* Tenji 671.5.5. *SNKBZ* 4:391.

21. For a history of the Tamai and the closely related Gosechimai down through later ages, see Hayashi Tatsusaburō, *Chūsei geinōshi no kenkyū*, 157–164. See also Fukutō Sanae, *Heian ōchō shakai no jendā*, 143–181. I will briefly discuss Tenji's role in the development of court ritual in Chapter 6.

22. Tenmu's close association with this dance is suggested by an entry in the *Shoku Nihongi* for the fifth day of the fifth month of 743, in which the retired ruler Genshō attributes the dance's origins to Tenmu. I will discuss this passage further below. Tenmu's association with imagery of immortals at Yoshino is also discussed in Bialock, *Eccentric Spaces*, 85–99. See also Ooms, *Imperial Politics*, 147–149.

23. I will discuss legends depicting the Queen Mother of the West's visits to sage rulers in Chapter 4. For the development of the concept of the sage king in the Japanese islands, see Como, *Shōtoku*, 75–92.

24. *Kojiki*, Yūryaku chapter. *SNKBZ* 1:345. Wada, *Nihon kodai no girei to saishi* 2:97.

25. For a discussion of Jitō's reign in conjunction with that of Tenmu, see Piggott, *Emergence of Japanese Kingship*, 127–166.

26. This thesis is discussed at length in Shinbori Shinobu, "Jitō Jotei to Yoshino Gyōkō." See also Ooms, *Imperial Politics*, 179–180.

27. For the history of rainmaking rites in the Japanese islands, see Yabu Motoaki, *Amagoi girei no seiritsu to tenkai*, and Namiki, "Heian jidai no amagoi hōbi."

28. One further indication of the deity's importance for the royal cult may be found in the Kōgyoku chapter of the *Nihon shoki*, in which the Soga kinship

group is depicted as repeatedly seeking to usurp royal ritual prerogatives. Here we are told that the Soga built a temple known as Hōkiyamadera on a mountain on which the Nihu deity was thought to reside (*NSK* Kōgyoku 3:11, *SNKBZ* 4:95–97). For possible connections between this temple and others in the region, see Tsuji, *Narachō sangaku jiin no kenkyū*, 201–220. I discuss this temple again below.

29. *NSK* Jinmu, Period Prior to Accession. *SNKBZ* 2:213.

30. *NSK* Jinmu, Tsuchinoe Uma, 9.5. *SNKBZ* 2:213–215.

31. Offerings at Jinmu's tomb are recorded in *NSK* Tenmu 1.7. *SNKBZ* 4:341. This is discussed in Ooms, *Imperial Politics*, 74.

32. This legend illustrating Jinmu's mastery of the fish in Yoshino is also mirrored in a series of legends of fishermen and immortals that were associated with lineages such as the Ōtomo and Kusakabe, which had large presences along the coastal regions both on the Japan/Eastern Sea and on the Inland Sea. I shall discuss this in greater detail below.

33. Wada, *Nihon kodai no girei to saishi*, 3:465. Recently Katō Kenkichi has argued that sites named Nihu across Japan were closely connected with metal production and cinnabar. As a result, there is an extremely high correspondence between such areas and the Hata, who were at the forefront of metal production during the period (Katō Kenkichi, *Hatashi to sono tami*, 120–129).

34. Katō Kenkichi, *Hatashi to sono tami*, 120–130.

35. Wada, *Nihon kodai no girei to saishi* 3:172.

36. Wada's suggestion that the court may have been interested in Yoshino for its red earth provides several further clues as to the transmission of continental conceptions of immortals to the Japanese islands. If he is correct, we should expect to find similar legends in other regions with similar climate and geology. We should also expect that lineages associated with the mining of minerals or metal-working would be prominent in such regions. Fortunately, we already have the remarkable research of Matsuda Hisao, who took the trouble of having geological analysis done in numerous regions across the Japanese islands to determine which areas contained the compound that the Japanese court appears to have identified as cinnabar. Among the most startling findings was that in every region where we find cinnabar, we also find a place name referring to "Nihu." Matsuda also demonstrates that the Nihu Atae must have lived in these areas and, almost certainly, mined for metal there (Matsuda, *Niu no kenkyū*). Katō Kenkichi, building on Matsuda's work, has further demonstrated that in every area where the Nihu atae lived, there were also members of the Hata kinship group. Katō concludes that the Hata, who are known to have been involved in metal-working, were most likely overseers of the Nihu Atae.

37. *Nihon ryōiki,* 1.26. Kyoko Nakamura, *Miraculous Stories,* 138–139. *SNKBZ* 10:87–88.

38. *Nihon ryōiki* 1.28. Kyoko Nakamura, *Miraculous Stories,* 140–142. *SNKBZ* 10:90–93.

39. More subtly, the *Nihon ryōiki* account of the goals and practices of En no Gyōja is also suggestive of the conceptual framework that lay behind such practices. The Spell of the Peacock was held in high regard by ascetic practitioners in pursuit of superhuman powers and the ability to control spirits. Although it is not clear which scripture this spell derived from, the most likely appears to be the *K'ung ch'üeh wang chou ching* (*The Scripture on the Spell of the Peacock King*; J: *Kujakuōshukyō*), *T* 982, 983, and 985, 19:446–458. Several other scriptures with similar titles are also known to have circulated during the Nara period and were among the most highly valued texts in the early Heian period. This spell also appears to have been associated with the monk Dōkyō, whose rise to power apparently began when he used the Spell of the Peacock to heal the retired ruler Kōken of a serious illness shortly before she retook the throne in 765 (Nemoto Seiji, *Tempyōki no sōryo to tennō*). I will discuss further connections between Dōkyō, Kōken, and Yoshino below.

40. For an extended discussion of Kokūzō's identification with Venus in popular Japanese religion, see Sano Kenji, *Kokūzō bosatsu shinkō no kenkyū*, 235–299. Kokūzō worship is also discussed briefly in Lucia Dolce, "Introduction," 7–9.

41. The translation is from Hakeda Yoshito, *Kūkai: Major Works,* 19–20. For the original text, see *NKBT* 71: *Sangō shiiki, Shōryōshū,* 84. The textual basis for the Gumonjihō is the *Kokūzō bosatsu nōman shogan saishōshin darani gumonji no hō*. The text may be found in *T* 1145, 20:601–603.

42. Each of these temples is discussed in Tsuji Hidenori, *Narachō sangaku jiin no kenkyū*. For Hasedera, see also Tsuji Hidenori, *Hasederashi no kenkyū*. For Murōji, see also Sherry Fowler, *Muroji*. See also Tsuji Hidenori, *Murōjishi no kenkyū*.

43. *NSK* Kinmei 13.5. *SNKBZ* 3:421.

44. *Nihon ryōiki* 1.5. Kyoko Nakamura, *Miraculous Stories,* 111–112. *SNKBZ* 10:39–46.

45. *Nihon ryōiki* 1.5. Kyoko Nakamura, *Miraculous Stories,* 113–116. *SNKBZ* 10:42–43. For Gyōki and his movement, see Nakai Shinkō, *Gyōki to kodai Bukkyō*; Nemoto, *Nara Bukkyō to Gyōki denshō no tenkai*; and Yoshida Yasuo, *Gyōki to ritsuryō*.

46. For the text of the *Gyōki nenpu*, see Inoue Kaoru, ed., *Gyōki jiten*, 255–275.

47. For the sutra dedication, see Takeuchi, *NI* 2:612. For temples purportedly built by Gyōki during this period, see Inoue Kaoru, "Gyōki no shōgai,"

17–18. Yoshida gives a list of temples attributed to Gyōki in the *Gyōki nenpu* in Yoshida Yasuo, *Gyōki to ritsuryō*, 318–320. For more on relations between the cults of Gyōki and Shōtoku, see Como, *Shōtoku*, 111–132.

48. For the relationship between Prince Kusakabe, the Kusakabe kinship group, and other, affiliated kinship groups, see Ōhashi Nobuya, *Nihon kodai no ōken to shizoku*, 199–207.

49. Ōtomo genealogies and their connections with the Korean peninsula are discussed at length in Mizoguchi Mutsuko, *Kodai shizoku no keifu*, esp. 176–211. See also Naoki Kōjirō, *Nihon kodai no shizoku to tennō*, 57–74.

50. Saeki, *Shinsen shōjiroku no kenkyū* 1:285. This is discussed in Shinkawa, *Nihon kodai no saishi to hyōgen*, 262–267.

51. *Hizen fudoki*, Matsuura district. *SNKBZ* 5:331.

52. I shall discuss this in greater detail in Chapter 5.

53. Variant renderings of the Uranoshimako legend are discussed at length in Shimode, *Kodai shinsen shisō no kenkyū*, 171–222. For a discussion of this legend as it relates to both the Kusakabe and the Shōtoku cult, see Como, *Shōtoku*, 94–97.

54. *Tango fudoki*, *SNKBZ* 5:476. Continental influences in the text are also discussed in Bialock, *Eccentric Spaces*, 89.

55. Thus the frequent use of the prefix "*kushitama*" in the names of deities. I will further discuss the relationship between combs (*kushi*) and elixirs of immortality (*kusushi, kushi*) in the context of several important legends in Chapter 7.

56. Shimode lists several Uranoshimako shrines from the region in Shimode, *Kodai shinsen shisō no kenkyū*, 189. During the Heian period increasingly elaborate versions of the legend continued to be produced. For more on the Uranoshimako cult during the early Nara period, see also Takioto Yoshiyuki, "Urashimako denshō no seiritsu kiban"; Hayashi Kōhei, *Urashima densetsu no kenkyū*; and Masuda Sanae, *Urashima densetsu ni miru kodai Nihonjin no shinkō*.

57. *Huai nan tzu*, fascicle six. Hsiung Li-hui, ed., *Hsin fan Huai nan tzu*, 300–301 and 358–359. Although the textual origins for the rabbit on the moon are obscure, the rabbit appears both in the Ma wang tui tapestry and more broadly throughout Han dynasty epigraphy (Loewe, *Ways to Paradise*, 127–133).

58. *Sou shen chi*, by Kan Pao, Book 14, #354. In *Sou shen chi*, ed. Huang Ti-ming, 486.

59. Just what sort of garment this would have been is unclear. Akimoto glosses it as a garment worn by beings in the Buddhist heaven Toriten (*NKBT* 2:447, n.11).

60. This remnant of the *Suruga fudoki* may be found in *SNKBZ* 5:575–576.

61. This remnant of the *Ōmi fudoki* may be found in *SNKBZ* 5:578–579. The legend is also discussed in Shimode, *Kodai shinsen shisō no kenkyū*, 130–134. For a discussion of this and other such legends of Heavenly Maidens from the point of view of folklore studies, see Miller, "The Swan-Maiden Revisited."

62. The Iga Muraji's claims to descent from this female immortal were repeated as late as the Kamakura period, although Shimode notes that by the time of the composition of the *Shinsen shōjiroku* the Iga Muraji had also constructed genealogical links with the Nakatomi kinship group (Shimode, *Kodai shinsen shisō no kenkyū*, 137–139). Further possible evidence associating the Iga Muraji with female immortals can be found in the *Iga fudoki*, which contains the tale of a Heavenly Maiden who, much like the female immortal who appeared before Yūryaku at Yoshino, descends to earth and plays a magical "Chinese harp" (*kara no koto*).

63. *Kaifūsō* #31. *NKBT* 69:100. The *Kaifūsō*, a collection of Chinese-style poems from the Nara period, contains several other poems concerning immortals as well. Because there is widespread agreement that the poems collected in this work reflect a high degree of familiarity with (if not dependence upon) Chinese models, however, Japanese commentators have long argued that motifs associated with Taoist immortals simply reflected the close adherence of Japanese poets to the tropes and allusions of Chinese literary works. As a result, there is a widespread tendency to dismiss virtually all references to Chinese cults and conceptions of immortality in the literature of the period as mere literary ornamentation. See, for instance, Shimode, *Kodai shinsen shisō no kenkyū*, 119–120.

64. *Nihon ryōiki* 1.13. Kyoko Nakamura, *Miraculous Stories*, 124–125. *SNKBZ* 6:92–93.

65. In addition, the *Nihon ryōiki* account of Nuribe Hime highlights the degree to which lineal affiliations helped shape cultic orientations even among Buddhist clergy. Nuribe no Hime, for instance, would have been considered a relative of Rōben, one of the most important monks of the Nara period and a member of the Nuribe kinship group.

66. *MYS*, Book 3, no. 385. *SNKBT* 1:252. The translation is from Edwin Cranston's *Waka Anthology 1*, 497. Note that I have altered Cranston's rendering of this maiden's name from "Mulberry-branch Nymph" to the more literal "Immortal Mulberry-branch Maiden" (Tsuminoe no Hijiri Hime) in order to emphasize her explicit designation as a female immortal.

67. For a discussion of textual sources for the Immortal Mulberry-branch Maiden, see Shimode, *Kodai shinsen shisō no kenkyū*, 110–120. See also Katata Osamu, *Nihon kodai shinkō to Bukkyō*, 39–55.

68. Literary references to female immortals at Yoshino are discussed at length in Shimode, *Kodai shinsen shisō no kenkyū*, 97–157. I will discuss other poems from the Immortal Mulberry-branch Maiden corpus in Chapter 6.

69. *Hizen fudoki,* Kishima district. *SNKBZ* 5: 515. Cranston, *Waka Anthology 1,* 144.

70. The Sumiyoshi Daijin, an aggregate form of the Sumiyoshi deities, in this regard, is particularly important. As we noted in Chapter 1, this deity was said to have flown over the Yoshino region while riding a dragon and wearing continental-style clothing.

71. In the *MYS* we also find a dialogue that purportedly occurs between Ōtomo no Yakamochi and local women in the Matsuura district of Hizen province in which Yakamochi playfully asks the women if they are not, in fact, "immortals of Matsuura." The text may be found in the preface to a series of poems set in Matsuura in book 5. See *SNKBZ* 1:479.

72. *Toyuke miya no gishiki chō,* in *GR* 2:53. This is also recounted in numerous later texts of importance for Ise Shintō. See, for instance, the *Toyuke kōtaijin gochinza hongi.* In *SZKT* 7:453.

73. This remnant from the *Tango fudoki* can be found in *SNKBZ* 5:483–484. Cranston, *Waka Anthology 1,* 150–151.

74. *NSK* Age of the Gods, *SNKBZ* 2:60–61. I will discuss this in detail in Chapter 7.

75. See, for instance, *Ise nisho kōtaijingū gochinza denki, SZKT* 7:439, also 453.

76. Shimode names fourteen Toyouke Hime shrines that are listed in the *Engishiki* (*Kodai shinsen shisō no kenkyū,* 156).

77. For more on the political background of Abe's dance, see Piggott, "The Last Classical Female Sovereign," 51–55.

78. *SNG* Tempyō 15.5.5. *SNKBT* 13:419–421. See also Ooms, *Imperial Politics,* 121–123.

79. Piggott, "The Last Classical Female Sovereign," 54. In due time the Princess Abe did in fact ascend the throne, not once but twice during the tumultuous final decades of the Nara period. Her fateful alliance with the monk Dōkyō, yet another healer-monk from the region, would have far-reaching consequences for the structure of court ritual and the balance of power at court for centuries to come. For Dōkyō, see Nemoto Seiji, *Tempyōki no sōryo to tennō.*

80. Shimode notes that although Nara-period sources are unfortunately silent on the topic, by the middle of the Heian period the linkages between

the Gosechimai, Tenmu, Yoshino, and immortality had grown to be so strong that texts such as the *Seiji yōryaku* traced the origins of the Gosechimai to a dance performed by the Chinese deity Takakara Megami for Tenmu at Yoshino. *Seiji yōryaku, Nenjū gyōji*, section 27. In *SZKT* 28:145. Shimode, *Kodai shinsen shisō no kenkyū*, 98. For more on the role of immigrant lineages in the formation of the concept of the sage king, see Como, *Shōtoku*, 75–92.

81. I discuss legends relating this deity to both the origins of sericulture and Amaterasu in Chapter 7. Legends relating this deity to Amaterasu within the Ise textual corpus can be found in the *Ise nisho kōtaijingū gochinza shidaiki, KT* 7:429–434, *Ise nisho kōtaijingū gochinza denki, KSTK* 7: 435–450, *Toyuke kōtaijin gochinza hongi, KT* 7:451–463, *Zō Ise nisho taijingū hō kihongi, KT* 7:464–479, and the *Yamato hime no mikoto seiki, KSTK* 7:479–508.

82. During the Kamakura period, of course, the outer shrine of Ise, where Toyuke Hime was housed, was to be a major source for the emergence of medieval understandings of Shintō (Teeuwen, *Watarai Shintō*).

83. Fukutō Sanae, *Heian ōchō shakai no jendā*, 154.

Chapter 4: The Queen Mother of the West and the Ghosts of the Buddhist Tradition

1. Gordon, *Ghostly Matters*, 190.

2. The *Gangōji garan engi narabi ni ruki shizaichō* may be found in *NI* 2:383–393. *Hōryūji garan engi narabi ni ruki shizaichō* may be found in *NI* 2:344–365. The *Jōgū Shōtoku hōōteisetsu* may be found in *STZ* 3:9–22.

3. For the early Shōtoku cult, see Como, *Shōtoku*; Hayashi Mikiya, *Taishi shinkō no kenkyū*; and Iida Mizuho, *Shōtoku taishiden no kenkyū*.

4. Helen McCulough, trans., *Tale of the Heike*, 315–317. For a fascinating discussion of the role of *onmyōdō* beliefs and practices in the shaping of the text, see David Bialock, *Eccentric Spaces*.

5. For the original text of *Atsumori*, see *NKBT* 40: *Yōkyokushū* 1:233–240. An English translation may be found in Arthur Waley, *Noh Plays of Japan*, 63–73.

6. The Buddhist founding legend has been discussed by a large number of Japanese scholars. For a brief overview, see Tamura Enchō, *Nihon Bukkyōshi*, 1:68–84. See also Hiraoka Jōkai, *Nihonjiin shi no kenkyū*, 22–43.

7. Much of my understanding of the Mononobe has been shaped by Mayuzumi Hiromichi, *Mononobe Sogashi to kodai ōken*. For the cultic activities of the Mononobe, see Hon'iden Kikushi, "Mononobeshi to Isonokami Jingū"; Izumiya Yasuo, "Mononobe to shūkyō"; Kamei Kiichirō, "Isonokami

Jingū to Oshisaka Ōnakahime"; Watanabe Katsuyoshi, *Chinkonsai no kenkyū*, 139–149; and Emura Hiroyuki, *Ritsuryō tennōsei saishi no kenkyū*, 76–109.

8. For more on the cycle of political violence and rites of propitiation, see Como, *Shōtoku*, 93–110.

9. For the formation of service lineages known as *be* in Japan, see Yoshie Akiko, *Nihon kodai no shizoku no kōzō*; and Takemitsu Makoto, *Kenkyūshi*.

10. Inoue Hideo, "Chiku, Toyo, Hi no gōzoku to Yamato chōtei," 157.

11. For *chimata* rites in Japan, see Maeda Haruto, *Nihon kodai no michi to chimata*. See also Wada, *Nihon kodai no girei to saishi* 2:269–364; and Como, *Shōtoku*, 111–132.

12. See, for example, *NSK* Sujin 10.9; *SNKBZ* 2:281; *NSK* Jinmu, Period Prior to Accession; and *SNKBZ* 2:215–217. Although I know of no explicit explanation in the primary sources as to why crossroads were a favored site for these rites, in China such sites were most likely regarded as especially volatile because the *yin* and *yang* elements flowing along each roadway would become turbulent as their paths crossed.

13. One of the most important *chimata* for the subsequent cult of Prince Shōtoku was in Kataoka at the intersection of the Great Lateral and Kusakabe/Tatsuta highways. I have discussed the legend of Shōtoku's encounter with an immortal at this *chimata* in *Shōtoku*, 93–109. Note also that the Kusakabe claimed as a founding ancestor Tamba no Michi Omi, who was in turn said to be a direct descendant of the deity Ama no Hoakari no Mikoto. This deity, discussed in greater detail in Chapters 5 and 7, was also claimed as an ancestor by several sub-branches of the Mononobe.

14. Hirano discusses the Inabe's genealogical connections with both the Mononobe and the Hata in his "Hatashi no kenkyū." The Fumi no Obito were a sub-branch of the Kawachi no Aya, an immigrant kinship group that traced its origins to a scholar of the Confucian classics who was said to have been sent to the Japanese islands during the reign of Ōjin.

15. The most prominent *chimata* prior to the Nara period are discussed throughout Maeda Haruto, *Nihon kodai no michi to chimata*; as well as in Wada, *Nihon kodai no girei to saishi* 2:295–324.

16. To give but one example, we saw in Chapter 2 that Azeko, the officiant said to have propitiated the vengeful weaving deity Akaru Hime in Kyūshū, was himself from just such a Mononobe sublineage.

17. Matsumae Takeshi, *Kodai denshō to kyūtei saishi*, 91.

18. The *Sendai kuji hongi* may be found in *ST*. For an English translation, see John R. Bentley, *The Authenticity of the* Sendai Kuji Hongi: *A New Examination of Texts, with a Translation and Commentary*. Bentley's claims about the early provenance of the text, however, are highly controversial. For a review of the issue, see Mark Teeuwen, "*Sendai kuji hongi*."

19. *Sendai kuji hongi.* Tennō hongi, Jinmu 1.11. *ST,* 125. Alternatively, the Spell of Furu can be taken to mean "the spell of shaking." Bentley renders the phrase *"yura yura"* not as a phonetic incantation, but as a stage direction for the officiant to sway while speaking.

20. For the relationship between court rites of spirit pacification and the Isonokami shrine, see Matsumae Takeshi, *Kodai denshō to kyūtei saishi,* 115–127. I discuss this further in Chapter 7. The text's reference to the rite as the Furu kotohoki contains broader implications for understanding Mononobe ritual practice. As Katata Osamu has noted, *"hoki," "hoku,"* and *"hokai"* are all terms for ritual speech in which the speaker seeks to effect some change in the world through the expression of the wish for that change (*Nihon kodai shinkō to Bukkyō,* 142–144). Although often translated as "prayer" or "charm," *hokai* were frequently used at *chimata* both to bring blessings and to subjugate the enemies—living or dead—of the court.

21. *NSK* Yūryaku 13.3. *SNKBZ* 3:193. This reference to the *tachibana* in conjunction with the Ega *chimata* is highly suggestive in light of the *tachibana*'s role as a symbol of *tokoyo*—a land beyond death closely related to millenarian cults and immigrant kinship group deities. Perhaps the most famous example of such cults can be found in another passage in the *Nihon shoki,* which refers to a popular religious movement that anticipated the advent of the *tokoyo* deity in the form of a worm on the *tachibana* tree. This millenial movement is of particular interest because its main figures were from immigrant kinship groups closely related to the formation of the cult of Prince Shōtoku; see Como, *Shōtoku,* 33–54. Ōfube's movement is also discussed in Ellwood, "A Cargo Cult in Seventh Century Japan"; and Katō Kenkichi, *Hatashi to sono tami,* 196–205.

22. The standard work on the Fumi no Obito and their kinsmen is Inoue Mitsusada, *Nihon kodai shisōshi no kenkyū,* 412–468.

23. *NST* 3: 213–214. For court purification rites in Naniwa, see also Okada Seishi, *Kodai ōken no saishi to shinwa,* 59–94. See also Uwai Hisayoshi, *Nihon kodai no shizoku to saishi,* 62–82. For a more speculative view, emphasizing the importance of *onmyōdō* in such rites, see Takikawa Seijirō, *Ritsuryō to daijōsai,* 223–328.

24. *Engishiki,* Book 8. Bock, *Engi-Shiki: Procedures of the Engi Era—Books 6–10,* 88–89. This liturgy also appears to have greatly influenced later developments in the history of Japanese religion. See, for instance, the *Nakatomi harae kunge,* a twelfth-century commentary upon the rite, which later served as a major source for the birth of medieval Shintō. For more on the commentary, see Mark Teeuwen and Hendrik ven der Veere, *Nakatomi harae kunge.*

25. For the Ōharae, see Miyake Kazuo, *Kodai kokka no jingi to saishi*, 163–214; and Obinata Kasumi, *Kodai kokka to nenchū gyōji*, 184–220.

26. In addition to examples from the *Po wu chih* cited below, these terms appear in such texts as the *Shan hai ching*, second fascicle. The text may be found in Yuan K'o, ed., *Shan hai ching chiao chu*, 21–66.

27. The *Engishiki's* instructions for the uses of these implements are discussed briefly in Bock, *Engi-Shiki: Procedures of the Engi Era—Books 6–10*, 88. Chapter 7 discusses the importance of these rites in conjunction with the development of the Chinkonsai.

28. *NST* 3:215.

29. This is discussed at length in Kominami, *Seiōbō to tanabata denshō*, 109–142. I discuss the ritual pairing of these days in greater detail shortly. I also discuss the Ōharae in greater detail in Chapter 7.

30. Just as the first fifteen days of the first month marked the beginning of the first half of the year (and the ascent of *yang*), so the first fifteen days of the seventh month marked the advent of the second half of the year (and the ascent of *yin*). As a result, the beginning, midpoint, and end of the new year cycle (that is, 1.1, 1.7, and 1.15), as well as corresponding days of the seventh month (that is, 7.1, 7.7, and 7.15) were among the most heavily ritualized in the festival calendar. These days were also thought to be moments of heightened interaction between the human and spirit worlds. I shall discuss the ritual significance of the seventh day of the seventh month (*tanabata*) and the seventh day of the first month (*jen-jih*) shortly. I discuss the importance of rites associated with the fifteenth day of the first month in Chapter 6.

31. *Shan hai ching*, fourth fascicle. The text may be found in Yüan K'o, ed., *Shan hai ching chiao chu*, 407. The Queen Mother has been the object of sustained interest among scholars of Chinese religion. For an extensive treatment of the role of the Queen Mother in T'ang religion and literature, see Cahill's *Transcendence and Divine Passion*. The Queen Mother's appearance is discussed in detail in Kominami, *Seiōbō to tanabata denshō*, 71–103. Virtually all aspects of the Queen Mother are also discussed with great erudition in Loewe's *Ways to Paradise*, esp. 86–134. For an extensive treatment of the origins of the Queen Mother's cult as well as the development of different means of representing her, see Fracassso, "Holy Mothers in Ancient China." The translation is from Loewe, *Ways to Paradise*, 91.

32. *Po wu chih*, eighth fascicle. The text may be found in Fan Ning, ed., *Po wu chih chiao cheng*, 97. The translation is from Loewe, *Ways to Paradise*, 116–117.

33. For more on the role of the Three-legged Crow and bird messengers for the cult of the Queen Mother of the West, see Cahill, *Transcendence and Divine Passion*, 91–98.

34. For Mount Kunlun, see Kominami, Seiōbō to tanabata denshō, 143–186. For the tapestry, see Loewe, *Ways to Paradise*, 17–59.

35. Similar iconographic motifs have been found in Japan as well. The Tenjukoku shūchō tapestry purportedly commissioned by Shōtoku's fourth wife, the Lady Tachibana Inabe no ōiratsume, contains an image of the rabbit in the moon in the upper left corner of the tapestry. Although the upper right portion of the tapestry no longer exists, making it impossible to tell if the rabbit was flanked by the Three-legged Crow, the Three-legged Crow is depicted on the Tamamushi shrine at Hōryūji. Intriguingly, the Lady Tachibana's name includes both the motif of the Tachibana and the surname Inabe. For a discussion of the tapestry, see Pradel, *Fragments of the Tenjukoku Shūchō Mandara*; and Ōhashi Katsuaki, *Tenjukoku shūchō no kenkyū*. For a brief discussion of various attempts to date the tapestry, see Lurie, "Origins of Writing in Early Japan," 416–417. For a discussion of the symbol of the rabbit, see Loewe, *Ways to Paradise*, 127–133. Excellent photographs of both the Tamamushi shrine and the tapestry may be found in the catalogue of the NHK Shōtoku exhibition in Ōsaka in 2001 (Tōkyōto Bijutsukan, ed., *Shōtoku taishi ten*, 72–77).

36. References to rites involving the calling back of the dead can be found even in the *Ch'u tz'u*. See Hawks, *Songs of the South*, 219–231. Rites of spirit-calling are discussed in detail in Yü Ying-shih's classic study "O Soul, Come Back." For a variety of viewpoints on Chinese death rituals from the late imperial period, see Watkins and Rawski, eds., *Death Ritual*.

37. Such spirits, of course, would then become the objects of rites of pacification such as the Ōharae.

38. For legends concerning the Queen Mother of the West and these and other rulers, see Cahill, *Transcendence and Divine Passion*, 108–142.

39. See, for instance, the *Han wu ku shih*, in Masuda Wataru, trans., *Dai Rojin zensho* 6:52–54; and the *Han Wu-ti nei chuan*, in Wang Kuo-liang, ed., *Han Wu t'ung ming chi yen chiu*, 50–51. For an extended discussion of the role of the Han Wu-ti legend corpus in early Chinese religious discourse, see Kominami, *Chūgoku no shinwa to monogatari*, 237–434. See also Cahill, *Transcendence and Divine Passion*, 143–189.

40. *CCSSC*, as quoted in Moriya, *Keisosaijiki*, 22. I will discuss this passage further below.

41. *NSK* Age of the Gods, *SNKBZ*, 2:55.

42. As we shall see shortly, the *Kojiki* explicitly identifies the *tachibana* as the Queen Mother's "fruit of immortality."

43. Kominami, *Seiōbō to tanabata denshō*, 109–142. I will discuss this in greater detail below. By the advent of the Sui dynasty there was a large corpus

of Chinese literature related to the Queen Mother of the West's visits to sage rulers on the seventh day of the seventh month (see Chapter 3), and as we shall see shortly the Queen Mother was in addition the focus of popular worship on the seventh day of the first month.

44. This issue is discussed in detail in Kominami, *Chūgoku no shinwa to monogatari*, 241–257. For the classic work on the ghost festival, see Stephen Teiser, *The Ghost Festival in Medieval China*. I discuss Taoist conceptions of the fifteenth day of the seventh month as a day for judging the dead shortly.

45. Kominami, *Seiōbō to tanabata denshō*, 118. As I noted in Chapter 2, weaving elements resembling the Queen Mother's *sheng* have also been found in substantial numbers in Hizen province in Kyūshū.

46. As I noted in Chapter 2, the introduction of classical Chinese divination texts to the court of Suiko was followed by an explosion of omen entries in the court chronicles. These omens were frequently taken to have political import, signifying everything from changes in the ruler's health to Heaven's pleasure or displeasure with the ruler's virtue. See Tamura Enchō, *Nihon Bukkyōshi* 4:419–441. See also Como, "Ethnicity, Sagehood and the Politics of Literacy."

47. *NSK* Hakuji 1.1. *SNKBZ* 4:181–183.

48. Images of the Weaver Maiden in Koguryō tomb paintings are discussed briefly in Hirabayashi Akihito, *Tanabata to sumō no kodaishi*, 44–49.

49. Shinkawa, *Nihon kodai girei to hyōgen*, 147.

50. *SNG* Taihō 1.1, *SNKBT* 12:33. Shinkawa, *Nihon kodai girei to hyōgen*, 141–147.

51. This is discussed at length in Shinkawa, *Nihon kodai girei to hyōgen*, 134–141.

52. The passage in question from the *Yu yang tsa tsu* can be found in a critical edition with Japanese commentary in Imamura Yoshio, trans., *Yūyō zasso* 4:208. The text also suggests that the omen was met with considerable skepticism. Although the significance of such an omen was not questioned, the text states that courtiers believed one of the bird's legs to be false.

53. For the origins and development of the cult of the Yatagarasu, see Nakamura Shūya, *Hatashi to Kamoshi*, 46–49.

54. *NSK* Jinmu, Tsuchinoe no Uma, 6.23. *SNKBZ* 1:204–205.

55. Shinkawa Tokio has noted that even in the court chronicles the Yatagarasu's role as emissary from the Sun Goddess Amaterasu has obvious parallels with the role of the Three-legged Crow as emissary for the Queen Mother of the West. Shinkawa also notes that Jinmu's explicit characterization of the Yatagarasu as an auspicious omen closely mirrors Chinese and Japanese conceptions of the auspicious nature of the Three-legged Crow (*Nihon kodai girei to hyōgen*, 151).

56. Ibid., 148–149.
57. *NSK* Suinin 90.7.14. *SNKBZ* 2:335.
58. *NSK* Suinin 99.3.12. *SNKBZ* 2:336–337.
59. See Nakamura Takashi, *Chūgoku saijishi no kenkyū*, 24–48; and Kominami, *Seiōbō to tanabata denshō*, 125.
60. Popular New Year's rites of spirit worship in the Japanese islands are discussed briefly in Chapter 2. The role of the rooster in New Year's rites at the gate is discussed in detail in Moriya, *Keiso saijiki*, 23–25.
61. *CCSSC* 1.1; Moriya, *Keiso saijiki*, 22.
62. Kominami, *Seiōbō to tanabata denshō*, 125–126.
63. *CCSSC* 1.7; Moriya, *Keiso saijiki*, 37–38.
64. *CCSSC* 1.7; Moriya, *Keiso saijiki*, 38.

Chapter 5: Shamanesses, Lavatories, and the Magic of Silk

1. The lavatory goddess is discussed at length in Nakamura Takashi, *Chūgoku saijishi no kenkyū*, 49–66. I will discuss legends associated with this goddess again in Chapter 6.
2. The text may be found in *Hsü chi chieh chi yen chiu*, ed. Wang Kuo-liang, 47. See also Nakamura Takashi, *Chūgoku saijishi no kenkyū*, 53–54.
3. For more on this, see Nakamura Takashi, *Chūgoku saijishi no kenkyū*, 24–48 and Kominami, *Seiōbō to tanabata denshō*, 125. I shall discuss rites related to the lavatory goddess again in Chapter 6.
4. *Li chi*, fascicle 6. Chiang Yi-hua, *Hsin fan Li chi tu pen*, 238–239.
5. Ibid., 352.
6. *NSK* Kōgyoku 3.7, 2. *SNKBZ* 4:93–95. I will discuss this cult briefly in Chapter 6.
7. As we noted in Chapter 2, archeological discoveries of large numbers of looms and weaving implements at shrines across the Japanese islands confirm that female deities were regularly propitiated with objects associated with weaving and sericulture. For archeological remains from the area including weaving implements and *hitogata*, see Yuba Tadanori, "Saishi ibutsu no naiyō."
8. Periodization and routes for the arrival of sericulture are discussed in Nunome Junrō, *Kinu no tōden*, 113–119. For a more technical discussion of the history of weaving in the Japanese islands, see Nunome Junrō, *Kinu to nuno no kōkogaku*.
9. Weaving maidens are said to have been given to the Munakata deities in *NSK* Ōjin 41.2, *SNKBZ* 2:497. Weaving maidens are said to have been installed at the Miwa shrine in *NSK* Yūryaku 14.3. *SNKBZ* 3:197.

10. Just what this entailed is unclear. For a recent discussion of the practice in the context of gender roles during the period, see Yoshie Akiko, *Nihon kodai no saishi to josei*, esp. 1–20.

11. For Wakateru's reign, see Piggott, *Emergence of Japanese Kingship*, 44–65. Throughout this paper I refer to the historical Yamato ruler as Wakateru, but the constructed figure of the texts as Yūryaku. In this way I hope to highlight the constructed nature of royal genealogies and ancestral legends. I also hope to reinforce the point that weaving and weaving cults helped shape the identity of not only various craft lineages but also of the royal house itself.

12. For diplomatic missions to both northern and southern Chinese dynasties during this period, see Inoue Mitsusada, "Yūryakuchō ni okeru ōken to higashi ajia."

13. The Hata were discussed extensively in Chapter 1. For more on Yūryaku and the Hata, see Katō Kenkichi, *Hatashi to sono tami*, 156–164. For Yūryaku and the Kazuraki paramounts, see also Saeki Arikiyo, "Yūryaku chō no rekishiteki ichi," 8–13.

14. For an extended survey of Japanese scholarship on the formation of the *be* system in ancient Yamato, see Takemitsu Makoto, *Kenkyūshi*.

15. *NSK* Yūryaku 15. *SNKBZ* 3:201.

16. *NSK* Yūryaku 16.7. *SNKBZ* 3:201.

17. *Shinsen shōjiroku*, Yamashiro. Saeki, *Shinsen shōjiroku no kenkyū* 1:306.

18. *NSK* Yūryaku 6.3.7. *SNKBZ* 3:167.

19. *NSK* Yūryaku 7.7. *SNKBZ* 3:168–169.

20. For the Miwa cult, see Wada, *Nihon kodai no girei to saishi* 3:19–84. See also Wada Atsumu, ed., *Ōmiwa to Isonokami*.

21. For more on this, see Chapter 1.

22. For the "Iwai rebellion," see Oda Fujio, "Iwai no hanran," and Oda Fujio, ed., *Iwai no ran*.

23. For archeological connections between the Yamato court and the Munakata shrine, see Mayumi Tsunetada, "Saishi iseki no keisei"; Yuba Noritomo, "Saishi ibutsu no naiyō"; and Tamura Enchō, "Munakata, Usa, Asō."

24. The major exception, of course, is the female ancestral deity Amaterasu no Ōmikami.

25. See, for instance, Kōnoshi, *Kojiki no sekaikan* and Kōnoshi, *Kojiki to Nihon shoki*.

26. Mishina, *Nissen shinwa densetsu no kenkyū*, 268–270. See also Mizoguchi, *Ōken shinwa no nigen kōzō*, 185–191. See also Matsumae, "The Myth of the Descent of the Heavenly Grandson."

27. Hirabayashi, *Tanabata to sumō no kodaishi*, 128–129.

28. See, for instance, *Samguk sagi,* Silla Pongi, Yuri Isagüm 9.7.15. Inoue Hideo, trans., *Sankoku shiki,* 13.

29. The appearance of this trope in the Korean legends of kingship is noted in Ōbayashi, "Japanese Myths of Descent," 173.

30. *NSK* Age of the Gods. *SNKBZ* 2:152–153. This is also a trope found in the nation-founding legends from the Korean kingdoms.

31. This is discussed in Hirabayashi, *Tanabata to sumō no kodaishi,* 165. Note also that Takuhata Chichi Hime was also worshipped together with the royal ancestor Amaterasu at the inner shrine at Ise. I will discuss this in greater detail in Chapter 7.

32. *NSK* Age of the Gods, Book 2. *SNKBZ* 2:143.

33. For more on this, see Hirabayashi, *Tanabata to sumō no kodaishi,* 164–168. The presence of the god Ama no Hoakari no Mikoto in this narrative is also of particular note, as he was claimed as the founding ancestor of the Kusakabe, an important service group that played a major role in the spread of weaving cults and technologies. In Chapter 7 we shall see that descendants of this deity also played an important role in the formation of the early cult of Amaterasu no Ōmikami.

34. I will discuss Ama no Hoakari and the Mononobe in greater detail in Chapter 7.

35. *Kojiki,* Jinmu chapter. *NKBZ* 167. *SNKBZ* 1:159–161.

36. Recall, for instance, the legend cited earlier in the chapter in which Sugaru is said to have seized the Miwa deity in the form of a snake before bringing him before a terrified Yūryaku. For more on Kamuyaimimi no Mikoto, who was claimed as a founding ancestor of a number of sacerdotal lineages associated with *chimata* spirit-quieting rites, see Como, *Shōtoku,* 105–108. Below we shall also see that Isukeyori Hime herself was said to have been born after a single encounter between her mother and the Miwa deity.

37. *Hizen fudoki,* Matsuura district. *SNKBZ* 5:331–333. The translation is from Cranston, *Waka Anthology 1,* 143.

38. The cultic interactions among these regions are discussed at length in Kadowaki, *Nihon kaiiki no kodaishi,* 160–300.

39. For a detailed examination of archeological remains from such rites, see Kaneko Hiroyuki, "Tojōto saishi," 198–213.

40. This remnant from the *Yamashiro fudoki* can be found in *SNKBZ* 5:569. The rites performed during the third stage of the festival included exhibitions of horse-riding and archery and are known to have attracted large crowds. The rites were so popular and so boisterous that the court eventually felt compelled to ban the participation of people from outside of Yamashiro province, apparently in order to preserve public order (*SNG* Monmu 2.3.21, *SNKBZ* 12:9).

41. The island of Iki, which is located off the coast of Chikuzen in close proximity to the Korean peninsula, is a virtual treasure trove of ritual implements from the continent. Archeological finds from the area are discussed in Sada Shigeru, "Oki no Shima Saishi to Hensen." I will discuss the Iki no Urabe again in Chapter 7.

42. The passage is quoted in the *Honchō gatsuryō,* an eleventh-century court document. The text may be found in *GR* 4:309–310.

43. The assertion that the father of Wake no Ikazuchi was the deity at the Matsuno'o shrine, is also highly suggestive; recall that this shrine was not only run by the Hata, it also housed Ōmononushi's wife, the female deity from the Munakata shrine.

44. *Kojiki,* Jinmu chapter. *SNKBZ* 1:157.

45. *NSK* Jinmu 1. *SNKBZ* 2:233. Such genealogical linkages go a long way towards explaining why Chiisakobe no Sugaru is able to pacify the Miwa deity. They also undoubtedly help explain the common thematic motifs in the ancestral legends of both kinship groups.

46. A great deal of evidence suggests that during the sixth century the Miwa were closely affiliated with the Mononobe as well. See Yuba Tadanori, "Miwa to Isonokami no saishi iseki"; Shirai Isamu, "Miwa Jinja to Isonokami Jingū"; and Wada Atsumu, "Saishi no genryū."

47. *NSK* Sujin 7.8.7. *SNKBZ* 2:273–275.

48. Wada, *Nihon kodai no girei to saishi,* 3:44–46.

49. Ibid., 44–45.

50. This process was discussed in Chapter 3. Note also the role of the Mononobe liturgist Hozumi Omi no Oya Ōminakuchi Sukune, whose dream helps provide the impetus for the search along the coast of the Japan/Eastern Sea. Since the Mononobe appear to have had a strong military and cultic presence in Hizen following the failure of the Iwai rebellion early in the fifth century, this appears to be strong evidence that this and the other legends in the chapter had already begun to take shape during the Mononobe ascendancy in the sixth century.

51. *Kojiki,* Sujin chapter. *SNKBZ* 1:185–188.

52. For more on the often fearsome nature of these deities and the court's response to them, see Chapter 1.

53. Yoshikawa Shinji, "Kodai Tajima no sen'i seisan to ryūtsū." For the Kusakabe in Tajima, see Yoshida Akira. "Kodai Tajima no gōzoku to bumin."

54. These are discussed in Kaneko Hiroyuki, "Tojō to saishi," 213–216, and Kaneko Hiroyuki, "Bukkyō, Dōkyō."

55. *Kojiki,* Ōjin chapter. *SNKBZ* 1:279–281.

56. This is discussed in Hirabayashi, *Tanabata to sumō no kodaishi,* 166–167.

57. The lone exception I was able to find was Mayumi Tsunetada, who rather heroically argues that the legend is reflective of metalworking technologies; see Mayumi Tsunetada, *Nihon kodai saishi no kenkyū*, 291.

Chapter 6: Silkworms and Consorts

An earlier version of this chapter first appeared under the title "Silkworms and Consorts in Nara Japan," in *Asian Folklore Studies* 64 (2005):111–131. I am grateful to the editors for their permission to include the material in this volume.

1. *NSK* Suiko 11.12.5. *SNKBZ* 3:541–542.
2. *NSK* Suiko 12.4. *SNKBZ* 3:543–551. Although there is no evidence before the *Nihon shoki* indicating that the Seventeen Article Constitution was actually composed by Prince Kamitsumiya or even during his lifetime, it was almost certainly a seventh-century document. Possible sources for the Seventeen Article Constitution are discussed in Ōno Tatsunosuke, *Shōtoku taishi no kenkyū*, 171–211. My understanding of the court's adoption of Chinese calendrical tropes has been shaped in large degree by Nishimoto Masahiro, *Nihon kodai girei seiritsushi no kenkyū*; Shinkawa, *Nihon kodai no saishi to hyōgen*; and Miyake Kazuo, *Kodai kokka no jingi to saishi*.
3. Nishimoto Masahiro, *Nihon kodai girei seiritsushi no kenkyū*, 9.
4. *Kaifūsō*, preface. *NKBT* 69:58–59.
5. *Sui shu*, Wo chuan. In *ES* 29: *Sui shu*, 1827.
6. For the Chinese festival calendar, see Nakamura Takashi, *Chūgoku saijishi no kenkyū*. For the ritual calendar of the Nara court, see Miyake Kazuo, *Kodai kokka no jingi to saishi*.
7. For the development of such practices, see Kuhn, "Tracing a Chinese Legend." For weaving cults in Japan, see Hirabayashi, *Tanabata to sumō no kodaishi*.
8. For this cycle of poems as well as a more general discussion of *tanabata* poetry from the period, see Kojima Noriyuki, *Jōdai Nihon bungaku to Chūgoku bungaku*, 2:1120–1153; and Watase Masatada, "Kakinomoto no Hitomaro."
9. This line has been repeatedly adopted by Shimode Sekiyo, one of the first scholars to discuss the role of Taoism in early Japan. See his *Kodai shinsen shisō no kenkyū* and *Nihon kodai no dōkyō*. On the literary front, much the same line is taken by Kojima in his *Jōdai Nihon bungaku to Chūgoku bungaku*. For an excellent discussion of current debates concerning the role of Taoism in Japan, see Kohn, "Taoism in Japan." As Kohn notes, legends of immortals and resurrection and so forth were not the exclusive provenance of

the Taoist tradition, and as I noted in the introduction, my concern here is not so much with Taoist tradition as with religious practices and beliefs that could be found across the Chinese religious spectrum during the period.

10. These texts were first identified as a set by Shinkawa Tokio in his *Nihon kodai no saishi to hyōgen*, 23–45.

11. The translation is from Katō Genchi and Hoshino Hikoshiro, trans., *Kogoshūi or Gleanings from Ancient Stories*, 39. This legend is also recounted in *Nihon shoki*, Yūryaku 16.7, after which the Hata were dispersed to collect silk taxes. I discussed a variant rendering of this legend in the *Nihon shoki* in Chapter 5.

12. This is suggested most famously in the fourth article of the Taika edicts (*NSK* Taika 2.1., *SNKBZ* 4:131–133). Although the historicity of the Taika reforms is greatly open to question, by the start of the Nara period there is little doubt that woven products were a mainstay of both taxes and salaries at court. Torao Toshiya states that during the period: "Produce taxes were paid in kind on goods produced locally and required by the central government. These were mainly textiles, especially silk and hemp cloth, but also included dyes, lacquer, paper and salt" ("Nara Economic and Social Institutions," 432). For more on the role of silks in provincial taxes paid to the Nara government, see Yoshikawa Shinji, "Kodai Tajima no sen'i seisan to ryūtsū."

13. These are listed and discussed in detail in Takebe Yoshito, *Nihon momenshi no kenkyū*, 59–121.

14. Numerous variations of this legend are presented in the *NSK* Age of the Gods. *SNKBZ* 2:75–91. I will discuss it at length in Chapter 7.

15. *NSK* Yūryaku 6.3. *SNKBZ* 3:167.

16. *Chiu T'ang shu*, fourth fascicle, Yung wei, 7.3. Chung-hua Shuju, 1:75.

17. *Chou li*, seventh fascicle. The text may be found in Lin Yi, ed., *Chou li chin chu chin fan*, 307.

18. *Sou shen chi*, by Kan Pao, The text may be found in Huang Ti-ming, ed., *Sou shen chi*, 481. I will discuss this passage further in Chapter 7.

19. This shrine later became a center of the *oshira* silkworm cult. For rites and legends associated with this most unusual cult, see Konno Ensuke, *Bajō kon'in tan*. I will also discuss this shrine further in Chapter 7.

20. Kōgyoku 3.7. *SNKBZ* 4:93–95. The translation of the song is from Cranston, *Waka Anthology 1*, 120.

21. The Tsuminoe no Hijiri Hime legend cycle is discussed at length in Shimode, *Kodai shinsen shisō no kenkyū*, 110–127, and Katata Osamu, *Nihon kodai shinkō to Bukkyō*, 39–56.

22. The translation is from Cranston's superb *Waka Anthology 1*, 83. *NSK* Nintoku 39.11.7. *SNKBZ* 3:49–50.

23. *MYS* 3:386. Cranston, *Waka Anthology 1*, 497.

24. *Kojiki*, Nintoku, part 4. *SNKBZ* 1:295–297.

25. Shinkawa also notes that the Wani appear to have been closely connected with the performance of *onmyōdō* rites for the Nara court (*Nihon kodai no saishi to hyōgen*, 32).

26. Ibid., 33.

27. I will discuss this aspect of the legend in greater detail in Chapter 7.

28. *Kojiki*, Keikō chapter. *SNKBZ* 1:235–237. Cranston, *Waka Anthology 1*, 24–25.

29. Shinkawa, *Nihon kodai no saishi to hyōgen*, 32–33.

30. *NSK* Age of the Gods, Book 1. *SNKBZ* 2:43.

31. *NSK* Ingyō 7.12. *SNKBZ* 3:115–117.

32. In this regard Shinkawa notes that Kuchiko was an ancestor of the Wani kinship group. Because later in the legend Ikatsu and Otohime are shown stopping at the residences of other Wani ancestors at the center of the Wani's main base, he suggests that the Wani may have played an important role in the construction of this legend (*Nihon kodai no saishi to hyōgen*, 29).

33. *NSK* Ingyō 8.2. *SNKBZ* 3:119. Cranston, *Waka Anthology 1*, 85.

34. Hirabayashi, *Tanabata to sumō no kodaishi*, 150–155.

35. *CCSSC* 7.7. Moriya, *Keiso saijiki*, 155.

36. Hirabayashi, *Tanabata to sumō no kodaishi*, 154.

37. *NSK* Nintoku 22.1. *SNKBZ* 3:45. Cranston, *Waka Anthology 1*, 80.

38. Cranston notes: "Why the cocoon should be considered 'double-layered' is not clear; it has been suggested that the reference is to silkworms that spin cocoons twice (i.e. go through two generations) in a season. The application of the *jo* to the human situation must envisage the happy husband enjoying the warmth of two bedmates at once" (*Waka Anthology 1*, 80).

39. *Kojiki*, Nintoku chapter. *SNKBZ* 1:297.

40. *Po wu chih*, fourth fascicle. The passage may be found in T'ang Chiu-ch'ung, *Po wu chih chiao shih*, 45. Moriya also notes other such references in classical sources in *Keiso saijiki*, 52.

41. Nakamura Takashi, *Chūgoku saijishi no kenkyū*, 49–65. As we saw in Chapter 5, the fifteenth day of the first month was also the date for worshiping the lavatory goddess.

42. For worship of the stove god, see ibid., 501–503.

43. *CCSSC* 1.15. Moriya, *Keiso saijiki*, 48.

44. *CCSSC* 1.15. Moriya, *Keiso saijiki*, 53–58. This legend can also be found in the fifth fascicle of the *Yi yuan* by Liu Ching-hsiu; see Fan Ning, ed., *Yi yuan, Tan sou*, 44–45.

Chapter 7: Silkworm Cults in the Heavenly Grotto

1. This is not to say that royal mythologies focused exclusively on Amaterasu. Another focus of worship for Yamato rulers was Takami Musubi no Mikoto, an agricultural deity that we met briefly in Chapter 5. Evidence for Takami Musubi's ascendancy can be seen in the legend of the descent of the Heavenly Grandchild, where most variations of the legend have Takami Musubi send the royal ancestor Ninigi no Mikoto down to the Japanese islands. Further evidence for the importance of this deity in the early royal cult can be seen in the Niinamesai (Festival of the Tasting of the First Fruits) and the closely related Daijōsai, a major rite of accession. In both of these rites Takami Musubi is the main object of worship. For more on Takami Musubi no Mikoto, see Mizoguchi Mutsuko, *Ōken shinwa no nigen kōzō*. The topic of the Daijōsai is vast and cannot be treated in depth in a single chapter. For more on the Daijōsai, see Kōgakkan Daigaku Shintō Kenkyūjo, ed., *Daijōsai no kenkyū*; Mayumi Tsunetada, *Daijōsai*; Okada Seishi, *Kodai saishi no shiteki kenkyū*, 85–138; and Okada Seishi, ed., *Daijōsai to niiname*.

2. Tenmu's role in the development of the Chinkonsai is also discussed in Bialock, *Eccentric Spaces*, 67–84. See also Ooms, *Imperial Politics*, 156–162.

3. The *Nihon shoki* provides several versions on this point. Some state that it is a maidservant of Amaterasu's who impales herself; others say that Amaterasu impales herself, but that it is the maid who dies. Matsumae has argued rather forcefully, however, that in the earliest versions in which Amaterasu appears in the myth and in later liturgies it was assumed that it is Amaterasu who has died and entered the cave ("The Heavenly Rock-Grotto Myth," 10). This legend has also been treated from the point of view of folklore studies in Miller, "Ame no Miso-Ori Me." See also Miller, "Of Weavers and Birds."

4. Several variants of this legend are listed in the *NSK* Age of the Gods. *SNKBZ* 2:75–90. For the *Kojiki* account, see *Kojiki*, Age of the Gods. *SNKBZ* 1:63–69. Although Ame no Uzume is often seen as a paradigm of early Japanese religiosity, Okada Seishi has argued that this goddess was not a part of the original Ise cult (*Kodai saishi no shiteki kenkyū*, 300–301).

5. For a sample of interpretive positions concerning Susanoo's role in this narrative, see Ebersole, *Ritual Poetry*, 88–101; and Naumann, "*Sakahagi*." I shall return to this topic below.

6. This theme runs throughout much of Kōnoshi Takamitsu, *Kojiki to Nihon shoki*. For a brief English-language summary of Kōnoshi's views, see Kōnoshi, "Constructing Imperial Ideology."

7. Kōnoshi, "Constructing Imperial Mythology," 55–56.

8. *Kojiki*, Chūai chapter. *SNKBZ* 1:245.

9. Liturgical prayers (*norito*) recorded in the *Engishiki*, an early tenth-century ritual compendium, indicate that liturgists regularly confessed to a similar list of sins and requested that the resulting impurities be carried away to the underworld. See, for instance, the *Tataru kami o utsusiyaru* liturgy, in Phillipi, *Norito,* 70. The *norito* have also been collected and annotated in *NKBT* 1: *Kojiki, Norito,* ed. Kurano Kenji and Takeda Yūkichi.

10. Matsumae, "The Heavenly Rock-Grotto Myth," 13.

11. Watanabe Katsuyoshi, *Chinkonsai no kenkyū,* 125–139.

12. Matsumae posits at least three separate layers in the rite. Citing later liturgical traditions as well as the court chronicles, he suggests that in its earliest form the rite may have been one of spirit-binding that involved the tying of knots (*musubi*), and that it was then merged with a spirit-shaking rite associated with the Mononobe and the Isonokami shrine. He also suggests that a third layer was added with the re-enactment of the dance of Uzume Hime by female members of the Sarume no Kimi, a liturgical lineage that claimed descent from this goddess. See Matsumae, "The Heavenly Rock-Grotto Myth," 13–14.

13. Ibid., 11. This is also briefly discussed in Ōbayashi Taryō, "Japanese Myths of Descent," 174.

14. This was first noted in Matsumae, "Origin and Growth of the Worship of Amaterasu," 1–3.

15. *NSK* Kenzō 3.4. *SNKBZ* 3:253.

16. Senda Minoru, *Ise Jingū,* 22.

17. Kenzō 3.2. *SNKBZ* 3:252–253.

18. *SNG* Taihō 1.4.3. *SNKBT* 12:39. For the archeology of this shrine, see Kyōto-shi Maizō Bunkazai Kenkyūjo, *Shiseki Konoshima ni masu Amaterasu Mitama Jinja (Kaiko no Yashiro) Keidai.* Note that I referred to this shrine briefly in Chapter 6.

19. Literally, "bath person."

20. One *jō* equals approximately ten feet.

21. *NSK* Yūryaku 3.4. *SNKBZ* 2:157–159

22. Ōbayashi Taryō, "Japanese Myths of Descent," 173.

23. As we shall see shortly, Matsumae, Okada Seishi, and many others have suggested that the deity at the Ise shrine was originally a male sun god who required a female shaman as a consort. This view is strongly opposed, however, by Mizoguchi Mutsuko. See Mizoguchi, *Ōken shinwa no nigen kōzō,* esp. 218–240.

24. Okada Seishi, "Ise Naigū sōdenkami no seikaku to seiritsu," 9–12.

25. Ibid., 12–16.

26. Mayuzumi Hiromichi, *Mononobe Sogashi to kodai ōken,* 91.

27. *NSK* Jinmu, 76th year. *SNKBZ* 2:237.

28. Ōbayashi, "Japanese Myths of Descent," 175–176.

29. Teeuwen, *Sendai kuji hongi*," 94.

30. The relationship between court rites of spirit pacification and the Isonokami shrine are discussed at length in Matsumae Takeshi, *Kodai denshō to kyūtei saishi*, 115–127.

31. *NSK* Jinmu, Period Prior to Accession, *SNKBZ* 2:225. For more on Mononobe legends related to Nigihayahi's descent from the Heavenly Plain as well as the role of Nigihayahi in the court chronicles, see Mayuzumi Hiromichi, *Mononobe Sogashi to kodai ōken*, 87–100.

32. Ōbayashi, "Japanese Myths of Descent," 176.

33. Ōbayashi notes this and other extensive overlaps in thematic content between Mononobe and Korean nation-founding legends in ibid., 171–176.

34. See, for instance, *NSK* Age of the Gods, *SNKBZ* 2:117, where Futsunushi is sent to pacify rebellious spirits across the land.

35. *Nihon koki* Enryaku 24.2. *SZKT* 3:39.

36. Watanabe, *Chinkonsai no kenkyū*, 139–158.

37. *Kojiki*, Jinmu, Period Prior to Accession. *SNKBZ* 1:145–147. This legend is also found in *NSK* Jinmu, Period Prior to Accession. *SNKBZ* 2:203–205.

38. For possible Silla influences on the Ise shrine, see Maekawa Akihisa, *Nihon kodai shizoku to ōken no kenkyū*, 262–284.

39. Izumiya Yasuo has also speculated that such rites were originally derived from the cult of Ame no Hiboko. See Izumiya Yasuo, "Mononobe to shūkyō." Similarities between accounts related to the Isonokami Jingū and the Izushi shrine of Ame no Hiboko are also discussed in Taketani Hisao, *Kodai shizoku denshō no kenkyū*, 279–311. For Korean influences on the legend cycles of Futsunushi and Susanoo, see Mishina Shōei, *Mishina Shōei ronbunshū* 2:255–329.

40. *NSK* Suinin, 39.10. *SNKBZ* 2:329–330.

41. Equally noteworthy is the fact that the text explicitly states that the founding ancestor of the Mononobe sublineage in charge of the shrine bore the name of Kasuga Omi. As we saw in Chapter 6, the Kasuga Omi were also an important branch of the Wani kinship group, which created a number of legends about royal consorts who were called out by rulers using the vocabulary of continental weaving and sericulture rites. See, for instance, the legend of Mononobe no Me Ōmuraji's intercession on behalf of Kasuga Wani Omi Fukame, a consort who fell into disfavor with the ruler Yūryaku when she became pregnant after having been with him for only a single night, in *NSK* Yūryaku 1.3. *SNKBZ* 3:150–152.

42. For an excellent illustration of how Mononobe ancestral legends were inscribed in the cultic landscape of the Wani, see the Muretsu chapter

of the *Nihon shoki*, in which the Mononobe ancestor Kage no Hime sings a funeral dirge for her deceased husband as she journeys to the base of Mount Miwa, recounting each step of a journey from Isonokami across a number of Wani villages. *NSK* Muretsu, Period Prior to Accession, *SNKBZ* 3:273–275. This is also discussed in Wada Atsumu, "Yamabe no Michi no Rekishiteki Igi," 9–14. Similarly, in the *Shinsen shōjiroku* the Kakinomoto branch of the Wani are explicitly said to have been descended from Ichikawa and the Mononobe Isonokami liturgical line known as the Furu Sukune. *Shinsen shōjiroku*, Yamato Kōbetsu section. Saeki, *Shinsen shōjiroku no kenkyū*, 191.

43. Naoki, *Nihon kodai shizoku to tennō*, 269–282.

44. This is discussed briefly in Okada Seishi, *Kodai saishi no shiteki kenkyū*, 301–303.

45. Suinin's genealogy, as given in the court chronicles, also states that his maternal grandfather was a Mononobe.

46. Further indications that the early cult of Amaterasu may have been linked to the Mononobe can be seen in accounts in the *Nihon shoki* and *Kojiki* that state that Amaterasu resided in the village of Kasanui in Yamato province until she informed Yamato Hime no Mikoto that she wished to move to a more congenial spot. Although this legend has drawn the attention of scholars interested in the history of the institution of the Saiō, one of its most important aspects for our purpose is the simple statement that Amaterasu was not originally from the region of the Ise shrine. By highlighting the village of Kasanui in Yamato province as the point of departure for the cult, the text provides an important clue as to early associations of the deity that perhaps were still present at during Tenmu's reign. Of further interest is the fact that the Kasanui appear to have been a service group associated with stitching sails for court ships. In addition an ancestor of the Kasanui is listed in the *Sendai kuji hongi* as a member of the Mononobe kinship group who descended to earth along with the deity Amateru Kuniteru Hiko Ama no Hoakari. The connections between Amaterasu, Yamato Hime no Mikoto, and Toyuke Hime, the goddess of the Outer Ise shrine, later became the subject of the *Yamato Hime Mikoto no seiki*, one of the fundamental texts of medieval Ise Shinto. This text may be found in *SZKT* 7:479–508.

47. *NSK* Suinin 32.7.6. *SNKBZ* 2:325–327; Aston, *Nihongi* 1:180–181.

48. This legend was discussed in Chapter 4.

49. For the Kusanagi sword of the Owari shrine, see Okada Seishi, *Kodai saishi no shiteki kenkyū*, 239–259.

50. Matsumae, *Kodai denshō to kyūtei saishi*, 271–283

51. The Owari Muraji are discussed in detail in ibid., 269–308. For the origins of the Atsuta shrine, see Maekawa Akihisa, *Nihon kodai shizoku to ōken no kenkyū*, 306–323.

52. *NSK* Sujin, 1.2. *SNKBZ* 2:268.

53. *NSK* Suzaku 1.9.27. *SNKBZ* 4:467. See also Ueda, *Kodai no Dōkyō*, 54–55. Further evidence suggesting that the Yamato Takeru legend cycle was prominent in the minds of the Tenmu court can also be seen from the *Kojiki* account of Yamato Takeru's funeral, which, as we saw in Chapter 6, concludes by stating of the dirges sung for the mythic prince that "even today they sing these songs at a *tennō*'s funeral."

It would appear in addition that the funerary rites for Tenmu, the first ruler to claim to be a manifest deity, were also used as an occasion to reassert the ruler's divine status. In this regard the legend of the Heavenly Grotto, which focuses upon Amaterasu's death and triumphant resurrection, may have served as an important ideological touchstone. Evidence for this can be seen in funerary odes composed for Tenmu and his successors that utilize such euphemisms for the ruler's death as *iwa gakuri* (hiding in the cave), an apparent reference to Amaterasu's death and resurrection.

54. *NSK* Suinin 25.3.10. *SNKBZ* 2:320–321.

55. *NSK* Keikō 40. *SNKBZ* 2: 386–387.

56. The motif of the immortal who leaves behind an article of clothing after achieving "liberation from the corpse" was an important element in a number of legends of Chinese immortals that appear to have little connection with any Taoist liturgical tradition. Robert Ford Campany has recently suggested that this belief can be traced to funerary rites involving figures that impersonate the deceased (*To Live as Long as Heaven and Earth*, 52–60).

57. See, for instance, *NSK* Jinmu, Period Prior to Accession, *SNKBZ* 2:225.

58. For a discussion of the immigrant "*Kushi no kami*" Sukuna Bikona no Mikoto and other such *tokoyo* deities, see Como, *Shōtoku*, 33–54.

59. *NSK* Age of the Gods. *SNKBZ* 2:167.

60. *NSK* Age of the Gods. *SNKBZ* 2:163.

61. *NSK* Age of the Gods. *SNKBZ* 2:175.

62. Matsumae notes in another context that in Heian-period liturgies for the Chinkonsai, this motif is also seen in the shaking of a "soul-box" ("The Heavenly Rock-Grotto Myth," 13). As we saw in Chapter 4, the Kusakabe also claimed to be direct descendants of Ama no Hoakari no Mikoto.

63. *Kojiki*, Keikō chapter. *NKBT* 215. For more on this and other legends concerning combs and immortality, see Como, *Shōtoku*, 99–100.

64. *Engishiki*, section ten. *SZKT* 26:312.

65. This legend is discussed in the context of early conceptions of *tokoyo* in Sugano Masao, *Kojiki setsuwa no kenkyū*, 192–229. For a detailed look at the relationship between this legend and legends concerning Yamato Takeru's mother and the Kataoka beggar, see Como, *Shōtoku*, 100–102.

66. *Harima fudoki* (Records of the customs and land of Harima), Kago district, Hire no Oka. *SNKBZ* 5:23.

67. *NSK* Suiko 21.11.2. *SNKBZ* 3:570–571.

68. Como, *Shōtoku*, 104.

69. I have derived Table 4 from Matsumae, "Origin and Growth of the Worship of Amaterasu," 1–3; and Senda, *Ise Jingū*, 17–22.

70. This is the conclusion of Matsumae, who argues that while the royal line may have originally used a rite centered on Takami Musibi, in which the ruler's spirit was bound with knots to prevent it from leaving during the winter solstice, the spirit-calling function of the rite was most likely a contribution of the Mononobe ("The Heavenly Rock-Grotto Myth," 17–19).

71. Senda, *Ise Jingū*, 20.

72. For a history of silkworm cults and goddesses in China, see Kuhn, "Tracing a Chinese Legend."

73. The passage may be found in Wang Kuo-liang, *Hsu chi chieh chi yen chiu*, 40.

74. *CCSSC*, 3rd month, 3rd day. Moriya, *Keiso saijiki*, 100.

75. *Sou shen chi*, Book 14, #351. In Huang Ti-ming, ed., *Sou shen chi*, 480–481. This legend is also discussed from a structural point of view in Miller, "The Woman Who Married a Horse." For a discussion of the role of the *Sou shen chi* in the formation of early Chinese tale literature, see Kenneth DeWoskin, "The 'Sou shen chi' and the 'Chih-kuai' Tradition."

76. The *oshira* cult has been well studied by Konno Ensuke in his *Bajō kon'in tan*.

77. *NSK* Age of the Gods. *SNKBZ* 2:59–60. There is some evidence that the linkage between the moon deity and sericulture may also have continental roots. In China the arrival of the first full moon of the New Year, on the fifteenth day of the first month, was also a festival closely associated with women and with silkworms. This is discussed thoroughly in Nakamura Takashi, *Chūgoku saijishi no kenkyū*, 49–66.

78. *NSK* Age of the Gods. *SNKBZ* 2:60–61.

79. The ancient Korean word for the top of the head is homophonous with horse, while the word for forehead is virtually identical with millet and so forth. This is discussed in *NSK* Age of the Gods. *SNKBZ* 2:60, n.4. Mishina Shōei, *Nissen shinwa densetsu no kenkyū*, 257–258.

80. *NSK* Age of the Gods. *SNKBZ* 2:61.

Works Cited

Reference Works

Dictionary of Sources of Classical Japan. Joan Piggott et al., eds. Paris: Collège de France, Institut des Hautes Études, 2006.
ES. Wei Zheng, ed. Beijing: Zhonghua Shuju, 1995.
Fudoki. In *SNKBZ* 5: *Fudoki*, ed. Uegaki Setsuya. Tokyo: Shōgakkan, 1997.
GR. Hanawa Hokinoichi, ed. 29 vols. 1959–1960.
Indiana Companion to Traditional Chinese Literature. William H. Nienhauser, ed. Bloomington: Indiana University Press, 1986–1998.
NI. Takeuchi Rizō, ed. 3 vols. Tokyo: Tokyōdō Shuppan, 1962.
NKBT. 100 vols. Tokyo: Iwanami Shoten, 1958–1968.
NST. 67 vols. Tokyo: Iwanami Shoten, 1970–.
SNKBT. Satake Akihiro et al., eds. 100 vols. Tokyo: Iwanami Shoten, 1989–2005.
SNKBZ . 88 vols. Tokyo: Shōgakkan, 1994–2002.
SZKT. Kuroita Katsumi, ed. 60 volumes. Tokyo: Yoshikawa Kōbunkan, 1972.
Shintō taikei. 52 vols. Tokyo: Shintō taikei hensankai, 1998–2001.
STZ. Fujiwara Yūsetsu, ed. 5 vols. Tokyo: Ryūginsha, 1944.
T. Takakusu Junjirō and Watanabe Kaigyoku, eds. 85 vols. Tokyo: Daizō Shuppan Kabushiki Kaisha, 1932.
ZGR. Hanawa Hokinoichi, ed. 37 vols. Tokyo: Zoku gunsho ruijū kanseikai, 1957–1959.

Primary Sources

Atsumori. Zeami. In *NKBT* 40: *Yōkyokushū*, ed. Yokomichi Mario and Omote Akira, 1:233–240. Tokyo: Iwanami Shoten, 1960.
CCSSC. By Tu Kung-chan. In *Ching ch'u sui shih chi*, ed. Wang Yü-jung. Taipei: Wen chin Chu pan she, 1988.
Chin kang po jo po luo mi ching (J: *Kongō hannya haramitsu kyō*). Kumarajiva, trans. In *T* 235, 8:748–752.
Chiu T'ang shu. Chung hua shu chu, Beijing, 1975.

Chou li. In *Chou li chin chu chin fan*, ed. Lin Yi. Taipei: Taiwan Shang wu yin shu kuan, 1997.

Ch'u tz'u. In *Hsin i ch'u tse tu pen*, ed. Fu Hsi-jen. Taipei: San min Shu chu, 1995.

Daianji garan engi narabi ni ruki shizaichō. In *NI* 2:366–382.

Denjutsu isshin kaimon. By Kōjō. In *T* 2379. 74:634–659.

Engishiki. In *SZKT* 26: *Kōtaishiki. Kōninshiki. Engishiki*, ed. Kuroita Katsumi. Tokyo: Yoshikawa Kōbunkan, 1972.

Gangōji garan engi narabi ni ruki shizaichō. In *NI* 2:383–393.

Gyōki nenpu. In *Gyōki jiten*, ed. Inoue Kaoru, 255–275.

Han Wu ku-shih. In *Ro Jin senshū* 6, ed. Masuda Wataru, 52–54. 6 vols. Tokyo: Iwanami Shoten, 1937.

Han Wu-ti nei-chuan. In Wang Kuo-liang, *Han Wu t'ung ming chi yen chiu*, 50–51. Taipei: Wenshih Chehsüeh Chupanshe, 1989.

Hiesha negi kudenshō. In *ST* 29: *Jinja hen: Hiyoshi*: 1–6.

Honchō gatsuryō. In *GR* 4: 302–320.

Hōryūji garan engi narabi ni ruki shizaichō. In *NI* 2:344–365.

Hsü chi chieh chi yen chiu. In Wang Kuo-liang, *Hsu chi chieh chi yen chiu*. Taipei: Wen shih che Chu pan she, 1987.

Huai nan zu. In *Hsin i Huai Nan tzu*, ed. Hsiung Li-hui. Taipei: San-min Shu-chu, 1997.

Ise nisho kōtaijingu gochinza denki. In *KT* 7:435–450.

Jōgū Shōtoku hōōteisetsu. In *STZ* 3:9–22.

Kaifūsō. In *NKBT* 69: *Kaifūsō, Bunka shūreishū, Honchō monzui*, ed. Kojima Noriyuki. Tokyo: Iwanami Shoten, 1964.

Kogoshūi. By Imbe Hironari. In *ST koten hen* 5: *Kogoshūi*, ed. Iida Mizuho. Tokyo: Shintō Taikei Hensankai, 1986.

Kojiki. In *SNKBZ* 1: *Kojiki*, ed. Yamaguchi Yasunori and Kōnoshi Takamitsu. Tokyo: Shōgakkan, 1997.

Hsü k'ung zang p'u sa neng man chu yuan zui sheng shin t'uo luo ni ch'iu wen ch'ih fa (J: *Kokūzō bosatsu nōman shogan saishōshin darani gumonji no hō*). In *T* 1145. 20:601–603.

K'ung ch'üeh wang chou ching. (J: *Kujakuōshukyō*). *T* 982, 983, and 985. 19:446–458.

Li chi. In *Hsin-i: Li chi tu pen*, ed. Chiang Yi-hua. Taipei: San min shu chu, 1997.

Lun heng. In *Hsin i: Lun heng tu pen*, ed. T'sai Chen-ch'u. 2 vols. Taipei: San min shu chu, 1997.

Lun yü. By Confucius. In *Hsin i ssu shu tu pen*, ed. Hsieh Ping-ying et al. Taipei: San min shu chu, 1995.

Manyōshū. In *SNKBZ* 6–9: *Manyōshū*, ed. Kojima Noriyuki, Tōno Noriyuki, and Kinoshita Masatoshi. 4 vols. Tokyo: Shōgakkan, 1971.

Nihon kōki. In *SZKT* 3: *Nihon kōki, Shoku Nihon kōki, Montoku tennō jitsuroku*.

Nihon ryōiki. In *SNKBZ* 10: *Nihon ryōiki kōchū, yaku*, ed. Nakada Norio. Tokyo: Shōgakkan, 1995.

NSK. In *SNKBZ* 2–4: *Nihon shoki*, ed. Kojima Noriyuki, Naoki Kōjirō, Kuranaka Susumu, Mōri Masamori, and Nishimiya Kazutami. 3 vols. Tokyo: Shōgakkan, 1994.

Pao p'u tzu. In *Hsin i: Pao p'u tzu tu pen*, ed. Li Chung-hua. Taipei: Chung hua shu chu, 2001.

Po wu chih. In *Po wu chih chiao shih*, ed. Fan Ning. Taipei: Mingwen Book Co., 1981.

Ryō no gige. In *SZKT* 22.

Ryō no shūge. In *SZKT* 23–24.

Samguk sagi. In *Sankoku shiki*, trans. Inoue Hideo. Tokyo: Heibonsha, 1980.

Sangō shiiki. By Kūkai. In *NKBT* 71: *Sangō shiiki, Shōryōshū*, eds. Watanabe Shōkō and Miyasaka Yūshō. Tokyo: Iwanami Shoten, 1965.

Sendai kuji hongi. In *ST, koten hen 8: Sendai kuji hongi*.

Shan hai ching. In *Shan hai ching chiao chu*, ed. Yüan K'o. Taipei: Lejin Books, 1995.

Shinsen shōjiroku. In Saeki Arikiyo, *Shinsen shōjiroku no kenkyū*. 6 vols. Tokyo: Yoshikawa Kōbunkan, 1962.

SNG. In *SNKBT* 12–16: *Shoku nihongi*, ed. Aoki Kazuo, Inaoka Kōji, Sasayama Haruo, and Shirafuji Noriyuki. Tokyo: Iwanami Shoten, 1989–1998.

Sou shen chi. By Kan Pao. In *Sou shen chi*, ed. Huang Ti-ming. Taipei: Chung kuo Ku hsi Ch'u pan she, 1996.

Sui shu. In *ES* 28–29. Beijing, Zhonghua Shuju, 1995.

Tōshi kaden. In *NI* 3:875–886.

Toyuke miya gishiki chō. In *GR* 2:52–83.

Yamato Hime Mikoto no seiki. In *KT* 7:479–508.

Yen lo wang kung hsing fa tsu ti (J: *Enraō kugyōhō shidai*). In *T* 1290. 21:374–376.

Yi yuan. By Liu Ching-shu. In *Yi-yuan, Tan-sou*, ed. Fan Ning. Beijing: Chung hua Shu chu, 1996.

Yōtenki. In *ST* 29: *Jinja hen: Hiyoshi*: 7–96.

Yu yang tsa tsu. By Tuan Ch'eng-shih. In Imamura Yoshio, trans. *Yūyō zasso*. Tokyo: Heibonsha, 1988.

Secondary Sources

Abe Ryūichi. *Weaving of Mantra*. New York: Columbia University Press, 1999.

Abe Shigeru. *Heian zenki seijishi no kenkyū*. Tokyo: Shinseisha, 1974.

Adolphson, Mikael. *Gates of Power*. Honolulu: University of Hawai'i Press, 2000.

Aston, W. G. *Nihongi: Chronicles of Japan from the Earliest Times to A.D. 697*. 2 vols. Tokyo: Tuttle, 1972.

Barrett, Tim. "Shinto and Taoism in Early Japan." In *Shinto in History*, ed. J. Breen and M. Teeuwen, 13–31. Honolulu: University of Hawai'i Press, 2000.

Bentley, John R. *The Authenticity of the* Sendai Kuji Hongi: *A New Examination of Texts, with a Translation and Commentary*. Leiden and Boston: Brill, 2006.

Beppu Daigaku Fuzoku Hakubutsukan, and Usa-shi Kyōikuiinkai. *Tempyō no Usa*: *Usa Kokūzōji to kodai Bukkyō*. Ōita-shi: Beppu Daigaku Fuzoku Hakubutsukan and Usa-shi Kyōikuiinkai, 1996.

Bialock, David. *Eccentric Spaces, Hidden Histories: Narrative and Royal Authority from* The Chronicles of Japan *to* The Tale of the Heike. Stanford: Stanford University Press, 2007.

Bock, Felicia, trans. *Engi-Shiki: Procedures of the Engi Era*. 2 vols. Tokyo: Sophia University, 1970–.

Bokenkamp, *Ancestors and Anxiety: Daoism and the Birth of Rebirth in China*. Berkeley: University of California Press, 2007.

Cahill, Suzanne. *Transcendence and Divine Passion: The Queen Mother of the West in Medieval China*. Stanford: Stanford Univesity Press, 1993.

Campany, Robert. *Strange Writing: Anomaly Accounts in Early Medieval China*. Albany: State University of New York Press, 1995.

———. *To Live as Long as Heaven and Earth: A Translation and Study of Ge Hong's Traditions of Divine Transcendents*. Berkeley: University of California Press, 2002.

Como, Michael. "Ethnicity, Sagehood and the Politics of Literacy in Asuka Japan." *Japanese Journal of Religious Studies* 30/1–2 (2003):61–84.

———. "Horses, Dragons and Disease in Nara Japan." *Japanese Journal of Religious Studies* 34, no. 2 (2007):393–415.

———. "Of Temples, Horses, and Tombs: Hōryūji and Chūgūji in Heian and Early Kamakura Japan." In *Hōryūji Reconsidered*, ed. Dorothy Wong, 263–288. Cambridge: Cambridge Scholars Press, 2008.

———. *Shōtoku: Ethnicity, Ritual and Violence in the Japanese Buddhist Tradition*. New York: Oxford University Press, 2008.

Cranston, Edwin. *Waka Anthology 1: The Gem Glistening Cup*. Stanford: Stanford University Press, 1993.

Denecke, Wiebke. "Topic Poetry Is All Ours: Poetic Composition on Chinese Lines in Early Heian Japan." *Harvard Journal of Asiatic Studies* 67, no.1 (2007):1–49.

DeWoskin, Kenneth. "The 'Sou-shen-chi' and the 'Chih-kuai' Tradition." Ph.D. diss., Columbia University, 1974.

Dolce, Lucia. "Introduction: The Worship of Celestial Bodies in Japan: Politics, Ritual and Icons." In *Culture and Cosmos* 10 and 11 (2006):3–45.

Ebersole, Gary. *Ritual Poetry and the Politics of Death in Early Japan*. Princeton, NJ: Princeton University Press, 1989.

Ellwood, Robert. "A Cargo Cult in Seventh Century Japan." *History of Religions* 23 (1984):222–238.

Emura Hiroyuki. *Ritsuryō tennōsei saishi no kenkyū*. Tokyo: Hanawa Shobō, 1996.

Farris, William Wayne. *Population, Disease and Land in Early Japan, 645–900*. Cambridge, MA: Harvard University Press, 1985.

———. *Sacred Texts and Buried Treasures: Issues in the Historical Archaeology of Ancient Japan*. Honolulu: University of Hawai'i Press, 1998.

Fowler, Sherry. *Muroji: Rearranging Art and History at a Japanese Buddhist Temple*. Honolulu: University of Hawai'i Press, 2005

Fracassso, Riccardo. "Holy Mothers in Ancient China. A New Approach to the Hsi-wang-mu Problem." *T'oung Pao* 74 (1988):1–46.

Franke, Bernard. *Kataimi to katatagae*. Trans. Saitō Hironobu. Tokyo: Iwanami Shoten, 1989.

Fukunaga Mitsuji. *Dōkyō to kodai Nihon*. Kyoto: Jinbun Shoin, 1987.

———. *Dōkyō to Nihon bunka*. Kyoto: Jinbun Shoin, 1982.

Fukutō Sanae. *Heian ōchō shakai no jendā: Ie, ōken, seiai*. Tokyo: Azekura Shobō, 2005.

———. *Ie seiritsushi no kenkyū: Sosen saishi, onna, kodomo*. Tokyo: Azekura Shobō, 1991.

Gordon, Avery. *Ghostly Matters: Haunting and the Sociological Imagination*. Minneapolis: University of Minnesota Press, 2008.

Grapard, Alan. "Institution, Ritual and Ideology: The Twenty-two Shrine-Temple Multiplexes of Heian Japan." *History of Religions* 27 (1988):246–269.

———. *Saichō*. Honolulu: University of Hawai'i Press, 2000.

Hakeda Yoshito. *Kūkai: Major Works*. New York: Columbia University Press, 1972.

Hawks, David. *Songs of the South*. London: Penguin Books, 1985.

Hayashi Kōhei. *Urashima densetsu no kenkyū*. Tokyo: Ōfū, 2001.
Hayashi Makoto, and Koike Jun'ichi, eds. *Onmyōdō no kōgi*. Kyoto: Sagano Shoin, 2002.
Hayashi Mikiya. *Taishi shinkō no kenkyū*. Tokyo: Yoshikawa Kōbunkan, 1980.
Hayashi On, and Marui Keiji, eds. *Myōken bosatsu to hoshi mandara: Nihon no bijutsu* 377. Tokyo: Shinbundo,1997.
Hayashi Tatsusaburō. *Chūsei geinōshi no kenkyū*. Tokyo: Iwanami Shoten, 1962.
Hirabayashi Akihito. *Tanabata to sumō no kodaishi*. Tokyo: Hakusuisha, 1998.
Hirano Kunio. "Hatashi no kenkyū." *Shigaku zasshi* 70, no. 3 (1961):25–47.
———. *Kikajin to kodai kokka*. Tokyo: Yoshikawa Kōbunkan, 1993.
Hiraoka Jōkai. *Nihonjiin shi no kenkyū*. Tokyo: Yoshikawa Kōbunkan, 1981.
Honda Jirō. *Shūrai tsūshaku*. 2 vols. Tokyo: Shūei Shuppan, 1977–1979.
Hon'iden Kikushi. "Mononobeshi to Isonokami Jingū." In *Kodai Nihonjin no shinkō to saishi*, ed. Matsumae Takeshi and Shirakawa Shizuka, 4557. Tokyo: Daiwa Shobō, 1997.
Hosoi Hiroshi. "Tenmondō to rekidō: Kodai ni okeru seiritsu no haikei to sono yakuwari." In *Onmyōdō no kōgi*, ed. Hayashi Makoto and Koike Jun'ichi, 87–108. Kyoto: Sagano Shoin, 2002.
Hung Shu-hui. *Niu-lang chih-nü yen-chiu*. Taipei: Hsüeh-sheng Shu-chu, 1988.
Iida Mizuho *Shōtoku taishiden no kenkyū*. Tokyo: Yoshikawa Kōbunkan, 2000.
Inokuma Kanekatsu, and Watanabe Akiyoshi, eds. *Nihon no bijutsu 217: Takamatsuzuka kofun*. Tokyo: Shibundō, 1984.
Inoue Hideo. "Chiku, Toyo, Hi no gōzoku to Yamato chōtei." In *Kodai no Nihon 3: Kyūshū*, ed. Kagamiyama Takeshi and Tamura Enchō, 138–158. Tokyo: Kadokawa Shoten, 1970.
Inoue Kaoru, ed. *Gyōki jiten*. Tokyo: Kokusho Kangyōkai, 1997.
Inoue Kaoru. "Gyōki no shōgai." In *Gyōki jiten*, ed. Inoue Kaoru, 9–22. Tokyo: Kokusho Kangyōkai, 1997.
Inoue Mitsuo. *Kammu tennō*. Kyoto: Mineruba Shobō, 1996.
Inoue Mitsusada. *Nihon kodai shisōshi no kenkyū*. Tokyo: Iwanami Shoten, 1982.
———. "Yūryakuchō ni okeru ōken to higashi ajia." In *Chōsen sangoku to Wakoku*, ed. Inoue Mitsusada. Tokyo: Gakuseisha, 1970.
——— et al., eds. *NKBT 3: Ritsuryō*. Tokyo: Iwanami Shoten, 1976.
Izumi Takeshi. "Hitogata saishi no kisōteki kōsatsu." In *Nihon kōkogaku ronshū*, ed. Saitō Tadashi, 144–191. Tokyo: Yoshikawa Kōbunkan, 1986.

Izumiya Yasuo. "Mononobe to shūkyō." In *Nihon shoki kenkyū*, ed. Yokota Ken'ichi Sensei Koki Kinenkai, 16:15–30. Tokyo: Hanawa Shobō, 1988.

Kadowaki Teiji. *Nihon kaiiki no kodaishi*. Tokyo: Tokyo Daigaku Shuppankai, 1986.

Kamei Kiichirō. "Isonokami Jingū to Oshisaka Ōnakahime." In *Nihon shoki kenkyū* 13, ed. Yokota Ken'ichi Sensei Koki Kinenkai, 107–158. Tokyo: Shōgakkan, 1994.

Kaneko Hiroyuki. "Bukkyō, Dōkyō no torai to banjin suhai." In *Kodaishi no ronten 5: Kami to matsuri*, ed. Kanasaki Hiroshi and Sahara Makoto, 167–191. Tokyo: Shōgakkan, 1999.

———. "Gakki, shuzōgu, bōshokugu." In *Kofun jidai no kenkyū 3: Seikatsu to saishi*, ed. Ishino Hironobu, Iwasaki Takuya, Kawakami Kunihiko, and Shiraishi Taiichirō, 152–160. Tokyo: Yūzankaku, 1991.

———. "Miyako o meguru matsuri." In *Nihon no shinkō iseki*, ed. Kaneko Hiroyuki, 187–211. Tokyo: Yūzankaku, 1998.

———. "Tojō to saishi." In *Okinoshima to kodai saishi*, ed. Oda Fujio, 198–226. Tokyo: Yoshikawa Kōbunkan, 1998.

Katata Osamu. *Nihon kodai shinkō to Bukkyō*. Kyoto: Hōzōkan, 1991

Katō Kenkichi. *Hatashi to sono tami*. Tokyo: Hakusuisha, 1998.

Katō Genchi, and Hoshino Hikoshiro, trans. *Kogoshūi or Gleanings from Ancient Stories*. Tokyo: Meiji Japan Society, 1926.

Kidder, Edward. *The Lucky Seventh: Early Hōryū-ji and Its Time*. Tokyo: International Christian University, 1999.

Kikuchi Yasuaki. *Ritsuryōsei saishi ronkō*. Tokyo: Hanawa Shobō, 1991.

Kikuike Kyōko, "Goryō shinkō no seiritsu to tenkai." In *Goryō shinkō*, ed. Shibata Minoru, 37–62. Tokyo: Yūzankaku, 1985.

Kiley, Cornelius. "Surnames in Ancient Japan." *Harvard Journal of Asiatic Studies* 29 (1969):177–189.

Kinoshita Ryō. *Kodai dōro*. Tokyo: Yoshikawa Kōbunkan, 1996.

Kleeman, Terry. "Licentious Cults and Bloody Victuals: Sacrifice, Reciprocity, and Violence in Traditional China," *Asia Major* 3rd ser., 7, no.1 (1994):185–211.

Kōgakkan Daigaku Shintō Kenkyūjo, ed. *Daijōsai no kenkyū*. Kyoto: Kōgakkan Daigaku Shuppanbu, 1986.

Kohn, Livia. "Taoism in Japan: Positions and Evaluations." *Cahiers d'Extreme-Asie* 8 (1995):389–412.

Kojima Noriyuki. *Jōdai Nihon bungaku to Chūgoku bungaku*. Tokyo: Hanawa Shobō, 1975.

Kominami Ichirō. *Chūgoku no shinwa to monogatari*. Tokyo: Iwanami Shoten, 1984.

———. *Seiōbō to tanabata denshō*. Tokyo: Heibonsha, 1991.
Konno Ensuke. *Bajō kon'intan*. Tokyo: Iwazaki Shoten, 1956.
Kōnoshi Takamitsu. "Constructing Imperial Ideology: *Kojiki* and *Nihon shoki*." In *Inventing the Classics: Modernity, National Identity, and Japanese Literature*, ed. Haruo Shirane and Tomi Suzuki, 51–70. Stanford: Stanford University Press, 2000.
———. *Kojiki no sekaikan*. Tokyo: Yoshikawa Kōbunkan, 1986.
———. *Kojiki to Nihon shoki*. Tokyo: Kōdansha, 1999.
Kubota Osamu. *Yasaka jinja no kenkyū*. Kyoto: Rinsen Shoten, 1974.
Kuhn, Dieter. "Tracing a Chinese Legend: In Search of the Identity of the 'First Sericulturalist.'" *T'oung-pao* 70 (1984):213–245.
Kurano Kenji, and Takeda Yūkichi, eds. *NKBT* 1: *Kojiki, Norito*. Tokyo: Iwanami Shoten, 1958.
Kuroda Toshio. "Shinto in the History of Japanese Religion." *Journal of Japanese Studies* 7, no. 1 (1981):1–21.
Kyōto-shi Maizō Bunkazai Kenkyūjo. *Shiseki Konoshima nimasu Amaterasu Mitama Jinja (Kaiko no Yashiro) keidai*. Kyoto: Kyōto-shi Maizō Bunkazai Kenkyūjo, 2002.
Loewe, Michael. *Ways to Paradise*. London: George Allen Unwin, 1979.
Lurie, David. "Origins of Writing in Early Japan." Ph.D. diss., Columbia University, 2001.
Maeda Haruto. *Nihon kodai no michi to chimata*. Tokyo: Yoshikawa Kōbunkan, 1996.
Maekawa Akihisa. *Nihon kodai shizoku to ōken no kenkyū*. Tokyo: Hōsei Daigaku Shuppankyoku, 1986.
Masaki Kisaburō. "Munakata san megami to kiki shinwa." In *Oki no shima to kodai saishi*, ed. Oda Fujio, 51–72. Tokyo: Yoshikawa Kōbunkan, 1988.
Masuda, Sanae, *Urashima densetsu ni miru kodai Nihonjin no shinkō*. Tokyo: Chisen Shokan, 2006.
Matsuda Hisao. *Niu no kenkyū: Rekishi chirigaku kara mita Nihon no suigin*. Tokyo: Waseda Daigaku Shuppanbu, 1970.
Matsumae Takeshi. "The Heavenly Rock-Grotto Myth and the Chinkon Ceremony." *Asian Folklore Studies* 39, no. 2 (1980):9–22.
———. *Kodai denshō to kyūtei saishi*. Tokyo: Hanawa Shobō, 1974.
———. "The Myth of the Descent of the Heavenly Grandson." *Asian Folklore Studies* 42, no. 2 (1983):159–179.
———. "Origin and Growth of the Worship of Amaterasu." *Asian Folklore Studies* 37, no. 1. (1978):1–11.
Mayumi Tsunetada. *Daijōsai*. Tokyo: Kokusho Kankōkai, 1988.

———. *Nihon kodai saishi no kenkyū*. Tokyo: Gakuseisha, 1990.
———. "Saishi iseki no keisei." In *Oki no shima to kodai saishi*, ed. Oda Fujio, 99–129. Tokyo: Yoshikawa Kōbunkan, 1988.
Mayuzumi Hiromichi. *Mononobe Sogashi to kodai ōken*. Tokyo: Yoshikawa Kōbunkan, 1995.
McCulough, Helen, trans. *Tale of the Heike*. Stanford: Stanford University Press, 1988.
McMullen, Neil. "On Placating the Gods and Pacifying the Populace: The Case of the Gion Goryō Cult." *History of Religions* 27 (1988):273–290.
Miller, Alan. "Ame no Miso-Ori Me (The Heavenly Weaving Maiden): The Cosmic Weaver in Early Shinto Myth and Ritual." *History of Religions* 24 (1984):27–48.
———. "Of Weavers and Birds: Structure and Symbol in Japanese Myth and Folktale." *History of Religions* 26 (1987):309–327.
———. "The Swan-maiden Revisited: Religious Significance of 'Divine-wife' Folktales with Special Reference to Japan." *Asian Folklore Studies* 46 (1987):55–86.
———. "The Woman Who Married a Horse: Five Ways of Looking at a Chinese Folktale." *Asian Folklore Studies* 54 (1995):275–305.
Mishina Shōe. *Mishina Shōei ronbunshū*. 6 vols. Tokyo: Heibonsha, 1973.
———. *Nissen shinwa densetsu no kenkyū*. Tokyo: Heibonsha, 1972.
Miyake Kazuo. *Kodai kokka no jingi to saishi*. Tokyo: Yoshikawa Kōbunkan, 1995.
Mizoguchi Mutsuko. *Kodai shizoku no keifu*. Tokyo: Yoshikawa Kōbunkan, 1983.
———. *Ōken shinwa no nigen kōzō: Takami musuhi to Amaterasu*. Tokyo: Yoshikawa Kōbunkan, 2000.
Moriya Mitsuo. *Keiso saijiki*. Tokyo: Teikoku Shoin, 1931.
Murayama Shūichi. "Gionsha no goryōjinteki hatten." In *Goryō shinkō*, ed. Shibata Minoru, 207–216. Tokyo: Yūzankaku, 1985.
———. *Nihon onmyōdōshi sōsetsu*. Tokyo: Hanawa Shobō, 1981.
———. *Shūgen, onmyōdō to shaji shiryō*. Kyoto: Hōzōkan, 1997.
——— et al., eds. *Onmyōdō sōsho*. 4 vols. Tokyo: Hanawa Shobō, 1991–1993.
Nakai Kazuo. "Satsuma girei to sono shūhen." In *Ōmiwa to Isonokami: Shintaisan to kinsokuchi*, ed. Wada Atsumu, 107–118. Tokyo: Chikuma Shobō, 1988.
Nakai Shinkō. *Gyōki to kodai Bukkyō*. Kyoto: Nagata Bunshodo, 1991.
Nakamura, Kyoko. *Miraculous Stories from the Japanese Buddhist Tradition*. Cambridge, MA: Harvard-Yenching Institute Monograph Series, 1973.

Nakamura Shōhachi. *Gogyō taigi*. Tokyo: Meitoku Shuppansha, 1973.
———. *Gogyō taigi kisoteki kenkyū*. Tokyo: Meitoku Shuppansha, 1976.
———. *Gogyō taigi zenshaku* 1. Tokyo: Meiji Shoin, 1986–.
Nakamura Shūya. *Hatashi to Kamoshi*. Kyoto: Rinsen Shoten, 1994.
Nakamura Takashi. *Chūgoku saijishi no kenkyū*. Kyoto: Hōyū Shoten, 1993.
Nakano Hatayoshi, *Hachiman shinkō*. Tokyo: Hanawa Shobō, 2001.
———. *Hachiman shinkō no kenkyū*. 2 vols. Tokyo: Yoshikawa Kōbunkan, 1975.
———. *Hachiman shinkō to shūgendō*. Tokyo: Yoshikawa Kōbunkan, 1998.
Namiki Katsuko. "Heian jidai no amagoi hōbei." In *Heian jidai no jinja to saishi*, ed. Nijūnisha Kenkyūkai, 111–176. Tokyo: Kokusho Kankōkai, 1986.
Naoki Kōjirō. *Nihon kodai no shizoku to tennō*. Tokyo: Hanawa Shobō, 1993.
Nara Bunkazai Kenkyūjo Asuka Shiryōkan. *Kitora kofun to hakkutsu sareta hekigatachi*. Nara-ken, Takaichi-gun, Asuka-mura: Nara Bunkazai Kenkyūjo Asuka Shiryōkan, 2006.
Naumann, Nellie. "*Sakahagi*: The 'Reverse Flaying' of the Heavenly Piebald Horse." *Asian Folklore Stories* 41 (1982):7–38.
Nemoto Seiji. *Nara Bukkyō to Gyōki denshō no tenkai*. Tokyo: Yūzankaku, 1991.
———. *Tempyōki no sōryo to tennō: Sō Dōkyō no shiron*. Tokyo: Iwata Shoin, 2003.
Nishimoto Masahiro. *Nihon kodai girei seiritsushi no kenkyū*. Tokyo: Hanawa Shobō, 1997.
Noguchi Tetsurō, and Sakai Tatao, eds. *Senshū Dōkyō to Nihon. Daiichi kan: Dōkyō no denpa to kodai kokka*. Tokyo: Yūzankaku, 1986.
Nunome Junrō. *Kinu no tōden*. Tokyo: Shōgakkan, 1999.
———. *Kinu to nuno no kōkogaku*. Tokyo: Yūzankaku, 1988.
Ōbayashi Taryō. "Japanese Myths of Descent from Heaven and their Korean Parallels." *Asian Folklore Studies* 43, no. 2 (1984):171–184.
Obinata Katsumi. *Kodai kokka to nenjū gyōji*. Tokyo: Yoshikawa Kōbunkan, 1993.
Oda Fujio. "Iwai no hanran." In *Kodai no Nihon 3: Kyūshū*, ed. Kagamiyama Takeshi, 159–175. Tokyo: Kadokawa Shoten, 1970.
Oda Fujio, ed. *Iwai no ran*. Tokyo: Yoshikawa Kōbunkan, 1991.
———, ed. *Okinoshima to kodai saishi*. Tokyo: Yoshikawa Kōbunkan, 1998.
Ōhashi Katsuaki. *Tenjukoku shūchō no kenkyū*. Tokyo: Yoshikawa Kōbunkan, 1995.
Ōhashi Nobuya. *Nihon kodai no ōken to shizoku*. Tokyo: Yoshikawa Kōbunkan, 1996.

Okada Seishi, ed. *Daijōsai to niiname*. Tokyo: Gakuseisha, 1979.

———. "Hiyoshi Jinja to Tenchichō Ōtsumiya. In *Nihon shoki kenkyū,* ed. Yokoto Ken'ichi Sensei Koki Kinenkai, 16:54–57. Tokyo: Shōgakkan, 1994.

———. *Ise Naigū Sōdenkami no Seikaku to Seiritsu*. In Okada Seishi, ed. *Saishi to kokka no rekishigaku*. 5–28 Tokyo: Hanawa Shobō, 2001.

———. *Kodai ōken no saishi to shinwa*. Tokyo: Hanawa Shobō, 1978.

———. *Kodai saishi no shiteki kenkyū*. Tokyo: Hanawa Shobō, 1992.

———. "Nara jidai no Kamo Jinja." In *Kodai saishi no rekishi to bungaku*, ed. Okada Seishi, 247–287. Tokyo: Hanawa Shobō, 1997.

Okada Shigekiyo. *Imi no sekai: Sono kikō to henyō*. Tokyo: Kokusho Kanōkai, 1989.

———. *Kodai no imi: Nihonjin no kisō shinkō*. Tokyo: Kokusho Kankōkai, 1982.

Okada Shōji. "Heian zenki jinja saishi no 'kōsaika.'" In *Heian jidai no jinja to saishi*, ed. Nijūnisha Kenkyūkai, 1–110. Tokyo: Kokusho Kankōkai, 1986.

Okimori Takuya, Satō Makoto, and Yajima Izumi, eds. *Tōshi kaden: Kamatari, Jōe, Muchimaro den chūshaku to kenkyū*. Tokyo: Yoshikawa Kōbunkan, 1999.

Ooms, Herman. *Imperial Politics and Symbolics in Ancient Japan: The Tenmu Dynasty, 650–800*. Honolulu: University of Hawai'i Press, 2009.

Ōno Tatsunosuke, *Shōtoku taishi no kenkyū*. Tokyo: Yoshikawa Kōbunkan, 1970.

Ōyama Seiichi. *Nagaya no ōkimike mokkan to kinsekibun*. Tokyo: Yoshikawa Kōbunkan, 1998.

Philippi, Donald. *Norito*. Princeton, NJ: Princeton University Press, 1990.

Picken, Stuart. *Historical Dictionary of Shinto*. London: Scarecrow Press, 2002.

Piggott, Joan. *Emergence of Japanese Kingship*. Stanford: Stanford University Press, 1997.

———. "The Last Classical Female Sovereign: Kōken-Shōten Tennō." In *Women and Confucian Cultures in Premodern China, Korea, and Japan*, ed. Dorothy Ko, Jahyun Kim Haboush, and Joan Piggott, 43–74. Berkeley: University of California Press, 2003.

Pradel, Maria del Rosario. "Fragments of the Tenjukoku Shūchō Mandara: Reconstruction of the Iconography and the Historical Contexts." Ph.D. diss., UCLA, 1997.

Sada Shigeru. "Oki no Shima Saishi to Hensen." In *Oki no shima to kodai saishi*, ed. Oda Fujio, 73–98. Tokyo: Yoshikawa Kōbunkan, 1988.

Saeki Arikiyo. *Shinsen shōjiroku no kenkyū.* 6 vols. Tokyo: Yoshikawa Kōbunkan, 1962.

———. "Yūryaku chō no rekishiteki ichi." In *Yūryaku tennō to sono jidai,* ed. Saeki Arikyo, 1–22. Tokyo: Yoshikawa Kōbunkan, 1988.

Sagai Tatsuru. *Hiyoshi Taisha to San'ō Gongen.* Kyoto: Jimbun Shoin, 1992.

Saigō Nobutaka. "Hachiman kami no hassei." In *Hachiman shinkō,* ed. Nakano Hatayoshi, 3–34. Tokyo: Yoshikawa Kōbunkan, 1983.

Sano Kenji. *Kokūzō bosatsu shinkō no kenkyū.* Yoshikawa Kōbunkan, 1996.

Sasō Mamoru. "Heian jidai ni okeru ekijinkan no shōsō." In *Heian jidai no jinja to saishi,* ed. Nijūnisha Kenkyūkai, 367–406. Tokyo: Kokusho Kankōkai, 1986.

Schafer, Edward. *Pacing the Void.* Berkeley: University of California Press, 1977.

Segawa Yoshinori. "Umakai shūdan no kami matsuri." In *Kofun jidai no kenkyū 3: Seikatsu to saishi,* ed. Ishino Hironobu, Iwasaki Takuya, Kawakami Kunihiko, and Shiraishi Taiichirō, 122–130. Tokyo: Yūzankaku, 1991.

Seidel, Anna. "Imperial Treasures and Taoist Sacraments: Taoist Roots in the Apocrypha." *Cahiers d'Extrême-Asie* 5 (1983):223–347.

Sekiguchi Hiroko. "The Patriarchical Family Paradigm in Eighth-Century Japan." In *Women and Confucian Cultures in Premodern China, Korea, and Japan,* ed. Dorothy Ko, Jahyun Kim Haboush, and Joan Piggott, 27–46. Berkeley: University of California Press, 2003.

Senda Minoru. *Ise Jingū: Higashi ajia no Amaterasu.* Tokyo: Chūkō shinsho, 2005.

Shibata Minoru. "Gion Goryōe: Sono seiritsu to igi." In *Goryō shinkō,* ed. Shibata Minoru, 217–250. Tokyo: Yūzankaku, 1985.

Shigeta Shinichi. *Abe no Seimei: Onmyōtachi no Heian jidai.* Tokyo: Yoshikawa Kōbunkan, 2006.

Shimode Sekiyo. *Kodai shinsen shisō no kenkyū.* Tokyo: Yoshikawa Kōbunkan, 1986.

———. *Nihon kodai no Dōkyō, onmyōdō to jingi.* Tokyo: Yoshikawa Kōbunkan, 1997.

Shimonaka Nisaburō, ed. *Shintō daijiten.* Kyoto: Rinsen Shoten, 1937.

Shinbori Shinobu. "Jitō Jotei to Yoshino Gyōkō." In *Asuka no rekishi to bungaku,* ed. Yokota Ken'ichi, 119–148. Tokyo: Shinshindō, 1980.

Shinkawa Tokio. *Dōkyō o meguru kōbō: Kunnō, dōshi no hō o agamazu.* Tokyo: Taishūkan Shoten, 1999.

———. *Nihon kodai no saishi to hyōgen.* Tokyo: Yoshikawa Kōbunkan, 1999.

Shirai Isamu. "Miwa Jinja to Isonokami Jingū." In *Yamabe no michi,* ed. Wada Atsumu, 154–182. Tokyo: Yoshikawa Kobunkan, 1999.

Sivin, Nathan. "On the Pao P'u Tzu Nei Pien and the Life of Ko Hong (283–343)." *Isis* 60 (1976):388–391.

———. "On the Word 'Taoist' as a Source of Perplexity. With Special Reference to the Relations of Science and Religion in Traditional China." *History of Religions* 17, no. 3, and 17, no. 4 (1978):303–330.

Slingerland, Edward. *Analects*. Indianapolis: Hackett Publishing, 2003.

Sonoda Kōyū. "Kokūzō shinkō no shiteki tenkai." In *Kokūzō shinkō*, ed. Sano Kenji, 143–166. Tokyo: Yūzankaku, 1991.

Stein, Rolf. "Religious Taoism and Popular Religion from the Second to Seventh Centuries." In *Facets of Taoism*, ed. Anna Seidel and Holmes Welch, 53–81. New Haven, CT: Yale University Press, 1979.

Strickmann, Michel. "History, Anthropology, and Chinese Religion." *Harvard Journal of Asiatic Studies* 40 (1980):201–248.

Suenaga Masao, and Inoue Mitsusada, eds. *Takamatsuzuka kofun to Asuka*. Tokyo: Chūō Koronsha, 1972.

Sugano Masao. *Kojiki setsuwa no kenkyū*. Tokyo: Ōfusha, 1973.

Suzuki Ikkei. *Onmyōdō: Jujutsu to kishin no seikai*. Tokyo: Kōdansha, 2002.

Tachibana Kyōdō. "Wagakuni ni okeru goryō shinkō to *Dai Hannya Kyō*: Shōmin Bukkyōshi to shite no isshiki ron." In *Goryō shinkō*, ed. Shibata Minoru, 79–100. Tokyo: Yūzankaku, 1988.

Takebe Yoshito. *Nihon momenshi no kenkyū*. Tokyo: Yoshikawa Kōbunkan, 1985.

Takemitsu Makoto. *Kenkyūshi: Beminsei*. Tokyo: Yoshikawa Kobunkan, 1981.

Taketani Hisao. *Kodai shizoku denshō no kenkyū*. Tokyo: Kasama Shoin, 1971.

Takikawa Seijirō. *Ritsuryō to daijōsai*. Tokyo: Kokusho Kankyōkai, 1989.

Takioto Yoshiyuki. "Urashimako denshō no seiritsu kihan." In *Kodai kokka no rekishi to denshō*, ed. Mayuzumi Hiromichi, 40–53. Tokyo: Yoshikawa Kōbunkan, 1992.

Tamura Enchō. "Munakata, Usa, Asō shinkō to sono seiryoku." In *Kodai no Nihon 3: Kyūshū*, ed. Kagamiyama Takeshi and Tamura Enchō, 302–315. Tokyo: Kadokawa Shoten, 1970.

———. *Nihon Bukkyōshi*. 4 vols. Tokyo: Hōzōkan, 1985.

Tanigawa Ken'ichi. "Torigata doki ni tsuite." In *Kodai Nihonjin no shinkō to saishi*, ed. Matsumae Takeshi, Shirakawa Shizuka, et al., 116–122. Tokyo: Daiwa Shobō, 1997.

Teeuwen, Mark. "From Jindō to Shintō: A Concept Takes Shape." *Japanese Journal of Religious Studies* 34 (2002):243–247.

———. "*Sendai kuji hongi*: Authentic Myths or Forged History?" *Monumenta Nipponica* 62, no. 1 (2007):87–96.

———. *Watarai Shintō: An Intellectual History of the Outer Shrine in Ise.* Leiden: Research School CNWS, 1996.

———, and Hendrik ven der Veere. *Nakatomi harae kunge: Purification and Enlightenment in Late-Heian Japan.* Munich: Iudicum, 1998.

Teiser, Stephen. *The Ghost Festival in Medieval China.* Princeton, NJ: Princeton University Press, 1988.

Toby, Ronald. "Why Leave Nara?" *Monumenta Nipponica* 40, no. 3 (1985):331–347.

Tōkyōto Bijutsukan, ed. *Shōtoku taishi ten.* Osaka: NHK, 2001.

Torao Toshiya. "Nara Economic and Social Institutions." In *Cambridge History of Japan,* Vol. 1: *Ancient Japan,* ed. Delmer Brown, 415–452. Cambridge: Cambridge University Press, 1993.

Tsuji Hidenori. *Hasederashi no kenkyū.* Tokyo: Gannandō, 1979.

———. *Murōjishi no kenkyū.* Tokyo: Gannandō, 1979.

———. *Narachō sangaku jiin no kenkyū.* Tokyo: Meichō Shuppan, 1991.

Ueda Masaaki. *Kikajin.* Tokyo: Chuō Kōronsha, 1965.

———. *Kodai kokka to shūkyō.* Tokyo: Kadokawa Shoten, 1998.

———. *Kodai no Dōkyō to Chōsen bunka.* Kyoto: Jimbun shoin, 1989.

———. "Satsu gyūma shinkō no kōsatsu." In *Kamigami no saishi to denshō: Matsumae Takeshi kyōjū kokinen henbunshū,* ed. Ueda Masaaki, 19–34. Tokyo: Tōmeisha, 1992.

———. *Ueda Masaaki chosakushū.* 3 vols. Tokyo: Kadokawa Shoten, 1998.

Uwai Hisayoshi. *Nihon kodai no shizoku to saishi.* Tokyo: Jinbun Shoin, 1990.

Wada Atsumu. *Nihon kodai no girei to saishi, shinkō.* 3 vols. Tokyo: Hanawa Shobō, 1995.

———. "Oki no shima to Yamato ōken." In *Oki no shima to kodai saishi,* ed. Oda Fujio, 164–198. Tokyo: Yoshikawa Kōbunkan, 1998.

———, ed. *Ōmiwa to Isonokami: Shintaisan to kinsokuchi.* Tokyo: Chikuma Shobō, 1988.

———. "Saishi no genryū: Miwasan to Isonokamiyama." In *Ōmiwa to Isonokami: Shintaisan to kinsokuchi,* ed. Wada Atsumu, 3–36. Tokyo: Chikuma Shobō, 1988.

———, ed. *Yamabe no michi.* Tokyo: Yoshikawa Kobunkan, 1999.

———. "Yamabe no Michi no rekishiteki igi." In *Yamabe no Michi: Kofun, shizoku, jisha,* ed. Wada Atsumu, 1–44. Tokyo: Yoshikawa Kōbunkan, 1999.

Wakamatsu Ryōichi. "Saisei no inori to jinbutsu haniwa." In *Kodai Nihonjin no shinkō to saishi,* ed. Matsumae Takeshi, Shirakawa Shizuka, et al., 147–167. Tokyo: Daiwa Shobō, 1997.

Waley, Arthur. *The Noh Plays of Japan*. Rutland, VT: C. E. Tuttle, 1976.
Wang Kuo-liang. *Han Wu t'ung ming chi yen-chiu*. Taipei: Wenshih Chehsüeh Chupanshe, 1989.
———. *Hsu chi-chieh chi yen-chiu*. Taipei: Wen-shih-che Chu-pan-she, 1987.
Wang Yung. *Shōtoku taishi jikū chōetsu*. Tokyo: Daishukan Shoten, 1994.
Watanabe Katsuyoshi, *Chinkonsai no kenkyū*. Tokyo: Meichō Shuppan, 1994.
Watase Masatada. "Kakinomoto no Hitomaro, Chinese Astronomy and Chinese Traditions Concerning the Seventh Night Story: The 'Seventh Night Poems' in the Hitomaro Kashū." *Acta Asiatica* 77 (1999):30–49.
Watkins, James, and Evelyn Rawski, eds. *Death Ritual in Late Imperial and Early Modern China*. Berkeley: University of California Press, 1988.
Yabu Motoaki. *Amagoi girei no seiritsu to tenkai*. Tokyo: Iwata Shoin, 2002.
Yamachika Kumiko. "Michi to matsuri." In *Nihon no shinkō iseki*, ed. Kaneko Hiroyuki, 211–236. Tokyo: Yūzankaku, 1998.
Yamamoto Kōji. *Kegare to ōharae*. Tokyo: Heibonsha, 1992.
———. "Onmyōdōryō to onmyōdō." In *Onmyōdō sōsho 1: Kodai*, ed. Murayama Shūichi et al., 341–352. Tokyo: Meichō Shuppan, 1991.
———. "Tenmon, reki, sukuyōdō." In *Onmyōdō sōsho 4: Tokuron*, ed. Murayama Shūichi et al., 411–425. Tokyo: Meichō Shuppan, 1993.
Yano Michio. "Bukkyō keiten no naka no reki, sukuyōkyō." In *Onmyōdō sōsho 4: Tokuron*, ed. Murayama Shūichi et al., 357–366. Tokyo: Meichō Shuppan, 1993.
———. *Mikkyō senseijutsu: Sukuyōdō to Indo senseijutsu*. Tokyo: Tokyo Bijutsu, 1986.
Yokota Ken'ichi. *Asuka no kamigami*. Tokyo: Yoshikawa Kōbunkan, 1992.
Yoshida Akira. "Kodai Tajima no gōzoku to bumin." *Tajimashi kenkyū* 25, no. 1 (2002):1–39.
Yoshida Yasuo. *Gyōki to ritsuryō kokka*. Tokyo: Yoshikawa Kōbunkan, 1987.
Yoshie Akiko. *Nihon kodai no saishi to josei*. Tokyo: Yoshikawa Kōbunkan, 1996.
———. *Nihon kodai no shizoku no kōzō*. Tokyo: Yoshikawa Kōbunkan, 1986.
———. *Nihon kodai no uji no kōzō*. Tokyo: Yoshikawa Kōbunkan, 1986.
Yoshikawa Shinji. "Kodai Tajima no sen'i seisan to ryūtsū." *Tajimashi kenkyū* 22 (2002):9–27.
Yoshino Hiroko. *In'yō gogyō shisō kara mita Nihon no matsuri: Ise Jingū saishi, daijōsai o chūhin to shite*. Kyoto: Jinbun Shoin, 2000.
———. *In'yō gogyō to Nihon no tennō*. Kyoto: Jinbun Shoin, 1998.

Yü Ying-shih. "O Soul, Come Back: A Study of the Changing Conceptions of the Soul and Afterlife in Pre-Buddhist China." *Harvard Journal of Asiatic Studies* 47 (1987):363–395.

Yuba Tadanori, "Miwa to Isonokami no saishi iseki." In *Yamabe no michi*, ed.Wada Atsumu, 129–153. Tokyo: Yoshikawa Kōbunkan, 1999.

———. "Saishi ibutsu no naiyō." In *Oki no shima to kodai saishi*, ed. Oda Fujio, 99–129. Tokyo: Yoshikawa Kōbunkan, 1988.

Index

Abe no Kotoshiro, 162–164, 166, 189, 197, 219
Abe no Kunimi, 164–166, 197, 218
Akaru Hime: Ame no Hiboko and, 43, 54, 131–132, 162, 197–198; animal sacrifice and, 45, 53; cowherd deities and, 44, 197, 221; epidemics and, 40, 197; Himegoso shrines and, 40, 44, 50, 111, 118, 197, 205; Jingū kōgō and, 216; as karakami, 41, 43–45, 51, 53–54, 78; as Kyūshū deity, 40, 78, 118, 135, 162, 197; Mononobe and, 40, 43, 106, 123, 260n.16; Munakata deities and, 40, 118, 123; Sumiyoshi shrine and, 216; sun deities and, 165, 249n.53; Tsunoga Arashito and, 44–45, 51, 53–54, 197; as vengeful goddess, 40, 54, 111, 118, 124, 131, 197; weaving implements and, 40–41, 43, 106, 111, 118, 123, 162, 197
Ama no Hoakari no Mikoto: Amaterasu and, 122, 163, 167–168, 180–183, 267n.33; Amateru shrines and, 163, 179, 181, 183; Heavenly Grandchild legend and, 122, 163, 167, 180–181; Ho no Suseri and, 121, 177–178, 209; Konohana Sakiya Hime and, 121–122, 163, 167, 180, 198, 209; Kusakabe kinship group and, 172, 198, 210, 260n.13, 276n.62; Mononobe kinship group and, 156, 163, 168, 172, 179, 181, 198, 212, 267n.34; Owari Muraji kinship group and, 122, 156, 163, 172, 181–182, 198, 213; Wani kinship group and, 156–157, 172–173, 179, 198; Yamato Takeru and, 156–157, 172, 174, 177, 181, 222, 275n.46
Amaterasu: Ama no Hoakari and, 122, 163, 167–168, 180–183, 267n.33, Amateru shrines and, 162, 163–165, 181–183, 189, 209–210; Chinkonsai and, xx, 60, 108, 156, 169, 180, 204; consecrated princesses and, 81, 175, 253n.19, 277n.46; Heavenly Grandchild legend and, 122, 163, 167, 180, 183, 185; Heavenly Grotto and, xx, 60, 141, 156, 158–159, 166, 181, 188, 204, 276n.53; horses and, 159, 184–186; immigrant lineages and, 183, 189–191, 198; Konoshima ni masu Amateru Jinja, 164, 209; Mononobe and, 181–183, 202, 275n.46; Niinamesai and, 82, 158, 167; Oshira cult and, 188; resurrection and, 60, 156, 158–159, 166, 192, 202, 272n.3; as royal ancestor, xx–xxi, 155; as silkworm goddess, xxi, 135, 183, 188–191; sun gods and, 197, 249n.53; Susanoo and, 141, 158–159, 181, 185, 204, 217; Takami Musubi and, 162–163, 167, 182, 217, 272n.1; Takuhata Hime and, 164–165, 167, 267n.31; Tenmu and, 155, 158–159,

185, 219, 253n.19; Toyouke Hime and, 81, 188–190, 218, 275n.46; Tsukiyomi Mikoto and, 163–164, 166, 188–189, 210, 219; as weaving maiden, 141, 158–159, 167; Uzume Hime and, 159, 220, 272n.4, 272n.12; Yamato Hime and, 175, 206, 221, 229, 277n.46; Yamato Takeru and, 156, 221, 276n.53; Yatagarasu and, 103, 222, 264n.55

Amateru shrines: Ama no Hoakari and, 163, 179, 181, 183; Amaterasu and, 162, 163–165, 181–183, 189, 209–210; immigrant lineages and, 164, 180, 182–183, 189; Konoshima nimasu Amateru Mitama Jinja and, 164, 181, 182, 189; Kyūshū lineages and, 162–163, 180; Mononobe kinship group and, 168–169, 182, 275n.46

Ama yorozu taku hata chi hata hime. *See* Takuhata Chichi Hime

Ame no Hiboko: Akaru Hime and, 43–44, 53–54, 132, 162, 197, 216; as cowherd deity, 43–44, 53–54, 197–198, 221; Izushi Otome and, 131–132, 198, 207; Izushi shrine and, 131–132; Jingū kōgō and, 207, 216, 241n.17; Mitoshi no Kami and, 43–44, 221; Miyake Muraji and, 173, 212; sun deities and, 162; Tajima Mori and, 173, 212, 217; Tsunoga Arashito and, 44, 53–54, 197

animal sacrifice, xi–xiv, xviii–xix, 25–32, 36–39, 41–42, 45, 47, 50–55, 105, 186, 196, 209, 248n.39, 248n.44

Atsumori, 86–87, 90, 107, 198

Atsuta shrine, 12, 174, 177, 199, 210, 213, 275n.51

Azeko, 40, 43, 123, 249n.49, 260n.16

Benshō, 16, 199, 204, 242n.37

Bu, Great King. *See* Yūryaku

Bureau of Yin and Yang (Onmyōryō), 219, 234

Chiisakobe kinship group: Hata kinship group and, 116, 126, 130–131, 193, 200; Kamuyaimimi no Mikoto and, 122, 199, 216; Miwa kinship group and, 117, 126, 131, 134, 193, 211, 216, 268n.45; Ōmononushi and, 117, 122, 124, 268n.45; as sacerdotal lineage, 117, 122, 124, 126–127, 130–131, 134, 193, 268n.45; sericulture rites and, 116–117; thunder deities and, 117, 127, 268n.45; weaving lineages and, 116; Yūryaku and, 116–117, 200

Chiisakobe Sugaru, 116–117, 267n.36, 268n.45

chimata: Hata kinship group and, 125; hitogata and, 33, 107, 199; Mononobe kinship group and, 91–94, 202, 261n.20; Ōfube no Ōshi and, 261n.21; purification and, 33, 199; spirit quieting and, 33, 199, 202, 206, 247n.45, 261n.20, 267n.39; strategic importance of, 91, 199, 246n.16

Chinese festival calendar: animal sacrifice and, xii–xiii, xix, 26, 35–39, 41, 45, 53–55, 105; *Ching ch'u sui shih chi* and, 38, 58–61, 98, 105, 111, 149, 152–153, 185, 231, 234, 238n.4; kusagari and, xix, 58, 60, 65, 185, 210; nodal days and, 58, 60, 62, 137, 184–185, 195, 210, 231–232, 248n.34, 248n.36; Queen Mother of the West and, 62, 99–100, 102, 104–107, 214, 264n.33; Suiko court and, xi, 33–35, 45, 58, 60, 83, 85, 89, 137, 146, 149, 153, 155, 210, 211, 216, 234; technologies and, xi–xiii, xviii, 34, 41, 45, 53–55, 84, 112, 117, 135, 153; Weaver Maiden and Cowherd and, xii, xix–xx, 26, 38–39, 105, 148–149, 184, 186, 221; yin and yang and, xi–xii, 34–36, 54–56, 60, 109, 114, 139–140, 153, 185, 195, 247n.24

Chinkonsai (Mitama shizume matsuri): Amaterasu and, xx, 60, 108, 156, 169, 180, 204; Futsunushi no Mikoto and, 170; Heavenly Grotto legend and, xx, 60, 156–157, 159–161, 180, 182, 184–185, 199, 204, 276; Hōzō and, 60, 161, 173, 175; Isonokami shrine and, 93, 169–171, 199, 261n.20; Mononobe and, 93, 108, 157, 161, 169–171, 175, 180, 182, 199, 206, 212, 220, 224–225, 261n.20, 273n.12, 277n.66; Umashimaji and, 93, 168, 220
Chūai, 12, 160, 200, 207, 216, 242n.27
cinnabar, 65–66, 222, 254n.33, 254n.36
combs, 72–74, 80, 177–180, 256n.55, 276n.63
consecrated princess (Saiō, Saiin): Ise shrine and, 81, 165, 173, 175, 253n.19, 277n.46; Kamo shrines and, 4, 22; Tenmu and, 155, 173, 175; Yamato Hime as, 174–176, 206, 221, 229

Daianji, 11, 19, 51, 68, 200, 202, 250n.58, 251n.69
Dōji, 10–11, 16, 19, 200, 202, 225, 235, 243n.50, 250n.58
Dōkyō, 196, 201, 204, 209, 229, 235, 255n.32, 258n.79
Dōshō, 19–20, 67, 201, 203
Dōtō, 46–47, 49, 51, 53, 100–101, 201, 250

elixirs. *See* medicine hunts
Ema kinship group, 46–47, 51, 201
Enma (King Yama), 48–49, 195, 250n.63
En no Gyōja, 66, 201, 203, 235, 255n.39

female immortals: Heavenly Maiden of Suruga as, 74–76, 184, 216–217; Nuribe Hime as, 75–76, 78, 83, 213, 257n.65; Takakara Megami as, 71, 76, 83, 176, 217, 259n.80; Toyouke Hime as, 57, 78, 80–81, 176, 229; Tsuminoe no Hijiri Hime as; 57, 78, 80–81, 176, 229; Uranoshimako and, 57, 72–75, 176–177, 180, 220; Weaver Maiden and, 74, 77, 120–121, 204, 216, 221, 234
fruit of immortality: peaches as, 97–99, 105, 185, 232; Queen Mother of the West and, 97–99, 104–105, 173, 232, 263n.42; tachibana as, 94, 99–100, 103–104, 107, 143, 261n.21, 263n.35, 263n.42; Tajima Mori and, 103–104, 205, 212, 214, 217
Fujiwara Fuhito, 75–76, 209, 215
Fujiwara Kadono, 17, 204
Fujiwara kinship group: epidemics and, 10–11; Hata kinship group and, 16–18, 21–23, 199, 242n.37, 243n.41; Hōryūji and, 10–11; Kusuko incident and, 17, 211; *Tōshi kaden* and, 226, 249n.54; Tsunoga and, 226, 249n.54; twenty-two shrine-temple system and, 21–23
Fujiwara Nakanari, 16–17, 202, 211
Fujiwara Tanetsugu, 16–17, 201–202
Fujiwara Umakai, 16, 201, 204, 242n.38, 246n.20
Fukunaga Mitsuji, xiv–xv, 2, 56, 251n.2
Fushimi Inari shrine: Hata kinship group and, 5, 13, 20, 193, 202; Kamo shrines and, 5, 18, 193, 202; Tōji and, 20, 202, 210
Futsunushi no Mikoto: Chinkonsai and, 170, Isonokami shrine and, 169–170, 202, 206; Jinmu and, 169–170, 170–171, 202, 206; as Master Shaker, 170–171, 202; Mononobe kinship group and, 169–170, 202, 206; spirit shaking and, 169–171

Gomyō: Gumonjihō and, 19–20, 67, 202, 243n.51; Hata kinship group and, 19–20, 22, 24, 67, 243n.51; Saichō and, 24, 202, 243n.51

Gonsō: Gumonjihō and, 19–20, 67, 202, 243n.51; Hata and, 19–20, 22, 24, 67, 243n.51; Saichō and, 24, 202, 243n.51

Gosechimai dance, 62, 80–81, 217, 228, 248n.36, 253n.21, 259n.80

Great Buddha of Nara, 10, 17, 200, 201, 215

Gumonjihō: Daianji and, 19, 200; Dōji and, 19, 200, 235; Dōshō and, 18, 201; Gomyō and, 19–20, 67, 202, 243n.51; Gonsō and, 19–20, 67, 202, 243n.51; Hata kinship group and, 19–20, 67, 202–203, 243n.51; Kūkai and, 18–19, 67, 210, 226, 243n.51; Yoshino and, 19, 67, 203

Hachiman, 14, 18, 20, 22, 196, 203, 242n.32

Hakuji, 100–102, 203

Hata kinship group: Amaterasu and, 164, 182–184, 189, 191, 197; Chiisakobe kinship group and, 116, 126, 130–131, 193, 200; Fujiwara kinship group and, 16–18, 21–23, 199, 242n.37, 243n.41; Fushimi Inari shrine and, 5, 13, 20, 193, 202; Gumonjihō and, 19–20, 67, 202–203, 243n.51; Heian capital and, xviii, 4, 6, 193, 203; Kamo shrines and, 4–5, 7, 18, 20–22, 103, 125–128, 131, 134; Kokūzō and, 18–19; Konoshima ni masu Amateru Mitama Jinja, 164, 182, 189, 197; Kōryūji and, 18–19, 201; Kūkai and, 6, 18–20, 24, 201–202, 243n.51; Matsuno'o shrine and, 5–6, 10, 18, 20–22, 42, 127, 135, 164, 189, 193, 202, 205, 211, 214, 220, 244n.54, 268n.43; Munakata deities, 13, 18, 42, 120, 125, 242n.30, 268n.43; Ōyamakui no Mikoto and, 20, 42, 205, 211, 214, 220; Saga and, 4, 18, 20–21, 134, 214; Shōtoku and, 8, 10, 19, 24, 183, 197, 241n.27

Hata no Asamoto, 16, 199, 201, 204, 242n.37

Hata no Shimamaro, 16–17, 204

Heavenly Grandchild (Ninigi no Mikoto): Ama no Hoakari, 122, 163, 167, 180–181; Amaterasu and, 122, 163, 167, 180, 183, 185; Konohana Sakiya Hime and, 120–122, 163, 180, 209; pregnancy in a single night motif in, 120–121; Takami Musubi and, 120, 217

Heavenly Grotto legend: Ama no Hoakari and, 122, 163, 167, 180–181; Amaterasu and, xx, 60, 141, 156, 158–159, 166, 181, 188, 204, 276n.53; Chinkonsai and, xx, 60, 156–157, 159–161, 180, 182, 184–185, 199, 204, 276; Ōharae and, 156–157, 159, 161, 204, 211; resurrection and, 60, 156, 158–159, 166, 192, 202, 272n.3; Takami Musubi and, 162–163, 167, 182, 217, 272n.1

Heavenly Maidens. See female immortals

Heizei: Fujiwara kinship group and, 16–17, 202, 211, 242n.38; Kusuko incident and, 4, 16–17, 202, 211, 214; Saga and, 4, 211, 240n.13

Hibasu Hime: fruit of immortality and, 173, 205; Inishiki Irihiko and, 172, 205–206, 221; Kusakabe kinship group and, 172–173, 210, 218; Tajima Mori and, 173, 205; Wani kinship group and, 173, 218; Yamato Hime and, 172–173, 205–206, 221

Hiei, Mount. See Hiyoshi shrines

Hiko Hoho Demi no Mikoto, 121–122, 209

Himegoso shrines, 40, 43–44, 50–51, 111, 118, 135, 197–198, 205, 249n.48

hitogata, xi, xix, 33, 48–49, 52, 54, 94–95, 107, 110, 205, 246n.21, 246n.22, 265n.7

Hiyoshi shrines, 5, 20–22, 42, 193, 205, 214–215, 220, 244n.54, 249n.47
hokai, 93, 206, 261n.20
Ho no Suseri no Mikoto, 121, 177, 209
Hōryūji, 11, 18–19, 101, 107, 200, 206, 209, 215, 225, 243, 263n.35
Hōzō: Chinese festival calendar and, 60, 173, 175, 206; Chinkonsai and, 60, 161, 173, 175; medicine hunts and, 60; Shōkonsai, 60, 161, 175, 206; Tenmu and, 60, 161, 173, 175, 206

Ikutamayori Hime, 129–130, 213, 215
Inishiki Irihiko: Hibasu Hime and, 172, 205–206, 221; Isonokami shrine and, 171, 206; Mononobe kinship group and, 171, 206
Ise shrines: Abe no Kunimi and, 164–166, 197, 218; consecrated princesses and, 155, 164–166, 169, 172–173, 197, 253n.19; Jitō and, 155, 210, 253n.19; regalia and, 39; royal cult and, 21, 155–157, 159, 164–165, 169, 227, 273n.23; Silla and, 166, 171, 274n.38; Takuhata Chichi Hime and, 165–167 218, 267n.37; Takuhata Hime and, 164–167, 218; Tenmu and, 155, 173–175, 181, 219, 253n.19; Toyouke Hime and, 57, 78, 81–82, 166, 219, 229; Yamato Hime and, 172, 174–176, 211, 229, 275n.46; Yamato Takeru and, 156, 173–176, 181, 211, 221
Isonokami shrine: Chinkonsai and, 93, 169–171, 199, 261n.20, Futsunushi no Mikoto and, 169–170, 202, 206; Inishiki Irihiko and, 171–172, 206; Isonokami chimata and, 92; Mononobe kinship group and, 93, 169–173, 175, 179, 206; regalia and, 170–171, 206; resurrection rites and, 93, 175–176, 220; twenty-two shrine-temple system and, 21
Isonokami chimata, 92, 206

Isukeyori Hime, 122, 128, 212, 267n.36
Iwa no Hime, 144–148, 150, 152–153, 212
Izushi Hime. *See* Izushi Otome
Izushi Otome, 131–134, 198, 207
Izushi shrine, xx, 112, 125, 131–132, 134, 154, 274n.39

Jingū kōgō, 12, 14, 22, 200, 207, 238, 241n.17, 242n.27, 244n.56
Jinmu: Futsunushi Mikoto and, 170–171, 202; Isukeyori Hime and, 122, 128; Mononobe kinship group and, 93, 168–170, 202, 207, 220; Ōtomo kinship group and, 64–65, 103, 207; Yatagarasu and, 102–103, 208, 222, 264n.55; Yoshino and, 64–65, 69, 82, 122, 207, 254n.32
Jitō: Ise shrine and, 155, 210, 253n.19; Prince Kusakabe and, 62–63, 70, 210, 224; Tenmu and, 61–62, 210, 253n.25; Yoshino and, 62–63, 75, 81, 210

Kamitsumiya, Prince. *See* Shōtoku
Kamo Agata Nushi kinship group: Hata kinship group and, 4–5, 7, 18, 20–22, 103, 125–128, 131, 134, 207; Yatagarasu and, 103, 208, 222
Kamo shrines: consecrated princess and, 4, 22; Hata kinship group and, 4–5, 7, 18, 20–22, 103, 125–128, 131, 134; Matsuno'o shrine and, 20, 42, 205, 211, 220; Mioaya Kami and, 5, 127, 208; Ōyamakui no Mikoto and, 20, 42, 205, 211, 220; Saga and, 4, 6–7, 18, 20–21, 134, 211, 214; Tamayori Hiko and, 126, 208, 218; Tamayori Hime and, 126, 208, 218; Wake no Ikazuchi no Kami and, 20, 211, 220, 268n.43
Kamu Yaimimi no Mikoto: Chiisakobe kinship group and, 122, 199, 216; Isukeyori Hime, 122, 128; Ōmononushi and, 122

karakami: animal sacrifice and, xviii–xix, 25–26, 41, 50; Chinese festival calendar and, 25–26, 41, 193, 196; continental technologies and, 26, 53; as cowherd deities, 43–44, 53–54, 197–198, 221; immigrant lineages and, xviii–xix, 21–23, 25–26, 41–42, 50–51, 54, 193–195, 208; as local deities, 25–26, 50; twenty-two shrine-temple system and, 21–23, 196

Kasuga no Omi kinship group, 172, 202, 221, 274n.41

Keikō: Hibasu Hime and, 205, 218; Waki no Iratsume and, 220; Yamato Hime and, 205, 221; Yamato Takeru and, 211, 220–221

Kitora kofun, 34, 208, 247n.30

Koguryŏ: Dōtō and, 201, 250n.58; immigrant lineages and, 47, 51, 125, 212, 220, 251; medicine hunts and, 58; omens and, 101; ritual calendar and, 58, 120; River Earl and, 214; Sui dynasty and, 136; tomb paintings and, 101, 198, 264n.48; Tsunoga and, 51, 125, 220; Yamashiro and, 47, 51, 125, 250n.58; Yūryaku and, 93

Kōgyoku (Saimei), 11–12, 30–31, 66, 209, 246n.18

Kōken (Princess Abe), 70, 196, 201, 202, 209, 215, 235, 255n.39, 258n.79

Kokubunji, 3, 9–11, 14, 17, 23, 200, 209, 215

Kokūzō (Space Buddha): astrology and, 67, 252n.53; Dōji and, 19, 200; Gumonjihō and, 18–19, 67, 200, 202, 209, 226, 235, 252n.54; Hata kinship group and, 18–19; Kōryūji and, 18–19, 201; Kūkai and, 18–19, 24, 200, 226; Yoshino and, 67, 243n.43

Kōmyō, 10–11, 200, 209

Kongō hannya haramitsu kyō, 31, 52–53, 235

Kōnin, 16, 18, 202

Konohana Sakiya Hime: Ama no Hoakari and, 121–122, 163, 167, 180, 198, 209; Amaterasu and, 121–122, 163, 167, 180, 198, 209; Heavenly Grandchild and, 120–122, 163, 180, 209; pregnancy in single night motif and, 121–122, 180, 209; as weaving maiden, 120, 135, 163, 180, 183, 209

Konoshima nimasu Amateru Mitama Jinja: Amaterasu and, 164, 209; Amateru shrines and, 164, 181–182, 189; Hata kinship group and, 164, 182, 189, 197; Oshira cult and, 188; silkworm cults and, 164, 183, 188–189, 209

Kōryūji: Dōshō and, 19, 201; Hata kinship group and, 18–19, 201; Kokūzō and, 18–19, 201

Kuchiko no Omi, 145–148, 150, 271n.32

Kūkai, 6, 18–20, 24, 67, 201–202, 210, 226, 240n.9, 243n.45, 243n.51

Kunlun, Mount, 97, 104, 214, 263n.34

kusagari (medicine hunts), xix, 58, 60, 65, 185, 210

Kusakabe kinship group: Ama no Hoakari and, 122, 172, 198, 210, 260n.13, 276n.62, Gyōki and, 69–70, Hakuji and, 100–102, 203, Hibasu Hime and, 172–173, 210, 218, Mononobe kinship group and, 83, 92, 101, 107, 180, 198, Ōtomo kinship group and, 70–72, 80, 82, 124, 254n.32; Prince Kusakabe and, 70, Shinohara no Otohime and, 122–124, 215, 251n.66; Uranoshimako and, 72–73, 177, 220

Kusakabe, Prince, 62–63, 70, 207, 210, 256n.48

Kusanagi Sword: Atsuta shrine and, 12, 174, 199, 210; Owari Muraji kinship group, 174, 181, 199, 213; Tenmu and, 12, 174, 181, 199, 211; Yamato Takeru and, 173–174, 181, 199, 211

Kusuko incident, 3–5, 16–18, 134, 211, 214
Kwallŭk, 33–34, 45, 211

Lavatory goddess: ancestral legends and, 124, 131, 133, 211; Chinese festival calendar and, 111, 113, 211, 271n.41; household deities and, 110, 124, 211; sericulture and, 110, 124, 133, 152, 211
liberation from the corpse: 176–177, 179–181, 221–222, 229, 276n.56; Ama no Hoakari and, 180–181; Chinese beliefs and, 276n.56; Kataoka beggar and, 179, 180; Oto Tachibana Hime and, 180; Toyouke Hime and, 229; Waki no Iratsume and, 180, 199, 221; Yamato Takeru and, 176–177, 180, 222

Matsuno'o shrine: Hata kinship group and, 5–6, 10, 18, 20–22, 42, 127, 135, 164, 189, 193, 202, 205, 211, 214, 220, 244n.54, 268n.43; Hiyoshi shrines and, 20, 42, 205, 214, 220, 243n.52; Kamo shrines and, 20, 42, 205, 211, 220; Ōyamakui and, 20, 42, 205, 211, 220; Tendai and, 20, 205
Matsuura, 71–72, 122, 124, 131, 258n.71
medicine hunts (kusagari), xix, 58, 60, 65, 185, 210
Michiae matsuri (Rite of Roadside Offerings), 51–53, 43, 47, 91, 211, 246n.18
Mitoshi no Kami: Ame no Hiboko and, 43–44, 221; animal sacrifice and, 41–44, 212; cowherd deities and, 43–44, 221; karakami and, 43, 221, *Kogoshūi* and, 41–42, 44, 212; Toshigoi matsuri and, 41–42, 212
Miwa kinship group: Chiisakobe kinship group and, 117, 126, 131, 134, 193, 211, 216, 268n.45; Kamo no Kimi kinship group and, 128–129, 213; Ōmononushi and, 117–118, 128; Ōtataneko and, 128–129, 213
Miwa shrine: Izushi shrine and, 133–134; Kamo shrines and, 128, 133–134; Mononobe kinship group and, 157; Munakata shrines and, 117–118, 265n.9; ōmononushi and, 117–118, 128; ōtataneko and, 128–129, 213; sacerdotal lineages and, 128–129, 135; weavers and, 113, 118, 265n.9; Yūryaku and, 117–118
Miyake kinship group: Ame no Hiboko and, 173, 212; fruit of immortality and, 103–104, 212; Hibasu Hime and, 173, 205; Queen Mother of the West and, 103–104, 173; Shōtoku and, 103; Tajima Mori and, 103–104, 173, 212
Mononobe kinship group: Akaru Hime and, 40, 43, 106, 123, 260n.16; Ama no Hoakari and, 156, 163, 168, 172, 179, 181, 198, 212, 267n.34; Amaterasu and, 122, 163, 167–168, 180–183, 267n.33; Amateru shrines and, 168–169, 182, 275n.46; Atsumori effect and, xix, 86–87, 90, 107; chimata and, 91–94, 202, 261n.20; Chinkonsai and, 93, 108, 157, 161, 169–171, 175, 180, 182, 199, 206, 212, 220, 224–225, 261n.20, 273n.12, 277n.66; founding legend of Japanese Buddhism and, xix, 69–70, 83–88, 90, 95–96 107; Fumi no Obito and, 94–95, 104; Futsunushi no Mikoto and, 169–170, 202, 206; Isonokami shrine and, 93, 169–173, 175, 179, 206; Jinmu and, 93, 168–170, 202, 207, 220; Korean Peninsula and, 91–92, 112, 157, 169, 171, 182, 193; Kusakabe kinship group and, 83, 92, 101, 107, 180, 198;

Ōharae and, 95, 104, 186; Owari Muraji and, 157, 163, 172, 177, 181, 213; *Sendai kuji hongi* and, 93, 163, 168–170, 172, 174, 198–199, 212, 220, 223–224, 297n.46; Wani kinship group and, 172, 176–177, 179–180, 182, 274n.41, 274n.42; Yūryaku and, 91, 93–94, 157, 170, 174, 222, 274n.41

Mononobe no Yuge Moriya, 69–70, 88, 95–96

moon deity. *See* Tsukiyomi no Mikoto

Munakata Cult: Hata kinship group and, 13, 18, 42, 120, 125, 242n.30, 268n.43; as Kyūshū deities, 14, 18, 39, 78, 118–119, 125; Matsuno'o shrine and, 13, 18, 42, 268n.43; Miwa shrine and, 118, 268n.43; Weaving deities and, 39; Weaving offerings and, 42, 113, 118, 249n.49, 265n.9

Nara Osa, 51, 53, 212, 251n.67
Nigihayahi no Mikoto, 163, 168–169, 171, 198, 212, 220, 224, 274n.31
Nihon ryōiki, 15, 26, 45–46, 48–51, 53–54, 66, 68–70, 76, 84, 100, 122, 180, 195, 200–201, 213, 225–226, 233–235, 250n.62, 255n.39, 257n.39
Nihu Kami, 63–66, 244n.57, 254n.28, 254n.33, 254n.36
Ninigi no Mikoto. *See* Heavenly Grandchild
Nintoku, 144–145, 150, 212
Norito, 159, 213, 227, 273n.9
Nukadabe kinship group, 200, 250n.58
Nunoshiki no Omi Kinume, 48–49, 52, 213
Nuribe Hime, 75–76, 78, 83, 213, 257n.65
Nurinomi, 150–151, 183

Ōfube no Ōshi, 143, 154, 183, 213, 261n.21
Ōharae (Rite of Great Purification): bestiality and, 160, 185; Chinese deities and, 94–95, 104, 108, 186; Chinkonsai and, 108, 156–157, 161; Chūai and, 161, 200; founding legend of Japanese Buddhism and, 95, 104, 108; Fumi no Obito and, 94–95, 104; Heavenly Grotto legend and, 156–157, 159, 161, 204, 211; hitogata and, 95, 104; Mononobe and, 95, 104, 186; Susanoo and, 159, 185, 204

Okinoshima shrine, 39–40, 170
Ōmononushi: Chiisakobe kinship group and, 117, 122, 124, 268n.45, Hiyoshi shrines and, 205; Kamo no Kimi kinship group and, 212–213; Miwa kinship group and, 118, 122, 124, 212–213; Munakata Deities and, 118, 268n.43; Ōtataneko and, 128–129, 213; Seyatadera and, 128; as thunder deity, 117–118, 128; Yūryaku and, 117–118

onmyōdō. *See* yin and yang
Onmyōryō (Bureau of Yin and Yang), 219, 234
Oshira cult, 187–188, 270n.19, 277n.76
Ōtataneko no Mikoto, 129–130, 208, 212–213
Ōtomo kinship group: founding legend of Japanese Buddhism and, 69–70; Gyōki and, 70; Jinmu and, 64, 103, 207; Korean peninsula and, 71–72, 122, 193, 215, 256n.49; Kusakabe kinship group and, 70–72, 80, 82, 124, 254n.32; medicine and, 71–72, 78, 82; Shōtoku and, 69–70; Tenmu and, 65; Yamato Kusushi and, 71–72, 78; Yoshino and, 64, 71, 80, 82, 103, 207
Ōtomo no Sadehiko, 71–72, 78, 122–124, 215, 251n.66
Ōtomo no Yasunoko no Muraji, 69–70
Owari Muraji: Ama no Hoakari and, 122, 156, 163, 172, 181–182, 198, 213; Atsuta shrine and, 174,

177, 199, 213, 275n.51; Kusanagi sword and, 174, 181, 199, 213; Mononobe kinship group and, 157, 163, 172, 177, 181, 213; Tenmu and, 174, 176, 181, 213; Yamato Takeru and, 156, 172, 176, 177, 181, 199, 213, 222

Ōyamakui no Mikoto: Hata kinship group and, 20, 42, 205, 211, 214, 220, Hiyoshi shrines and, 20, 42, 205, 214, 220, 243n.52; Kamo shrines and, 20, 211, 214, 220; Matsuno'o shrine and, 20, 42, 205, 211, 220; Munakata deities and, 42, 268n.43; Tamayori Hime and, 20; Tendai sect and, 20, 205; Wake no Ikazuchi and, 20, 211, 220, 268n.43

peaches. *See* fruit of immortality

pregnancy in single night motif, 43, 121, 123, 127–128, 133–134, 274n.41

Queen Mother of the West: Chinese festival calendar and, 62, 99–100, 102, 104–107, 214, 264n.33; Chinese mythology and, 62, 73, 82, 85, 96–98, 104, 109, 214, 232–233, 248n.37, 262n.31, 264n.33; founding legend of Buddhism and, 86, 96, 106–107, 214; fruit of immortality and, 62, 82, 98, 104–105, 205, 214; Han Wu-ti and, 62, 97–99, 232, 248n.37; land of immortals and, 83, 98, 104, 109, 176, 205, 214, 262n.31; Ōharae and, 95–96, 186; sage rulers and, 62, 73, 82, 98, 104, 214, 253n.23, 264n.33; sheng and, 97, 99–100, 105–107, 264n.45; Three Legged Crow and, 97–98, 100–101, 214, 262n.33, 264n.55; tombs and, 98, 100–101, 106; weak waters and, 96, 104; Weaver Maiden and, xii, xx, 105, 214

rain making: animal sacrifice and, 31–32, 209; Chinese festival calendar and, 36, 140; kingship and, 30–32, 85, 209, 246n.19; markets and, 31–32; Nihu Kami and, 85; River Earl and, 31, 214, 246n.15

resurrection, xx, 80, 93, 121, 139, 143, 145, 154, 157–158, 168–169, 174, 176, 179, 180–182, 184, 186, 188, 190–192, 199, 212, 220–221, 269n.9, 276n.53

River Earl, 31–32, 39, 214, 246n.15, 248n.44

Saga, 4, 6–7, 15, 18, 20–21, 134, 211, 214, 242n.38

sages: Chinese conceptions of, 7, 82, 98, 104, 155, 214, immortality and, 82, 104, 214, 225; kingship and, 15, 62, 82, 98, 104, 155, 214; Queen Mother of the West and, 62, 82, 98, 104, 214; Shōtoku and, 85, 107, 216, 225, 229; Tajima Mori as, 212; Tenmu and, 81–82

Saichō, 6, 14–15, 20, 24, 202, 205, 215, 225, 242n.33, 243n.51

Saigū. *See* consecrated princess

Saiin. *See* consecrated princess

Saimei. *See* Kōgyoku

Saiō. *See* consecrated princess

san yuan, 104, 111, 152

Seiwa, 19, 201

Sendai kuji hongi, 93, 163, 168–170, 172, 174, 198–199, 212, 220, 223–224, 297n.46

Seyatadera Hime, 128, 130–131, 133, 212, 215

Shinohara no Otohime, 71, 122–124, 130–131, 135, 215, 251n.66

Shinsen shōjiroku, 7–9, 14, 51, 71–72, 116, 163, 174, 200, 212–213, 230, 240n.12, 244n.54, 257n.62, 275n.42

Shōkonsai, 161, 185

Shōmu, 9–11, 16–17, 67, 80–81, 200, 203–204, 209, 215

Shōtoku (Prince Kamitsumiya), 8, 10–11, 14–15, 18–19, 24, 70, 83–85,

88–89, 92, 94, 96, 100, 103–104, 106–107, 136, 179–180, 183, 197, 200, 203, 206, 209, 215, 215–216, 225, 229, 241n.21
Soga kinship group, 31, 66, 69, 84, 87–90, 92, 94–95, 106–107, 157, 216, 246n.18, 253n.28
Space Buddha. See Kokūzō
Spell of the Peacock, 67, 235, 255n.39
spirit quelling rites. See Chinkonsai
Sui empire: *Ching ch'u sui shih chi and*, 53, 61, 111, 231, 260n.4; Koguryŏ and, 136; Queen Mother of the West and, 263n.43; Suiko Court and, 216; *Sui shu* and, 234
Suiko: astrology and, 33, 35, 45, 85; Chinese festival calendar and, xi, 34, 58, 137, 142, 149, 216; *Ching ch'u sui shih chi* and, 153, 216; court ritual and, 142, 146, 153, 155, 216; Kwallŭk and, 45, 211, 216; medicine hunts and, 58, 210; roadways and, 47; Shōtoku and, 84, 89, 137, 216; Sui and, 234
Suinin, 171–173, 175, 206, 275n.45
Sujin, 129, 153, 212, 217
Sumiyoshi deities, 12, 14, 18, 78, 200, 216, 241n.27, 258n.70
Sumiyoshi shrine, 14, 22, 198, 216
Suruga, Heavenly Maiden of, 74–76, 184, 216–217
Susanoo no Mikoto, 141, 158–159, 181, 185, 204, 217

Tachibana. See fruit of immortality
Tajima Mori: Ame no Hiboko and, 173, 212, 217; fruit of immortality and, 103–104, 205, 212, 214, 217; Hibasu Hime and, 173, 205; Miyake kinship group and, 103–104, 173, 212; Queen Mother of the West and, 103–104, 173, 214; tokoyo and, 103–104
Takakara Megami (Exalted Chinese Goddess): female immortals and, 76, 83, 176; Yoshino and, 71, 217, 259n.80

Takamatsuzuka Kofun, 34, 217, 247n.22
Takami Musubi no Mikoto: Ama no Hoakari and, 162, Heavenly Grandchild and, 120, 217; Ise shrine and, 167; moon deity and, 163, 197; Niinamesai and, 217, 272n.1; royal cult and, 217, 277; sun gods and, 162, 167; Takuhata Chichi Hime and, 120,
Takuhata Chichi Hime (Ama yorozu taku hata chi hata hime), 120, 163, 165–167, 218, 267n.31
Takuhata Hime, 165–167, 218
Tamayori Hiko, 126, 208, 218
Tamayori Hime, 20, 130, 207, 208, 218
Taoism: animal sacrifice and, 25, 37–38, 248n.39; Chinese festival calendar and, xiv–xvi, 46–47, 105, 264n.44; Fukunaga Mitsuji and, xiv, 2, 46, 239n.9, 252n.2; immortality and, 146, 176, 232–233, 257n.53, 270n.9, 276n.56; Kūkai and, 226; literature and, 257n.53, 259n.9; Queen Mother of the West and, 95, 104, 214, 232; spirits and, 45
Tasting of the First Fruits (*Niinamesai*): Amaterasu and, 82, 158, 167; Gosechimai and, 82; Takami Musubi and, 167, 217, 272n.1
Tenchi: court ritual and, 62 137, 226, 230, 253n.21; Jitō and, 207; Tamai and, 62, 253n.21
Tenmu: Amaterasu and, 155, 158–159, 185, 219, 253n.19; animal sacrifice and, 27–28; astrology and, 34–35; Atsuta shrine and, 12, 174, 199, 211, 213; Chinkonsai and, 60, 161, 173, 175; consecrated princess and, 155, 173, 175; Gosechimai and, 62, 71, 80–81; Hōzō and, 60, 161, 173, 175, 206; Jitō and, 61–62, 210, 253n.25; Kusanagi sword and, 173–174, 181, 199, 211; Ōtomo kinship group and, 64–65;

Owari Muraji kinship group, 174, 176, 181, 213; Yamato Takeru and, 156, 174–175, 199, 211, 222, 276n.53; Yoshino and, 61–63, 71, 80–81

Three Legged Crow: court ritual and, 102; Empress Wu and, 102, 234; Hakuji and, 100; Ma wang tui and, 98; omens and, 101; Queen Mother of the West and, 97–98, 100–101, 214, 262n.33; sage kingship and, 102; Tamanushi altar and, 101, 263n.35; Yatagarasu and, 103, 264n.55

Tōdaiji, 10, 14, 200, 203, 215

tokoyo (land of immortals): Amaterasu and, 180; combs and, 179, 180; female immortals and, 177, 178, 180; fruit of immortality and, 103, 261n.21; Ōfube no Ōshi and, 143, 180, 213; Oto Tachibana Hime and, 180; Queen Mother of the West and, 103; silkworms and, 143; Tajima Mori and, 103; Uranoshimako and, 178, 220; Waki no Iratsume and, 178

Toshigoi matsuri, 29–30, 41, 212, 223, 250n.62

Tōshi kaden, 223, 226, 234, 249n.54, 252n.10

Toyouke Hime: Gosechimai and, 81; as a Heavenly Maiden, 78–83; immortality and, 57, 78, 80–81, 176, 229; Ise and, 81, 166, 173, 190, 219, 259n.82; medicine and, 79, 81, 189; sericulture and, 80, 166, 188–189, 219; Tamba and, 78–80, 189, 219, 229; Tsukiyomi no Mikoto and, 188–189, 219; Uranshoshimako and, 57, 78, 80, 176; Yoshino and, 78, 229

Tsukiyomi no Mikoto: Amaterasu and, 163–164, 166, 188–189, 210, 219; Kadono district and, 163–164, 189; Korean peninsula and, 163–164, 166; Toyouke Hime and, 166, 188

Tsuminoe no Hijiri Hime (Immortal Mulberry-branch Maiden), 144–145, 154, 219, 257

Tsunoga, 44, 51, 53, 125, 249n.54

Tsunoga Arashito, 44–45, 50–51, 53–54, 197, 200, 220–221, 226, 249n.54

twenty-two shrine-temple system, 21–22, 196

Uji bridge, 46–47, 51–53, 201

Umashimaji: Chinkonsai and, 93, 168, 220, Mononobe kinship group and, 93, 168, 220; resurrection spell and, 93, 220

Uranoshimako: combs and, 73, 177, 180, 220; immortals and, 57, 72–75, 176–177, 180, 220; Kusakabe kinship group and, 72–73, 177, 220; medicine and, 73, 80; Tamba cults and, 57, 80, 220, 256n.56; Tokoyo and, 73, 177, 180, 220; Toyouke Hime and, 57, 78, 80, 176

Uzume Hime, 159, 220, 272n.4, 273n.12

Wakateru. *See* Yūryaku

Wake no Ikazuchi no Kami, 5, 20, 127–128, 207–208, 218, 220, 268n.43

Waki no Iratsume, 176–178, 180, 220–221

Wani kinship group: Ama no Hoakari and, 156–157, 172–173, 179, 198; Hibasu Hime and, 173, 205, 218; Kuchiko no Omi and, 150–152, 272n.32; Kusakabe kinship group and, 182, 198, 205, 221; Mononobe kinship group and, 172, 176–177, 179–180, 182, 274n.41, 274n.42; resurrection and, 176–177, 179–180, 221; Waki no Iratsume and, 176–178; Yamato Takeru and, 146, 157, 172–175, 178, 222

Wani no Kuchiko. *See* Kuchiko no Omi

Weaver Maiden and Cowherd: Akaru Hime and, 44; Amaterasu and, 141, 158–159, 167; animal sacrifice and, xix, 26, 39, 54, 186, 221; as astral deities, xii, xx, 38, 138, 221; Chinese festival calendar and, xii, xix–xx, 26, 38–39, 105, 148–149, 184, 186, 221; consorts and, 149, 153; Heavenly Maidens and, 74, 77, 120–121, 204, 216, 221, 234; human sacrifice and, 39, 186; poetry and, 138; pregnancy in single night motif, 121; Queen Mother of the West and, xii, xx, 105, 214; weaving regalia and offerings and, 39; weaving technologies and, xii, 184

Yamato Hime: Amaterasu and, 175, 206, 221, 229, 277n.46; as consecrated princess, 174–176, 221, 229; Hibasu Hime and, 172–173, 205–206; Inishiki Irihiko and, 172, 205–206, 221; Kusangai sword and, 173–174, 221; Mononobe kinship group and, 173, 275n.46; Wani kinship group and, 173, 221, 229; Yamato Takeru and, 173–175, 211, 221
Yamato Kusushi kinship group, 71–72, 78
Yamato Takeru: Ama no Hoakari and, 156–157, 172, 174, 177, 181, 222, 275n.46; Amaterasu and, 156, 221, 276n.53; Atsuta shrine and, 177, 199, 211, 213; Kusanagi sword and, 173–174, 181, 199, 211; Owari Muraji kinship group and, 156, 172, 176, 177, 181, 199, 213, 222; resurrection and, 146–147, 176–179, 222, 276n.65; Tenmu and, 156, 174–175, 199, 211, 222, 276n.53; Waki no Iratsume and, 176–178; Wani kinship group and, 146, 157, 172–175, 178, 222; Yamato Hime and, 173–175, 211, 221

Yatagarasu: Amaterasu and, 103, 222, 264n.55; court ritual and, 103; Jinmu and, 102–103, 208, 222, 264n.55; Kamo Agatanushi kinship group and, 103, 208, 222; Three Legged Crow and, 103, 264n.55; Yoshino and, 102–103, 208, 222
yin and yang, xi–xii, xvi, 32, 34–36, 54–56, 58, 60, 109, 121, 140, 146–147, 153, 185, 195, 219, 232, 234, 246n.16, 247n.24, 260n.12, 261n.13
Yoshino: female immortals and, xix, 57, 59–60, 62, 66, 72–78, 80, 82–83, 124, 131, 144–145, 213, 219, 222, 253n.22, 259n.80; Gosechimai and, 62, 81, 217, 228, 259n.80; Gumonjihō and, 19, 67, 203; Jinmu and, 64–65, 69, 82, 122, 207, 254n.32; Jitō and, 62–63, 75, 81, 210; medicine hunts and, xix, 58, 60, 65, 185, 210; Nihu Kami and, 63–66, 244n.57, 254n.28, 254n.33, 254n.36; Nuribe Hime and, 75–76, 78, 83, 213, 257n.65; rain making and, 63–66; red earth and, 65–66, 82, 131, 222, 254n.36; Takakara Megami and, 71, 217, 259n.80; Tenmu and, 61–63, 71, 80–81; Toyouke Hime and, 78, 229; Yatagarasu and, 102–103, 208, 222
Yūryaku (Wakateru, Great King Bu): Chiisakobe kinship group and, 116–117, 200, 267n.36; consecrated princess and, 164–165, 197; Heavenly Grandchild legend and, 119; Koguryŏ and, 93; Miwa shrine and, 117–118, 267n.36; Mononobe and, 91, 93–94, 157, 170, 174, 222, 274n.41; sericulture rites and, 116, 141, 145, 153, 222, 266n.11; weaving lineages and, 114–119, 141, 174, 200, 203, 222, 270n.11; Yoshino and, 62–63, 257n.52